Invading Hitler's

Invading Hitler's Europe

From Salerno to the Capture of Göring –
The Memoir of a US Intelligence Officer

Roswell K. Doughty

Introduced and Edited by Reiner Decher

FRONTLINE BOOKS

First published in Great Britain in 2020 by
Frontline Books
An imprint of
Pen & Sword Books Ltd
Yorkshire – Philadelphia

ISBN 978 1 52677 322 7

Typeset by Mac Style
Printed and bound in the UK by TJ Books Limited,
Padstow, Cornwall.

MIX
Paper from
responsible sources
FSC® C013056

Pen & Sword Books Limited incorporates the imprints of Atlas,
Archaeology, Aviation, Discovery, Family History, Fiction, History,
Maritime, Military, Military Classics, Politics, Select, Transport,
True Crime, Air World, Frontline Publishing, Leo Cooper, Remember
When, Seaforth Publishing, The Praetorian Press, Wharncliffe
Local History, Wharncliffe Transport, Wharncliffe True Crime
and White Owl.

For a complete list of Pen & Sword titles please contact

PEN & SWORD BOOKS LIMITED
47 Church Street, Barnsley, South Yorkshire, S70 2AS, England
E-mail: enquiries@pen-and-sword.co.uk
Website: www.pen-and-sword.co.uk

Or

PEN AND SWORD BOOKS
1950 Lawrence Rd, Havertown, PA 19083, USA
E-mail: Uspen-and-sword@casematepublishers.com
Website: www.penandswordbooks.com

Contents

Acknowledgements

A word of thanks is due to many people; Ros Doughty's daughter Ann Doughty Bunting, her husband Charles, and to his grand-daughter Laura Landsiedel Ford, who all made material available for this memoir, written almost completely in the author's own words. His diary from which these words evolved has not been found, but luckily with the help of his wife El and daughter Martha, its content has been saved in the form of this memoir. Special thanks is hereby given for the family's trust in my delving so intimately into its history. A special thanks for the map-making skills of Andreas Illert.

… and a dedication …

Most books begin with a dedication. R.K. Doughty did not leave one for this memoir, although his words are intimately reflective. An event as tumultuous as war surely leads to the full range of human emotions and interactions. As you read this, you will see that a lot of feelings, human feelings, are expressed. Perhaps we can dedicate this writing, these stories, to the good in people and whatever good can come out of war.

Reiner Decher, with my diligent proof reader
and life partner, Mary
September 2020

Maps, Photographs, and References

M aps are provided to orient the reader. The artist is Andreas Illert who noted points in the journey of the 36th Division from the text.

Photos are attributed to the source in the captions. Where such attribution is not provided, the images are from a scrapbook kept by the author with the identity of the photographer unknown.

The reader might benefit from consulting a book produced by the US Government Printing Office: *Riviera to the Rhine* by J.J. Clarke and R.R. Smith, Center for Military History, Washington DC, 1993.

A more general review of the history of the 141st Regiment and 36th Division, including shorter stories that are rewritten (by the author) versions of this memoir, is available at: http://www.texasmilitaryforcesmuseum. org/36division/archives/141/ps3.htm.

Another excellent book covering this part of the Second World War is *The Day of Battle: the War in Italy and Sicily, 1943–1944* by Rick Atkinson (Henry Holt, 2007). It describes the larger movements of the 36th Division and its regiments with excellent pictures and maps. This (second) volume is part of a trilogy about the war.

Key Officers

US Officers

Omar Bradley (1893–1981)
Mark W. Clark (1896–1984)
John E. Dahlquist (1896–1975)
Roswell K. Doughty (1909–2001)
Dwight D. Eisenhower (1890–1961)
Otto F. Lange (b. 1891)
Alexander Patch (1889–1945)
Robert I. Stack
Fred L. Walker (1887–1969)
William H. Wilbur (1888–1979)

German Officers

Walther von Brauchitsch (1881–1948)
Hermann Göring (1893–1946)
Erwin Rommel (1891–1944)
Gerd von Rundstedt (1875–1953)
Karl Wolff (1900–1984)

Abbreviations

AA	Anti-Aircraft – *see* Ack-Ack in the Glossary
AG	Adjutant General (G-1: administration)
BU	Boston University
CCB	Combat Command B
CIC	Combat Information Center, also Criminal Investigation Command
CG	Commanding general
CO	Commanding Officer
CP	Command Post
DSC	Distinguished Service Cross
FFI	Forces Française de l'Intérieur (French Interior Force)
FTP	Francs-Tireurs et Partisans (French shooters and partisans)
GI	General Issue: American soldier
I&R	or I and R, Intell and Recon (Intelligence and Reconnaissance)
LCT	Landing Craft, Tank
LCVP	Landing Craft Vehicle and Personnel
LST	Landing Ship, Tank
M., Mme.	In French: Monsieur and Madame
MLR	Main Line of Resistance
MP	Military Police
OD	Officer of the Day
OP	Observation Post
Pfc	Private first class (military rank)
PR	Public Relations or Personal Reconnaissance
PW	Prisoner of War
PX	Post Exchange
R and R	Rest and Relaxation
ROTC	Reserve Officer Training Corps
SOP	Standard Operating Procedure
SP (gun)	Self Propelled (gun)
TAC	Tactical Air Command
TD	Tank destroyer
UPI	United Press International

Note from the Editor

The words you are about to read are almost exactly those of R.K. Doughty. Thus, I hardly qualify as an editor. He dictated these words in 1979 to his wife Eleanore who took them in shorthand. His daughter Martha transcribed the shorthand notes to approximately what is presented here. The original text was preserved on thin typewriter paper that was transformed into a digital Microsoft Word file. This process allowed correction of spelling (especially the names of European towns and people), a very few grammatical errors, and formatting for print production.

The only additions to the original text (in the form of footnotes, pictures, and maps) are those that draw in the larger context of the war and some important events at the times described. Some clarifications are also noted with added words in square brackets. The Internet is a rich resource which I consulted and mined to enhance the presentation of the text.

About the subject of war. Battles seem to me to be notoriously difficult to describe in a way that makes their evolution clear. Doughty's very candid words describe the experience from his ground-level point of view in a vivid way. Words and names from the text are readily available to execute searches on the Internet for more information on the larger picture of the war, world events, as well as technical details.

The larger picture one may read about in the literature is indeed much larger. The 36th Division is but one unit, yet it was an important part of the war. The writers of all histories are understandably centered on the units in which they served and thus there is the potential that the larger picture may be seen to be less than it was. Reading about these other units in parallel with this story allows one to better grasp the magnitude of this war. For example, the Battle of Monte Cassino was actually four battles, only the last of which finally turned the tide. The first three were disasters for the Allies, according to the assessment of historians and Doughty. Photographs about the Battle of Monte Cassino paint a picture of its ferocity. In an Internet search or a visit to the area, one cannot be but overwhelmed by the silent witness embodied in the square miles of military cemeteries located in the area.

It is the personal side of this tale that paints a troubling picture of war as a human undertaking. We are very fortunate in many ways that it is available so many decades after the Second World War. Since the manuscript is dated 1979, more than three decades after the war, it must have been composed with the aid of extensive diary notes.

Doughty's survival seems a product of his native ingenuity, guts (or, as he might have said, sangfroid), and luck, as may be the case for all survivors of such violent events. What strikes me as miraculous is that, despite traumatic experiences, Doughty, like so many and unlike some, especially those with serious injuries, was able to put these experiences aside and proceed with his life, hopefully not drawn back to these events to fruitlessly ruminate on them. Reading this memoir is certainly cause for reflection about courage, camaraderie, and the nature of war.

In addition to this memoir, Doughy left behind a notebook containing correspondence with editors of the *Historical Quarterly* (dated 1988–9) and articles he sent them for publication. The publication is put out by the Texas Military Forces Museum in Austin (www.texasmilitaryforcesmuseum.org) with its strong connection to the 141st Infantry Regiment and the 36th Division as, initially, many of its soldiers were from Texas. The published stories are relatively short and essentially those told in this memoir. The complete memoir, of which this book is a shortened version, is available from the library of this museum. He also leaves behind in the family archives a collection of poetry, some of it related to war experiences, as well as a tale describing his military journey to Korea. The man had a way with words!

Introduction – The Military
Aspects of the Story

Doughty's tale is of the 141st Infantry Regiment (36th Infantry Division, 7th Army; General Mark Clark was its CO in Italy, General Alexander Patch in France) during its campaign in North Africa, two invasions of Italy, an invasion of France on the Riviera, its push up the Rhône, crossing the Vosges Mountains, into Germany and finally into Austria during the Second World War.

From a letter to the author's grandson Matt Bunting dated 26 September 1989, we have the following details about the author's military unit.

To give you background on army structure, then in existence, a division was made up of three regiments. In our case the 141st, 142nd, and 143rd Infantry Regiments comprised our Division. There was also a regiment of artillery consisting of three battalions of 105mm howitzers and a fourth battalion of 155mm guns. The 105s were light artillery and were designated as the 131st, 132nd, and 133rd Field Artillery Battalions. Each of the light battalions was earmarked as a member of a regimental combat team. In other words, the 141st Infantry Regiment and the 131st FA Battalion operated as a combat team. The same applied to the 142nd and the 132nd, etc. The medium artillery 155s were under division control and later in the war we had some 8in (about 200mm) guns assigned to the division as heavy artillery. These were also under division control. Most of the time, all artillery was under division control and fired en masse from a Fire Direction Center. However, should a mission arise calling for a regimental combat team, we always knew who would operate with us.

In addition, each division had an aviation unit attached to the artillery, a Medical Unit, Quartermaster Company, Engineer Battalion, Ordnance Company, Reconnaissance Troop, and other units for special services. When we were combat ready and joined by other troops, such as anti-aircraft batteries, armor, chemical mortar outfits and the like, we numbered in the neighborhood of 18,000 men.

The typical regiment is under the command of a colonel and this one consists of three battalions, named, appropriately, first, second, and third. Each battalion consisted of 4 companies. Companies were comprised of platoons and platoons of squads.

In each of those battalions there was a group of individuals charged with 'Intelligence and Reconnaissance', I&R. This group was termed the S-2 and, in the 141st, was under the command of the author, Captain Doughty, promoted to Major during the campaign.

In the text, the reader will encounter S and G numbers. The S numbers apply to *battalion* (or *brigade*) level functions while the G numbers apply to (*corps* or) *division* level. The number that follows the letter refers to the organizational function. Thus, very generally, 1 applies to administration, 2 to intelligence, 3 to operations, and 4 to logistics, supplies, etc. There are other numbers, although these are not particularly relevant to this text.

The role of the I&R people is to learn whatever they can by any means available: where are enemy strengths, mine fields, where are usable roads, etc.? The means include individuals going behind enemy lines, interrogation of prisoners, discussions with partisans, and observation. Late in life, Doughty is quoted by his daughter as describing the work of an I&R platoon:

They carry machine guns and mortars. In secret, they get as close to the Germans as they can. They do not fight, unless they have to. They are there to collect information. I trained every squad member to write coded messages on Red Cross paper, ... in case they are captured. Germans gave prisoners paper once a month and, using code, they sent back a story to me of something they had seen. They provided invaluable information.

In a campaign, the I&R groups establish a command post (CP) linked to observation posts (OP). The information gathered is critical to the effectiveness of artillery and troop movements. You will easily conclude that the S-2 folks are continuously in the thick of the action. After all, it is the infantry that has the final say as to whether a military objective has been achieved and artillery cannot contribute much to the effort without knowing where enemy strongpoints are.

During the Second World War, the 36th Division had 3 infantry regiments (141st, 142nd and 143rd of about 3,000 men each). In battle, two fought and the third was held in reserve. According to the author's notes, a battalion had roughly 200 men and a company consisted of 100 men.

Prologue

In the interest of brevity, the story begins in North Africa. Scholars wishing to see the complete work are welcome to browse the archives of the Texas Military Forces Museum in Austin.

A few dates are important to put Roswell Doughty's story in historical context. Doughty graduated from Boston University in 1931 and married his wife Eleanor in 1936. Three children were born to them and the war started for him when he was called up following the Pearl Harbor attack in late 1941.

Six initial chapters of his complete work are omitted from this telling of his story. They describe his university education with the Reserve Officer Training Corps (ROTC, for short) with the peacetime, stateside training for service as a reserve officer. After he was called up, the training intensified at various US army bases followed by more live-ammunition training in North Africa.

The complete story weaves in details of raising a growing family during the time spent training in the US.

Chapter 1

Prelude to Combat

T he war ended in North Africa[1] with Allied victory over the Axis and training for assaulting the coast of Europe, somewhere, was on everyone's mind.

I had just settled into the routine of amphibious training when I received orders to report to an officers' training camp near the desert. It was, I thought, a welcome relief to get away from the routine of embarking on large ships, being transported out of sight of land and then, after climbing down nets fastened to the sides of ships, entering small boats for the trip to shore in waves of ten or more

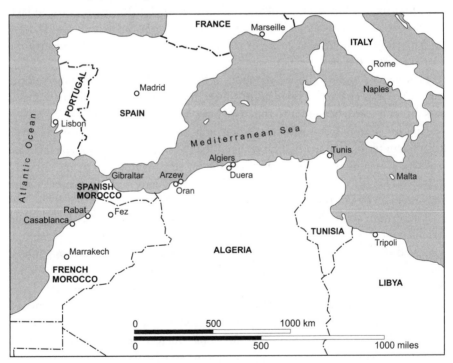

---

1. Historical background: Germany occupied North Africa between 12 February 1941 and 13 May 1943. The German Afrika Korps was under the command of General Erwin Rommel who was suspected to have been involved in an assassination attempt on Hitler's life. He was forced to commit suicide (10/14/1944) to accommodate Hitler's need to preserve the reputation of an admired and honorable German general. The German command headquarters were located in Tripoli. The Second Battle of Al Alamein in Egypt (23 Oct–11 Nov 1942) was the turning point for the German Army in Africa with surrender on 5 May 1943.

such boats. We also had areas on the shore where we could practice climbing up and down nets, launching and landing from small boats, paddling rubber rafts and developing techniques for organizing our units on shore in the darkness after landing. We learned, too, about naval support techniques and tactics, what we could expect and not expect in this regard. However, there were questions in our minds as to how to communicate with support ships, particularly cruisers and battleships, and we were told that this problem was exacerbated by a shortage of certain radios that could lock into the navy networks. However, we were assured that shore parties would be with us to direct naval fires, once we landed.

I arrived at the special training camp and was, to put it mildly, surprised to learn that it was being conducted by Brigadier General William H. Wilbur[2] who had been my professor of military science and tactics at Boston University (BU). I had heard of his winning a Congressional Medal of Honor (see plate section) at the North African landings when he had delivered the terms of surrender to the French and then, as the story went, returned to find French artillery still knocking out our landing craft. Apparently he had commandeered a tank and had run over and knocked out of action several French batteries of guns. In fact, so considerable were his actions, which any of us who knew him would have anticipated, that he received one of the longest citations ever entered into the Congressional Record.

I had fenced under Wilbur's coaching at BU and, while I always respected the man, there was an aura of invincibility about him that was so protuberant that it was difficult to see beyond it to the basic man. Yet, on one occasion when he was leaving his post at BU during my junior year, he called me to his office and in very warm terms told me that he realized that I had lost my father several years earlier and that he would be glad to stand in for that relationship to me, should I ever need his help. I had no idea, then, that I would later serve in combat under his orders on one of the most difficult of fighting fronts.

There were about 200 officers present at the school which was designed to produce mental toughness, the postulate being that we were already physically seasoned and ready for the rough and tumble of warfare. All of us were assembled on a ridge the first morning, when I descried the familiar walk of General Wilbur as he came down a path to give us our first orientation on what to expect. I was not aware until that moment that he was the commandant, and I was surprised when he walked directly up to me, as we stood at attention, and shook hands with me. He hadn't seen me since 1930, some thirteen years earlier, and in the meantime I had put on some weight and a moustache. While I never knew for

---

2. RKD's words (from the letter to Matt Bunting, 1989): General Wilbur had (by war's end) won every medal the U.S. offers and some of them two or three times. He kept all of them except the Congressional Medal of Honor in a shoebox, a fact I learned at his funeral a few years ago when I went to West Point for the occasion. His widow had the box of medals with her, each of which was wrapped in tissue paper. The general, unlike many others, never displayed them.

certain, I believe that he'd seen my name on a roster and was looking for me when he joined the group.

We got the immediate impression from the general that the outlook for the term of the school was, to say the least, parlous. He greeted us with the statement, 'Men, you are in fine physical condition. The training in this camp will prepare you mentally for battle!' This would include enough doses of peril and sleeplessness, he said, to closely simulate battle conditions. In fact, he added that nothing in combat would exceed the stress under which we would operate at his school which, for obvious reasons, we came to know as 'Wilbur's School of Torture and Dirty Tricks.'

We were to operate 24 and 12-hour shifts on alternating days without any opportunity to catch up on sleep missed on those days when we kept moving around the clock. We were also subject to water discipline, reserving our canteens full of water until each evening when they would be inspected before we could use their content.

We would be subjected to overhead fire by German machine guns on a so-called 'Crack and Thump' course, when we would learn to listen for the 'Thump' of the gun after hearing the 'Crack' of bullets passing close overhead.

We would be taught the hard way to look for and avoid booby traps. We would also learn to shoot at targets of fleeting opportunity, to 'read' terrain in order to know how to use its variations to best suit our own purposes. And, finally, assuming that we were successful in learning these lessons, we would follow artillery fire closely as a means of approaching hostile positions while bursting shells dampened the spirit of any defenders.

In short, we were to engage in the closest approximation to warfare that General Wilbur and his aides could devise for us. Furthermore, just to test our endurance to the utmost, we would run 4 miles a day – 2 miles downhill, 2 miles back up – in the blazing sun, with full packs and equipment while the general rode his jeep behind us looking for stragglers.

Should we not stand up under this abuse we would be returned to the states for reclassification, subject to being drafted as buck privates or some such rank.

We returned to our tents fairly certain of one thing: we'd be better off anywhere else in North Africa, no matter what role we might play.

The 'fun' started that day and went on throughout the night and through the evening meal the next day. While I had been tired in my life, I never quite reached the same pinnacle of exhaustion, before or after, of that 36-hour stretch. The sun sapped at our vitals and the lack of water made our bodies ache as we went through problem after problem, situation after situation, and punishment after punishment.

Nothing would have prompted me to cut a corner, sneak a nap, ease off running, or phoney up a response as many of the officers did. I remember that during the second day's run I felt light-headed and ready to drop as I jogged through the sand with the pack on my back weighing a ton. However, the sight of my old mentor riding his one-starred jeep kept me moving while my heart pumped like a sledgehammer, jarring my breathing.

When we were finally released from that miniature purgatory, I went to take a shower and was stunned by the water which, even though it had stood for days in 100 to 110-degree heat in a tower, 'it felt frigid because of the disparity between its 80-degree temperature and the atmospheric heat of 110 degrees. It revived me considerably and surprisingly enough, we all felt as though we had proved, not only our mental tenacity but our physical toughness too. We slept under blankets that night and were chilly when we awoke the next morning.

We were led toward our next 24-hour stint by an officer who, one could see, was overly proud of his muscles. It was obvious that he had spent hours improving them with barbells, push-ups, weights, and all manner of paraphernalia. His attitude was somewhat imperious as he ordered us about like vassals, and while I had no idea that the time would come when I might one day even the balance, I nevertheless promised myself that, if I ever had the opportunity, I'd straighten out some of the muscle-bound tissue between his ears. His chances for learning a few lessons were better than average, since all members of the class felt the same toward him.

We arrived at what is known in Africa, and possibly elsewhere, as a 'wadi.' It was a ravine cut into the soil and hard rock by wind and water over the centuries. As we approached it, the conclusion was inescapable that this was a special gully, drafted into the scheme of making better officers and men of all of us. There were signs all along its rim that extended, so far as we could see, for over a mile from the outlet which we were approaching. Clusters of the school's cadre were gathered near the de-busing point and as we got off the buses, the groups disappeared, some dropping into the wadi, others marching off to points unseen behind a number of ridges in that vicinity.

We were armed with carbines and live rounds of ammunition and taken single-file to a ledge that formed a depressed trail along one side of the wadi. A sign there read to the following effect: 'Crawl on your guts along this pathway until you come to the next sign. Keep your butt close to the ground since you will receive rifle fire as you crawl.'

We crossed, single file, along the path which was about 2ft below the general ground surface of that area and 10ft above the floor of the wadi. As we did, several bursts of Browning sub-machine-gun fire were directed at the edge of the gully just above our heads. Anyone who hadn't learned to slither along the ground with a minimum of air space under his gut got the message that day. My elbows hurt as did my knees, dragging the rest of me along the route with the greatest amount of friction possible. There was something about the solid thud of bullets striking rocks and ricocheting across the wadi that prompted a desire to burrow one's way ahead.

Near the end of the crawl-path I waited while the man ahead of me poked his head above the rim of the wadi in response, I assumed, to instructions on a sign

I could see near him. Suddenly, he ducked back and ran a hand over his face as though rubbing something from his eyes.

At that moment I saw General Wilbur's head and shoulders as he leaned over to speak to the officer who was still rubbing his face. The general withdrew and the man on the ground, again, put his chin up over the rim of the wadi. I could see him jump as a shot rang out followed by two more. I couldn't tell from where I lay who was shooting at what, but I gathered that it was an unpleasant predicament.

As the man moved down into the wadi I crawled to the sign I'd seen and read, 'Raise your head and rest your chin on the edge of the cliff until three shots have been fired. If you flinch, three more shots will be fired until you have completed the test properly.'

Not knowing what I'd see, I did as ordered and looking straight ahead saw the jut-jawed face of General Wilbur who showed no sign of recognizing me. Out of the corner of my eye I could see a man sitting on a rock about 10ft to my right. He was aiming a Garand rifle in my general direction. Under my chin was a boxed-off sandpit about a yard square. I saw the general nod and the next second I felt a series of stinging sensations as the sand in front of me was blown by the force of a .30-caliber bullet into my face. I had shut my eyes instinctively but even so had the uncomfortable feeling that my right eye might have been injured. I could feel a trickle of wetness down my right cheek but in the 100-degree heat, thought it was sweat. I did not flinch as two more shots were pumped into the sand but I kept hoping that the man doing the shooting had no nervous afflictions endemic in his family. His position was such that only a freak ricochet would cause me to be struck by a bullet.

As I jumped down to the wadi floor I brushed my right cheek with my hand and was relieved to find that it was wet with nothing but sweat. I spit out some grit that had been blown into my mouth to set my teeth on edge. As I did so I jumped half out of my hide as a ¼lb block of dynamite went off around a corner some 5ft behind me. The explosion half deafened me for the remainder of the day.

I caught sight of a sign that admonished me to be alert for booby traps of all kinds and 'hostile' ambushes as I proceeded up the wadi. By the time I started on this leg of the exercise, the man ahead of me had disappeared around a bend in the wadi but I could make out, over the crashing of the sub-machine gun and Garand rifle behind me, the sounds of a carbine shooting and decided I'd keep an eye peeled for ambushes up ahead.

Watching every move, I went slowly and almost at once saw wires leading to a flat rock lying to one side of a fairly well-defined trail along the floor of the wadi. I recognized that this was so poorly concealed that it might have been left to distract me from something more dangerous. I studied the footing and saw three small wires protruding from the pathway just across the flat rock. Since I had to move on I jumped clear of the rock and small wires and found I'd cleared the first obstacle.

The noise in the wadi was almost unbearable since it echoed and re-echoed with percussive effect which magnified the sounds beyond belief. I stepped along as lightly as possible and on rounding the bend where I'd heard the carbine firing I got down low and almost duck-walked while watching everything, high and low. I saw two ropes that were blended pretty well into the side of the wadi move and a target, comprising three silhouettes of helmeted heads, rose abruptly behind a series of rocks. I fired at them from a kneeling position to which I'd sunk as soon as I saw the movement. I hit all three since they fell over when I released a shot at each one. I was concerned about slugs from my gun ricocheting to hit one of my teammates ahead and also about shots hitting me from the rear. However, the routing was so tortuous up the wadi that each man was protected by the wadi walls. I also found that once when I sped up my pace a little I was warned by a disembodied voice to hold in place for a count of three.

Even so, the whole enterprise was pretty close to the knife edge of great personal danger. It went on and on with targets appearing momentarily and then disappearing. Split-second timing was required to hit all targets in the allotted time which, in turn, meant catching sight of the various dummies as they were hoisted into place or as they were encountered, assuming that they were not of the disappearing type.

All through the hour-and-a-half of running the wadi gauntlet my uniform was sopping wet; for a while, initially, the walls of the gulch shaded a portion of the route, but the sun – as it rose higher – made the place an inferno.

I expended some 200 cartridges on my noisy way up the wadi and was very happy when I finally reached the end of the course, where I was directed along a route, below a ridge, that led back to our initial point. En route back I passed several officers who were being worked on by medics for heat prostration.

We felt sorry for a number of officers who were 'washed out' of the school for failure to meet its standards. But like a lot of things in the army, they were rewarded, rather than punished, for their failure. It was purely happenstance but at that time a new organization was being beefed up and all officer material, not otherwise employed, was being sought to fill the ranks of the military government organization. As a result the drop-outs from Wilbur's special training course were not only put into plush jobs (many of them later took over the operation of hotels in such playgrounds as Sorrento and Capri) but were promoted before those of us who entered combat. It was just another of those things about military foul-ups that test the mettle of men dedicated to the job of fighting a war, instead of pretending to fight one.

The time we spent on the 'Crack and Thump' course was merely a precursor of things to come. We trooped out to the range which was a long ridge running downhill to a crossing ridge that rose, at the juncture, some 50ft above the range. We stood on the range at various distances from the crossing ridge. Several German machine guns were positioned to shoot from the crossing ridge over our heads. At first, we stood in a group around General Wilbur at about a 300yd distance from the guns.

The sound of bullets passing close overhead was not new to any of us who had served in target pits on ranges in the US. It is a smacking sound in both ears like a giant handclap. The German guns were fired in short bursts and the cracking in our ears made several of the officers hit the dirt, while those of us who continued to stand tried not to look superior about it.

We had been cautioned to listen for the 'thump' of the gun which, because sound travels slower than bullets, would follow the 'crack' of the bullets a few seconds later. The guns were sufficiently far apart that their 'thumps' could be distinguished one from the other and we learned very quickly that, by consciously listening for the deep thumping, we could identify which of four guns were firing at us and its approximate location.

We moved to various ranges to learn the different timings of 'thumps' at the longer ranges. However, in reviewing the experience later with some of my tent-mates I learned that they, too, had had the sensing of being terribly vulnerable on the 'crack and thump' range, for it was the first time any of us had stood openly in front of such weapons with no chance of avoiding injury or death if the gun clamps had failed and the gun muzzles had dropped at a critical moment.

General Wilbur, of course, stood with us as we moved along the range and when, later in the war, he joined our division as assistant division CO he continued to stand when taken under fire. While this contemptuousness for his personal safety was part and parcel of the image he projected, I always felt that it was somewhat vainglorious and a poor example to set for the dough-feet who, had they followed his lead, would soon have been knocked out of the war, one way or another.

We approached the end of our 'durance vile' with a sense of elation, knowing that those of us who had survived its rigors were cut from a different stripe than those who had, for whatever reason, begged off and gone back to their units. The grand finale of our testing was the exercise whereby we would follow artillery fire closely as we advanced across open terrain toward an 'enemy-held strongpoint.'

As the day of the 'big shoot,' as it was called, came, General Mark W. Clark[3] made an inspection tour of the camp. He was, without doubt, the biggest pain in the ass we'd ever encountered. Everything about him, from his entourage to his posing to get his left profile into pictures that were taken by his PR men, bespoke an egocentric, arrogant personality, one which later was to show up poorly in combat despite his constant effort to keep his name, rank, and profile before the public and to hell with the men who were doing the fighting.

We saw him, first, as he drew up to the range where our class was assembled, preparatory to undergoing the nerve-wracking ordeal of maneuvering under artillery fire. Wilbur, who was older than Clark but who did not have the

---

3. General Clark's performance in this campaign has been judged controversial by historians and the reader may wish to examine the history in greater depth. Clark was replaced by General Alexander Patch for the Riviera landings and southern France campaign.

advantage of classmates in higher echelons to push and pull him upward, saluted Clark and the exercise began.

I was a squad leader and had deployed my men across a portion of a field that was covered with a low-growing ground shrub. In the distance – some 1,000yd – was a rock pile which represented the 'enemy' position. We had been rehearsed as to the manner in which we would proceed, by echelon, across the intervening terrain.

When it came to my turn to order my squad to set out toward our objective, I yelled 'Up,' and we all ran as hard as we could go until I heard a flight of shells shearing through the air over our heads when I shouted 'Down,' and we plunged together to the earth, bouncing somewhat at the force of the landing. We moved in successive dashes in the same manner. When we were about halfway to the rock pile, I heard feet pounding along behind me after I yelled 'Up!' Turning to see what I assumed was a laggard from my squad I was surprised to see General Clark bowling along with us. I yelled 'Down' and heard him crash to the ground together with the rest of my squad.

When we were almost at the final objective, I became aware of a savage burning on my chest and thighs as well as my forearms. I actually thought I was having a seizure of some kind but delayed trying to inspect my skin until I passed the rock pile. There I found men tearing off their clothing and looking at great blisters all over their bodies. I found the same condition on myself and felt that I could hardly stand it in the heat of the day. Someone yelled, 'Hey! Stinging nettles!' Sure enough we'd ploughed our way across a field of poisonous barbs that no one had earlier identified.

General Clark was so winded that he could not conduct a critique of the problem when asked to do so by General Wilbur who, true to form, had dashed along in front of our group, standing the whole time even when shell fragments were whizzing past him from detonations occurring anywhere from 30 to 50yd beyond his position. A spent shell fragment had struck my boot heel, with no damage, when I was some 25yd behind Wilbur.

We were happy to learn that we would go home the following day. I'm sure that the 'American Eagle,' as Clark liked to describe himself, had something to do with shortening our sentence. We rode out in 2.5-ton trucks singing and proclaiming our 'freedom' once again.

In a very real way, General Wilbur prepared us for that moment in our lives when we passed from ordinary existence to a living where being alive from moment to moment seemed a miracle. To anyone who has not passed the line and had the curtain of war come down behind him, blotting out all meaningful security and destroying values that make civilized life a prized possession, there can be no comprehension of the changed outlook that henceforward throughout the rest of their lives dominates the hearts and minds of combat soldiers.

Chapter 2

Guarding a Frontier

Once I had returned to the regiment near Arzew I sensed that the preparatory stages for our division's entry into combat were about at an end. We were living in pup tents near the sea, and tied up in the port were a number of Allied ships awaiting orders.

Just at dusk one evening I heard the sudden roar of airplane engines and dove for a slit trench just outside my tent. Several planes streaked over our heads, their machine guns chattering, and the sensation was one of noise in six dimensions, echoing and re-echoing. Anti-aircraft fire from the ships and gun emplacements along the shore added to the din and fragments of shells whirred into our bivouac area.

Shortly, we saw the flashes of bombs and then heard their explosive sounds. From our position we could not be sure of their targets but were glad to learn the next day that they had fallen on a cemetery in a classic case of overkill, missing the shipping completely but disinterring some old bones. Apparently, the sortie had evaded our radar, located on a promontory overlooking Arzew, by skimming across the water below the radar's scanning rays.

We were happy to see the ships up-anchor and leave port and happier to receive orders to move, secretly, to Rabat, Morocco. It seems that the Allied High Command had become worried about a possible attack from Europe, through Spanish Morocco, as a means of relieving the pressure on the Axis troops near Bizerte. We were ordered to conceal all identifying marks on our vehicles, equipment and uniforms and make a dash for the Atlantic Coast where Rabat, the capital of both French and Spanish Morocco, lay. It took us several days of hard running through mountainous roads for part of the way as we paralleled the Mediterranean coastline.

All communication with civilians was prohibited. We had reason to believe that there were many double agents at large in North Africa who plied their trade of selling information to both sides. In addition we limited to emergencies all radio signals with our column of vehicles that stretched for miles along the road.

When I arrived at our destination I found a beautiful forest of large cork trees that were owned by the Sultan of Morocco and which were patrolled by his special guards. They rode beautiful Arabian horses known throughout the world for their speed, endurance, and beauty. As they circulated among our troops, identifying areas that were off-limits, we were impressed with their colorful uniforms and turbans. Large aisles had been cleared through the forest to help reduce fire hazards. Flying squirrels, whose webbed bodies permitted them to sail for several hundred feet, were everywhere and it wasn't too long before our men had tamed some as pets.

Our first night there we were congratulating ourselves for having made the run from Arzew to Rabat in record time and, we felt, secretly as well. After mess that night, as I was working in the command tent assigned to my section, one of the I&R boys tuned a radio to Berlin, as we usually did, because 'Axis Sally' played the best music on the air, including tunes sung by 'Der Bingel,' as Bing Crosby was known by the Germans. Her attempts to harm our morale were so corny that most everyone laughed them off as she intimated that wives and sweethearts back home were having a high old time with 4Fs and goldbricks who were 'sitting out' the war.

She managed to jolt us, however, that night for her first words were, 'Hello, you men of the 36th Texas Division. We've been watching your secret run across North Africa. Welcome to the cork forest at Rabat and all the little green worms you found there.' This meant that spies had been right in our camp that day, and we wondered about the sultan's guards who had made bold to chum up with some of our men.

She was correct about the green worms that let themselves down on silken strands from the trees all around us. As I was eating a sandwich that first day, I managed to avoid biting into one of the crawlers who swung onto the sandwich just as I was about to take another bite of it.

Axis Sally had managed in a few sentences to make the war a very personal matter by singling out the 36th Division for commentary directly from Berlin.

On our second day in the forest I took off for Rabat and found it an attractive city, particularly in the European section and near the Sultan's palace. There were magnificent homes in fine settings with bougainvillea climbing all over them in clusters of blossoms that were dazzling to look at under the desert sun. While I was there I thought I'd get some wine for our regimental mess and, upon inquiry of some of the American officers I ran into, went to a Jewish quarter which was part of the Medina, a native zone. My driver and I finally found a Jew who spoke English. He looked very much like an Arab and he watched my face, almost furtively, as I explained what I wanted. He directed us to drive to the next street corner and loped along beside us, barefooted, as we moved ahead.

I went up a series of stairways with my guide and entered a building that was more like a maze than a business establishment. In an inner court I was told to wait, and as I stood there I was the center of many hostile gazes from old men who sat at tables talking. I was beginning to get concerned when 20 minutes had passed and nearly started out of the place, only to be stopped by a young boy who, apparently, had been posted to see that I did not leave.

A few minutes later the English-speaking Jew hove into sight carrying four bottles of red wine. The bottles were dust-covered and appeared to represent a fair buy. I paid the man in French francs and gave him a tip for his pains which brought a real smile to an otherwise somber face. 'I was afraid you might not pay for the wine,' he said, 'Germans simply took it from us without payment.'

'We're trying hard to be as different from Germans as we know how,' I said. 'I think you can count on selling as much as you wish to part with as long as my unit is here.'

He didn't ask me my unit which was a good sign but he did, upon query from me, direct me to a French restaurant which he said was not off-limits to American GIs. It was called the 'Chanticleer,' and I had already learned that it was the one civilian restaurant where we might eat without much risk of contracting disease. I ate at it on several occasions during our stay near Rabat and brought home from it the recipe for preparing tomato slices with grated blue cheese, onions, and salad dressing.

I went one day into the Medina where the smell of open sewers blended with rotting meat hung from overhead trellises near vendors' stalls. At the far end of the native quarter I found a beautiful old palace reached by threading one's way through an intricate passage built to make entry difficult, should the owners desire to repel attack. The palace had been converted to a museum filled with beautiful furniture and furnishings and its gardens were brilliant and well tended. A blindfolded horse, hitched to a long bar, walked in endless circles as small buckets, actuated by a turnstile moved by the horse, delivered water to an irrigation system that kept the plants alive and thriving in oppressive heat.

On top of the high walls that surrounded the palace grounds were storks' nests, stiff and bristling with large sticks, in the center of which young birds clacked their bills whenever a parent hove into sight carrying food. It was a lovely spot to visit, and I went there several times by horse and buggy driven by a native in loose and smelly robes. I also tested the hot mint tea that was supposed to alleviate the torpor of the day and found it surprisingly refreshing. It seemed to balance inner and outer heat making the outer less oppressive. No self-respecting germ could have lasted long in the carafes of boiling water with which the tea was brewed by bearded Arabs, high on a terrace overlooking the Atlantic Ocean across a sea of flat roofs.

Our job in that area was to patrol the border between French and Spanish Morocco to guard against surprise attack. At the same time some of the division's units were put to work guarding the thousands of PWs who were herded into compounds along the coast. No one seemed sure what Spain and its colonies might do at that time. We were on the edge of wild country, mountainous and sparsely populated. The only way in which we could efficiently cover the border between the two countries, which was marked by a river, was to fly planes along the boundary. The only available planes were the light-artillery spotter planes that carried the pilot and, behind him, the observer. Their motors were so small that I was reminded of toy planes propelled by elastic bands.

In order to try to fool the Spanish Moroccans, who had several mountain divisions located fairly close to the river, we flew six planes around in a great circle, one portion of which encompassed the river. However, each time we got out of sight of the Spaniards, we would land the planes near our camp, change their symbols and markings and fly the route again. Our hope was to convince the Spanish commanders that their proximity to the border was a matter of concern to several American divisions. Since it took about 2 hours to complete one circuit, we found that three trips a day was about all we could manage with each plane.

I was not happy with what my pilot considered to be an adequate landing field from which I took off each day for the grand tour. It was a small field surrounded by trees like cedars of Lebanon and, while I had little to judge by, I was convinced that there wasn't adequate take-off room to clear the trees. My first flight out of that rough pasture did little to change my mind. Peering over the pilot's shoulder while keeping my feet out of the way of pedals that operated the ailerons, I knew that we would crash before we could clear the barrier ahead. Just before we did, though, the pilot pulled back on the stick, causing a similar movement of the dual control in front of me, and we literally jumped over the trees.

This was my first flight in such a light plane that responded to every vagrant breeze that blew. I found myself trying to counterbalance the various shifts in the center of gravity by leaning one way and another as we climbed higher above heavy slopes that sent thermal drafts to dog us as we flew our orbit of the potentially hostile positions.

I was sitting on a parachute that was strapped to my back and yet, confined by the plane's canopy, I had no confidence in my ability to get out of the confined space should an emergency arise. The land was so convoluted that the only hope of landing the plane, should it be forced down for any reason, was to hit the river or the beaches along the Atlantic Coast.

We droned along some 4,000ft above the highest prominences and occasionally we would spot a camel caravan or a herd of sheep or goats with, here and there, a small village of ancient homes, deserted from all appearances, and cheerless.

On the first day we landed at a French fortress overlooking the river in one area. The commandant, as I recall him, was a large, silver-haired man who invited us to lunch and, from certain spy holes in one of the casemates, pointed out Spanish Moroccan defensive zones. I had begun to exercise my school French by that time and was pleased to find that I could follow his explanation easily and in detail. He taught me a number of military terms that stood me in good stead for the rest of the war.

After we took off again, the prospect seemed less perilous as we now were aware of the French dispositions on our side of the river and the size of their force, which was not inconsiderable. I later made a report of such matters for use by my regiment should occasion require action by our troops. We flew on, that first day, to the confluence of the river with the ocean, circled back away from Spanish Morocco, and landed again at the miserable field we'd left earlier in the day. Landing was a matter of scraping through the treetops, dropping suddenly and with heavy impact into the rutted runway, and praying that the brakes would hold before we reached the far side of the field. I was very happy to get out of the plane, unstrap the parachute, and drink a cold beer that one of the air crew provided from a jury-rigged refrigerator set up in a tent.

I found it necessary, during our stay near Rabat, to work until late at night preparing intelligence estimates of the situation east of us where the war was ending in North Africa and to plot potential hostile defenses on the Spanish Moroccan border. We were also constantly bombarded with 'Order of Battle' data, supplied by higher headquarters, which gave us background information on many of the Axis military leaders. I kept the I&R platoon busy, as well, practicing their techniques of patrolling, encoding and decoding messages, identifying hostile planes and tanks from silhouettes prepared for that purpose and operating observation and listening posts, the latter to be used at night on positions as close to enemy lines as possible.

During the day I strapped on my parachute, climbed into a fragile plane, prayed a little as we hopped over our tree barrier and watched the controls sliding beneath my feet as we soared aloft. Most of the patrols were uneventful, and I began to appreciate the wild beauty of the African landscape. On several occasions I saw herds of between 50 and 100 wild boars and sows running from the noise of our plane with their rocking-horse gait.

Suddenly one day the pilot, who was constantly in touch with our base by radio, cut the motor, which gave me quite a start and as we commenced a long glide toward a forbidding looking mountain slope, he shouted over his shoulder, 'Red alert! Enemy planes in this area. Watch toward the sun.' I was glad when I heard the motor sputter back to life to replace the whining of the wind in our struts and under-carriage.

I held one hand up to blot out most of the glare of the sun and looked toward that yellow, blazing orb for the first sign of an enemy aircraft, most of which I had learned to distinguish on sight from having worked with the I&R platoon on its identification program. It was a well-known German tactic to dive on a target from out of the sun and since we had no chance against an armed fighter, my pilot decided to circle low between several steep hills where, if required, we could dodge around a shoulder of one of them depending on the direction of attack. While he was busy keeping us away from dangerous peaks, I swiveled my neck to watch in all directions although, because of the plane's canopy, I could see nothing directly overhead. Mainly I watched the edge of the sun from behind my hand and was quickly aware of sweat streaming down my back and legs as I realized that my first sight of the enemy's power, applied to me personally, might be my last one. It was a relief to get the pilot's signal that all was, once again, safe – a report he made by poking his right thumb up.

That same day, after having landed again at the French garrison's headquarters, I learned that the Spanish troops had withdrawn from the border and, according to French patrols, had re-established their defenses 10 miles into the interior of their country. This was good news and, strangely enough, I was the first to report it that night at our division headquarters whose personnel kept busy doing garrison duty, rather than the sky patrolling I was engaged in. This was the first of many such occasions during the war when I found myself doing the job of the division staff.

As we were about to take to the air again from the French landing strip our pilot received another radio report calling for all spotter planes in the vicinity to patrol out to sea some 50 miles in search of a German submarine that was thought to have been crippled by depth charges the night before. He didn't ask me if I wanted to accompany him but if he had, I would have agreed to go since he would have had a tough time alone trying to observe the ocean in all directions while flying. Furthermore, over the water we were bound to be more conspicuous from shore watchers than when flying through the hills. It was a distinct possibility that we could be fingered for air attack, particularly if a hostile submarine actually were in trouble on the surface.

We made our way toward the Atlantic while gusts of wind from the ocean slowed us down and caused the plane to bounce around considerably. It was a lonely feeling to see the shoreline disappear from sight as we floated along toward the ever-receding horizon and, while we could still see the hills and mountains behind us, when we made our turn to the south, it dawned on me that a fighter plane – should one put in an appearance – couldn't miss us in that locality. Fortunately, none did but it was getting dark by the time we hedge-hopped over our tree-lined landing strip and crashed to a halt with my leg muscles cramped, as usual, from applying the non-existent brake to avoid hitting the trees on the far side. I never did get used to flying into and out of that rat trap. It was, I thought, a good thing that we had seen nothing in our search of the deep water, since a German U-boat could easily have brought us down with its deck guns, had one been out there.

We weren't in Rabat's vicinity very long before we were ordered to return to Arzew to continue with our amphibious training.

Chapter 3

Intelligence School and Intelligence at Work

We had just settled into amphibious training once again and had even arranged an officer's club in one of the Arzew villas, all of which were pastel colored and quite modern in architecture, when I was alerted to attend the NATOUSA (North African Theatre of Operation, US Army) Intelligence School, at Duera in the mountains, a few miles south of the city of Algiers.

I had just missed out on a similar assignment to attend such a school in Cairo, Egypt, where the British had established an intelligence center but, for reasons never explained to me by Colonel A.B. Crowther, the division G-2 at the time, my orders were cancelled.

An officer from the armored infantry regiment of the First Armored Division, who had also been ordered to Duera, called at our headquarters and I drove with him in a chauffered command car from Arzew to Algiers, a distance of about 250 miles over poor roads crowded with military traffic of all kinds. It took us the better part of two days, and on the way we were alerted several times by reports of escaped German PWs in the area. We slept in the car overnight with one staying awake while the other two slept. In the morning, as we were burning a waxed K ration package over which to heat a canteen cupful of water for coffee (the package having been designed for that purpose), three small Arab boys followed by a shy little Arab girl approached us. In the distance we could see and hear a herd of goats which, I assumed, were under the surveillance of our visitors.

It was evident to anyone who had been in North Africa very long that Arabian children were undernourished and, consequently, always hungry. These four were no exception and shortly I spoke to them in French and asked if they were hungry. All heads bobbed up and down rapidly so I offered each a box of K rations which consisted of cheese, coffee and what the GIs euphemistically called 'dog biscuits' – very hard, round crackers hyped up with vitamins and tasteless.

The children moved to a point along the roadside some 50ft from where I was shaving out of my helmet which I was using as a wash basin. I saw that they were having difficulty opening the packages so called for them to come back and as each handed me his ration box I could see that he did not believe I'd give it back. I cut the end off each package and showed them what was inside. I also showed them how to heat water by burning the package and their eyes shone excitedly as we heated water in two canteen cups for their use.

They chattered like a flock of birds in their native tongue, throwing in a French question now and then to let me know they were interested in us. I learned that they drove the herd all day, every day, and that for all practical purposes they were on their own so far as concerned finding food and a place to sleep each night. Their families would find them every month or two but leave again in a day or so taking some of the goats with them. They had never seen the inside of a school and had little or nothing but their ragged clothing to keep them warm at night. They often stole grapes, in season, from the vast vineyards that were growing in many areas along the North African littoral. They also said that they were glad the war had come along for they'd eaten better, once the Americans had arrived, than ever before.

We gave them the rest of our K rations for I was certain we could get more from installations along the way, assuming that we couldn't do better than K rations for future meals. The last we saw of the goatherds found them sitting in the road dividing up the case of K rations for ease of transportation.

At Fez we took the time to visit the Medina, after talking with some of the French officers we met who were stationed there. This, of course, was the native quarter and I had the distinct impression of riding through biblical scenes as we circled down a long hill from the modern part of the city to approach this high-walled area. Olive trees were growing here and there and under the hot sun everything danced in heat waves. In the distance we could see minarets and domes of the old city but the ancient wall finally blotted out the view and the approach began to take on overtones of danger. I had the sensation that if we passed the forbidding wall we could disappear forever and no one would know what had happened to us.

We found the street crowded but there was an entrance-way to a courtyard from which, after leaving our vehicle, we could walk down a stairway to the Palais Jamai, a Cook's Tour Hotel of which we'd heard. Everything there was breath-taking since every surface was covered in mosaics – walls, ceilings, floors, terraces, fountains, and even table tops beneath palm trees. There were fountains and small irrigation canals and beautiful gardens descending in terraces toward a cast-iron fence beyond which rose minarets in the distance.

We ate a meal on a tiled terrace in the shade of a tree and were joined by the wives of three French officers who had been on leave at the hotel but who had, that morning, returned to their regiments. I did the translating as we sat for an hour after our meal and learned that the officers in question had originally opposed the Allied landing at Oran but had been glad when the Vichy French government had been overruled by the French High Command in North Africa.

We took our leave, hating to venture out beyond the walls that earlier we had found so forbidding. However, I was always well armed and hadn't really anticipated trouble when we entered the thick-walled native city. It was simply the play of imagination on the possibilities that might occur in a jumbled rabbit warren of a place that had made our entry something less than enthusiastic.

Before leaving I talked with a British air officer who was billeted in the hotel since his squadron operated out of a nearby airfield. He agreed that the British Air Ministry had done well by him and his group – his one beef, so to speak, being that they were, knowingly, eating mule meat at meals that were otherwise superb. I told him I'd be glad to give him some K rations if he thought they'd be an improvement. He declined with thanks and added that, beyond being a mite 'grainy,' mule meat wasn't that bad to eat.

When we arrived at Duera I reported to a British major who was in charge of the Intelligence School. I found him in the officers' mess, it being about noon when we drove into town. The town was not too large but did contain a sizeable French hospital. The major invited us to have lunch, which was a mixture of American, British and French fare, as I recall it. I admired the British way of doing things throughout the war. They always appeared to put down roots wherever they landed, even if only for a fortnight. The officers' mess was in a pyramidal tent with netting enclosing the bottom area where the flaps had been rolled up to let the breezes through. It had a wooden floor and comfortable chairs and tables with a sideboard where one could choose from a selection of foods. In one corner stood a bar but, unfortunately, no ice.

The school, itself, had been set up in a school building at the edge of town where there was quite a stand of palm and olive trees as well as oaks and other deciduous trees. Around the school were rolling hills and set up in firing positions were German 88mm anti-aircraft, anti-tank guns, howitzers of several calibers, tanks and self-propelled guns, most of which had been camouflaged with desert browns, tans and greys since they had been captured from the Afrika Korps. Machine guns and Schmeizer machine pistols were also on display in the school building.

Before I went to the school, however, the major advised me to go to a certain home near the hospital where I would be billeted with the family of a hospital orderly, a middle-aged man who lived with his wife and young daughter in a two-and-a-half-story stone house. I did so and received quite a welcome when I introduced myself in French and thanked them for making a room available for my ten-day stay.

The daughter, who was 12 or 13, showed me upstairs to a bedroom where mosquito netting surrounded the bed. Lighting was by candle and I was warned by the youngster to be careful about fire. I assured her I would be very cautious and she showed me the bathroom where, strangely enough, there was running cold water and fairly modern plumbing. If I wanted a bath it would be necessary to advise them a day ahead. I told the girl that I would try to take care of my ablutions elsewhere, which I did, once I learned that there were showers set up by a quartermaster company in the town square.

I had been troubled by an open sore, something like a large boil, on my right leg, which I'd had lanced at a French hospital at Mostaganem just after leaving Arzew. It had been irritated for some time and I realized as I set out for Algiers with my friend from the First Armored Division that it had suddenly grown worse overnight.

We drove to the permanent hospital, where I had to wait for more than 2 hours, while French wounded were cared for, before a doctor could see me. He took me into an examining room and after inspecting the festered area called several other doctors in, one of whom appeared to be the chief surgeon. While their talk was technical and too fast for me to understand completely, I found myself beginning to worry when I realized that the chief surgeon was concerned about my losing my leg. He felt it possible that one of several roots had attached itself to a main artery of my leg.

I told them that there would be no question of my losing my leg there as I would remove myself, pretty damned quick, to the nearest US hospital. The chief surgeon, whose face was masked in a black beard, laughed to show huge yellow teeth and said he'd see what he could do to save my leg.

They put me on an operating table and proceeded to cut at the infected area with very small scalpels while I did my best to keep from groaning since there was no thought of anesthetic of any kind. It hurt like hell and I could feel myself getting faint until, all at once, there was a hot cascading of liquid across my thigh and the world seemed bright and gay once more. It was a hydra-headed monster, I gathered from the talk, emanating from several channels deep within my leg. Finally, after about half an hour of considerable effort, a drain was inserted in the wound and a dressing applied to it.

The doctors informed me that I would be in their care for about a week. I replied that I was leaving at once for Algiers as I had already delayed my host for several hours. The chief surgeon shook his head when I announced my imminent departure but then relented and gave me several large dressings for use on the road, provided that I would agree to go to a hospital in Algiers for further examination within the next two days. He feared that the incision would close before the infection was drained off and he also thought that the jouncing around on the road would be detrimental to my well-being.

I was in the best condition of my adult life and while I had occasion to think about a soft bed and a good night's rest, whenever we struck a heavy bump, I felt little the worse for wear when I arrived at Duera.

I decided to visit a hospital the day following my arrival at Duera and went by jeep to Algiers which I had never seen before. As we approached the city, I was dumbfounded at the millions of rounds of artillery ammunition that were stored in bays along the roadside together with thousands of aerial bombs of every description. The depots ran for miles and seemed very poorly guarded, under the circumstances. As we entered the city there came sounds of small-arms fire in increasing volume. We were at the top of the series of hills that form the main part of Algiers and I could see for miles out across the Mediterranean Sea. The harbor was full of ships of all kinds, and the city was throbbing with a mixture of civilian and military traffic.

Suddenly an electric streetcar came racing along the street we were traveling on, and in it were a number of GIs wearing the Big Red '1' of the First Division, my old unit. A GI was at the controls waving a bottle with one hand and doing a poor job of controlling the speed of the car with the other. Other soldiers fired pistols and carbines into the air as they passed my vehicle and shouted obscenities to anyone who would listen.

Fortunately I found the street I was looking for and turned off to the hospital located there. Again, I was forced to wait several hours because civilians and soldiers, hurt by the marauding GIs, were being brought to the emergency room where I was located. I was given a perfunctory examination by a US medical doctor who changed the dressing on my leg, pressed the sore area that was healing rapidly, and pronounced me fit. So far as I can now recall, that was the last of my disability.

The next day the Duera school began its curriculum and I was immersed in all kinds of studies based on both British and US approaches to combat intelligence. It was somewhat perplexing to hear the British instructors speak in terms of 'enemy intentions' while our approach to such matters was one aimed at learning 'enemy capabilities.' Basically, I learned, before the war was over, that we were striving to establish similar conclusions and while it seemed to some of us that hostile 'intentions,' being rather amorphous at best, could change very rapidly, hostile capabilities were limited by such finite considerations, as strength of opposing units, supply problems, transportation facilities, supporting arms, length of time in combat, availability of reserves and other realities. We, of course, were also concerned with other less definitive hostile concerns as morale factors and leadership qualities of top generals.

However, if we took into consideration all aspects of the enemy's 'intentions,' it would boil down to an examination of all of the factors that concerned our system of analysis and not alone the cast of mind of the enemy leaders, as seemed to be implied in the use of the term 'hostile intentions.'

None of us, who had yet to enter combat, felt comfortable querying proposals put forth by such men as the white-haired major who, at age 26, had been into and out of Europe several times in such actions as Dieppe, Dunkirk, and Greece. He was old before his time and yet there was a conscious quietude about him that commanded respect and evoked credibility.

On one occasion the major surprised us while discussing the best techniques for interrogating prisoners of war. He said:

You men will be operating on the knife-edge where prisoners will be at their 'softest,' immediately after capture. Do not discredit reports that part of the German method of training men against divulging military information has been to convince them that they will be killed by us, if they are captured. While this may steel them against easy surrender, it acts as a boomerang once they are taken. Then, they are thinking mainly of some way to save their necks.

Watch their eyes. You'll see every emotion running through them as you study them. You'll have them where they are most vulnerable, on a fighting front where men can disappear without anyone really knowing what happened to them. Play on this isolation, this sense of aloneness but, and this is important, control the interrogation. You'll be in a cellar or a cave somewhere, or possibly in a house or barn and since you'll interrogate the prisoners, time and circumstances permitting, one at a time, you'll have them outnumbered. Do not let them talk, even if they try to, until you direct the questioning for that purpose.

While I was somewhat skeptical of this approach, it being the first time in my army career that I'd heard a man skilled in the art of interrogation initiate instruction by saying, 'Don't let them talk,' I later put it to very effective use, to the point where 90 percent of the solid intelligence available to my regiment in the normal course of combat came from prisoners of war.

We learned of a technique in obtaining corroboration of facts we were not sure of through use, for example, of 'a show of knowledge' wherein our interpreters would reel off a series of facts we already knew, throwing in some of the more conjectural matters, to gauge the prisoner's reaction to the display of knowledge. Many times it was evident to us, who were watching a prisoner's eyes, that he was impressed with our knowledge. This, in turn, would help break down barriers to giving us further information on the premise that if we were already aware of much of the German situation in front of us, little harm could come of telling us more.

We were told of tell-tale signs to watch for, when a group of prisoners was taken, in order to isolate the 'weak sisters' or the 'soft touches' for immediate interrogation, assuming the tactical situation to be in need of fast help. Officers and enlisted men were to be segregated to obviate the weight of the officer personnel's presence on the ordinary soldier's desire to save his own neck by talking.

We were given demonstrations taken from actual combat experiences where hard nuts, like some German officers, had been cracked because they had given the impression that they were willing to talk but had lied consistently from square one. Part of the technique of interrogation, of course, is to ask questions the answers to which have already been reliably established.

The major added:

If you can get a prisoner to talk at all, the chances are good that you can bring him to a point where further lying, assuming that his initial answers have been lies, will appear foolish to him, too. There is something psychologically chilling about a sudden silence on the part of the usually egotistical officer or enlisted man who thinks he can delude you with a lot of lies and half-truths. Since he's already talked and has been found out, his reaction may well be to give you everything he knows. It may, however, be difficult to distinguish between what he knows and what he thinks he knows.

You will have trouble with some of the radical units such as the SS and units comprised of men who grew up as Hitler Jugend[1] and who are fanatical in their support of the Nazi regime. You may have to give up on them, so don't hold them too long at the front since they will be subjected to more sophisticated techniques in other places.

I assumed that this meant that such PWs would be infiltrated by US intelligence men acting as German PWs or would be exposed to electronic devices used for listening in on conversations between prisoners. Although his words regarding fanaticism were prophetic, I was to encounter only one prisoner who refused to talk after capture by my regiment, and even he was capable of changing his mind when we promised him a quick trip to the French Colonial Army's Goums[2], whose reputation for successful interrogation was well known to German troops.

I was awakened each morning by the young daughter of the household who would bring me warm water for shaving and upon tip-toeing out of my room would slam the door loudly enough to awaken the dead. The days passed very quickly and since we had a full day's break between courses, I managed to return to Algiers to look around.

I encountered two of my former BU professors on duty at Ike Eisenhower's headquarters in an old hotel in the heart of the city. Both were full colonels in the reserve and were busy planning future operations. I also saw Ike in his sedan talking with Marlene Dietrich, who was part of a USO troop entertaining the GIs.

The Red Cross building in Algiers was a spacious, modern building where several of us went to get oriented on what to see in the city. I met a British naval captain, quite a lot older than me, who volunteered to take us on a jaunt through the Casbah, renowned in Hollywood offerings. The captain was all decked out in his dress uniform replete with ribbons, connoting long and hazardous service. His full beard gave him the look of Prince Albert, Queen Victoria's consort, a fact of which he was aware when I mentioned the resemblance to him.

We walked downhill from the Red Cross building toward the waterfront and turned into a foul-smelling alley through a high gateway in a wall. There were four of us from the Intelligence School and the captain, who rolled as he walked, a holdover, he said, from walking a plunging deck. We hadn't gone far before sirens sounded and the captain, along with the rest of us, ducked up another alley and into a cellar doorway. The stench was terrible and we agreed that we'd take our chances returning to the modern part of the city, although the captain said he had something else in mind and left us, after seeing to it that we knew where the entrance to the Casbah was located.

---

1. Hitler Youth.
2. Fighters consisting of individuals native to French colonies.

Bombs crashed into the harbor area as we scurried uphill again but the all-clear sounded shortly thereafter and we were free to roam the city. I wanted to buy some souvenirs to send home and went to a bazaar area where there were hundreds of artisans making leather items from camel skin, carving sandalwood boxes, making the turned-up-toed shoes that some Arabs wore and, in general, developing touristy items to include clothing on which they'd sewn some of the American and British unit identification patches.

I watched an old man sitting shoulder high on a ledge behind which was a cubbyhole in which he kept tools and camel skins. This was his place of business and it was quite a sight to watch him split a camel's skin into two pieces, thus reducing his costs but also reducing the value of his wares.

In a fairly large store occupied by several merchants in their Arab robes and hoods, I saw some poufs which I thought would make good presents to send home since the leather exterior could be stuffed after arrival in the states. I spoke in French to a fairly young man who was clean-shaven and full of business. We had been warned to haggle over price as no merchant ever asked, initially, what he would finally take. So I made quite a to-do over his asking price and started on my way around the shop. He grabbed me by the shoulder and in half Arabic, half French recited the extraordinary skills that went into making a pouf, fitting the pieces to make a perfectly round shape and sewing them with special leather thongs for longevity.

I told him I'd seen better for half the price and he invited me to show him where. I declined and walked on to another merchant where, after some haggling, I bought a pair of Arabian woman's shoes as souvenirs. I started out the door when the pouf dealer caught up with me and in a torrent of several languages beckoned me to come back to his stall. We finally settled on a price and when I'd paid him and had the bundle wrapped for mailing, he said in the clearest English, 'Come back again, old fellow, it's been a pleasure doing business with you.' It was so unexpected that I had to laugh with him and learned from him that he had lived ten years in Chicago, Illinois, and had sold Arabian goods at the Chicago World's Fair during that time.

That taught me not to assume that a person spoke no English, at least until I'd asked if that was the case. In another instance of language problems, I ran into a reverse situation in Duera a couple of days later when I entered a barber shop and found, to my surprise, two female barbers. Both were French women and fairly young and good-looking. I made signs that I wanted a shave and a haircut and one of the lady barbers motioned me to a chair. While she shaved my face she went to great lengths to tell her companion all about her desire to go to bed with an American, preferably like the type in the chair, but that her husband had threatened to do her bodily harm if she so much as looked at an American and all that, she said, in spite of the fact that she knew he was keeping a mistress in another part of town.

She went on and on describing my virtues to include my moustache, which she liked, but all the time keeping her voice on a completely objective and matter-of-fact key as though discussing the day's shopping. It was so intriguing that I pretended to sleep as she shaved me and applied hot towels before trimming my hair. She even asked her friend if she thought I looked like the kind of fellow who would object to advances by a female and received an answer in the affirmative.

As I left and after pretending not to understand the value of the French franc, I paid her an amount twice what she'd asked and said in French, 'I wish I could stay longer to hear more about myself but the war calls and I have to answer.' The woman stared into my eyes with her mouth open wide and then threw a towel over her head and ran off into another room while her co-worker collapsed in gales of laughter over her memories of the intimacies that had been mentioned in the monologue. That was my only experience with a woman barber during the war or after, but it wasn't all bad, at that.

The Intelligence School broke up on schedule and I decided to return to my unit at Arzew via Algiers and got my traveling companion to agree. We stopped for a snack at the Red Cross center and then proceeded westward, again, toward Arzew. A few miles outside of Algiers I saw an officer whom I had known as Captain Cunningham when he was an ROTC instructor at BU. He was now a Brigadier General and was very active at a road-block running back and forth and barking orders.

On a hill above the road I saw what looked like a PW enclosure. I had the driver stop and walked back to where Cunningham was talking with a group of MPs. I saluted and stuck out my hand which he ignored. 'I'm Doughty,' I said. 'You were an instructor at BU when I was there.'

'Right, Doughty,' he said. 'Now please drive on!'

'Would you mind telling me what's going on here?' I asked.

'Nothing that you need to know about,' he snapped. I got the message, real clear, and left. Later I learned that the 1st Division had mutinied in Algiers upon hearing that it would make the amphibious attack against Sicily. I had met and talked with several of my old friends from the 1st when I had spent some time in Sidi Bel Abbes, thse headquarters of the French Foreign Legion. They had told me, as we drank at the Officers' Club one night, that General Teddy Roosevelt Jr had indicated to them that, once the war ended in North Africa, the Big Red One[3] would head for home to instruct others in how to fight Germans. How he had come to this opinion was not clear, according to my friends, but I could understand why men would be disappointed if the general's prediction proved false. I could not understand a mutinous reaction, part of which I had observed my first day in Algiers. The whole story was never told abroad so far as I could determine, but after the 1st Division helped complete the conquest of Sicily it was moved to England to be reconstituted, preparatory to landing, once more, in Normandy. As one of the most impressive of the regular army divisions, with a history of heroic action in warfare, the 1st could not possibly have been withdrawn from combat so early in the war without charges that the regular establishment, as many of us had long ago surmised, was too good to die.

---

3. 1st Infantry Division.

Chapter 4

A Breach of Security

There was a very different feeling in the air when I returned to the 141st Infantry from Duera. Everything was moving at a faster pace and I learned that certain shipping in Oran Harbor had been earmarked for the 36th Division. Rumors were heard on all sides as to our ultimate destination. Sicily was in the process of being subdued with heavy competition between the slow-moving British invasion force and the dashing, daring thrusts of General Patton, who couldn't stand the sight of Montgomery and who, consequently, did all in his power to show him up.

Some of my fellow officers, after listening to British officers, were betting on the Balkans, after a fast sortie through the Adriatic Sea. This, of course, was Mr. Churchill's grand ploy to cut Russia off from overrunning Eastern Europe. Some officers even thought we'd make a direct run for France which, as I viewed it, would leave our supply lines vulnerable to attack from Italy. It also seemed contrary to fairly obvious plans to mount a very large-scale invasion of Europe from the British Isles.

As I viewed the situation I felt that Italy was our only logical target, but while I didn't know where we might strike, it seemed plausible to me that we would hit near Rome in order to reduce one major Axis capital as soon as possible. I was very busy adapting intelligence reports for regimental use, since it seemed, at times, that we might be thrown into the Sicilian fight, as reports sifted back of heavy German resistance.

I was also appalled at certain rumors of a foul-up on the landing beaches of Sicily and of casualties inflicted on our air force by our own and British naval guns when, contrary to plan, the airmen flew directly over the invasion fleet. It also appeared fairly wise to study the Sicilian topography, as well as that of the toe of the Italian peninsula, in case we were moved through those areas to combat positions.

Our efforts to keep our plans secure were often the cause of hundreds of hours of work, planning for all foreseeable contingencies. While higher headquarters were aware of eventual landing operations, the fighting troops were kept under the pressure of ignorance of target areas and, therefore, were often forced to double and quadruple their efforts to be ready for any development. This meant spending 18- and 20-hour days in the process.

The division had moved, in my absence, to the outskirts of Oran, fairly close to the area where we had first bivouaced in the middle of April and where the Arabs had stolen, and then returned, our anti-gas underwear. The place at that time of year was a dustbowl with red dust, raised by heavy military traffic, filtering into everything, including our working papers, which would then smudge under sweaty hands and arms, into our food and our lungs. My section was located practically at the edge of the main road where we caught the full burst of every dust cloud raised. This, of course, had occurred because I had not been present to guard against such poor siting. I had the tent moved to a spot several hundred feet from the road where life became much easier, once we could raise the tent flaps to let the breezes through.

One day Lieutenant Bill Schroebel, who had been away learning a transport quartermaster's job, came to me to ask for assistance in plans to load our regiment and its attached troops onto ships that would take us into combat. I was busy with various aspects of the intelligence annex that would accompany any operation instructions that would be issued by the regiment, and so I suggested that he seek help elsewhere. I didn't give the matter another thought until Colonel Werner, the regimental commander, called me to his tent. There I learned that I was to assist Schroebel. I mention it here because it, too, was an augury of things to come, later. As I now recall the problem, it concerned the allocation of troops to the assault ships, and it took but a few hours to straighten it away by calling on the port authorities in Oran and getting their suggestions.

As I worked developing overlays of hostile positions being reported from the Sicilian front and those located in Italy by air reconnaissance, I became certain that we would strike Italy. Suddenly, too, after years of map problems in which the only enemy was comprised of such symbols, I began to realize that, behind the symbols, were flesh and blood men and steel weapons. I could begin to see the enemy in three, rather than two, dimensions. While this may appear simplistic and obvious I learned, the hard way, that my most difficult assignment in the war was to convince a number of regular army officers who, throughout their careers, had fought nothing but paper 'enemies,' that the enemy had three dimensions.

Colonel Crowther, division G-2, called me one morning from his headquarters, further east of our position, to come over for a briefing and to accompany him to Oran where we would discuss certain counterintelligence measures with the Base Section G-2, located in that city. I arrived at division headquarters and talked with Crowther about maps that we would need before entering combat. He told me that the division engineers were already sorting such maps at a warehouse in Oran, preparatory to placing them on board the various assault ships just before we sailed for our, to me, unknown destination.

We left Crowther's tent and, as we approached the carpool area, a command car came to a halt near us and General Omar Bradley stepped out. We saluted and he asked us both to accompany him to the Situation Tent where General Walker and other members of his staff were assembled.

As we entered, someone shouted 'Attention!' and all present stood fast, as General Walker saluted and shook hands with Bradley. Shortly, a situation map, previously covered with canvas, was undraped and, for the first time, I learned that we would strike Italy in the Salerno Bay area. I had had a few seconds to study the symbols representing attacking forces, as well as known hostile dispositions, but in those moments I saw that the British X Corps would form the main assault force, and somehow this helped allay the shock of such an important assignment: the first solid blow against the main continent of Europe by the Allies.

General Bradley, for my money the best strategist and tactician in the war, took one look at the map and said, 'You're too near Agropoli! Move the landing area 1 mile north otherwise you'll have enfilade fire down your landing echelons.' With that he returned to his vehicle and took off for his next port of call.

This knowledge brought the war palpably closer to me. Now I knew where we would first meet the enemy and in approximately what force. As Colonel Crowther and I were driven to Oran, we talked of the impending invasion and he warned me about telling anyone of the contents of the map I'd seen. I told him that certain officers of the regiment claimed that they'd already been briefed on the landing site, a matter he knew nothing about but which he said he would look into.

Crowther also mentioned the fact that the Base Section G-2 was very much concerned about spying within the Base Section's own ranks where a number of civilians had been put to work after superficial security clearance. In fact, it seemed that there was a girl typist in the G-2 section there who was being watched because of certain activities she'd been engaged in, the nature of which Crowther did not know.

I said that, if I were the Base Section G-2, I'd get rid of the girl without a moment's delay, since the success or failure of our invasion could depend on keeping its destination from her eyes and ears. Crowther agreed and we discussed the difference between precautions taken by fighting units, whose members' lives depend so heavily on the maintenance of tight security, and those taken by units whose main job is to send others off to do the fighting. It seemed that the Base G-2 was anxious to catch more important agents than the girl typist, and therefore was, in effect, using her as bait. This smacked too much of the cloak-and-dagger crap that we were subjected to from time-to-time by the OSS[1] who, doubtless, did a great job throughout the war, but whose agents, all too often, could not refrain from exaggerating and romanticizing their work. Some of them were straight 8-balls who, I believe, were practically useless once they began to believe their own propaganda.

We talked with the Base Section G-2 and observed the girl who was suspected of being an enemy agent. Later we visited the warehouse where maps were being sorted. It was a huge place and well-guarded by sentries all around its exterior. Everywhere on tables, floor and walls were piles of maps which engineers had duplicated by the thousands from old Italian maps. We talked with some of our own engineers, who were stripped to the waist working in the stifling heat of a North African August. They were sorting maps in accordance with a cumbersome list of map numbers which identified the respective terrain sites

---

1. Office of Strategic Services (today's CIA).

covered by the maps. Some maps were drawn to a 1:50,000 scale while others, more useful for the tactical detail they offered, were drawn to a 1:25,000 scale.

Crowther, of course, had already received a set of maps for his purposes and assured me that each regiment would be given an intelligence overlay that would show enemy installations and concentrations of troops and weapons sufficient to assist their tactical planning while en route by ship to their objectives. This was a necessary precaution but one which left me concerned about overall control of our regiment's attacking echelons, since its units would be scattered on a number of ships before their commanders would know their final targets. Communications at sea would be limited at best and, very likely, unavailable for such things as tactical planning.

It is not an apocryphal story to say that there was a leak in the security covering the invasion of Salerno. It happened, despite the fact that Ike Eisenhower, in his book *Crusade in Europe*, alludes to the possibility of such a leak. It occurred as a result of a breach of orders by one of the engineers preparing maps for the 36th Division's use. He, apparently tired of referring to an involved list of numbers to identify maps needed by the various fighting teams of the division, copied off his own, shorter list for convenience of reference. Even that would not have been too great a breach of security if the copied list had been confined to use in the warehouse. However, as is almost inevitable in such cases, the short list found its way into the engineer's pocket and then, inadvertently without doubt but nevertheless, directly, into the hands of an enemy agent.

No one was the wiser that the breach had occurred until the suspected girl typist in the Base Section was observed returning the list to a locker used by the engineers of the Base Section several days later. Why, if this was true, nothing was done to punish the offending officer, is difficult to understand. It's very likely explained by one of several hypotheses: no one was sure, except by inference, that the list had been compromised; it was too late to change plans since, as was later to be made known, arrangements were then about clinched for Italy to surrender before we drove our attack home on the Italian mainland; a court martial would have divulged the security leak with consequent political and spiritual upheavals at home, once the details were known.

One thing was fairly certain in my mind, and that was the sense that forces opposing us in Italy already knew where we would strike. It prompted me to scan intelligence reports crossing my desk with the greatest care to try to learn whether reinforcements were moving toward the projected Salerno beachhead. Anyone obtaining a list of map numbers of the type in question could, by reference to widely available indices of such numbers, spot our target exactly. Added to the normal nervous pressures of my fighting debut was the worry that we would be walking into a death-trap.

During the first week of September 1943 a situation was brought to my attention by Colonel Werner which led to a monumental misunderstanding between a GI from New York and me which, to this day, I believe the former GI considers to have been deliberate on my part. It concerned Sidney Z. Searles, a lawyer with absolutely no qualifications as a rifleman. He was a very bright man but with little muscular coordination and possessed of an attitude toward fighting that could only be described as negative to the nth degree.

I was working in my quarters when Colonel Werner, together with Searles' company commander, dropped by to ask my advice about Searles. Werner, I believe, felt that I, as a Yankee, might be able to solve the dilemma of what to do with Searles better than he or some other Texan might do. I finally said that, under no circumstances did I think it fair to Searles or to those who would serve with him in an infantry squad, to put him in the front lines. I agreed to take him in my section for the landing and said I had a particular assignment that I was sure he would handle well.

The matter was left like that and Searles reported to me just before we loaded for Salerno, bag and baggage. I charged him with the security of the field safe which was part of the intelligence section's equipment. It was a very heavy steel box with handles on either end to permit ease of transport by two men. I warned Searles to chain himself to the safe because it contained the 'Top Secret' Corps Plan of Maneuver for the first few weeks of the invasion together with a number of other highly classified documents, all of which were numbered and for which I was personally responsible. Searles was very happy with this turn of events and set about familiarizing himself with the men and officers of the section.

While it anticipates my story by a week or so, nevertheless I think the misunderstanding should be made clear at this juncture. After landing at Salerno, a subject to be covered in detail later, and not knowing what would happen minute-by-minute, after having been shot at for a number of hours plus having been bombed and strafed, I suddenly looked up and saw Searles and another man from the I&R platoon struggling across the beach with the safe. I had apparently done Searles no favor leaving him aboard ship for a later landing because enemy planes had worked over the armada fairly well during the day.

He dropped the safe at my feet and despite my being distracted by trying to direct naval fire at several gun positions in the hills, demanded that I inspect its contents. I finally found a moment to do so and when I opened the safe with a key I had retained, I found it full of soap and candy! I could not believe my eyes and Searles' face was pitiful to look at. He couldn't say anything, nor could I. I located Corporal B.P. Hobday of my section and, pointing to the safe, asked him how come? It seemed that he had thought it safer to leave the Top Secret papers in a crate on the dock at Oran for shipment a week later. Since every password for the next two weeks, every operation and intelligence instruction for the whole corps was also there and since it was possible that Hobday's action had compromised our security, for which I alone could be held responsible, I raised hell in spades. I further told Hobday to wait on the beach until the crate showed up if it took nine years. I was never so surprised and shocked in three years of warfare as I was when Hobday's 'tradin' material' took precedence over top-secret materials. I scrounged necessary data from the artillery and drew a full breath again some ten days later when Hobday showed up with my secret papers – still in their crate.

I was caught up almost immediately following Searles' assignment to my section with the combat loading of our troops on board ship in Oran Harbor. Finally, we were all on board ship and awaiting sailing orders. I was on the combat transport *O'Hara* with the rest of the regimental staff and many of the regiment's fighting echelons. The ship was stuffed to its internal overhead with war gear of all kinds. There was scarcely room to move or to sit down anywhere, except in the wardroom. As I sat talking with other staff members my name was called over the intercom. 'Captain Doughty, report to the bridge,' came the summons.

I picked up my gear and went to the bridge, where the ship's captain told me a small boat was waiting at the foot of a ship's ladder, ready to take me to the command ship where I was to report to Colonel Crowther. I climbed down to a float and got aboard an open whaleboat-type ferry that was operated by a crew of four sailors. It was full dark at the time and the only lights observable were blue ones identifying gateways through the anti-submarine nets guarding the harbor. As we picked up speed to run toward the command ship, sister to the *O'Hara*, lying at anchor about a half-mile away, anti-aircraft batteries all around the harbor commenced firing. We were caught in the open with no chance of taking cover from falling bombs or the flack that fell back with quick hissing sounds into the water. The sailors put on helmets and the pilot of the boat wore a wider helmet equipped with radio earphones. He reported a light raid primarily against the submarines lying low against the shoreline at the far end of the bay.

Gun flashes lit the water brilliantly as did some bomb blasts that appeared to emanate from beyond the palisades that ringed the harbor's southern edge. I found that I was practically blinded from some of the bright flashes and wondered if we weren't fairly visible from the air. We could follow the route that was apparently being taken by the enemy planes as search-lights converged on them some miles to the west of our position.

By the time I reached the command ship the raid was over, and I climbed to the deck where I received permission to go aboard after saluting the stern where the flag was located and then the officer of the deck. Blue lights on deck showed me where the wardroom lay since I had been told by my escorting crew of sailors that both this ship and the *O'Hara* were built to identical plans.

I was not surprised when I opened the wardroom door to find total darkness since, in wartime, all doors that open onto open decks are rigged to extinguish all lights that might show through when the doors are opened. I stepped over the threshold and found myself falling free through space. Instinctively my arms flew out and my right hand struck and for a moment grasped an iron railing. However, the weight of my body carried me on down and I struck the steel plates of the deck below on my left shoulder and jaw. My helmet saved me some of the blow but it was forced down over my face and cut the bridge of my nose. My neck nearly snapped under the impact and for a moment I lay stunned with a great ringing in my ears.

No one had seen me fall since everyone was getting ready to leave port and I learned later that the movement of ships had been delayed by the need to hold for my return to the *O'Hara*. I climbed back up the ladder, fully aware that there was at least one difference between the sister ships: the wardroom doors and a door to the lower deck were in opposite positions.

When I cautiously entered the wardroom several men came up to me, when the lights went on again, to see if they could help. I had bled all over my uniform and both eyes were turning black. My jaw hurt like thunder and I was certain I'd broken some teeth. I found out that I'd cracked a molar when my old friend Dr. Tony DeMuth inspected my jaw the next day, as we rolled across the Mediterranean. In fact, he removed the molar in six pieces by setting me on a bale of some kind and without benefit of anesthetic, other than a slug of whiskey, by tugging at the shards until they were removed. Everything in the ship, including the clinic, had been loaded to the beams with war materiel.

Colonel Crowther took me in tow and led me to his stateroom several decks below the wardroom. When we got there, he turned to me and said, 'Doughty, there's hell to pay!' I had figured that only something drastic would have warranted this last-minute meeting.

'What's wrong?' I asked.

'The Germans know exactly where we are going to land,' Crowther replied. 'Look at these aerial photos.'

He handed me several blown-up glossies which showed nothing but a convoluted series of vehicle tracks in what looked like a sea of mud.

'These were taken by reconnaissance planes today,' Crowther went on. They show the movement of several armored units from Bari on the east coast of Italy to Eboli which lies in the center of our landing site.'

Crowther discussed the fact that there appeared to have been a leak as to the identifying numbers of maps we had had distributed to the various ships.

'As a result we're going up against far stiffer opposition than we had originally thought to be the case,' the colonel said.

'Where the hell is the alternative plan that every combined operation as a primary rule should have?' I asked.

'There isn't any,' he responded, and I realized that there was a great discrepancy between theory and practice in this field of military planning, as I would find to be true of most military operations before the war ended.

'Not only that,' Crowther added another bit of information that has always caused me to doubt the good sense of General Dwight D. Eisenhower. 'Ike is going to announce the surrender of Italy when we're just 40 miles off the Salerno beaches. It couldn't come at a worse time because our men are going to think the landing will be easy. In addition, in order not to kill a lot of civilians, there'll be no bombing of the beach areas and only a limited amount of naval preparatory fires.'

'Just how many strikes are they putting on us?' I asked. 'Are we supposed to perform miracles?'

'I don't know about that,' Crowther answered, 'but your job is to convince your regimental officers of the fact that the fight will be the toughest one yet, since we shall now be up against odds that no one foresaw. I estimate that there will be another three German divisions opposing us, at least one of which will be an armored unit.'

'I'll tell the regimental staff, colonel,' I said. 'But who's going to tell the officers who are on other ships?'

'That is all attended to,' Crowther said and gave me a grim smile as I started to leave. 'Take care of that face,' he admonished as I went out the door wondering why he had, as seemed obvious in the light of his last remarks, given the respective unit S-2s separate briefings on such an important matter, at such a late hour in our leave-taking, all of which had delayed our departure.

I rode back through the star-studded night, nursing my jaw, neck and shoulder, finding no position that was comfortable. No one spoke to me as we sped between ships where engines were already turning over and, upon reaching the float alongside the *O'Hara*, I thanked the sailors who took off into the darkness of the ship's shadow.

In the wardroom, the regimental staff gathered as word spread that I had returned from the command ship with an important message. I had already told Werner most of the bad news, and the worried look on his face must have reflected the same sick feeling I'd had when Crowther gave me the word.

I gave the staff and some of the ship's officers the story as I had received it from Crowther. 'Jesus H. Christ,' someone cursed from the back of the wardroom. By this time my mouth was so swollen I could scarcely talk.

'The important item,' I said, 'is to warn all personnel of the danger in thinking that our landing will be unopposed now that Italy is out of the war. We will be fighting the worst kind of odds under circumstances where there is every reason to believe that the Germans already know of our landing site and are reinforcing their positions there.'

'What did the aerial photos show?' Major Willman, S-3, asked.

'Nothing,' I said, 'but tank tracks. However, from the stereo studies made of the pictures it was easily established that the tanks were heading across Italy from Bari. Reports from agents in the Bari area have identified armored units that left Bari under forced march several days ago. Some of them have already reached Eboli. These, by the way, are elements of the crack [German Army] Afrika Korps that made it out of North Africa at the last minute.'

'Another tidbit you'll enjoy,' I went on, 'is that Ike will announce the surrender of Italy just before we hit the beaches. How do you like that for lousy timing? Our guys are going to think they can put a flagpole in their navels and march around Vesuvius to Naples without firing a shot!'

'Jee-s-us H. Christ,' someone said. 'How can they make the odds against us any worse?'

'Only with a blueprint,' I answered. 'It looks like the high brass has forgotten we can bleed!'

Werner asked why something hadn't been given me in writing.

I said, 'I don't know, but he trusted me to report exactly what I learned. However, I did ask him for written confirmation and he refused it.'

Werner grumbled. 'I don't doubt what you've said is exactly what you were told,' he added, somewhat hastily, 'but, Christ, this raises hell with everything we've planned to date.'

I had a lot of trouble with Werner from the very beginning. He didn't like anyone who, with lesser rank than his, failed to shrink when addressing him or any other higher rank. He didn't like my independence of thought and spirit.

'I have a better question than that, colonel,' I said. 'Why did Crowther take us S-2s, one at a time, and brief us in his cabin where no one else could hear what he said? I think he's been put under wraps by higher headquarters who don't want their linen dirtied with talk of a security breach. I should think, too, that the British would be damned unhappy with these developments, assuming that they've been made aware of them.'

As I looked at the faces around the table where we were gathered I could sense the pounding concern that men who, having been told the odds, had taken them on gladly, only to find that the odds were now doubled, when it was too late to do anything about reducing them.

'Looks like we're walking into a goddamned trap,' one artillery forward observer said as he hit the table with his fist.

'Right,' I agreed. 'That was my first impression but the worst thing about it is that there appears to be more concern about injuring the Italian populace than in helping us establish a beachhead against practically unbeatable odds. Now that we have evidence of a security breach, I'd expect the top brass to pour on all kinds of fire-power to knock the hell out of everything in our way. I have half a notion that the bombing has been called off to substantiate later denials of the existence of the breach or, at least, of knowledge on the part of the high command, of such a breach.'

'You have a job to do,' I said to Werner, 'of briefing your troops on this latest turn of events and of convincing them that, with Italy out of the war, the fighting will be more, not less, severe. They're going to go ashore completely relaxed unless you do the job right.'

By the time our meeting ended we were underway, heading out to sea where the swells were beginning to sway the deck beneath our feet. I went to bed and woke up before daylight with an excruciating toothache that, in spite of Dr. DeMuth's ministrations, went with me onto the Salerno beach.

Some 40 miles off Italy we were all awaiting Eisenhower's announcement, which came on schedule. We sat quietly after the transmission ended, some 200 officers crowded into the wardroom seemingly unwilling to comment except for one long, drawn-out 'Shh-i-i-i-t!' accompanied by a Texan accent which gave the word several syllables. As had been expected and despite everything the regimental officers had done to dispel the notion that our landing was to be a cinch, the GIs set up a holler that ought to have been heard on the Italian mainland. 'Finito Benito!'[2] was the catchword as men, finding some stashed bottles among their barracks bags, carried on a stealthy drinking bout for most of the evening. No one I knew on board that ship that night thought much of Eisenhower or anyone on his staff. It was a fiasco, so far as we were concerned, and we were pawns in a game that had more sociological than military overtones.

---

2. Fascist Italy surrendered on July 10, 1943. The Allied invasion of Sicily, codenamed Operation *Husky*, began on the night of July 9–10, 1943, and ended August 17. The Salerno invasion (Operation *Avalanche*) went ahead after Sicily was secured. The dictator Benito Mussolini lost his government's support and was arrested on July 24, 1943. On September 12, 1943, he was rescued and subsequently protected by German paratroopers in the Italian North. He was captured by partisans, tried, and executed on April 28, 1945.

Chapter 5

Battle

On September 9, 1943,[1] I went into combat. As we had sailed past Sicily's mountainous silhouette the night before, I'd stood on deck in the darkness watching the stars. I could make out the ship's booms and rigging swaying gently against the sky. In the far distance, too, I could see what I took to be flashes from artillery barrages and possibly some bombing, but I could hear no sounds beyond those of the boat's passage through the water. Everything seemed too nice to leave. The wind was warm on my face and the movement of the ship's deck was soothing. I wondered, then, if I would live to see the day when I might, once again, stand on a ship's deck free of worry about war.

As we approached our anchorage well outside of Salerno's harbor, the ship slowed perceptibly and then came to a halt as great anchors splashed into the water and chains rattled for a long time until the anchors were lodged on the ocean bed. Blue lights, invisible from the air, cast deep shadows around the companionways and suddenly the decks were alive with bustling naval and army groups preparing to load our troops, by way of heavy nets put over the side of the ship, onto small boats that quickly appeared alongside from wherever they had been stored for the voyage. Speed was essential since we were to land our first wave on the beach at 3 am. There wasn't time to do more than give a fleeting thought to the hundreds of men who had preceded us to the landing site and to hope that they had successfully accomplished their missions of clearing sea mines, posting picket ships and advance shore parties, charting underwater obstacles, and, where necessary, preparing them for destruction at the right moment.

I had been informed through G-2 channels that British commandos had been active along the Salerno coast for at least two weeks. If our reports were correct, they had been landed from the submarine *Shakespeare*, which had brought them to the vicinity of Salerno and sent them to shore in collapsible kayaks which they were to conceal while they reconnoitered the whole landing site. It was their job to check out hostile gun emplacements and strongpoints, staging areas, and supply depots and to report their findings to any of the ships they could reach in the dark on the morning of our landing.

I was in the *O'Hara*'s wardroom strapping on my musette bag[2] and pistol when I received a call to come onto the ship's top deck. A few moments before,

---

1. Operation *Avalanche*.
2. Purse-like pouch.

I'd had something to eat and had talked with Captain Hersel Adams, a Texas officer who had once served with the Texas Rangers. He had acted and talked strangely, and I had attributed his attitude to the general nervousness we were all feeling, not alone because this was to be our fighting debut, or as the army says, 'our blooding,' but also because of the probability that the Germans were ready and waiting for us.

Finally, Hersel turned to me and said that he knew, absolutely, that he was going to die at Salerno. Since I had known him as a well-adjusted, happy man with all the qualifications of a fine officer, I felt that this was a reflection of the misgivings we all had about the outcome of the invasion, in the light of the information I'd received from Colonel Crowther just before we had sailed from Oran. I said as much to him, but he gave me a quizzical kind of smile and went about getting ready to go ashore.

It was then that I was called to the deck where I found an officer I knew standing at the ship's railing while he peered into the darkness below. He turned to me and said, 'There's a couple of Limeys down there in a kayak. They want to come aboard.' Since he had, as he explained, refused them permission, they'd asked him to call me, for they were aware that their operations would have been circulated to the intelligence sections of the various fighting organizations.

I called down to the men, who were not visible except that there was a darker shadow where I assumed their craft to be, and said, 'Come up the rope ladder but keep your hands empty and in sight when you reach this railing.' We had been taught at Duera not to trust British accents, since many Germans had learned to speak English in British schools. I stood to one side with my pistol ready and followed the sounds of their progress up the ladder. Shortly there appeared in the dim blue light a beret, followed by a huge set of shoulders and the summer uniform of a British commando. As he jumped to the deck, I relieved him of a heavy revolver hanging in a holster at his side. I could see a white flash as he smiled. 'Taking no chances, I see,' he said. Behind him appeared the head and shoulders of another huge man who jumped lightly to the deck where the officer, who had stood by after calling me, relieved him of a similar weapon.

The men towered over me as we walked through the companionway to the wardroom. One of them was a major who stood 6ft 6in while the sergeant with him, we learned, was 6ft 9in tall. I checked out their IDs and units with a list I had been given of the group who'd gone ashore to reconnoiter and, satisfied that they were genuine commandos, returned their weapons.

They had been delayed by hostile activities, which they said had been increasing all week long. They reported much armor in and around Eboli, and while I had food brought to them, since they'd been on short rations for many days, they plotted positions they had observed on a map. Included in their findings was the location of a 280mm railroad gun, which was later known as an 'Anzio-Annie.' Its barrel, as I had learned from various intelligence reports, was as long as the nine railroad engines it took to tow the weapon. Italian and German supply depots were located at Agropoli on the outermost southern tip of Salerno Bay. When the commandos had finished with grease pencils on overlays, they had given us the positions of many guns of all calibers to include 88s, 105s, and 150s,[3] together with self-propelled monsters. In the meantime, they had put away enough food for a squad.

I got the information to an artillery forward observer and had men of the S-2 section prepare other overlays for later distribution to battalions, showing hostile positions completely encircling Salerno Bay and well up into the mountains beyond. As we had feared, the trap was there before our eyes, waiting only to be sprung!

Because of the political situation surrounding the capitulation of Italy, and Eisenhower's decision to spare the Italian civilians the effects of heavy bombing, our troops were faced with the need to clear mines, barbed wire, and booby traps while undergoing their baptism of fire. Normally, much of the clearing would be accomplished by bombing and bombardment. I did not relish this thought as I took leave of the British commandos, of whom I never heard another word, and climbed down the rope net attached to the *O'Hara*'s flank and dropped into a bobbing LCT[4] that was to take part of the command group ashore in the fourth wave of the assault echelons.

Our plan of attack found my regiment, the 141st, on the extreme right of the entire landing operation. To our left was the 142nd Infantry, and in floating reserve, awaiting commitment in accordance with the flow of battle, was the 143rd

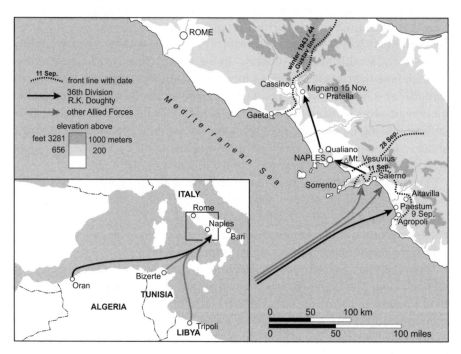

---

3. All these mobile gun calibers are in mm (100mm = 4in).
4. Landing Craft Tank.

Infantry. Each regiment had its own artillery battalion to form, between them, the main elements of a Regimental Combat Team. On the left of the beachhead and comprising the main assault force was the British X Corps, with the difficult task of storming and reaching the city of Salerno itself.

It was a somber moment when I found myself in the LCT looking out across the water where I could make out the bowwaves of a number of similar craft ploughing a huge circle well away from the *O'Hara*. This was the real test of nerves for, now, everything was under naval control. As time wore on it began to get lighter, and we were still circling well out away from land.

On signal our wave formed a line with boats separated from each other by 50 to 100ft. We then headed for shore where the outlines of mountain crests were beginning to show against a brightening skyline. Wisps of fog began to curl up from the water as daylight approached. It gave the scene a nightmarish quality as boats on our flanks penetrated small fogbanks, disappearing completely and appearing again as we pressed forward.

We had observed no signs of firing from the shore despite the fact that three waves had preceded us. I had no illusions that this meant there were no Germans awaiting us. It was, I felt sure, only a matter of time before we would feel the full weight of German fighting units, veterans in every respect but nevertheless vulnerable to our firepower if we could bring it to bear.

Looking back, I found that we had proceeded to a point where we could no longer see our transports. I could barely make out the bow waves of the next line of boats following at a cautious distance behind us. The sound of planes in the air made us aware of danger from that direction, although nothing came near us so far as we could determine.

All at once several green flares arched up from the direction of the shore, and I felt that this was some signal from German ground forces acknowledging aerial reports of our invasion fleet. A deep muttering sound came to my ears from a great distance off to the port side of our boat. I realized then that it was probably a naval bombardment by the British against their portion of the beachhead.

Because we had had a jeep loaded onto our boat, there had only been room for about twenty-five men and their equipment. I sat in the jeep and was suddenly aware that the whole scene had been lit up by dozens of flares dropped from a plane directly over the command ship, whose guns went into action, slamming hot steel into the heavens. There could no longer be any doubt that the invasion was on and that we were about to be welcomed to Italy by waiting enemy troops.

Sitting under those flares brought visions of clattering runs by strafing planes but none came. It began to brighten very considerably about this time, and I could see that we still had a long way to go to shore. We passed the outjutting cape where Agropoli lay and at about that time a destroyer, controlling the landing, signaled us to stop as enemy resistance had been met on Blue and Yellow[5]

---

5. The colors refer to military designations of beach segments.

beaches. We were held in place for 10 minutes while the daylight increased and, with it, the tension of waiting.

While we had been cautioned to keep our heads below the boat's gunwales, for whatever protection they might afford, I continued to watch ahead where, suddenly, machine-gun tracers cut their dotted lines across the background. I could not distinguish their colors nor could I determine the direction of their flight. All I knew was that fighting was going on along the shoreline. As we moved swiftly toward the beach I could make out the dune line behind the white sands of the beach and began to realize that all was not proceeding well, since the machine-gun tracers were flaring toward us from the dunes. If so, where the hell were the three waves that had gone ahead as assault troops?

Artillery shells began to fall, striking the water behind us with heavy explosions, and we were made aware of the worst military position to befall anyone: helpless on the water with no possibility of returning fire. An added danger arose as mortar shells, those silent messengers of death, began to explode around us. Every moment, crouched, now, below the blunt bow of the LCT, seemed forever as we awaited a direct hit. It seemed that gunners would have to be blind not to hit us as the range closed.

I was awaiting the rasp of the keel on sand and the release of the bow to open the way to relief from the inaction which seemed to be sapping at my strength. When we touched bottom, the boat lurched, sprang forward and stopped with the motor going full blast. The coxswain released the bow and after moving downward a few inches it stuck. I shoved against it with all my might and yelled for others to do the same before some alert gunner, seeing our predicament, zeroed in on us. Slowly, the ramp went down – grudgingly and with sudden jerks that nearly threw us off balance.

When I looked out I was stunned to see that we were still a couple of hundred feet from the shore where an uncharted reef had stopped us. Even so, I jumped into the water and finding it too deep, shucked off my harness which we had learned to keep unbuckled and let it go with my musette bag into the water into which my helmet also disappeared.

Plunging and half swimming I headed for shore, my only weapon the .45 caliber pistol I'd stuck into my pants belt as I let everything else go. It was worse than a nightmare of trying to run and being unable to move. Every step was an agony of suspense as machine-gun bullets zipped overhead and mortar fire struck all around me. My breath became labored as I lifted my knees high to try to improve my speed. I bent low to the water, at the same time, and realized later that there had been a kind of exhilaration in betting my life against the guns, that I could make it to the beach. I crawled up on the shore and on looking back toward our LCT found that its crew had finally backed it off the reef and were heading out for more troops.

Other men from the contingent I'd come ashore with had taken a slanting course to come in on the section of the beach where the rest of our wave, now under savage fire, had landed. Some of them were hit and others were trying to bring them ashore.

While we had been warned about getting off the beach as rapidly as possible, since enemy guns had, without question, been zeroed in on it and could hit it at any time day or night, I found that I could not do so. Instead, I dropped into a foxhole that someone had started to dig but which was now half full of water. It was located partway up the beach and beyond it lay my problem. There, in solid bands, were double-apron barbed wire fences interlaced with shining wires that led to mines and booby traps. I was several hundred feet south of the main landing beach and little had been done to render the footing safe in my area.

Sand filtered into my clothing and made life more miserable. Over the top of the dune I could see Mount Soprano, which had been a reference point for much of our planning. I wondered if I would ever reach some of the initial objectives we had set for the regiment.

Off to my right, about 1,000yd away, I saw the low silhouette of a German tank. Its operator slewed it around so that it was facing our landing area and shortly bullets from its machine guns were zapping the air just above my head. Lying low I brought an entrenching tool to bear on the foxhole's interior and managed to dig it several inches deeper although the water, by that time, was caving in the sand all around the perimeter. I was fairly certain that, for me, it was going to be a very short war.

I looked out on the water again and saw an LCT hit and burning about a mile from shore. A speedy navy boat was rescuing survivors. Another fast boat, moving parallel to the shore, fired some rockets that I could see arching overhead. In a short space of time a pall of black smoke began to block the German gunner's vision from where the rockets had landed and started to release smoke.

Nearer at hand and broaching against the shoreline was another landing craft on fire and abandoned. Other navy craft began to generate smoke from their stacks and as they moved across the landing site, the smoke blotted out the scene of landing craft still coming into the shoreline. This, in turn, prompted the German defenders to adopt new tactics, and shortly they were firing heavy concentrations of shells all along the shoreline.

Just before this happened, however, an anti-aircraft gun that had been landed on our beach opened fire on the tank that had been firing over my head. While the shells could not penetrate the tank's armor, they came fast enough to influence the tank commander to pull back out of sight but only after he had let loose with about ten rounds of 75mm ammunition at the anti-aircraft crew.

I was, to put it mildly, groggy with the muzzle blast and concussive effects of the duel, but I suddenly saw salvation in the form of a gaping hole through the barbed wire where a short round from the tank's gun had battered the barbed wire and exploded some mines.

One of the men near me, who had dug a hole similar to mine, yelled 'Captain Doughty, it's me Hobday!' He was a corporal in my intelligence section. He had always taken an interest in my family and had sent cards to our daughter, Martha, on special occasions.

I stepped up onto the beach with water and sand dripping from my uniform and said, 'Let's get out of here.' As I stepped toward the gap in the wire I saw movement and spotted a helmet and the shoulders of someone coming down a small gully on the other side of the wire barricade toward our position. In the seconds it took me to recognize the man's German helmet, I threw myself through the opening in the wire and fired my .45, which had been wrapped in a waterproof container until I first hit the beach. Whoever it was paused a second or two and then started to raise his rifle to his shoulder. A shot rang out as I flung myself forward onto the sand. The man pitched forward in the act of bringing a rifle to his shoulder. Although I was expecting to be shot any second and possibly the burning of a slug striking me, nothing happened.

'Hot Damn! Cap'n.' Hobday yelled. 'You got him!'

I lifted my head and saw the man lying flat on the ground and the man's rifle, barrel-first in the sand. I had shot him without realizing it. Apparently I had fired without thinking as I dropped on to the sand. 'Let's go!' I said. 'Right through the gap in the wire.' We jumped through the barbed wire and started to walk north behind the dunes. I was certain that there were Germans in the immediate vicinity.

It would be difficult to imagine what went through the German soldiers' mind when he approached our postion on the beach. Possibly someone in the German army had observed our experience of landing on a reef only to swim and wade ashore. It's possible they thought to get prisoners who, under the circumstances, would be quite easily captured having lost, one could presume, their weapons.

Until he saw the weapon in my hand, our would-be captor could have counted on taking us with little difficulty, although how he could have expected to get through the barbed wire and booby traps is hard to conceive unless he knew something we didn't.

While I did not thank God for such a deliverance, I felt no compunction in what had occurred. As a matter of fact, I felt nothing, for it happened so fast and so automatically that I couldn't even be sure I had fired the fatal shot until much later when I cleaned my pistol.

I took off, behind the barbed wire and in front of the dunes, toward the busy part of the beach. For a moment I felt that I had, at least, gotten ashore and might have a shot at staying there, to do some damage. My teeth were chattering and my hands shaking at the near brush I'd had with death. The next day, when I had an opportunity to look at the spot where I'd last seen the German I'd shot at, I found only a helmet. The man's body and rifle had been taken away. In the helmet, which I now have in my den at home, was the name 'Swiersey.'

When I reached the anti-aircraft gun (AA gun), I was somewhat surprised to see that Colonel Werner had pulled his pistol on the gunner in order to get him to fire at the German tank. I figured this to be some kind of Texan histrionics and it, in no way, improved the colonel's image in my mind, even though I was glad that the tank had been driven off.

Bulldozers were operating at full tilt beyond the AA gun, pulling wire mats into place on the sand to form a roadway for vehicles which soon would be arriving. Others had dug away great areas of the dune and had scooped out bunkers for the storage of ammo, gasoline, foodstuffs, and all of the rest of the paraphernalia on which an army operates. Still others were making a roadway off the beach to a pasture near an Italian farmhouse.

Battle sounds were making a hellish din so that when we spoke to each other, it was necessary to yell. Werner was sending men all over the place. We had moved off the beach and were behind a wall near the farmhouse where General Lange joined us.

The news reached us by radio that the shelling of our beach was so great that all further landings, including our supporting artillery, were to be diverted to the 142nd Infantry's landing beach to our left. This was a serious situation, since we had but one artillery piece ashore and it was being manhandled to a position near the ruins of an ancient Greek city called Paestum, on the left of our zone of responsibility.

Our first battalion had failed to report its position and Colonel Werner, after dispatching several officers to locate it, finally turned to me and ordered me to do the same job. This was about as I had anticipated he would act under fire. He was edgy, on the verge of panic, and, as we learned during the next ten days, was happy to have Colonel Joe Crawford make most of the important decisions. Crawford, recovering from wounds received in North Africa with the 1st Division, had come in to bolster our command group and was a tremendously stalwart operator.

I took Pfc Charlie Lane of the I&R platoon with me and jumped through an opening in a stone wall on the far side of which stood a clump of low-growing trees. Just as I ducked through an opening in the trees and was about to traverse a slope down to a garden, something ripped over my head, tore through the trees, and struck a stone shed some distance away. It was a blood-congealing sound with the promise of death riding with it, and I dove forward and rolled into a ditch at the edge of the garden. Lane smacked down beside me. 'What the hell was that?' he whispered. 'I don't know,' I whispered back. 'Lie still. There's something moving under those piles of vines near the house.'

I could see several huge piles of brush and vines and as I moved my head a little to see further to our left, machine bullets tore up the ground around us. We had been spotted and again, it looked like a short war. Fortunately there were many tomato vines in the garden as well as other leafy vegetables, and by lying low I felt we might be able to wait out help.

We were very shortly made aware of the fact that we had landed on the spot where someone had earlier evacuated his bowels. Olfactory adaptation took place after a while, but in the heat, dirt, and danger, I was miserable.

It was about a half hour later that we heard sounds of men crawling toward us from our right flank. In the meantime Lane and I had been cautioning each other to play 'dead.' I was concerned about the sounds we'd heard until Lane, who had the ears of a wild animal, said, 'They're Mexicans. Probably E Company. We ought to warn them.'

'Stay put,' I said in a low tone. 'There's nothing we can do to warn them. You make a move and we've had it.' We were actually in a lull in our pest-hole while everywhere around us the battle reached a crescendo.

Suddenly, the deep bark of an American machine gun broke the lull. Tracers flew into one of the stacks of brush and set it afire and we could see movement among the flames and smoke. A German SP gun was backing off from its camouflaged position, its guns blazing. A bazooka rocket struck the front of the SP and bounced off, its yellow casing flashing in the sunlight. 'Forgot to pull the pin,' Lane said. Another bazooka rocket flew into the moving brush pile, and this time there was an explosion followed by several others as the gun's ammo blew up, making a funeral pyre of the scene. The Mexicans had lived up to their reputation of being the best damned fighting unit in the 'Fightin' 36th.'

As Lane and I stood up, satisfied that no other SPs or tanks were under the brush piles, someone back near the CP yelled, 'Tanks.' Without trying to clean our uniforms, Lane and I dashed back over the embankment and through the hole in the wall. There we found Werner and Lange digging holes with their helmets behind the wall. It was quite a sight.

'Where've you been?' Werner shouted.

'In a shit-hole,' I said. 'We've been pinned by an SP that E Company just ran off.' I went to get some water at a well to sponge the crap off my blouse.

'Where's the 1st Battalion?' Werner asked.

'No one knows,' I responded. 'We couldn't get out to an area where we could see a thing. There's no way to find them except to stumble into them.'

Werner looked at me as though he doubted I'd even tried, and I looked him up and down and asked him if he'd like an entrenching tool to help with his hole. He stood up, looking a little sheepish, and General Lange walked off toward the left flank of our position.

Later, I heard the story of what happened to Lange shortly thereafter. He apparently went to see what had happened to the 155mm howitzer that had made it to our beach before the beach was closed. He found it in the Paestum area, where a young corporal was about to pull one of the fanciest moves of the war. Lange, according to the gun crew, stood around watching them getting the gun ready for firing. The gun sights had been lost in the shuffle and the corporal was sighting on a road junction, by looking through the barrel, a method called 'bore-sighting.'

Lange touched the corporal on the shoulder and when the man turned, asked him, 'Do you know who I am?'

The corporal, who was busy getting ready for tanks that had already been spotted moving along a road to the central road junction, said, 'Never heard of you before,' and went on working.

Lange, of course, was looking for a salute in the middle of a battle. 'I'm the assistant division commander,' Lange said.

'Good job, if you don't screw it up,' came the rejoinder. Just how apt a response this was became clearer as the battle went on. By the time we had won the beachhead, Lange had so screwed up our troop dispositions with half-baked measures, that he was summarily relieved of his position by General Eisenhower.

In any event, the corporal managed to knock out the first of thirteen tanks moving nose to tail along the main road paralleling the coast in that area. He then had the crew manhandle the gun to where he could knock out the last tank, creating a cul-de-sac for the rest of the tanks, all of which were destroyed in turn. His exploit was reported as a lesson learned in combat and written up in army journals for others to emulate.

Word came to us at about noon that Hersel Adams had been killed near the main road where the tanks had been blasted. In the meantime, Werner, in an effort to prove his leadership, was still sending men all over the place to try to learn where different elements of the regiment were located and what their status was.

Shortly after I had talked with him about Lane's and my sortie, he sent me to the beach where Colonel Crawford was using a special radio for contacting the navy's gunnery officers at sea. Here, again, was a snafu of the most heinous type. With every part of the landing reliant on good communications with the navy's firepower, particularly during the initial stages of a landing before artillery could be landed and sighted-in, there was but one radio that could be meshed into the navy's communications system.

I found Crawford sitting at the edge of a lagoon that had cut deeply into the beach, wearing a headset and talking into a microphone. Two officers who had been sent to accomplish the mission set for me by Werner had been killed by artillery bursts. I worked with Crawford most of the afternoon relaying messages to our troops and getting targets from two of our battalions, the third one having been unaccounted for during the day.

Shortly after I got to the beach, which was a ferment of activity with an LST drawn up to the shore and discharging cargo, I heard our anti-aircraft guns firing and I hit the edge of the lagoon as three German fighters roared over the beach just above the trees. Machine guns hammered at us and the sand spurted with the impact of bullets. It was a close call and still I didn't feel tired, the urge being to do everything possible to try to reduce the chaos of pitched battle to something more like normalcy.

Doctors were working in a corner of the beach where wounded were being brought in on litters. Some of the less badly wounded men were immediately evacuated by boat to the ships at the rendezvous area at sea.

I heard a peculiar noise and looked up to see a British fighter plane throwing smoke and apparently headed for a landing at the edge of the beach. The plane's markings were clearly visible, and the pilot waggled his wings to signal an emergency. Suddenly an anti-aircraft gun opened fire on the plane and immediately hundreds of guns took up the cudgel, bringing the poor bastard down in flames. It was the kind of tragedy that made everyone I talked with later feel guilty and ashamed. The plane struck the shore in a ball of fire, rolled wing-over-wing, and killed several GIs in the process. Only a trigger-happy bunch of scared men would shoot down a plane bearing allied markings and in trouble.

As soon as this emergency ended, another arose when a heavy German shell entered the nose-door of the LST and detonated a load of ammunition that shook the ship and gutted its interior.

In mid-afternoon a couple of prisoners of war were brought to me where I was working on the beach with Colonel Crawford. They were miserable looking men, and I learned through an interpreter that they had been warned by their officers that they were fighting the 'wild men' from Texas who would kill them should they be captured. They actually fell on their knees and begged for their lives under circumstances where I couldn't be sure I'd live another minute.

From them I learned that they had been apprised of our coming to Salerno for about a week. They even claimed to have dug foxholes in solid rock with pneumatic tools. Later that same day a captured map, showing the German plan of defense, indicated that our first three waves of infantry would be allowed to land and move inland. They would be cut off by a double envelopment by German infantry and tanks at first light and succeeding waves of boats were to be taken under fire from the dune line. A large circle below Mount Soprano had been designated in German 'Killing Area.' The plan nearly worked.

It was scarcely credible that the day was finally drawing to a close and I was still alive and unhurt. To say that I had lived through a maelstrom would only hint at the thousands of vignettes of courage and daring, foolhardiness and obstinacy, luck and ill-fortune, joy and sorrow, fear and horror that I observed that day. On one occasion I had run to a point on our far right flank where an aqueduct had been built by Mussolini as part of a system that drained the marshes behind the dunes and carried water by pipes over the dunes to the sea. It was a mound 30ft through at the base, several hundred feet long and about 20ft high. German tanks had done their best to pass that obstacle, but men with bazookas had knocked them out and killed the crews who managed to get out of their ugly mounts.

Observers on that flank had hinted at the possibility that our lost battalion was lying beyond the aqueduct in the gridwork of ditches that had been dug as drainage conduits, where there were many trees and much underbrush in the area. The action of German tanks in straddling some of the ditches to strafe down their lengths had been observed and the conclusion seemed logical that many of our troops were using the grid as shallow trenches. This proved to be the case as we later learned. As far as I was concerned, the one good deed performed by Mussolini in his lifetime was to have had built a sturdy bastion that bolstered our right flank at Salerno.

When the sun had almost disappeared into the sea, I was working at digging a slit trench for my night's lodging when I saw some boards moving about 10ft away. I pulled out my pistol and stood over the spot until two Italian men pulled themselves out of what proved to be a covered well. They had dug a cave into the side of the well where their family had hidden during that furious day. They showed me by pointing down into the well where the entrance to their cave was located and then, in a great show of friendship, dug my trench – both wide and deep – and for good measure gave me several tomatoes, which was the first food I'd eaten since leaving the ship.

I don't know how others fared that night, but I slept in my uniform without cover of any kind and when daylight arrived, I woke up with a sore throat and a chest cold that grew worse for several days and stayed with me for weeks. Despite all that, I was inwardly jubilant that I'd become a veteran the hard way and had lived to tell the tale.

Certainly the events of September 9, 1944, crowded the day with more thrills, spills, and chills than would be found in an ordinary lifetime of peaceful pursuits. Those of us who made it through the day felt and acted like well-seasoned veterans thereafter. While later warfare proved almost as difficult and hazardous, the contrast to prior experience was never again as soul-shaking as that we endured on the day the 36th Division was 'bloodied.'

Chapter 6

Monte Cicerale

Someone, and I believe it was Colonel Joe Crawford, gave the 2nd and 3rd Battalions of our regiment the assignment of infiltrating through German lines on the night of September 9, thereby breaking out of our confined bridgehead and seizing some of the high ground that had given the German defenders such an advantage over us. Colonel Werner, trying to act as though he had brought the regiment through the day when actually Crawford had made all the decisions, ordered me to establish an observation post (OP) on the mountain crests inland from Agropoli.

By the time the morning came we had firm control over the 2nd and 3rd Battalions but were still unaware of the 1st Battalion's position and status. I set out on foot to the south, just behind the dune line, taking with me four men of the I&R platoon. We came to the dike that had thwarted German tanks the day before and found evidence of a very severe fight there. Several tanks bearing swastikas were rammed into the base of the dike where they'd been stopped by bazooka fire. All of them had been gutted by fire and the smell of burned flesh was nauseating.

Since I was not sure of where the German defenders were located, I kept to pasture land where trees and shrubs gave us some cover. At the opening in the dunes, where I had shot the German soldier from the beach, I found only a helmet which I took along with me.

As we started inland from the dune area I rounded a clump of low shrubs and stopped short. In front of me was a German in a kneeling position with his gun, across a fallen tree trunk, aimed directly at me. It took me a second or two to realize that he'd been shot through the forehead and had frozen in a firing position when death took him.

Here and there, and particularly on a hill ahead of us, we could hear small arms fire crackling from time to time as our attacking echelons flushed out a machine-gun nest or some snipers left behind to report our actions. My general impression, however, was that the defenders had taken off and were no longer on our right flank or, so far as I could determine, anywhere on our front except for those cut off by our two battalions infiltrating to positions behind them in the night.

I reached the main road with my men after passing a number of well-dug-in gun positions, some of which had been taken by our Mexican-Americans in daring maneuvers climaxed, I later learned, by a man named Ugly Gonzales. He had single-handedly crawled to within grenade-throwing distance of an 88mm gun crew and, with his pack on fire from where a shell had grazed it, reduced the position, killing the crew with grenades and bullets. He earned one of the first DSCs[1] the division awarded to its heroes.

On the road I ran into Captain Herb Eitt of A Company, part of our missing battalion. From him I learned that the battalion had been caught in an open area by the enveloping German attack aimed at cutting off reinforcements. They had spent D-Day in the corners of the ditch-grid, dodging one way and another, depending on where German tanks took strafing positions. Bazookas had helped keep the tanks from completely overrunning the battalion, even though it had been unable to take any of its initial objectives. Some men had been crushed to death beneath tank treads or otherwise killed. Even later attempts to put together what occurred there have produced a patchwork of stories, due to the fact that each individual had a very restricted view of the actions that transpired that day.

I sent word back to Colonel Andy Price that I had located the 1st Battalion and then proceeded on my way, along the road. At a bridge site I came across another German soldier, dead on the bridge. He had been hit by fragments from naval shells, so far as I could determine, for his body was gelatinous and as we moved him to the roadside, it seemed as though every bone in his body was shattered. It was a gruesome sight and beyond the bridge we found a German tank tilted up on one side and its entire interior burned to cinders and in which three charred skeletons lay.

Ahead of us the 2nd and 3rd Battalions were encountering resistance at a farmhouse that was in plain view on a hillside. As I watched I saw some of our troops jump very quickly to the ditches beside the road as gunfire erupted from the farmhouse. We also laid low while several squads circled the house and then took prisoners from it. I sent a man back to get more men and jeeps from the I&R platoon.

The prisoners were members of the 26th Panzer Division and from them we learned that, with them at the beachhead, had been elements of the 15th Panzer Grenadier Division, the 29th Motorized Division, and the 16th Panzer Division. These units had opposed the 36th Division's landing and should, by all odds, have won the day since conventional military wisdom dictates that attackers, in an invasion, should outnumber defenders, two to one.

There wasn't much doubt in my mind that two elements worked in our favor. We had lost the overall element of surprise, although a lesser, but very effective, surprise had been our ability to wipe out tanks with bazooka fire until we could get our artillery ashore. The chief component of our victory was the naval fire I'd helped deliver onto targets throughout the German defensive zone. This was confirmed by the PWs who said their ranks had been shattered by the volume of heavy caliber bombardment and the extreme accuracy of guns that were controlled by electronic systems to insure that accuracy. I saw on the flank of

---

1. Distinguished Service Cross.

Monte Cicerale before the day was over three great tanks smashed beyond all hope of repair by direct hits from naval shells.

The other element that contributed to our success was overconfidence on the part of the German defenders, which prompted them to adopt the tactic of letting our first three waves ashore. In essence, then, a case could be made for the view that – as things turned out – the leak of the identity of our landing site actually worked in our favor. I would hate to think of the consequences had our force been taken under fire from the first moment that its vanguard came into firing range.

We also learned from the prisoners that the main German force opposing our division had pulled out in the night and moved south to a point where they could strike inland and then north again, to reinforce the defenses against the British X Corps, thereby putting practically the whole burden of establishing the beachhead on our allies.

The regimental CP was set up in a cave near the beach and was located at the end of a ravine from which a German mortar crew had lobbed shells at us throughout the previous day. It had a sandy floor and was a most tempting place to sit out the war. I, however, did not see it until early in the morning of our third day in combat.

As soon as the resistance was cleared at the farmhouse on the hill, the whole I&R platoon caught up with me and we started a reconnaissance for an OP. We, at first, went out onto a rather low hill near the base of Monte Cicerale, but I felt that the only place to really observe the countryside for miles around was on the crest of Cicerale. With us was a driver from regimental headquarters who had come along because one of the I&R jeeps had been damaged while being transferred to an LCT and was being repaired. I mention this because it became the focal point in a controversy that I was imvolved in a couple of days later with General Lange.

In any event, I sent the spare driver back to report to regiment that, while I was establishing an OP at the first location, I was setting out to put another one on top of Monte Cicerale. I left four men at the first position, where they had taken over a house at the edge of a small settlement and were comfortably situated in an upstairs bedroom, the family having left for parts unknown. There were gardens full of ripe tomatoes, melons, and other crops which would supplement the K and C rations we were living on so that the men, after connecting a phone line to the nearest battalion CP, were in good shape.

From that point on we proceeded with great caution, since we soon passed the leading units of our battalions and were in the open, a place I found myself all too often from then on.

The road was precipitous and we used the technique of leapfrogging our vehicles as we wound our way, over steep and winding roads, all of which, of course, were unpaved and dusty. Anyone observing our progress would have had no trouble following the dust cloud that rose high about our heads. We wore goggles and dust masks, but it wasn't long before we all appeared to have aged considerably what with a grey pall covering our helmets, faces, and uniforms.

We found a number of dead Germans in ditches along the road and as we gained altitude, it occurred to me to look back for the view the Germans had had of our landing. It was somewhat frightening to realize that they could see what I next saw so clearly. Boats were plying back and forth from ship to shore bringing in our supplies. Every movement was observable even without field glasses. I could see dozers still working to improve the beach and the road net. Supply depots were easily recognized. Thousands of bidons[2] of gasoline were piled high in one place. Artillery shells in their cases were also obvious. Jeeps and 2-ton trucks, artillery emplacements, tents, latrines – all were in evidence, and I figured the Germans had made a mistake leaving our front. I believe that they were worried that Montgomery's march from the tip of Italy would catch them, if they delayed, where they could not rejoin their main force which eventually would have to fall back to the north, once the beachhead at Salerno was secured by us.

We neared a little town of Monte just below the crest of Cicerale, and the people gathered there came out in swarms when someone yelled, 'Americani, Americani.' A priest told me, once we found that we both spoke French, that the Germans had pulled out the previous afternoon, taking several of the town's young girls with them. He sadly noted that the girls were not kidnapped but chose to go.

I said that we were establishing a curfew as of 7 pm each day for the protection of the civilians. I told him that this was our first combat and that green troops were apt to fire at anything that moved after dark. He agreed and said that the people were still nervous about the Germans returning, as they had promised they would. Therefore, he felt they would be only too glad to stay indoors at night.

The priest stood on a small stoop and told the Italian people who were crowding around our I&R boys, offering them food and fruit, about the curfew. Heads nodded agreement and then I suggested to the priest that he tell them that Montgomery's army was coming up the Italian peninsula and that any fear of the Germans driving us out of Italy was groundless. I felt that once Montgomery drew abreast of our position, the curfew would end and the people could resume normal living.

At about that time a small Italian man, with his coat flying out behind him, came running out of a side street shouting, 'Me American! Me American! Me come-a from Pitts-a-burgh, Pennsylvania.' He , Nick Negro, ran up to me and hugged my shoulders, with tears running down his face. I learned that he had been detained in Italy by the Fascists when war broke out, even though he was a naturalized American citizen. Poor chap had contracted TB working in a mine in Pennsylvania and looked sickly. He told me that several of his relatives had come

---

2. A bidon was a small portable container, today known as a Jerry (for German) can.

to his house in Monte to escape the war, which they had felt sure would envelop their homes in Salerno.

Negro invited me to have dinner with his family that evening and I said I would but wanted a couple of my men with me to operate a radio and the jeep. First, however, I told him, I would have to climb further up the mountain to establish an OP. I left and finally made it to the crest of Cicerale on foot, where I found the view magnificent. We dug in a couple of slit trenches below the crest but from which we could see in all directions for miles. From there men ran telephone wire to the jeeps and then drove, laying wire, to a battalion switchboard which was connected to our regimental CP. I checked in with the regiment once the phones were in operation and said I'd be back sometime before morning.

Upon returning to Monte, I went to Nigro's home after learning that the rest of the I&R platoon had staked out a claim on a vacant house where they were enjoying home-cooked food prepared by some of the townspeople. My driver elected to stay with the platoon. I also called the four men on the lower OP and told them to prepare to join us at Monte, where a jeep would collect them shortly and bring them up the mountain.

At Nigro's home, reached only after a very rough descent down a cobbled street where the houses were built with common sidewalls, I was given a very warm welcome by Nick and a couple of dozen people whom he introduced as relatives. I was tired from all the exertions of the past two days, and my uniform looked grey like those of the German army. I asked if I could clean up, and Nick led me and my radio man out onto a back porch where I saw one of the loveliest sights of Italy. The porch was built over a sharply descending slope and stood on pilings some 50ft high. All around its edge, suspended over space, were slanting racks that held fruit and vegetables of every description. Beyond was the most spectacular scenery I'd ever seen. The snow-covered Appenines ran straight down Italy on the left of the scene. In the distance were old ruins on several hilltops, an aqueduct at the base of a mountain many miles away, and several bridges spanning mostly dry beds that probably were filled with water when spring floods cascaded from the melting snow. I could count some fifteen or twenty spans on one of the bridges. To the right lay the Tyrrhenian Sea, sparkling in the last rays of the sun.

Nick brought out a waist-high tripod with a circular rim into which was fitted a washbasin. I dusted off my field jacket and stripped to the waist as a young girl, one of the Salerno relatives, brought out a pitcher of hot water for my use. From the doorway and a window I could hear women whispering and giggling as I set about to wash away the furrows of dust that had collected around my goggles and dust mask. When I removed a bar of soap from my musette bag, there was an increase in the volume of whispers, punctuated by a gasp or two. It was a wonderful feeling to sponge the dirt of battle off my chest and arms after I had cleaned my face and hair.

I beckoned to the girl who had brought the water and gave her the bar of soap together with two other bars I'd brought along. This, of course, was some of the 'trading material' that Corporal Hobday had brought to Italy in the S-2 field safe. I'm sure it was received as though it were gold-plated.

My radioman, a huge hulk of a corporal with the biggest feet I'd ever seen, took his turn at the washbasin when another pitcher of hot water was brought out from the kitchen. I mention his feet, which were size 15! although he stood only about 5ft 8in tall, simply because I noticed that his boots had broken open and the heels were so slanted that his walking was impaired. I asked him what was wrong with getting some new boots, and he told me they'd been on order for over six months and that he was now in bad shape. The army, it seemed, did not issue boots of that caliber. The upshot of the subsequent inquiry I initiated, when I returned to the CP, was the man's relief from further service. He was shipped home because the army had, at last, met its match in the kind of a problem it could not handle. The I&R platoon also lost one of its most stalwart members, all for want of a shoe last that would equip a short, heavy man with long, wide footwear.

When I had donned a clean shirt and neckerchief, which I carried in my duffle, I went back into the house and found that a number of the younger women spoke French so that I could talk directly with them instead of using Nick as an interpreter. Nick's English, despite his fifteen years in the states, had a lot of extra syllables in it that made it difficult to comprehend.

As sometimes occurs in the older social strata of Italy, the men of the household eat first and as a group while the women wait on them. I was not aware of this custom and did my best to convince Nick that I wanted the women to join us. He clucked at me and waved his finger across his face and said, 'She's-a not done lak-a dot. Men eats – den woman.'

The women must have scoured the village for food because we were inundated with macaroni and cheese, vegetable salad, baked egg and potato pie and veal. This was the first real meal I'd eaten after landing in Italy and I was starved. However, I had to take it easy, despite their protests that I must eat more, because the absence of food had caused my stomach to shrink and I could hardly breathe even though I'd eaten sparingly. Wine was served with each course and I felt its effect at once.

I ate some fresh figs, which were a novelty to me, and grapes that Nick had picked from his own vines that afternoon. While we sat there among a dozen or so Italian men, some of them with drooping moustaches, I was aware of a certain amount of tension in their attitudes. Even the women, who were peering at us from the kitchen where they were in each other's way, sensed that the men were uneasy about something, for they whispered constantly among themselves.

Nick finally stood up and said something to the following effect: 'Capitano Dody,' (his word for my name) – 'Whatcha you theenk the Presidente Rooseavelt, he's a gonna do to Eetaly now that-a we queet the war?'

'Why,' I responded, 'didn't you hear General Eisenhower's talk the other night?' All the heads shook negatively as Nick translated. 'We no listen-a to the radio when-a de Germans stay here,' he said.

'Italy has come into the war on our side and will be treated as an ally, not an enemy,' I told the group.

The effect of Nick's translation was electric; the men stood up and cheered and the women came crowding in to shake my hand. All of a sudden life had taken on a different meaning for everyone there. The result was that hours passed as the corporal and I brought the group up to date on what was happening in the world.

Nick finally said, 'I'm-a tell-a everybodys it's-a no good we fight America. Too many Italians-a live dere. It's-a almost like-a fight our own-a peeple.' We finally left after midnight and I promised Nick, as I went out the door, that I would bring him some food the next morning to make up for what we'd eaten. He tried to wave me off but when I mentioned coffee, sugar and white flour, his shoulders slumped for the women, who could understand part of what I said, let him know how welcome it would be. 'We no drink-a da real coffee,' he said, 'for two-a years.'

The ride down the mountain flank that night was memorable for several reasons. The moonlight was as bright as day and the sultry air of the Italian countryside was like a tonic. Partway down we suddenly heard gunfire, and off to the south a well-lit hospital ship, blazoned with red crosses, was strafed by German planes that flew at an altitude below our level. The air attack was met with anti-aircraft fire in such volume that we were impressed as the Germans must also have been, for their air attacks from then on were light and fast, doing little or no damage.

While I couldn't return to Monte the next day, I got word to the I&R boys there and they relayed the news to Nick. They also managed to get some 10 in 1 rations from one of the anti-aircraft crews and brought them to Nick with my compliments, even though I knew nothing about the deal.

When I returned to Monte, it was at the behest of Colonel Price who had been entertaining General Lange at our CP. He wanted me to show Lange the OP on Cicerale. Fate took a hand at that juncture, for Lange's driver had gone off to visit some of his friends in our regiment. A driver was assigned from the regimental motor pool, and I took off leading a convoy of four jeeps with Lange in the one behind me.

The dust was terrible and I had warned the general to take along goggles and a mask. I also told him to follow at some distance as it would ease the dust problem. He indicated that he'd been around enough to handle such situations without advice, which lent a certain coolness to our relationship. I got into my jeep and told my driver to gun it for Monte and to hell with anything!

We took off in a hurry, and it wasn't until we were halfway up the mountain that I realized that no one was following us. We turned and went back along the road and met the rest of the convoy just returning from a side trip. The general was fuming about my negligence in leaving him in the lurch. I looked at his driver and, sure enough, it was the one man in the whole regiment who could be counted on to take a wrong turn. He was the 'extra' driver we'd had to use when one of the I&R jeeps was sidelined and, so far as he knew, the OP was the one we'd put in as an interim measure before we scaled Monte Cicerale.

The general said he'd have me court-martialled even after I told him that only his temporary driver, who after all had been dragooned into taking Lange because his permanent driver was goofing off, could have made the mistake that had caused our problem.

I looked Lange squarely in the eye and said: General, it was your idea, if you'll recall, to follow at such a great distance that you lost sight of my vehicle. There is no way you can lead me to the OP and there's no way I can keep dust out of your vision. Now I'm prepared to go on and, this time, I'll give you a map so that if you get lost again, you can follow it to the OP. I'm also prepared to stand court martial for what can only be considered the most unreasonable grounds I've ever heard of.'

'Don't you challenge me, Captain,' he said with heavy emphasis on my lesser rank. I returned to my jeep and took off again. We finally made it to the OP with the general's lower lip still curled into a tight grimace as he, obviously, was still rankled by what he considered to be an insult to his august presence. I was disgusted with him and his efforts to prove himself something just short of a god.

I walked his butt off after we left the jeeps and got so far ahead of him on the rough peak of Cicerale that he became exasperated with me again and yelled for me to come back. I simply waited as I heard him gasping and cussing as he half crawled, half walked up toward me.

'General,' I said, 'you shouldn't be here to begin with. There is no certainty that German troops aren't hiding out in some of these ravines nor can we be sure that we won't receive artillery fire in any event.'

He stood beside me for a moment and then looked off to the south. 'I wanted to see if Monty's army was in sight,' he said.

'I could have told you that it was not,' I responded. 'We're keeping a sharp lookout for his approach.'

'Good enough,' he said, his crustiness re-appearing. 'I want to return to your CP now and I'll lead the way.'

'Begging your pardon, General, I'm not returning to the CP as I have something to attend to here.'

He stomped off down the mountain nearly falling with each step. His uniform was grey as was his face, and I could tell by his stiff back that he couldn't wait to report me to Colonel Werner.

I climbed to the OP and called the regimental CP, where I got Colonel Price on the line. I told him of the situation and he began to suggest that I was wrong in what I'd done.

'Look, Colonel,' I said. 'I'm damned tired of the toadying that goes on in this regiment simply because you people don't know what the hell you're doing, nor do you know the regulations. I'd just as soon be shipped out to another outfit as to go on living in fear of some egotistical idiot who, long ago, proved to me that he is unfit to command. You know exactly what I mean for we've discussed it before. You cool him off or I'll raise hell in spades to include the censorship he received on the Carolina maneuvers.'

Price was a nice guy at heart, and he began to see the funny side of my run-in with Lange.

'Did you really challenge him to court-martial you?' he asked.

'I sure as hell did,' I responded.

'When are you coming back?' he asked.

'I'll be in at mess time,' I said. I stopped in Monte for a few minutes after checking out the men on the OP, who were laughing about the Lange affair when I left.

At the CP I ran into Colonel Price and Lange at the mouth of the cave. He and Lange had been talking about me, it seemed safe to assume, and Price gave me a high sign so that I stopped before reaching them.

'The general has decided not to court-martial you,' Price said in a low tone as he grabbed my elbow and ushered me out onto the beach where we could talk.

'Big deal!' was all I could think to say.

'Take it easy,' Price admonished. 'He wants an apology, though'.

'You give him one for me,' I said, half jokingly.

'Jesus, man,' Price came back, 'I've gone all out to defend you, ...'

'Hold it right there, Colonel,' I said. 'I don't need defending. I'm not bucking for anything but I'll be goddamned if I'll play up to Lange's vanity. He's a horse's ass and he'd be laughed out of any court called to try me. I refuse to apologize for something he brought on himself. His person is not sacred to me, and it's damned near time someone in this outfit stopped kissing his butt.'

'How'm I going to tell him?' Price asked.

'Look, Colonel,' I said. 'I appreciate your trying to help me but you can't seem to see that Lange needs to recognize that his reactions are nearly always based on a false appreciation of his own worth. Suppose you go back and tell him that the story is already around that he stopped his jeep today and woke up some soldiers sleeping beside the road when they failed to salute him.'

'What are you telling me?' Price asked. 'He actually did that?'

'I didn't see him,' I said, 'but enough people did to make him the laughingstock of the whole army, if the word gets out.'

Price disappeared back into the cave and I went to where a meal of sorts was being dished out for the staff by Colonel Werner's striker.[3]

An hour later Price came to where I was sitting and said that Lange had returned to the division headquarters.

'Am I suspended from duty?' I asked. 'If so, I'll sleep for the next couple of days.'

'I don't know what happened,' Price said as he chewed on a cigar butt. 'I sort of alluded to the story you told me, and Lange seemed to get the message

---

3. A personal assistant.

without me saying more. He hemmed and hawed for a while, and I could see him getting worried. He finally said something like, "Well, my fine Marine (Price had served in the Marine Corps in the First World War), guess I'll do all my fighting against the Germans" and walked out.'

That was the last I ever saw of Lange although some of his harebrained tactics in deploying troops, in a sector where he was given command when our forces were split, between the right flank and a supporting role to the British 56th – Black Cat – Division from London, confirmed my belief that he was unfit for such duty. He was summarily relieved from his position with the division when Ike Eisenhower saw the mess we were in after the beachhead was finally secured.

Chapter 7

Shooting Some Birds

As those German units that had left our front entered combat, again, near the city of Salerno, the fighting there grew fiercer while in our zones everything was fairly quiet. The sun shone brightly while birds began to sing again. Figs ripened on trees were delicious, as were great bunches of grapes on the vine. Unharvested crops like tomatoes and melons were everywhere for the taking.

On one of my sorties to the village of Monte I was taken by Nick Nigro out to visit a 93-year-old man whose family had gathered at his farm for safety. The old fellow had a beard down to his waist and a fringe of long hair that hung down from under a farmer's straw hat he wore. He was busy working in his vineyard when we got there and leaned against one of the vine supports as we talked, with Nick interpreting.

The old farmer shook his head over the name 'Mussolini' and mumbled a few words that Nick either couldn't or wouldn't translate. The unusual thing about the man was the fact that he had spent all ninety-three years of his life within 3 miles of the place where we were talking. I could scarcely credit the story and indicated some skepticism. The old man waved his arm around the scene that spread out in all directions and said that he was sure, from all he'd heard of others' travels, that there was no prettier sight anywhere. With fresh air, good soil and good health, a fine family and a church nearby, what did he need from the rest of the world? Not only had most of the war passed him by, but so had the world, and he still seemed happy and strangely above and beyond many earthly cares. I've often thought of him standing there, gnarled hands on a hoe, and wondered if he felt sorry for those people who could not spend their whole lives on Monte Cicerale.

We returned to the regiment and I learned that we would probably be moved to a position nearer the British 56th Division and the 179th Regimental Combat Team of the 45th US Division that had been brought in to help expand the beachhead. In the meantime the 142nd Infantry Regiment was engaged in taking the town of Altavilla, which lay at the top of a mountain that was connected by a saddle to a higher mountain called Hill 424.

The fight for Altavilla that went on for over a week during which time the town changed hands several times was the critical battle for the Salerno beachhead. Below it lay the Sele and Calore rivers and before we were through with the German counterattack that eventuated, the Germans had nearly penetrated to the shoreline in that area, debouching from a very large tobacco factory that everyone on the Allied side of the beachhead came to know before the fight was ended.

By September 13, 1943, engineers from every available echelon finally completed a new landing strip north of Paestum and west of Highway 18, the main road paralleling the coast. This, in itself, became a lynchpin in the change of momentum that occurred shortly thereafter because our planes, instead of flying from a squadron of aircraft carriers in the Gulf of Salerno or from distant Sicily, could take off, bomb and return to base in a matter of a few minutes. I watched them perform this jumping-jack maneuver many times over the succeeding days.

It was sometime around September 13 that my regimental headquarters accompanied our 3rd Battalion to a position at the base of the Sele–Calore River corridor in the worst kind of terrain, full of swamps and water buffalo wallows, mosquito-ridden, and very close to the shoreline. Our division at that time was so split up that it was no longer a cohesive unit. Even regiments were operating piecemeal as witness the fact that, while our 3rd Battalion was located in the swamps, our 2nd Battalion, having been sent to the extreme left flank of VI Corps, was now brought back to the southern slopes of Mount San Chirico, some 3 miles southeast of our 3rd Battalion. Our 1st Battalion was on another ridge called Tempore di San Paolo, another 4 or 5 miles from the 2nd Battalion. Since this line might well have become a final defensive position for preservation of the bridgehead, there was some justification for the false rumors, that were picked up and broadcast by war correspondents still on ships at sea, to the effect that the Allied troops were planning a shore-to-ship maneuver. Evacuation under fire would have been a murderous undertaking and, so far as I have ever learned, it was not contemplated.

The German counterattack started on September 14 with heavy reconnaissance in force to feel out our soft spots. However, readjustments in our positions during the night found the enemy, unwittingly, advancing parallel to our lines. This, of course, resulted in German assault tanks and troops being decimated as unit after unit of our defense forces took them under fire from the flank. All of the attacking tanks were destroyed and the infantry soon retreated.

I had had a good deal of difficulty trying to locate a position for an OP. In the first place, on the day we moved to the new, wet location beside the British, I went northward from our old CP to a road junction that was under heavy German tank and artillery fire. In a triangular-shaped wooded area I talked with the S-2 of one of the 45th Division regiments and while we were discussing hostile positions, shells came ripping in and wounded him before I could learn all that I needed to know. I ducked out of that hot spot and went by jeep down a lane that had just been converted to a main supply route. It was practically overgrown and its boggy base was soon churned to mire as our trucks moved over it. Before our engineers were through with it, however, it stood up under two-way traffic supplying all units on the left of the bridgehead.

I found a fairly reasonable area for our CP where a small brook wound its way, below steep embankments, to the sea. At a stream junction nearby was a spit of flat sand where a command tent could be erected and have some protection from shell bursts, since it was well below the general level of ground in that vicinity.

We were about to have something to eat at dusk, after the headquarters group had moved into our new site, when the sound of planes put me into a swan dive through heavy brambles into the center of the brook. They were on us in seconds and we could hear small bombs falling through the trees, for they did not go off on contact but had some kind of delayed fuse on them. The ensuing detonations were deafening and they seemed to last for a long time.

I finally came out of the brook in which I'd lain with only my head out of water while I clung to a tree root. That no one was hurt was a minor miracle as many of the vehicles and tents were destroyed. My face and arms were torn by briars but I felt that I'd done the only thing possible to avoid being hit.

That night, because we were expecting another round of bombs at daylight, I dug a small cave in the embankment of the brook and put my bedroll into it after bracing some boards against the top of the dug-out area to try to avoid a cave-in. The top of my cave was over 10ft below ground level. Malaria was a problem in Italy, and since I'd given up on Atabrine and couldn't get anything else to suppress malarial symptoms if I contracted that disease, I used gloves on my hands at night, a netting over my helmet and tied under my field jacket, and a mosquito repellent. In spite of such impedimenta, I managed not only to avoid malaria but to sleep well each chance I got.

I expected to be awakened the next morning by sounds of an air attack but since none came, there being many more remunerative targets all along the line, I slept through until mid-morning. No one knew where I was, it seemed, and I was tired.

Colonel Crawford was busy with the tactical situation when I looked into the command tent. He had the 3rd Battalion commander on the telephone, so I went looking for breakfast somewhere. We had not gotten ourselves together well enough to have an organized mess, so it was practically everyone for himself. I ran into a small group sitting around a small gasoline stove where Colonel Werner's striker was heating some C rations. I hated the smell of those cans of hash and lost my appetite from the odor of preservative every time I opened one.

Someone had really put one over on the army when they sold them such a bill of goods. In some cans were biscuits and candy, and if one were lucky, a package of powdered coffee. Such are the vagaries of human existence that the men who did the front-line fighting (located as they were at the end of the supply line) usually got powdered lemon juice, the coffee rations having been short-stopped at army or army group where men not only ate better, in any event, but stored the coffee tins in their quarters against the need to have a late-night snack.

The colonel's striker, who was not only an Englishman but a butler to boot, had somehow been drafted into the US army and was about to be demobilized, the army having but recently acknowledged its error. He came from New York, where he had served as butler to some wealthy family and was going to return to that city as soon as possible.

In any event, as we sat eating beside a gasoline stove at Salerno, a British brigadier general strolled up to our group and when we stood at attention, he asked us to resume what we were doing and ate some of our heated C rations with us. He sat on the ground and queried us as to how we liked combat, and when I said that we'd like it better if we could see anything, he inquired of me as to my job. I told him I was the regimental intelligence officer, at which he assumed a less informal manner and said, 'Come with me!'

We were under his command at the time so I took off with him after checking out with the headquarters group. We drove along the marshy road where engineers were working, and en route we stopped at an artillery headquarters where I met a British officer named Captain Hamilton. It was interesting to learn that Hamilton had been directing the fire of a number of British 25-pounders, as some of their artillery guns were called, as well as the fire from naval batteries offshore. He had held the sector practically single-handedly with gunfire until readjustments had been made in the disposition of troops to block a gap in our lines.

Hamilton showed me a chart of the front lines in his sector and I was impressed with the British method of firing artillery concentrations on an overlay that was fitted to a map of the terrain in front of the British and our positions was a series of abutting rectangles, 100 by 200yd in size, which were named for birds. I could see 'Robin,' 'Lark,' 'Grey goose,' 'Linnet,' 'Kestrel' and many others. While I watched, Hamilton signaled by radio for the Bruisers patrolling offshore to fire 'Robin.'

'I don't dare let them go very long without calling for fire or we'll lose them to other units,' he said. 'I know that the Germans are forming up behind that old tobacco warehouse to counterattack, and we've got to keep them off-balance.'

The brigadier complimented Hamilton on his work and we left for his brigade headquarters where we had an atrocious meal of corned beef, bread, and tea brewed in what I recognized had once graced the underside of some Italian bed. It was a huge porcelain thunder-jug which the brigadier said had been thoroughly cleansed before being used for tea.

It was getting on toward dusk when I said I ought to be returning to my regiment.

'Hold on,' the brigadier said. 'I'm taking you out to our observation post so that you can see what I mean when I say there's no excuse for going blind in a combat zone.'

Apparently he had been waiting for the sun to get low enough to interfere with German observation, for we started toward the front and after 10 minutes we passed his brigade's outpost line. By this time my ears and eyes were honed to a fine degree. As we passed a dug-in machine gun, the brigadier stooped down and said something in a low tone to one of the crew.

We continued on until I was practically certain he was quitting the war by surrendering to some German sentry. However, we finally reached a farm where artillery had wrecked just about everything there. As we rounded the corner of a barn I saw three British soldiers, stripped to the waist, doing their best to milk an intransigent cow. Two had her by the head and tail and a third man was throwing a box around, which I took to be a milking stool, while he tried to grab her teats. She wasn't cooperating in any degree and her back hoofs flashed out barely missing the tail-holder.

In a silo near the top, where there was quite an opening reached by an iron ladder, three other British soldiers were cheering on the trio beneath them. Since I had estimated that we were within easy range of enemy guns, I wasn't keen about all the noise that was rising from that dusty barnyard.

'Jerry knows we're here,' the brigadier said. 'He's tried hard to knock us out.' He pointed to a hole in the silo that an armor-piercing shell had made, taking part of the ladder's handrail with it.

'We have a special welcoming committee for his patrols each night,' the Brigadier said, 'and we've caught several of them with booby traps that we try to rearrange daily just to make it interesting for them.'

'Up we go,' he added, and swung up the iron ladder like a sailor going aloft. I followed him and had a moment's pause as I passed the shell-hole, for the ladder was barely attached to the silo at one side while at the other side the rail was gone altogether for a distance of about 2ft.

On a platform that the observation team had built at the top of the silo I found five men in all. Two were working while the others yelled at the cow-wrestling group. One man was peering through a scope of the kind artillerymen usually employ, so mounted on a tripod that it could be used to look over a hillcrest or large rock while the viewer remained out of sight. The other man was speaking quietly into a radio microphone.

From our position I could see German vehicles moving past a road juncture, and we could hear tanks making their peculiar track-laying squeals somewhere off to our right in the Sele–Calore rivers corridor. I was convinced that this group had been at war too long.

The brigadier sat in full view of enemy observers who must have been blinded by the sun for we received no fire. 'Got the idea?' he asked and I'm sure he knew how scared I was. I said I did, more to get the lesson over with than to go along with what I considered the last stages of someone's death wish.

We remained there for about a half hour, and in that time the men below managed to subdue the cow long enough to get about a quart of fresh milk.

I had a great desire to look over my shoulder as the brigadier and I worked our way back through a grassy field where there was a small path leading to his outpost line. I heard a rifle bolt being drawn back and the brigadier said something which I took to be a password, for we went on with no further talk of any kind. It was some weeks later that I learned that my host, that day, was the most highly decorated officer in the British Army. I was very happy when I finally reached my regimental headquarters.

All along I had considered putting an observation team in a similar silo that stood at the top of a small rise in front of our 3rd Battalion's position. Suddenly, after my indoctrination by the British officer, I realized that, as with patrols, observers were the ones who had to take whatever risk was involved in order to try to preserve the mass of our troops from surprise and annihilation.

I checked with our command group, told them where I'd been and what I was going to do that night. I put an I&R platoon observation team at the top of our silo and warned them to take no chances of being seen during the day. Before long there were eight observation teams from Allied artillery units operating from the vicinity of the silo. At no time were they taken under fire.

During that day I learned more about OPs from the British than I'd ever heard from any other source. 'Don't always put your OP in the one best spot, particularly if there are several other places that may serve almost as well,' the brigadier had said to me as he sat dangling his legs from the silo platform.

'However,' he went on, 'disturb the setting around the best place to make it look as though it were occupied. Don't overdo it. Put one rock on top of another or haul in a log and put it where it appears to be concealing your observers.'

I don't know how many times I've thought of that cool brigadier since that day, but on many an occasion I blessed him for the trickery he taught me as I lay in an OP and watched German artillery shell the hell out of a decoy we'd set up for them a safe distance away.

We were not only aware of the hostile moves being made to dislodge us, but Axis Sally was good enough to let us know that the main attack would come between the Sele and Calore rivers just about opposite the position I was in with the regimental headquarters.

Between us and the shore, the British 25-pounders were firing from hub-to-hub positions and near them were the Royal Scots Greys, an armored unit, whose weapons were in constant use, firing over our heads as artillery. Beyond them to the west were the cruisers and battleships adding their strength to our defenses. For several nights I went to sleep in my mosquito-infested cave above the brook with the sound of 15in shells slithering over our bivouac to the enemy positions.

The day came when the German counterattack was launched, full-scale, against us. At the time I had gone forward to a secondary OP that I'd had installed on the second floor of a pigeon coop. It was limited in its outlook but covered a small defile where I was convinced German armor could approach our defensive network without being seen from our silo OP. When I arrived and poked my head up through a trapdoor into the observation portion of the cote, I found several observers talking excitedly into field phones. I climbed up and looked out to the front, where I could make out a partially concealed object moving toward us at about 150yd range. Trees were being pushed over, and I finally got a full view of the flash-hider on a large German tank gun. As the tank butted its way forward, its swastikas came into my glasses, which I had focused on the spot. This was my first face-to-face confrontation with a nasty fighting machine, and my guts felt fully exposed.

The gun fired and I dropped to the floor as the shell barely missed our fragile structure and burst somewhere behind us with a loud explosion. I grabbed a phone and called for Captain Hamilton, who radioed the navy to fire a ladder – three shells in direct line with each other from the ship so that I could indicate necessary adjustments to bring fire to bear on the tank, which I expected, momentarily, to blast me to kingdom come. I never knew what delayed the next shot from the tank, but observers said that its gun barrel appeared caught in a small tree. In any event, the tank had been forced to back away and take a new approach.

The navy's three shots were not visible to me, although I caught one of them which was not far off target. Taking a chance on how to direct the next round, I called for 100yd left and down 50yd, to fire for effect. I really wasn't sure of how to call the shot nor was I going to stick around to find out what happened.

I jumped from the loft, followed by everyone there, and ran straight back from the pigeon coop, swinging myself around trees and finally diving for cover behind a small knoll completely covered with moss. A heavy explosion sent shock waves over us, and I was close enough to the moss to smell its dankness. A soldier who had stopped short of my position started to sneak back toward the pigeon coop as debris fell all around us. 'Goddamn!' he yelled. 'The navy busted the tank.'

We could hear the roar of a pitched battle as we moved back to where the pigeon coop lay battered to splinters. Apparently the tank had let one go into the OP just as the navy shell struck its left track and upended the tank, leaving it burning. There was nothing else to be done there, since our telephone lines had been destroyed and besides, the place was getting hotter than a pistol.

Back of us the British guns and tanks were beating a heavy tattoo on our eardrums. I raced back to the CP and got in touch by radio with the I&R boys in the silo. I could hear excited voices calling map coordinates as I listened to the radioman describe the sight. Tanks and infantry were coming at our position from all angles and our artillery was tearing up the cabbage patch, knocking out everything that moved. It was a tense moment that went on and on until, as inevitably happens in warfare, something had to give way. Our planes were there, operating out of the nearby landing field that had been taken under artillery fire. I watched them rise steeply into the air, straighten out at a fairly low level, and toggle their bombs, followed by a strafing run and return to base.

We beat the tar out of the German counterattack and later, when our artillery spotter planes flew over the tobacco factory that Captain Hamilton had belabored for days, the stench of rotting bodies lying there reached the pilots several thousand feet in the air.

The I&R observation team called me and reported that red-shirted men and ambulances bearing red crosses could be seen moving about the German positions. I called the British brigade and asked the S-2 there what was happening. 'Jerry's pulling out,' he said.

I tore over to the brigade in my jeep, the firing from both sides having fallen off to a few harassing rounds in each direction. British reaction was typical. The brigadier waved goodbye to me with his swagger stick and as he took off in a small Bren Gun Carrier he said in a calm voice, 'After them, men! Don't give them a chance to stop and dig in.' I watched him go down a lane toward German lines until I lost sight of his beret that had protruded above the carrier.

Chapter 8

Altavilla

Just before the Germans pulled out of the beachhead I was sent to Altavilla to learn what the situation was in that belabored town. It was quite a sizeable village near the top of a mountain range and had been the refuge for many people fleeing from the city of Salerno when our attack, from the sea, focused on that center. Our troops had taken Altavilla for the final time on September 18, the day I went up the steep, tortuous road leading to it.

On the way up my driver had trouble making the grade in several places. As we rounded one turn I saw an Italian woman sprawled on her face beside the road, and beside her was a little girl with long brown curls and dressed in a blue dress with a blue ribbon in her hair. Both were dead and had been left where they fell for days. It was one of the most brutal sights of the war for me, for it was obvious that the mother had been trying to reach a place of refuge when she and her baby were brought down by artillery shell fragments.

I passed a church on the left side of the road on the outskirts of Altavilla and saw a large stone cross erected on the opposite side of the road. The town itself was a shambles with masonry, tiles from roofs, trees, vehicles, and dead animals strewn all over its main plaza. I got out of the jeep and walked to a building that bore a CP sign for one of the units of the 143rd Infantry Regiment.

People were just beginning to emerge from their hiding places deep in cellars and from caves and other shelters they'd dug. There was a lot of activity by our soldiers, who were moving out to form a defensive perimeter around the town. I wanted to see the far side of Hill 424 facing the hostile lines and found that, as I walked along the saddle between Altavilla and that terrain feature that loomed above all else in the vicinity, I found myself alone as my driver was staying with our jeep.

I came out on the nose of a spur overlooking the valley to the east where the German lines were located and found a company of paratroopers lying in slit trenches and watching for hostile movement below their position. A corporal pointed his .45 pistol at me and cried, 'Get down!' He motioned sharply with his weapon and I went down on one knee.

'What's wrong?' I asked.

'The Kraut are still down there,' the corporal said.

'No, they're not,' I said as I remained kneeling. 'Montgomery's army is abreast of us now and the Germans are pulling to the north.'

'That's what another officer said yesterday,' the corporal said as he did a duck-walk toward me keeping low as he moved. 'These Joes are dead because he walked all over our position and attracted artillery fire.'

He pointed at about a dozen troopers, whom I had thought were sleeping, and I could see blood on their uniforms. All of them were dead. Just then a runner came up from Altavilla and announced that the Germans had, in fact, pulled out and were well on their way to Naples some 30 miles away across a mountain range.

The paratroopers relaxed and started to police their dead. A couple of them said they wanted to see the top of Hill 424 because of all the hell they'd received from it. I went along with them, stepping as lightly as possible because there was always the chance that defenders of a hillcrest might have put out minefields to bolster their defenses.

We had to circle the hillside as we moved because of very steep embankments, and as I pushed past some low-growing bushes I stopped short, for the umpteenth time since landing on the beach. There on their knees and leaning forward onto their rifles were two US paratroopers – stone dead. A machine-gun burst had hit them in such a way that, as they dropped to their knees on the steep slope, their bayonets had penetrated the ground and supported them in that position after they expired. It was a weird spectacle. The paratroopers with me called for some of the others to help move the two bodies while I went on up the slope to the very crest of the hill.

There, again, I saw another chilling sight: the German defenders, some ten in all, were still sitting at their machine guns located in four corners of a square that encompassed the crown on the hill which was quite heavily wooded. While I did not inspect their bodies, I did remove several soldbuchs[1] from their tunics to identify their organization. The awful part of the scene was the fact that the eyes of all the men there had been blasted out of their heads as though a great naval shell had struck the center of their position and killed them all simultaneously with its concussive power. The ground was ploughed into shreds and the place smelled of death. I got out – and rejoined the paratroopers as they carried off their dead comrades toward Altavilla.

Back at the town an old woman whose face, shrouded in a black shawl, bore the strain of all she'd been through, spoke to me in Italian. I couldn't understand her so she took me by the hand and pulled me toward a blasted home at the edge of the town square. We entered the place and, after stumbling over smashed furniture and stones from ruptured walls, we went into the basement where there were still a number of people, crying and whimpering.

Across the basement was the entrance to a tunnel that had been dug, I gathered, by some of our troops or possibly by the Germans during the long fight to control Altavilla. The old woman held a candle she'd lit for me and, again, I had an unpleasant surprise. Bulging through the ceiling of the tunnel was the ugly snout of a huge shell which I estimated to be a 15in naval dud. It was a very unhealthy place to be. I backed off, treading lightly, and after making sweeping signs with my arms, moved everyone out of the cellar and into the square. I

---

1. Paybooks.

called an engineer to the place and told him what I'd seen. He immediately got other engineers to cordon off the whole square and to move everyone away from the dangerous area.

I talked with some officers I knew from the 143rd Infantry, and as we stood on the far side of the square we heard what sounded like applause. I looked down a side street that sloped up to the square and saw an old man guiding a burro on which a young woman sat, clapping her hands. A knot of people pressed forward toward her and apparently asked what had caused her reaction. The old man said something and everyone in the group started the same rhythmic clapping of their hands. No one cried that I could see or hear; they simply expressed their grief by pounding their hands together and shortly others around the square responded in the same way. We were told by an Italian-speaking GI that their priest had been found shot through the head, a fact I never could substantiate.

Altavilla had been the target initially for the 3rd Battalion of the 142nd Infantry which went on the attack at 5:45 am on September 13, 1943. Nearby were two other battalions of infantry: the 1st Battalion of the 142nd Infantry and the 3rd Battalion of the 143rd Infantry. A company of tanks and two battalions of artillery were in support. While the attack went well, at first, a counterattack threw the 142nd Battalion off the hill. The 1st Battalion, 142nd, moved in to reinforce the attack but got caught in a hostile artillery barrage that disorganized its companies until after midnight.

At the same time, the 143rd's 3rd Battalion drove up the ridge northwest of Altavilla, reaching the top by 9 am only to be driven off by a strong counterattack. A new attack on that strongpoint could not be organized until September 16, when the 504th and 505th Parachute Infantry Regiments, that had been dropped during the night of September 14 and 15 into the Mount Soprano area, patrolled the approaches to Altavilla and found them lightly outposted by the Germans.

The 504th moved out in the late afternoon of the 16th and launched an attack against the Altavilla heights but could not take their objectives because of heavy artillery fires falling on their positions along the slopes, where they were unable to move out of their foxholes during the day and night of September 17. It was only after the withdrawal of the German defenders, who had held Altavilla in a rearguard action while many of their other units began a retreat toward Naples, that our forces finally took and held that commanding position.

In the meantime, my regiment maintained its spread-out position, after having assisted in repelling the German effort to split the beachhead in two along the Sele–Calore rivers corridor.

At about this time General Lange was replaced by General Wilbur of the School of Torture and Dirty Tricks in North Africa. Generals Wilbur, Iron Mike O'Daniel, and Lange had been in command of three separate sectors of the US defensive zone when the Germans had mounted their counterattack. I later learned that Ike had arranged for Lange's and others' replacements when he saw the loss of coherence in all of our units because of the way they'd been deployed.

I was sleeping in my tent one night when someone pulled at my boot. I was fully dressed and lying on my bedroll beneath which my striker, a Mexican by the name of Pete, had put my air mattress. He had finally found a way to patch it from where a machine-gun bullet had put two holes through it when the German planes had strafed the beachhead.

It was normal to sleep with a pistol at hand in those days. I shoved mine under the nose of someone whose silhouette I could make out against a brilliant moonlit night and a voice yelled, 'Don't shoot, Cap'n! Don't shoot!' It was a sergeant who, until we reached the battlefield, had been real macho about what he planned to do to the enemy. I'd seen him quite often, in the vicinity of Djebel Khartoum, walk out onto a plateau and suddenly pull two pistols (one wasn't enough for him) from their holsters and blaze away at boulders and bushes. He also carried two knives and was famous for sharpening them, at every opportunity, against the leather of his boots.

The sergeant said he wanted to talk with me because he felt I knew more about the enemy situation than anyone else in the headquarters.

'Where've you been?' I asked since I couldn't recall having seen him during the fight. He told me that he'd been guarding supplies at the beachhead. His teeth were chattering even though the night was not cold. I very quickly sensed that he was panicky and ready to fall apart.

'I heard the Germans are dropping parachutists near here tonight.' he finally blurted out. 'I can't sleep for thinking about it.'

When I asked him where he'd gotten his information he said he'd overheard Colonel Crawford talking on the telephone in the command tent while he, the sergeant, stood guard outside. I told him he'd misinterpreted what he'd heard because the paratroopers involved were units of the US 82nd Airborne Division who had been dropped into the beachhead to support the fight for Altavilla.

The sergeant moved off into the night and later, having been tested beyond his endurance, was transferred to a rear echelon. In the early stages of the war there was a tendency on the part of some officers to subject men who had become physically and emotionally exhausted in combat to ridicule and contempt. It didn't take too long, however, to realize that the sooner such men were removed from the fighting front, the better their chances of recovery. Furthermore, fear and desperation are contagious and one man displaying inordinate signs of such reactions could quickly infect a whole unit. It was also fairly clear that the reverse often occurred, when a man showed tremendous guts in tackling a dangerous job and brought dozens of men with him because of their admiration for his nerve.

We found, too, that when men were taken to rear areas where they could get a couple of nights' sleep, some hot food, and a bath they would be eager to return to their units for fear that they might, otherwise, be assigned to a strange outfit whose members were unknown to them and whom, therefore, they could not trust. Eventually this led to the establishment of a rest area at Division Rear where men could recover their will to go on in combat, while still under division control. Once a man was evacuated through medical channels, his services would be lost to the division for weeks and he might thereafter be shunted to a Replacement Depot (Repple Depple, in GI parlance) and transferred out of the 36th Division.

When I returned from Altavilla on September 18, 1943, I saw dozens of women gathered around the great stone cross at the edge of town. They were on their knees with eyes turned upward and lips moving. They had very little to be thankful for, on the whole, except that they had lived through a maelstrom. On September 20 our regimental CP moved out of the pesthole we'd occupied for days and took over an Italian farmhouse that had just been vacated by General O'Daniel. I was delayed for some reason in making the move so that I pulled into the farmyard at about midnight. I simply stretched out on the ground beside a covered well and went to sleep.

At about dawn I was wakened by the low voices of two men talking on the other side of the well coping and it was fairly obvious that they did not know of my presence. I identified the voice of Colonel Werner when he said, 'What happened to you?'

'Colonel, so help me Jesus,' a man's husky whisper replied, 'I couldn't tell you or anyone what happened.' I did not recognize the voice but by this time, of course, I was fully awake.

'I must have panicked,' the voice went on. 'All of a sudden I just couldn't help myself with so many men getting killed and wounded. I tried to run up a white flag, and a couple of men jumped me and held me down.'

'Who took over from you?' the colonel asked. 'Damned if I know,' the voice replied. 'I must have passed out somewhere along the line. I don't remember a damned thing. I just want out, that's all!'

At about that moment a jeep drove into the yard and stopped near the two men whose conversation had caught my ear. Someone got out of the jeep and walked, with Werner and the man I had not identified, into the farmhouse. I decided I did not want to know who had been involved in an attempted surrender and, since it was light enough, I prowled around until I located most of the I&R platoon boys sleeping in their tents and in a barn. With them I had some coffee and grub that they'd scrounged from civilians along our route.

During the day we held a regimental staff meeting to learn of our next assignment, and it came as a pleasant surprise to find that we were to rest for a while until we could reorganize and rebuild our depleted ranks. As I studied a map of the terrain north of Naples I realized that we would have a difficult time later, not only with the ubiquitous mountains but with the Volturno and Garigliano rivers and I pointed this out to the staff as we discussed future potential operations.

The next day we moved, again, to a point near the Calore River where the ruins of a Roman aqueduct dominated our bivouac area. There we learned that our rest period would be filled with tactical walks, supervised by General Wilbur, whose job it was to point out strong and weak aspects of our tactics as we had employed them during our various battles. I attended several such sessions and found Wilbur's commentaries well taken and designed to improve the leadership capacity of the combat commanders. One or two of them took umbrage at certain of his criticisms and shortly thereafter were replaced with men who had earned promotion the hard way.

I put the I&R platoon through its paces and among other assignments went with its members to inspect the outposts we had established along the southern flank of the beachhead near Agropoli. On all such trips we managed to return with vegetables and fruit to improve our menus. In addition to sleeping well each night, after two weeks of having caught a nap of an hour or two between battles, we enjoyed the return to more normal conditions when our meals were served in a mess tent and latrines provided some privacy for nature's calls.

Rumors were once again prevalent concerning our return to the front, which by that time had moved far enough north that we could no longer hear the artillery duels, although, at night, we could see gun flashes that looked like heat lightning in summer.

Major Willman, the regimental S-3 of the 141st Infantry, and I were given the task of bringing the journals of the various headquarters sections up to snuff by reviewing and editing them. I noticed that great emphasis had been placed by all sections on the activities of Colonel Crawford during the battle for the beachhead. However, later, when I had occasion to inspect the journals of that period for some purpose – no longer remembered – I found that Crawford's name had been deleted in nearly every instance. I could only speculate on the reasons for such treatment of the official records of our combat experiences and on the perpetrator's identity.[2]

I heard that messages all along our front lines told of a number of German troops, dressed in completely red-colored uniforms, that were seen policing the battlefield of dead and wounded. I called the British 56th Division headquarters and learned, to my surprise, that the red-hued men were German graves registration and medical troops who, it seemed, always made their appearance just prior to a German withdrawal from a position. It seemed to me that such a practice was, first, an unlikely giveaway of projected operation and, secondly, a gut-busting operation on the part of its participants to offer themselves as such conspicuous targets on the battlefield. It was but the first of many highly courageous acts I saw German troops perform during the war. Our troops were ordered not to fire on the action of the scavengers. The British brigadier came on the phone to tell me to have our troops ready to 'dash after the bastards' without delay so that they'd have no opportunity to prepare delaying positions along the route of their withdrawal north through Naples.

I arranged to meet the brigadier along the roadway, at a juncture near his right flank, to get his plan of 'dashing after the bastards' as a matter of facilitating our own movements.

---

2. In other writing, RKD suggests that Colonel Werner was the perpetrator.

Arriving before him in my jeep, I had my driver pull over to the side of the road to a point from which I could use my field glasses to look the length of a gravel road leading directly into the German-held positions about a mile away. In the distance, I saw a small vehicle coming toward me at a fairly slow pace. When it reached the road juncture where I was waiting, I got out of my jeep and signaled what proved to be a British Bren Carrier to stop.

This was a small vehicle manned by a crew of two, a driver and a machine-gunner who appeared to be asleep with his head down on one arm.

'Sir?' The driver queried.

'I am awaiting your brigadier,' I said. 'We're getting ready to follow after the Germans. What can you tell me about their defenses out there about a mile?'

'They're gone!' he replied. 'Not a soul there now. I heard the sound of some shooting further on though.'

The brigadier rolled up to where we were talking at that point and questioned the driver some more.

'You been out here longtime?' he finally asked. 'Your gunner seems tired.'

'He's dead, sir,' the driver said. 'I was just returning his body to the rear when the captain stopped me.'

I was somewhat taken aback, although I realized that, a few days earlier, I probably would have been astounded. It wasn't that death was something taken casually and without regard for its nuances at the front, it was simply that death was so omnipresent that it was taken for granted solely as a means of ignoring it in order to complete one's present mission and get on with the next one. Deploring death was a luxury, I suppose, for which the day's schedule allowed no time. Some men, of course, could not dissociate themselves from each corpse they saw and as a result, their capacity to carry out each day's assignments grew smaller with each cadaver until only a shadow of a man was left. At that juncture they went under, mentally, spiritually, physically, and had to be removed from the scene.

That there may have been dissenters and con artists in the group who left the battlefield cannot be denied. On the whole though, there was very little of that kind of hypocrisy where the fighting took place. It was a different country where shot and shell set the parameters of living. Men knew that their lives depended on others and that the reverse was true. It was an entirely different citizenship than any other. To escape death, it was felt would be a miracle, but the only chance would be to react toward others as they would wish others to do for them. It was a real Golden Rule society, divorced as it was, in reality, from most of the other trappings and truisms of religion.

While many have said they found God in a foxhole, many more when weighing the absolutes of warfare coined a new thought after witnessing the slaughter, the maiming, the inhumanity, the degradation, the crassness, the lawlessness, the roar, the blindness, the injustice, the corruption, the sin, the privation, the loneliness, the heartbreak, and the many more deformities of warfare. That thought is sometimes expressed: 'God abhors a war as Nature abhors a vacuum.'

In effect, given the abject unholiness of war, no matter its cause, there can be little doubt that its outcome is not decreed by God for, to my mind, He ignores a war and all who fight it. In His firmament, a war is a great black hole.

On my way out of Altavilla, I heard people clapping as though applauding. It was, however, their way of expressing their grief on learning from a young lady of the death of her parents and of the village priest whose bodies had just been found. I passed a church whose doorway was guarded by a large rough stone cross standing alone in the churchyard. Kneeling around the cross was a number of old women and ancient men, their lips moving in silent prayer.

We moved out of the farmhouse where we had our headquarters the day after we had seen the German men, dressed in red, policing the battlefield. Our move was at night and we were to proceed to the ruins of an aqueduct where we would encamp pending further orders. We were not going to pursue the Germans through Naples.

At about midnight something happened to hold our column in a large field after we had moved but a short distance. We 'circled the wagons,' so to speak, by pulling our vehicles into an all-round defensive position and went to sleep.

I woke up in bright sunlight the next morning and, upon arising from the ground where I had spread my bedroll, I was astounded to see our regimental column, all elements of which had been drawn together in the night, in full sight with no one awake. It spoke only too well of our complete air superiority for a couple of German planes could have wiped us out.

It was actually about 9 am and everyone was so fatigued that we had just gone to sleep and to hell with everything! I alerted everyone by horn blowing and, in short order, we were on the move away from the area which, until that moment, we had referred to as '88 Alley' because of so much German high-velocity[3] fire falling on it.

There was no sound of gunfire in our vicinity nor could we hear much from the north. We reached our assigned area and made camp.

General Wilbur took the occasion, while we licked our wounds, to walk each unit of the division back over the battlegrounds to discuss tactics as they had been practiced during the fighting and to critique them. Some of the older National Guard officers from Texas took rank exception to what they considered 'kid's stuff' and were, therefore, relieved of their assignments. They, for the most part, of course, were the ones who had fouled up. Their replacements were, generally, better officers, by far.

I arranged, while training the intelligence sections of the regiment, to send the I&R platoon out to Agropoli on the southwest shore of Salerno Bay. I went with them, and after encountering an Italian supply depot, traded off some cigarettes and food stuff for a beautiful Italian tent that was larger than the pup tent that Major Williamson (regimental S-3) and I were sleeping in. It was large enough for

---

3. The 88mm shells traveled faster than the speed of sound so that no sound warning could ever be heard before they struck.

us to stand up in and it also accommodated cots for our bedrolls. It apparently had never been used, and when I pulled it from a storage bin, the Italian sergeant in charge had pressed me to take it. I gave him a pack of cigarettes, which he shared with some other Italian soldiers nearby.We also saw some huge glass flagons of olive oil that the Italian army employed for cooking purposes. These were so large and fragile and it is hard to believe that anyone planning army equipment would have considered them practicable. I'm sure they had to be hoisted around by cranes. Certainly they were terribly vulnerable to any kind of gunfire. I would hazard a guess that they contained a hundred or so gallons of oil.

When we encountered the Italian supply depot, soldiers there were lounging around, smoking and waiting for someone to tell them what to do and where to go. They were friendly and quite happy to be out of the war.

Early in the first week, before my element of the regiment had been moved to the flank of the British zone, the 141st headquarters had received word from Italian sources that that an Italian general, reputedly a giant of a man, was under siege by the German paratroopers at his home well to the south of our bridgehead. He was the leader of Italy's crack Alpine troops, trained in mountain fighting. Apparently, the Germans wanted him out of the way by one means or another, since their plans for the Italian campaign would be seriously impeded were he to regain command of troops in the Alps and from there disrupt German supply lines to the Italian front.

Colonel Werner deputized me to take a platoon of men to the south to affect release of the general and his return to our CP. Here again was a sign of Werner's misuse of troops and officers and his unstated reliance on me for what looked like a tough assignment. I went to the command tent and asked him why he wanted me to do the job. His answer was a classic, 'Because you speak French,' he said.

I was to go parading off to the south of Italy with a platoon of men[4] to rescue an Italian general who, since he was of great interest to the Germans, certainly should have been of similar interest to the Allies.

'How does speaking French affect the situation, Colonel?' I asked.

'If the general is as important as he sounds,' Werner responded, 'he probably speaks French.'

'What's wrong with sending more men together with an Italian interpreter?' I asked, 'I am not against going with the I&R platoon, but I think the situation calls for greater strength, since our objective is 75 miles away and should we require reinforcement, none will be available.'

'I can't spare any more men from our operations,' he said.

'Does division know of this request?' I asked.

'They think it's a fake,' he said.

'I'd like it as a matter of record,' I said,' that I don't consider it a fake and that, if we are unable to affect the rescue called for by the Italian government of Badoglio, I asked for an adequate force to make the effect.'

---

4. Typically twenty-five to fifty-five men in two squads.

I left with the I&R platoon a few minutes later, having tried unsuccessfully to telephone the British 10th Corps to learn of Montgomery's position, if possible.

We followed normal patrolling techniques of leapfrogging vehicles as a means of guarding against loss of the platoon from encountering hostile roadblocks or ambushes. While there was no sign of hostile presence, I kept up the practice of jeopardizing one vehicle at a time until reconnaissance could establish the safety of the terrain ahead before moving the group forward.

We advanced along Route 6, the main coastal road, but because of the need for caution, took a lot longer to reach the small town of our search. It was a bright, sunlit autumn day with no signs of warfare anywhere. Populated centers were sparse since the land was poor and mainly rural.

Finally, we turned off the route toward the shore. I had been told that the general lived in a somewhat isolated place near the sea, without near neighbors. The map I used was an old tourist creation with very little detail and none of that trustworthy.

As my jeep came up over a rise I could see, in the distance, a lone house of fairly moderate appearance. Near it was a detached garage and a couple of sheds. Nobody was in sight anywhere.

I stopped the platoon and ordered the vehicles off the road and while one squad got ready to advance on foot, the remainder moved to a stone wall a hundred feet or so to the right of the roadway. The squad deployed as skirmishers and moved toward the house. I went with those behind the wall where we crawled along the wall, down an incline screened by underbrush, and worked our way toward the garage at the right side of the house.

I did not expect to encounter any Germans. There was no sign of hostile activity so far as I could see. I caught up with the platoon leader still on his knees behind the wall. He was using field glasses and looking at the house.

'See anything?' I asked.

'Think someone's there behind the curtains,' he said in a low voice.

There were still no sounds. Finally I heard someone laugh. It was a male laugh, loud and harsh. Then there were the sounds of talking, but I couldn't understand what was being said.

A GI came running around the garage, which partially blocked our view of the front of the house.

'It's okay!' he said. 'The general's there! He's quite a guy. Big, bearded!'

I signaled the men to stay where they were and left with the soldier to go to the house. The squad of men was lolling around near the door until I showed up where they stood.

'Have you checked these buildings?' I asked.

'No need, sir,' the sergeant said. 'The general's men took care of the German paratroopers two days ago.'

I stepped up to the door where the general appeared carrying a bottle of wine. He was quite a guy, standing well over 6ft tall with a huge beard and a ham-size hand which he struck out to me while giving the wine to the sergeant I had spoken to.

I tried my French but, Werner to the contrary notwithstanding, it was a lost cause. I motioned to one of the Italian-speaking I&R men and went into the kitchen where the general's wife, herself built to similarly large proportions, waved to me to sit down.

Through the interpreter I learned that the general had, indeed, been the subject of a German effort to take or kill him. He had been defended by a squad of the Alpine troops who lived nearby, and in the process, several German paratroopers had been killed. The general had no fear of the Germans but felt that they had treated their Italian allies shamefully. He was ready when plans could be made to reorganize his Alpine troops and set them to harassing the German rear for the rest of the war.

When he saw my map, he roared at its inadequacy. He insisted on my taking a map he had on a linen backing of the Salerno area. His signature appears on the lower right corner but it is practically illegible. It looks like E.I. Paveza. I have the map in my desk among my souvenirs of the war.

I never heard of the general again, so I don't know whether he was able to organize the Alpini or harass the Germans. I doubted that such a plan was feasible.

Chapter 9

A Feint

During our stay near the old aqueduct, we learned that several infantry divisions had been brought into the beachhead area, among them the 3rd and 45th. From that time on, until the war ended, we were to be closely associated with those two divisions, not only as part of the 5th Army but as the nucleus of the 7th Army, under General Alexander 'Sandy' Patch, when we invaded Southern France on August 15, 1944. It took time to develop a sense of unity with other outfits, like the 3rd and the 45th, but there came a moment when I realized, as did almost everyone involved, that we could feel secure when we had those units on our flanks. Their leaders reciprocated that feeling.

We watched a situation map each day and posted the advances made by the 5th Army (US) and the 8th British Armies which, after they joined at Salerno, stretched across the Italian mainland with the 5th Army occupying the western sector of the front. The Germans, masters at delaying tactics and possessed of the best terrain in Europe for practicing such tactics, were slowly falling back to the vicinity of Monte Cassino, where aerial reconnaissance had detected a vast defensive system under construction. This was known as the Gustav Line, which was anchored at the eastern end on Mount Caira, a formidable peak[1] that was snow-covered year round. From there the line ran along a crest line, which we referred to as Castellone Ridge, through Monte Cassino and on out to the Tyrrhenian Sea near Gaeta.

It was a costly kind of warfare for our troops, since the Germans held mountaintops, and the job of climbing to those bastions and routing them out was measured in casualties per yard gained. Our training period ended on October 11, the anniversary of El's and my wedding, and on October 12, 1943, we boarded trucks and made the 30 to 35 mile run to Naples. On the way I caught my first daylight view of Vesuvius against a dappled sky. It was an unusual sight with the great cone looming above surrounding mountains and a white plume setting off the whole vista like a feather in its cap.

Everywhere along the route were signs of war's devastation, even though the passage had been a fast one when our troops drove the Germans backward after the beachhead was taken. Factories and large mercantile buildings appeared to have been dynamited by the retreating army and the few Italian civilians we saw were a pitiful sight. There were a number of gaily painted two-wheeled carts on

---

1. Mount Caira, at a height of 5,500ft, was part of the defensive boundary of what the Nazis called 'Festung Europa,' fortification Europe.

the road as people started to return to Naples and its environs. We even saw an electric streetcar running and it was jammed with people, some of whom rode on its top, while others clung precariously from its windows.

Our destination was Qualiano, just north of Naples and reached by a precipitous route out of Naples. In the center of Naples, however, our convoy stopped in front of a beautiful building which we learned was the general post office. I noticed that all of the homes and shops in that area appeared deserted, and when someone said that our division headquarters ought to set up shop there, I suggested that it looked too perfect a place, in the midst of the shambles surrounding it.

We drove on out of the city and by mid-afternoon had set up our regimental CP in a farmhouse surrounded by an apple orchard and a walnut grove. Apples were everywhere, as no one had had a chance to harvest them. This was true, also, of the walnuts so that we ate both crops at meals and for snacks. On the roof of the farmhouse we found an anti-aircraft mount the Germans had built with brass points of the compass set into concrete at the gun base. From that vantage point that night we could see the artillery flashes to the north and hear the low rumble of the guns.

On our way into Qualiano we had traversed a road cut very deeply into the terrain, from use over the centuries, and at a junction we had trouble getting our vehicles past an ugly cement casemate that had been built there to control the approaches to Qualiano.

Just after our evening meal we heard the anti-aircraft batteries of Naples and its perimeter go into action. It was quite a sight from our rooftop. That night, too, I received a telegram from El's mother saying that a son had been born to us and that mother and child were doing well. We celebrated in the farmhand's house, which some of us had taken over for sleeping quarters, not far from the CP. There was a fireplace in one room which would have been a welcome addition except that the chimney had been ruptured by shellfire and, although we lit a fire, we were finally driven out by smoke and had to finish our wine in the yard.

We hadn't been at Qualiano very long before we learned that the general post office had been blown to smithereens by a heavy explosion occasioned by the detonation of about a ton of dynamite the Germans had secreted behind one wall by tearing out the wall and rebuilding it to make it appear seamless and untouched. That taught me to avoid tempting shelters from then on, and I was glad that our division headquarters had kept out of the place. The lesson stood me in good stead many times when others would have fallen for a trap. It is probably little to wonder that I came out of the war with a deep-seated notion that a very heavy streak of sadism ran through the German army. I saw many signs of it all over Europe, and on at least one occasion in the Vosges Mountains nearly lost my life to a particularly diabolical scheme.

I went into Naples one day, by way of another training mission for the I&R platoon, and among other things had my hair cut at a barbers' school located in a glass-covered arcade near the waterfront. It took several months to restore those areas where the student barber managed to pull hair out in solid clumps.

Before returning to the front[2], in Naples one morning, I could hardly believe the scene before my eyes. There was a great deal of typhus in the city and our Military Government establishment decided to reduce the conditions conducive to lice propagation by powdering the populace with DDT. Since that time we've learned to be careful with that substance.

Notices had been posted in advance requesting people to appear at a certain large plaza for a swap of clothing and a dose of DDT. I thought that the convocation I was witnessing was on the order of a Roman orgy! Tens of thousands of Italian men, women and children were standing in the plaza and along avenues leading to it without a stitch of clothing on them! A cloud of dust, mostly DDT, was rising from the central area where GIs stripped to the waist were using motors and hoses to blast DDT onto the poor Italians.

It seems the civilians didn't like the idea of swapping their clothing for something the army would provide, so they left their things at home. There was also a lot of misunderstanding of the regulations put out by the Military Government.

What a debacle! I've often wondered how many of the Italians suffered ill effects from such gross applications of DDT. I can only say that it's a wonder that there wasn't a riot before the day's work was completed. The Italian people were basically gentle and grateful for anything we could do to relieve their suffering. I never found out what was done about their clothing which, of course, harbored the lice causing typhus. Unfortunately there were many civilian deaths from that disease. The military services were inoculated against it.

As we drove back through the hills to Qualiano an air raid started, and I stopped at a restaurant near the top of a hill. The owner and several customers came barreling out and motioned me and my driver to follow them across the road to an air-raid shelter. It was an enormous cave where several hundred people apparently were still living, having been bombed out of their homes. I took one whiff of the place and begged off, as did my driver.

Some of the ack-ack guns were located just below our position in a field and their shells and tracers came whizzing past us, too close for comfort. By that time it was dark, and anti-aircraft lights were searching the skies for the hostile planes. As I watched, a plane was caught in the glare of a light, where it shone like a moth fluttering around a candle. Several beams converged on it and the pilot, in trying to evade them, spiraled downward, only to be knocked out of the air to crash into the sea. When the raid ended, we had a good meal at the restaurant which specialized in fish. German raids were frequent and planes coming toward Naples from the north usually came down over the sea, guiding on an unfailing beacon – Mount Vesuvius.

---

2. The DDT story was found in a letter dated 17 October 1989 to Doughty's grandson Matt Bunting.

For the most part, the port of Naples was the bombers' chief target. When I had first seen it, there was a mad quality to the scene, due to the forest of masts protruding from the water where the Germans had scuttled ships to block the entrance to the dock areas. The docks had also been dynamited. Our engineers did a great job restoring facilities, though, once we retook the port.

Several of our battalion commanders were relieved and replacements made while we were at Qualiano. I've often thought that we might have done better to have kept certain of the relieved commanders because their background was in infantry whereas, for example, a Lieutenant Colonel Wyatt, who took over our 2nd Battalion, had been trained as an engineer. His limitations became evident to us when, as regimental CO on the Rapido River, he made some mistakes which probably would have been avoided by a well-grounded infantry officer.

During that time, too, we were involved in a feint that was designed to influence the German High Command in Italy to withdraw some of its troops from the front lines in order to defend against a possible amphibious end-run. I was on a special planning staff that met nearly every day in a building in Naples where Brigadier General O'Daniel gave us the background for a maneuver that was the crux of our feint.

One regiment was involved in amphibious maneuvers that included a lot of radio traffic, both from the sea and our training area, in a special code that we knew had already been compromised. I read scripts over the air at given times as part of the scenario that had been written by a special strategic intelligence group out of London and, while I was never sure of it, Douglas Fairbanks Jr was reputed to have worked on its content.

The difficult part of the whole operation was to deceive our own officers and enlisted men with some semblance of verisimilitude, while keeping them from becoming panicky over the dearth of vital information they would need to know if we were actually going to outflank the German line by water.

We went so far as to place logs in a position to simulate artillery pieces under camouflage nets, knowing full well that modern aerial photography would detect the sham. The premise on which we operated was that there were hundreds of double agents in the Naples area who were in a position to report to the Germans our daily staff meetings in that city which took place from 1–4:30 pm each day. During that time, once we had the scheme of things in mind and operating instructions issued, we would sit and spin yarns in order to pass the time that a serious planning session would have entailed. Later, when I went to Korea, I spent some interesting hours with General O'Daniel who, in Korea, was a lt. general and I Corps commander, reminiscing about the fake staff sessions we'd held in Naples.

When the day arrived to load on ships at Pozzuoli, where a former Italian amphibious plane base had been located, the officers of the regiment descended on me in droves and asked me how in God's name they could organize an attack based on the limited information they had received. If the plan was to succeed, it was absolutely essential that its true nature remain secret until after troops were aboard ship. I asked them to trust the amphibious staff that had prepared operating instructions which would be disseminated when the units were at sea. I hinted, too, at the possibility of compromise of our security if the full plan were disclosed prematurely. I told them that, since I was going aboard ship with them, I was in a position to know that the plan was workable and as safe as such things could be expected to be.

We moved our regimental combat team to the loading zone in the late afternoon and found a number of LSTs tied up there awaiting our arrival. We wanted all suspected agents in the vicinity to see the number of men involved, together with the fact that we had artillery with us.

It was a tedious job getting men into the ships, and in the meantime I had developed a team of officers who would break the news to the men that, while the ships would depart, after dark, there would be no troops aboard. I cautioned the members of that team to be absolutely certain that no outcry greeted the announcement. I was also to bring the glad tidings to the ship lying nearest the mainland. The disposition of LSTs was alongside a jetty opposite a huge hangar which also figured in our plan.

I entered my LST and stood on an inner-balcony overlooking the vast main hold of the ship while a hush fell over the hundreds of men as they looked up at me.

'When I give you the basic plan of this maneuver,' I said, 'I want to hear no sound whatsoever from you. It is absolutely essential that you not even whisper, and when I'm through you will have another assignment of equal importance which you must fulfill, noiselessly. If that is understood, raise your right hands and keep quiet!'

All hands shot into the air and I could see some officers directly below me moving restlessly as they wondered what in the hell I was talking about.

'Not a sound now!' I warned. 'This proposed amphibious operation is only a feint!' I held my right hand up and stopped everything but a loud exhalation of breath as the import of what I had said filtered into their minds.

'These ships will move out of here at 2100 hours but they will be empty.' I said and again held up my hands as a warning against sound. 'We have been feeding the Germans a false radio line for weeks, and we think they have fallen for it.'

I could sense the release from anxiety that swept over the group, many of whom, now, stood on tiptoe to hear what I had to say.

'There are dozens of double agents in and around Naples who will report our loading for an amphibious assault. The Germans, we believe, will also have been deluded into thinking that our landing site is near Gaeta because of the similarity of its crescent shoreline to the beach where we've been practicing.'

'Everything now depends on your absolute silence! All of the plans we've made, all of the logistical support, all of the false radio scenarios we've been feeding the enemy will go for nothing, if even one of you makes a sound of any kind.'

I was impressed with the fact that there hadn't been a peep from anyone.

'You will debark from this LST in a column of twos and move directly across the pier to the old hangar. There is to be no talk, no noise from equipment, no smoking, no light of any kind to be shown. You will not move across the pier until ordered to do so, since we will unload the ships in rotation starting with the ones furthest out on the pier.'

'Once in the hangar it will be crowded since the whole regimental combat team will be there. You are to remain quiet until you are called to board a truck toward morning for infiltration back to camp. If you feel uncomfortable during the night, remember how much better off you'll be than if you'd been called on to make another landing.'

After disembarking the troops in an almost ghostly silence, and reassembling them in close quarters within the hangar, the line of LSTs cast off and steamed north on schedule. Our troops were taken, a truckload at a time, to our bivouac area during the remainder of the night. They closed into position just before dawn.

The plan succeeded beyond all of our expectations as the Germans moved a division out of the front lines and sent it to outpost the coastline. Furthermore, subsequent captured maps showed the existence in our lines of a 'phantom' division that had been conjured up from radio scenarios. We also found evidence of a 'phantom' Allied fleet operating on the Tyrrhenian Sea whose existence also arose from German radio intercepts of false information deliberately given over a period of time.

Chapter 10

The Pink House

On November 15, 1943, my division was returned to the fighting front, then located in the vicinity of the town of Mignano,[1] in the Mignano Valley. The 141st Infantry relieved the 15th Infantry Regiment of the 3rd Division to which Lieutenant Colonel Crawford, who had been of such great help to my regiment during the Salerno fight, had been posted as exec officer.

While I can't be sure of the connotations involved, Colonel Crawford, in leaving the CP which we took over, offered us some Italian liquor that he had acquired locally. It was labelled 'Cognac' and appeared to be of ancient vintage, a factor the Italians apparently found easy to counterfeit with a little dust and soot. We paid him for it and someone put the three bottles under a table.

During the first evening I happened to look under the table and found that one of the bottles had not only been knocked over but was leaking its contents onto the floor. Peculiarly, too, smoke was rising from the floor where the 'Cognac' was eating its way through the wood. That taught all concerned a lesson about Italians and about Crawford.

Our CP was located in the upper room of a house of pink-colored stucco that, from the moment of our entry until this day, when veterans of our regiment reminisce over the Italian Campaign, has been referred to as the 'Pink House.' In the same house, on the lower floor, was located the CP of the 143rd Infantry Regiment. The troops of my regiment were disposed with the 1st Battalion on Mount Lungo, and the 3rd Battalion on Mount Rotondo, almost directly in front of the 'Pink House.' The 2nd Battalion was in reserve.

As the men of the 15th Infantry left for a rest area, one of them turned over to me a map that had been captured earlier from a German artilleryman, in which the area where our new CP was located was shown as defiladed from German artillery fire. Since the Germans could move their self-propelled artillery to any area along their front, I was inclined to doubt the safety of the house in that respect, and so stated.

We were shortly made aware of the fact that German observers had seen all of the activity around the CP from their high peaks that looked down on every move we made. Several heavy rounds landed on a slight rise just in front of the 'Pink House' and jarred our eyeteeth just as we were sitting down for our evening meal. Colonel Werner at that moment chose to tell me off in front of the

---

1. About 10 miles southeast of Monte Cassino. About 5 miles further ahead lie San Pietro and San Vittore.

rest of the staff by saying that I had been insubordinate to him. I looked at him and asked the circumstances he referred to.

'It's just your general attitude, Doughty,' he said.

'I'm sorry if you don't like my attitude,' I responded, 'but that is scarcely a basis for calling me insubordinate.'

'You never report to me on how the training of the I&R platoon is going.' he said.

'Have you found the platoon wanting in any respect?' I asked.

'That's what I mean!' Werner reported. 'You answer questions with questions.'

'Colonel,' I said, 'since you've chosen to reprimand me in front of others, I'm now going to let you in on something. At no time, since we landed at Salerno, have you commanded this regiment and I don't propose to be your whipping boy while you try to reestablish your authority. I think you've chosen me for that purpose because you know I do not stand in awe of your or anyone else's rank. Some of your Texas boys do.'

At just that moment a tremendous explosion occurred immediately outside the east end of our CP. It shook the house and knocked several bricks out of a fireplace at that end. A loud outcry reached us from downstairs and in the next few minutes we were busy tearing downstairs to see what had happened.

We found one of the officers of the 143rd's staff dead and several others wounded. The dead man, a medical major, was sitting in a chair near the lower fireplace and while he did not appear to be wounded, nevertheless he was dead. Near his head, which had dropped forward onto his chest, was a narrow window – more of a slit than a window – which contained no glass. It was later established that a steel splinter had come through the narrow opening and penetrated his neck, severing his spinal cord. The shell had struck an embankment outside the house and the force of the explosion had been toward the house. So much for defilade!

When we reassembled in our upstairs headquarters I noticed that Colonel Price had gone into Colonel Werner's office, where he was in earnest conversation with the latter. I wasn't about to be pilloried by anyone as puerile as Werner had shown himself to be. If he'd taken me to one side and indicated what he wanted change in my attitude, I would readily have complied. Since he had elected to try to nail my carcass to the barn door in order to impose his presence on the rest of the staff, most of whom came to me later and said they had been ashamed of his action, I let him have it.

He never again mentioned the incident due largely, I believe, to Price's influence but due in no small part, either, to my readiness to call a spade a spade. I was fortunate that I did not have to put up with his small-minded behavior for very long.

We began to realize just how inferior our positions were as casualties mounted. The first battalion, under a Lieutenant Colonel J. Trimble Brown, was exposed to the most hazardous situation of all. He had taken over a portion of

Mount Rotondo's southern slope where German artillery, mortars, and machine guns could rake his whole area with heavy fire, day or night. It was practically impossible for his men to get any rest and, as a result, his casualties – including men whose nerves had been shattered – exceeded those of the other battalions. I was sent by Werner to visit the 1st Battalion headquarters one night, another measure of his own lack of intrepidity – signs of which we'd seen at Salerno. I took a squad of I&R platoon men with me and at dusk we threaded our way, single file, through the devastated town of Mignano, down to a river where the trail to the 1st Battalion headquarters began.

The trouble with following the river was that the Germans held the opposite bank and several times an hour would send up flares that would light the area like a carnival midway as parachutes, carrying the glowing magnesium, would slowly settle to the ground.

As we stumbled through the darkness I could feel my boots sink up to my ankles in the muddy trail that had been the only means of access and egress to the salient we were visiting. It was spooky going with every sense alert to sound, sight, and smell. Tall, reedy grass grew along the embankment and offered a fragile cover for our movements. Against the sky we could catch an indistinct view of the round-topped hill toward which we were moving. When the first German gunner fired his machine gun across the river, we all thudded to the ground until the few short bursts were finished. I noticed that there were no tracer bullets in the fusillade, making it almost impossible to locate the gun's position, even though I could distinguish the 'thump' of the gun. Flash-hiders, used to a far greater extent by the German army than by ours, assured concealment of a gun's location.

We had moved quite a distance along the river's edge when we were almost blinded by the first flare thrown up for our benefit. I went down fast, since it was fairly certain that observers would be nearly as blinded as we were in the initial moments of glare. A mortar fired three rounds that were not intended for us, since they landed fairly near the base of Mount Rotondo, where I knew the entrance lay to a wine cave that the 1st Battalion headquarters had appropriated. Again, it was the German way of harassing our troops.

In dropping to the ground I must have moved off the trail for when I arose, after the flare had died out, I found myself in the reeds. Apparently, too, there was an eroded place on the embankment for I suddenly plunged straight down for about 10ft and landed in water up to my neck. The splash was enormously loud to my ears as I worked to keep my carbine above my head after its first immersion.

When I tried to climb out of the river, which was not over 30ft wide at best, I found the embankment straight up and down, although I sensed that I was in a small fold of ground away from the main stream. I moved slowly around the miniature cove finding no foothold anywhere for climbing the embankment. It was colder than blazes and my teeth vere chattering as I wondered what had happened to the I&R men who must have heard my entry into the water.

As I waited for another flare, I moved in close to the banking and faced away from the hostile shore. Above me, I heard the reeds rustle and looking up I made out a white blotch that was low to the ground.

'You down there, Cap'n?' a voice whispered. It was Sergeant Flowers, a wrinkled-face man of the plains of Texas, a tiger in a fight despite his small but wiry stature.

'Yes,' I whispered back. 'I can't climb this embankment. It's too straight and too slippery.'

'Hold on a minute,' he said and I heard him move away.

Shortly there were sounds of several bodies moving above me and Flowers' face appeared again, barely discernible in the gloom.

'They's three of us here now,' he whispered. 'Grab this rope and we'll pull you up.'

I heard a slap in the water and fumbled around until I found a fairly stout rope. I slung my carbine over a shoulder, took a couple of bights of the rope around my hands, and whispered, 'Pull away!' My feet dug at the banking as I went flying up it, and in about three seconds I was lying among them. We crawled to the path and I heard a snicker.

'Geez, Cap'n,' Flowers said, 'I know it ain't funny but, Christ, if I don't laugh, I'll die.'

'Laugh away,' I said and I could hear subdued chuckles as the men who had rescued me joined in the merriment. I had to smile myself in spite of the chilled condition of my clothes and body.

'Let's get going,' I said and we went on our way, reaching the CP and ducking into the curtained doorway to a cave just as more mortar shells landed outside. Inside, we passed a second curtain and came into a large wine cavern that had tunnels radiating off it in several directions, penetrating deep into Mount Rotondo.

A sentry had challenged us just short of the cave, and we'd given the countersign in guarded tones. I knew, from having studied a chart of the German position, that a bulge I could just make out at the top of the hill was a German bunker. Below it, in terribly exposed positions, were the foxholes of our troops which I couldn't see at night, but which I knew were there. We hadn't seen the sentinel who challenged us, either, but once inside we learned that he was in a covered foxhole as was another one whose job was to cover any one challenged with a sub-machine gun until they'd given the correct countersign.

We found the rest of our I&R squad inside, together with Lieutenant Colonel Trimble Brown and his staff. There were several Coleman lanterns hissing away, as well as a couple of small gasoline stoves where men were brewing coffee. I learned that Werner had talked with Trimble Brown on the telephone and had discussed with him the several questions I'd been asked to clear.

A number of men were sleeping in one of the galleries leading into the mountain. I set about peeling off wet clothing, while everyone guffawed at my predicament. It was fairly comfortable in the cave, and I was soon feeling better as I sat on a chair wrapped in a blanket with my feet on an ammo box in close proximity to one of the stoves.

Suddenly we could hear a strange rustling, rushing sound like nothing I'd ever heard before.

'Here they come again,' someone yelled as around a corner came thousands of rats that looked and acted like a miniature herd of buffalo, crowding and stumbling and squealing. Men struck at them with guns, pistols, and clubs they'd fashioned against such raids. I was in a good position with my feet up, although I was nearly knocked into the swirling mass of rodents by a soldier who fell backwards as rats started to nip at his legs.

The rats barreled into another tunnel where I could hear sounds of heavy whacks as the Joes, trying to sleep there, fought them off. Several men were bitten in the melee and had to be treated by a medic stationed in the cave. This rat foray occurred two or three times a night, according to Trimble Brown, and appeared to be occasioned by hunger.

I re-checked German positions and went into some of the questions bearing on morale that I'd been ordered by Werner to raise. Trimble Brown had nothing but the highest admiration for any man who could stay in a foxhole day and night for weeks while being subjected to heavy machine-gun, mortar and artillery concentrations endlessly. He had taken to rotating his companies on position practically daily and bringing the support company into the cave for relief from the incessant shelling. Even the rats were better than the constant exposure to death.

It wasn't until several days later that I began to understand why Werner had sent me to the 1st Battalion on what I had conceived to be a useless mission; one designed primarily to expose me to trial and tribulation, let alone death. He indicated at breakfast that the army was sending in a team of psychiatrists to learn why our battle fatigue cases were greater than others on the line.

'You, Doughty,' Werner said, 'will go to division and lead them up here and from this CP to the 1st Battalion. You're the only one who knows the route to the 1st Battalion.'

'That makes it real convenient, doesn't it?' I responded and he had the grace to bat his eyes, but to say nothing. He knew exactly what I meant. He hadn't stirred out of the CP for days. I ran the gauntlet to the division CP in daylight and was fired at by a battery of German guns that tried to outsmart my driver, who knew better than to maintain even speed. We'd rocket along at 50, then slow to 10 and jump again to 40. Shells dropped ahead of and behind us until we reached a screened area behind a large hill.

At division I ran into the assistant G-2 who couldn't understand why I was the one to undertake this medical mission. 'Look, Reese,' I said, 'I'm not a Texan. Does that tell you anything?' He, a Texan, went off scratching his head.

The team of psychiatrists was the saddest group of men I'd seen in years. Their helmets didn't look right on them, and I could tell that they were scared to the point of panic. One of them, with a straggly moustache, was the chief of the team.

'How was it coming back here?' he asked and his eyes appeared watery.

'We ran the gauntlet,' I said. 'Why are you men coming up to the fighting front? Don't you have enough to do in the rear areas?'

'Ran the gauntlet?' he asked. 'What do you mean?'

'The whole route is under German observation once we pass the other side of this hill where division headquarters is located. They shoot at us, but don't worry. Have your drivers follow my driver's lead. When he speeds up, you speed up. When he brakes, you brake. Don't stay too close though, for that would offer a target for more guns than they normally employ and we might get a real barrage on us.'

His eyes were bleak as he turned to discuss this turn of events with his confrères, two of whom announced, on the spot, that they were not going to come any further.

Two of the team decided they'd go, but in my jeep since they did not trust their drivers to know how to handle artillery fire. We headed back to the 'Pink House' at about 10 am under a cloudless sky. The doctors were huddled in the back seat, their teeth chattering in the cold breeze, made colder by the fact that we had the windshield down and covered with canvass and, of course, this necessitated putting the vehicle's canvass top down, as well.

As we pulled into full view of the hostile OPs that I knew existed on every crest on a great arc from west to east, I cautioned the doctors to hang on. My driver put on a burst of speed and then braked and the two rear-seat occupants nearly fell into my lap. Sure enough, four shells fell about 20yd ahead of us.

'Now go like hell!' I yelled at Bennett, my driver. He accelerated and we hit 50 with the wheels bouncing high off the road's surface when they struck some of the more dangerous potholes. Two shells fell behind us and two ahead. The Germans were practicing the naval strategy of bracketing a target by splitting their gun battery.

'Keep going,' I yelled, and the jeep began to sway as we hit maximum speed. All four shells landed behind us but too close for comfort.

As we approached a tree-lined portion of the road, I told Bennett to slow down as though about to turn off on a side road some 100yd ahead. He braked the jeep, hard, and pulled the wheel to the right. I looked back and saw the chief psychiatrist holding his assistant by one arm, as the latter nearly fell out of the jeep.

Part way around the curve Bennett spun the wheel back left and we plummeted out of the tree-lined defile, jounced over a high bump, and accelerated again. Two shells landed up the side road and two back in the defile. We were nearly home free, for I could see the turn-off coming up to our CP. I was hoping that other German guns would not join in the spirited game we were playing.

'Slow down,' I yelled and Bennett braked again causing a great commotion in the rear. I looked back and found that the helmet of each man had come down over his eyes. We were being analyzed by men who hadn't learned how to fit their helmet liners to their own heads!

I was working on the assumption that only four guns were trying to knock us out and that it took them as long to adjust their sights to new target areas as it took us to move about ⅕ mile. Of course, our variable speed made my analysis a ballpark estimate.

'Stop!' I yelled, and Bennett stopped the jeep in the middle of the road. I got out and pretended to be looking at a rear tire. My gamble was that the guns had been re-trained on the juncture of the road to our CP. I felt that we might wait just long enough for the Germans to shift onto us as a stationary target, at least with one or two guns, and give us a chance to get around the corner to the CP without being blown to bits.

The psychiatrists, by this time, were reduced to jelly. They ducked behind the front seats and I could hear one of them blubbering.

'Go!' I yelled and Bennett nearly lost all three of us when he let out the clutch. We must have moved about 50yd when two shells crashed just about on the spot where we had waited.

'Slow to 10,' I yelled and Bennett complied. Two shells struck the road junction about 50yd ahead of us.

'Now go like hell again.' I said and we nearly turned over as we careened around a corner, up over a rise, down onto a railroad crossing and up into our CP motor pool.

'Get inside.' I directed the visiting team. 'We're upstairs.' Our staff welcomed the two men who were too frightened to speak for nearly half an hour. They had some coffee and food and appeared to be coming out of their blue funk until I told them we should leave for the front shortly, to avoid the German noontime salute that the village of Mignano, just ahead of the 'Pink House,' received each day.

'How much further forward are you going?' the chief psychiatrist said. 'About 3 miles.' I responded.

'Why can't we interview the men and officers here?' he wanted to know.

'Because,' said Colonel Werner who had been listening, 'you can't understand the pressures our front lines are under until you see where they're located. It will be somewhat dangerous to go up in daylight but otherwise, it will be practically impossible for you to complete your assignment.'

I led them out the door and down to the motor pool where I had left Bennett. 'I'm going up to the 1st Battalion with these officers,' I said to Bennett. 'You stand by for a return run to division after dark.'

'Yes, sir!' Bennett said, relief in his voice that we weren't going to match wits with the German gunners again in daylight.

We started out to the main road and just as we reached it, the noontime tattoo by German artillery rolled over Mignano about 200yd away from our position. I jumped into the righthand ditch and laid low. Both psychiatrists were in the same ditch behind me. About 10 minutes later the barrage lifted and I said, 'Let's go.'

'I'm not going any further,' the assistant psychiatrist said. I could see he had just vomited.

'Suit yourself,' I replied, 'but you haven't seen one-thousandth part of what our infantrymen have been taking each hour for weeks.'

'They're trained for it,' the chief said.

'How do you train men to face death, loss of sleep, insufficient food, loss of comrades, maiming, freezing weather, and an army leadership that sends out psychiatrists to learn what that leadership hasn't the guts to find out for itself?' I shot at them.

'I think we've seen all we need to,' the chief said. While I was not itching to make the dangerous trek, I fought down the chance to turn back and said, 'You go back now and I'll write a report about yellow psychiatrists that'll follow your record for the rest of your lives. I'm going on up to the 1st Battalion Aid Station, and one of you'd better get there with me.'

I strode off, keeping to one side of the road, and then dog-trotted through Mignano just in case the Germans changed their regular pattern of clobbering the place.

'Hold on,' I heard a voice say and around a corner came the chief psychiatrist. He was pale and shaky but he rose in my estimation a long, long way for I was sure that he, with his background, was much more sensitive to the fearful conditions than were those of us who had had a chance to work into the situation.

We made the trip without a shot being fired at us. The German outposts must have been sleeping, for there was no way we could avoid detection in the ordinary course of events. I warned the doctor of all of the pitfalls as we stopped from time to time to catch a breath.

Outside the 1st Battalion Headquarters I ran into Colonel Trimble Brown and members of his staff, who said the aid station was farther along the base of Mount Rotondo in another entrance to the cavernous wine cellar, part of which I'd seen on my first visit. We skirted the mountain and shortly found the second entrance. Inside I found the battalion doctor working with a sergeant, who was sitting in a chair repeating over and over, his teeth chattering and his arms clasped around both knees to keep them from shaking. 'I've gotta get back, Doc! My men need me, Doc. I just gotta get back!'

The doctor was about to give him an injection, but the sergeant fended him off. 'Don't knock me out, Doc! Just let me get back on the hill. Please, Doc!'

We learned that the sergeant had been brought in by his men after he had been seized with such shattering shudders and quakings that he was a danger to them and himself. His nerves were shot after a month of such terrible exposure to the elements and hostile fires that he had no control left.

'I hope you noticed, doctor,' I said, 'that the man was still anxious to return to his men in order to bolster their morale, even when he'd lost all control over himself.'

We were in the 1st Battalion CP by that time after the psychiatrist and the Battalion medic had talked for about 2 hours, while the former took notes.

'I don't know why or how any man puts up with a situation like this.' the psychiatrist said to the group listening. 'I'm going back to write my report, and you can be sure that I shall fill it with nothing but praise for every man here.' He shook his head and looked at me. 'Thanks for the push,' he said.

We returned to the 'Pink House' after dark, with only one startling event to chill us when several flares were shot up over us in quick succession, to cause us to hug the trail by the river for nearly an hour. The psychiatrist had gotten his second wind by that time, and I could sense that he had steadied down to a point where he could feel the challenge to make it safely through a tough experience.

The reason for our holding such a grim and dangerous position became clear, although it made even less sense then, when we learned that, as a psychological ploy, the first Italian army unit to fight on our side after the surrender was coming into our position to relieve us. Apparently it had taken some time to locate a sufficient number of officers to command the Italian troops and to equip the First Italian Motorized Regiment, as it was called.

Just before the relief took place I established an OP on a mountain flank, overlooking the town of San Pietro, where a great deal of enemy activity had been observed by our front-line units. The mountain rose to the east of the 'Pink House' and the OP was reached by a trail from the CP along the mountain's base, under cover of many olive trees. It wound its way up over terrace after terrace and finally emerged in full view of hostile observation, about a hundred yards from the OP. This, of course, necessitated entering and leaving the place under cover of darkness. There was a natural declivity that had been deepened so that four or five men could occupy the post without crowding. Care had been taken to leave no telltale signs in or around the area. All earth had been removed from the site at night in sandbags, except for one low wall of such bags at the rear of the OP behind which a man could stretch out in a small dugout and get some sleep. A natural rock barrier provided crevices through which a telescope could be trained to watch the terraced approaches to San Pietro and through which men could also watch the scene with field glasses or the naked eye.

Overhead camouflage was provided by the branches of an olive tree. Low wires had been strung by the I&R boys along each side of the trail to prevent its being widened by careless use and each night men also walked to a point 100yd beyond the OP to a spot where, having learned the lesson well from the British brigadier, I had had a likely position for an OP slightly altered by the emplacement of a log beside a heavy boulder. If aerial photography were used against us, which I assumed would occur, the beaten path would soon be discovered and I wanted it to terminate well away from our active OP.

The brigadier's prophecy as to the efficacy of such deception proved prescient, for the Germans fired at the dummy position incessantly during the day, knocking the log to bits. At night some harassing fire was also tossed into the decoy OP. Each night men carted a new log to the spot and we learned to anchor it more securely by digging in stakes behind it to keep it from moving unless directly hit. We learned to replace the log toward morning, for the nightly harassing action ceased about then.

I was in the OP one day in order to confirm the reports of several hundred automatic weapon emplacements in San Pietro. There was no doubt in my mind as to the accuracy of the I&R observations, but Werner was all for committing me whenever he could. It was difficult to use the power scope because the slightest tremor threw off the image even though the instrument was mounted on a short tripod.

I caught a movement out of the corner of the telescope's image and, by a slight adjustment to the left, brought into focus a lumbering command car on the main highway. I alerted others to the situation and one of the observers said, 'Gawd-a-mighty, that dummy is out in front of our lines.' We watched the car ease up to a blown-out bridge where the driver got out and walked up to survey the waters below, hand on hips. At the same time another of our observers whispered, 'There's a German anti-tank gun zeroing in on the car.' I could also see the German gunner working hand cranks to bring his weapon onto the target.

The driver walked slowly back to the car and leaned against it while he talked with someone inside, for we could see movement in the rear seat.

'He's going to turn that crate around and there's mines every three feet on the road shoulders,' someone said. I had a feeling that the anti-tank gun would settle things first. We watched, scarcely breathing, as the driver backed across the grass verge on the right side of the road, pulled ahead and put both wheels over the left shoulder, reversed again and drove back from whence he'd come. Nothing happened! We could not account for the actions of the damned fool driver or of the German gunner. It's possible the latter thought that the mines would blow the command car and its occupants to eternity or that it was a gutsy ruse to get him to expose his position by firing at the car.

We were still talking about the incident when, after dark, I bailed out of the OP and descended the mountain to the 'Pink House.' There I learned the identity of one of the people who'd driven into No Man's Land. Sitting at our mess table was Margaret Bourke-White, the famous photographer. I asked her if she, by any chance, had been in a command car that had been driven up to a burned-out bridge beyond our lines. Even then, she was not aware of the close call she'd had.

'Yes,' she responded. 'My driver was sure there would be a sign telling us where the front lines were.' We all laughed at such naïvety.

'I watched your driver,' I said, 'and at the same time, when he walked to the bridge site, I could see a German gunner bringing an anti-tank gun to bear on your vehicle.'

Miss White seemed properly alarmed at that statement. 'You mean,' she said, 'that I was actually in range of a German gun?'

'Not only that,' I said, 'but your driver backed over a road shoulder, drove up onto the other shoulder and started back to our lines without seeming to recognize that there were German Teller[2] mines every 3ft along both sides of the road.'

'Good Heavens,' she gasped, 'I might have been hurt.'

'You would have been blown to bits,' I responded, 'by 21 pounds of dynamite except for the most incredible kind of luck I've ever seen.'

'I shall report that man,' she said as she took up reloading film into a large camera, a task she'd been at when I walked in.

I learned from others on the regimental staff that she had taken a look at the German charcoal pornography that we'd found on all the walls of the rooms we occupied and had simply glossed the embarrassing moment over by saying, 'Oh my, I must have some shots of that!' She had done just that and the situation was saved.

She stayed with us for several days and while she must have heard some vile language from time to time, she never commented on it or on the conditions under which we lived. She was dressed in the olive drab uniform of a war correspondent, with tunic and slacks. She was more daring than was wise but got some front-line action photos that were prize-winners.

We needed some aerial photographs of Mount Sammucro, for our efforts to take San Pietro had failed shortly after I reported some 300 automatic gun sites in the town. A Polish aviator who flew a P-38 for such photo reconnaissance missions refused to fly over Mount Sammucro because of the heavy flak thrown up from surrounding areas. Margaret White asked and got permission from our commanding general to fly with an artillery spotter in a light plane and spent several hours ranging back and forth by the flank of Sammucro, taking the shots we needed for a planned attack up its steep slopes. I sweated out that mission, too, from the I&R OP, and thought the plane would be destroyed by anti-aircraft fire before she signaled a return to base. I still have one of her excellent photographs of Sammucro in my den.

After the war Miss White wrote a book about our division and her experiences with it in the Mignano Valley and called it *Purple Heart Valley*.[3] She wrote that many people had asked her how it was possible for her to live with fighting men at the front. Her response was that she had never received more courteous and kindly attention anywhere in her life, and while there were inconveniences (latrines, no doubt) and considerable danger, she treasured every moment, or words to that effect.

I read the book after returning home from Europe and found in it a fairly spicy remark that anyone unacquainted with the situation would fail to grasp.

---

2. *Teller* is a German word for dinner plate – the size and shape of these mines.

3. This book is still available to purchase and borrow, and is probably worth a read. There is no mention of Miss White encountering the 36th Division as she traveled the area as a war correspondant for *LIFE* magazine. There is, however, a rich collections of pictures of other units on the same campaign.

She indicated that we had even told her the story of the one man any of us knew who had completely understood his reason for fighting. She left it at that.

Our medics had first broken the news of this unusual situation; unusual because, regardless of public relations ventures by the military forces to romanticize the GIs' understanding of basic issues in the war, few of the doughboys could give any cogent reason for being in the middle of such a fracas.

The unusual man had landed at Salerno and within an hour was back on the beach looking for a prophylactic station!

One more dramatic development occurred on or about December 5, 1943, while we were at the 'Pink House.' The First Italian Motorized Regiment came to replace my regiment. The news had come to us by telephone from division headquarters and Scotty and I were delegated to act as guides to get the Italians into the proper tactical positions at night. I, naturally enough, was to take in tow the unit that would replace our 1st Battalion on the slopes of Mount Rotondo.

Scotty and I went out to the main road on foot just before dusk, expecting that there would be no movement of the Italian troops until after dark. We had tried to talk with the staff hastily put together for the new unit but the Italian general, whose last warfare had occurred in 1918 and who had been ignored by Mussolini, could scarcely deign to look at us. The labor minister under Badoglio had donned a uniform, too, but his knowledge of infantry tactics was lacking. We learned, just before Scotty and I went out as guides, that the Italian staff was not going to assist in any way since their general had termed a passage of lines at night as 'purely automatic.' Since it is one of the most dangerous moves to be caught making, we knew just about how good the Italian war effort would be.

Scotty and I had just about reached the spot we'd chosen to meet the Italian troops when we heard the damnedest racket I'd heard in a long time. Down the road came huge Italian trucks under full observation by the Germans. Their blackout lights weren't blue like ours but, I was convinced, could be seen for miles. In the trucks were the Bersiglieri uniforms I'd seen, here and there, during my stay in Italy. The item, however, that had Scotty and me transfixed was the long, graceful, curling feather each man wore in his helmet. We could hardly believe that this was for real. I'd brought some Italian-speaking men from the I&R platoon with me to act as interpreters. Any thought of moving into the lines by stealth went glimmering as the sound of the trucks, with mufflers blaring, was enough to wake the dead. One of our enlisted men took a look and started to howl.

I was concerned about the column being hit by artillery fire and got some of the Italian officers down off their vehicles where I could talk with them through an interpreter. When I told them that the crests all around us to the north were German-held, they ran back along the road and cautioned drivers to put off their lights, which they didn't need in any event since it was still daylight.

That night stands out in my memory as remarkable for a number of reasons. Where we had not dared to strike a match while on the road at night, I was to see bonfires burning before the night was half over, where Italian kitchens were set up around the fields beside the town of Mignano. I gathered the officers of the battalion I was guiding to Mount Rotondo and in a defiladed spot under a culvert, I showed them the position they were going to occupy. This was the first they'd heard about a salient surrounded on three sides by Germans. The effect on them was anything but buoying. They thought that they should talk this over with their regimental staff officers, until I told them that their staff had retired.

I had all I could do to take the comic-opera quality of the scene seriously. It was pathetic in a way for, if these men were captured, the Germans had promised them instant death. I told the officers that we would soon enter the salient and I wanted them to tell their men of the probable reception we might get from Germans just across the river to our left.

In my life, I never was so edgy as I was on that trip to the base of Mount Rotondo. The thing that made it most harrowing was the fact that the Germans never fired a round despite the noise of trucks, the fires, and the squabbling of the troops as we moved toward our 1st Battalion CP. The Italian enlisted men were damned unhappy about their tactical situation and made no bones about it. They talked in excited tones as though they were on a Sunday stroll. I barked at them a number of times and wondered what would happen if a flare went up. All remained serene.

At the battalion CP I again warned the Italians that we were, now, in a very ticklish situation, since we would have to crawl up over the slope of Mount Rotondo and, as we encountered the foxholes of the 1st Battalion troops, an Italian would be dropped off at every spot from which we removed one of our GIs. I had no faith that any of us would make it back to the battalion CP alive. I shall never be able to account for the absolute lack of German reaction that night. I was covered with sweat after making the rounds of the foxholes from which I had the American GIs and non-coms individually move directly back to the CP, preparatory to leaving the position.

When I got back to the cave, I found that the I&R boys were already moving out with the 1st Battalion but as I stood there, I suddenly realized that the language I was hearing was Italian. Every last Italian, feigning a misunderstanding of what foxhole he was to occupy, had simply tagged along and was now ready to quit the vicinity of the salient.

Needless to say, we had a terrible time getting them back in position and, as a result, it was dawn before many of us could leave the site. We suffered many casualties returning to our regimental CP since the German reaction, though delayed until daylight, was punishing. I almost got it as I passed through the town of Mignano at about 7 am when a barrage was laid on us that lasted for 15 minutes. I sweated it out in a cellar, the stench of cordite strong in my nose.

For my night's work I received, much later in the war and after we'd made the Southern France landing, an Italian Cross of Military Valor. As a postlude to that situation, the ancient artillery of the Italian unit, when positioned where our guns had been, didn't have enough range to reach our own front lines, let alone German fortifications. The Germans, upon capturing a large number of Italians, manacled their hands and then shot them through the head, leaving them in clusters on the hillsides where we found them.

The following comments are relevant to RKD's role in the situation as he fought his way in a northwest direction from the 'Pink House' toward Monte Cassino. RKD was in a pretty tough business where good information was critical.

RKD was in the infantry, but artillery played a very important role in that it had to be integrated with the infantry. On-the-ground observers, like him, together with light observation airplanes as Margaret Bourke-White described in her coverage, are very often the eyes for the artillery.

Consider you are a manning a cannon team, well camouflaged. Knowing what to fire upon is typically a matter of having the observers tell you where the target is. Thus their function is critical. When you do fire, you risk revealing your position because you might be seen by the enemy. The next possible event is a shot landing near your position. While that may be miss and you consider yourself fortunate, the observers are probably using the miss distance and vector direction on the gridded maps that RKD mentions so often so that the next shot may be right on your position!

Chapter 11

Rest, Rats, and Agonies

On the day before the Italian unit came on line, we had been told to expect an important visitor but had no idea that he would arrive in daylight in a huge, chauffeur-driven blue limousine with eight outriders on motorcycles. The entourage was so impressive that the German observers couldn't help but recognize the arrival at our CP of a VIP.

Crown Prince Umberto stepped out of the limousine near our CP, and the Italian officers who'd joined us early nearly ruptured themselves saluting and fawning over him. If he was meant to be a morale raiser, I can only say I found him foppish and effeminate.

Our staff had decided to move into the basement of the 'Pink House,' once the Italian staff joined us, since there was insufficient room for both groups in the confined quarters we'd been occupying. I was standing near Umberto talking, in French, with the former minister of labor for the Italian government under Bodoglio, when I heard the sudden, almost overwhelming and deadly roar of planes right on top of us. They'd come around Mount Summucro to the east, at low level, and were strafing as they powered over us.

The only entrance to the cellar of the 'Pink House' was a door at the rear of the building from which a long ramp, over which wine barrels could be rolled, led to the basement floor about 15ft below ground level. I dove for that ramp in a desperate move that had to be controlled if I wished to avoid going over its edge onto the cellar floor. With me went three other forms and together we rolled down the incline, tangled head and foot. At the bottom we began to untangle just as anti-personnel bombs started to detonate in an ear-crushing racket, like the one I'd experienced at Salerno when I'd had to dive into a brook. For small bombs they made a hellish racket and one went off just inside the cellar doorway, throwing metal and stone chips over our heads.

It wasn't even embarrassing to find that the crown prince was one of the four of us who had had the same inspiration that probably saved us from being badly wounded or killed. I could only think that he had been responsible for the bombing with his foolish jaunt up to the front under circumstances where the Germans would be constrained to give him a royal welcome. We dusted ourselves off and, as we started up the ramp, several more bombs detonated. We waited a half hour while listening to cries for 'medic' from men who had been wounded. Before we were through with the German donation to our day, we identified three types of bombs: those that went off on impact, those with a delayed fuse, and a third type that were triggered when they were touched by a warm human hand. To make the touching almost a cinch, such bombs were shaped like metal pens and pencils.

After the bombing I talked with Colonel Price who, when he got nervous, would shift a cigar stub from one corner of his mouth to the other in rapid succession. I had been teed off by the fact that men, who had not been exposed to danger, were receiving rest and rehabilitation leaves at Sorrento while those in contact with the enemy were, apparently, forgotten. Price was dealing the leaves out of his vest pocket, so I walked up to him during the evening after Umberto had returned to the rear areas and said, 'Colonel, how would you like an investigation into this regiment's administrative procedures?'

He had dark eyes that snapped, on inner command, in a way that was supposed to warn all and sundry that he wouldn't take much guff from anyone. It was a reflexive response that hid a big heart and camouflaged uncertainty.

'What've you got in mind?' he asked, removing the cigar butt.

'We have some medical officers who have had one hell of a time working at battalion aid stations. They've saved life, after life and no one has thought to send them on leave.'

'Who would take their places?' he asked.

'There are medics with the reserve battalion,' I responded. 'And yet ours haven't had a moment of peace and quiet since we landed over two months ago.'

'Doughty,' Price responded, 'I'll have to handle this business the best way I know how.'

'Colonel,' I replied, 'you don't seem to grasp my meaning. I could expose the favoritism you've been practicing, by bringing to the attention of the division G-1 or the army inspector general a list of the rear echelon men you've been sending to Sorrento. It's time this regiment was administered on some basis other than rewarding peacetime service in the National Guard. I just thought you'd like the impressions of a non-Texan who is not a member of the "Old Buddy Club"?'

He grunted and we parted. The next morning he called me to one side and said in a conspiratorial tone, 'You're leaving for Sorrento today.' I said, 'Colonel, you still aren't getting the message. I wasn't speaking for myself when I criticized the regiment's practices. I believe in this outfit and I think it will establish one helluva war record. I just think you ought to stop being so damned provincial, particularly now that more than half of the division's complement is non-Texans.'

He looked at me with one eye closed against the perennial cigar smoke and said: 'You ain't going?'

'Not if there's a doctor around who's free and can spend a week away,' I responded.

'We got one goin' with you,' Price said. 'We shifted a couple of slots to make room.'

'Mind if I look at those who are going?' I asked.

'What's an S-2 got to say about who's going?' he asked.

'The same as he's got to say about all of the non-S-2 functions he's been saddled with whenever a problem arose,' I stated.

'Such as?' he wanted to know.

'Such as quartermaster problems of loading troops in Oran; such as medical surveys involving psychiatrists; such as operations of a feint out of Pozzuoli,' I replied.

'Doughty, you old bastard,' Price said, his laugh showing tobacco stains on his teeth and both corners of his mouth, 'you really got a lot of answers, don't you?'

'Isn't it true?' I asked. 'You've turned to me on all kinds of sticklers, expecting me to handle them, but in return for which I'm supposed to take your crap just to be kept in line.'

'I think you're right,' he responded and clapped me on the shoulder. 'I'm redoing the list and you can go if you want to.'

'I'm ready,' I responded. From that moment on things started to get better within the regimental zone of influence. I know that my outspoken attitude was often the cause of complaints, but I also had reason to believe that my talk with Price, with whom I was on excellent terms from then on, broke through the chauvinism that had previously marked the handling of administration within the regiment. It was a matter of pride with me when, several years after the war on a visit to Fort Worth, Texas where Price lived, he said to Walt Buehler of the GM legal staff who was with me when we visited Price's home, 'Doughty was the most professional officer ever to serve with the 141st Infantry.' Whether he was right or wrong was not as important as the fact that Price reflected a more catholic attitude than had existed in the regiment during the initial stages of the war.

A doctor, Captain Joe Cunningham, and I took off for Sorrento the next day having been ordered there for a week's stay. We were as excited beneath the surface as a couple of kids going to the circus. Joe had won the Silver Star with his efforts at Salerno when, under heavy fire, he went wherever he was needed in the beachhead and as a result was credited with saving many lives.

It was interesting to observe, as we made our way back through the communities we'd passed on our way north, that many of the damaged houses were already in the process of being rebuilt. Bridges, too, that had been blown, causing us long delays, were in the process of reconstruction by masons who were using as much of the old material as possible in the restoration effort. It not only was a sign of Italian industriousness but exhibited a faith in the capacity of the Allied armies to bar the return of the German army.

The port of Naples was humming again, and everywhere we saw huge depots of war materials that had sprung up since our earlier passage. Crops that could be salvaged after the trampling of armies were in evidence in stores and along the way, in the colorful two-wheeled carts that the Italians decorated with painstaking designs. People were on the move in all directions, it seemed, as we neared Sorrento at the end of the Amalfi Peninsula.

We pulled up in front of the Albergo Vittore, our assigned hotel [where a week was spent enjoying the relatively peaceful and beautiful environment and the company of other Allied personnel away from the war. The week included a close encounter with an Italian family with whom Doughty maintained contact long after the war had ended.].

The time for our departure [from Sorrento] came on a fast track and on December 15, 1943, I got up early and packed preparatory to visiting our friends before leaving in the late afternoon. However, those officers replacing us on R and R came in at breakfast time and relayed orders for all of us to return at once since our 2nd Battalion was to attack San Pietro under Major Milton Landry the next day.

We also learned that Colonel Werner had been wounded by anti-personnel bombs in another German air raid when he'd run out of the CP to see what was happening. Since Colonel Price had let it be known that he did not want to take over the regiment, Colonel Wyatt had been named temporary CO.

Hard driving brought us to Presenzano where Colonel Price had established a regimental rear CP which, to put it nicely, was an unorthodox establishment. It was located behind a hill where the division's forward CP was dug in. Only that morning the building in which the regimental group was located had been hit by a bomb at one corner and while the damage was minimal, all of the windows had been blown out, making it difficult to keep warm.

I learned that Colonel Wyatt had ordered Price and the rest of the rear echelon forward to the new CP, which had just been moved to the base of Mount Rotondo. Wyatt had also ordered me forward, in daylight, to get into the I&R OP as soon as possible for the next day's big shoot.

I put on a new combat suit, heavily padded and practically waterproof, which had arrived in my absence, strapped on my .45, which I carried in a shoulder holster that Corporal Hobday had made for me from the leather of a German officer's courier case and which was large enough to fit over my heavy outerwear, and took off. When I passed our own artillery positions, the noise was incessant, as the preparatory fires were then in process of softening up the defenses of San Pietro. In my gut I knew that an attack against San Pietro was practically suicidal and it made me feel no better when I overheard Wyatt say, after my arrival at the forward CP, that he had heard General Clark say that he wanted to give San Pietro to his wife as a birthday present! What a crock of egotistical hooey that was!

On approaching the new CP, which was located in a one-room stone house and not in the rat-infested cave, a number of German guns were throwing shells over my head at some 8in guns located just behind the 'Pink House.' It reminded me of something that had happened just before I left for Sorrento. I had had an infected spot, a small cyst really, under my Adam's apple that was beginning to bother me.

Captain Sam Goldstein of our medical detachment took a look at the infected area and said it ought to be removed. He had me lie on a cot at the back of the 'Pink House' and after spraying something on my neck to deaden the pain, he was just about to cut around the cyst to remove it, when the house almost caved in under an explosion that sent Goldstein to the floor. Only cool nerves had kept him from cutting me. Unbeknown to any of us in the CP, a battery of 8in 'Long Toms' had dug in just behind the house and the first shot fired was the one from which we'd received the muzzle blast. Any time big guns like those went into action they attracted heavy counterbattery fires from the German artillery. Unfortunately some of that counterbattery shelling of the Long Toms caught our senior medical officer, Major Joe Coopwood, in a tent near the 'Pink House' and killed him instantly.

I left the CP on the reverse slope of Mount Rotondo the next morning, as soon as I learned that Colonel Wyatt and Ross Young were in an OP on Mount Maggiori, not the one higher up on Sammucro. Upon arrival I told Wyatt, an engineer officer, that the OP was too distant from the fighting echelon and was immediately invited to join him in a move nearer to San Pietro. I had already seen that several tanks that had been sent in to assist the foot soldiers had been knocked out of action at the outskirts of San Pietro, where they'd been confined to a road on which they'd been sitting ducks for German anti-tank guns whose positions I had long ago marked on an overlay.

The automatic fire from San Pietro was appalling. The battalion had suffered severe casualties from the outset and was unable to penetrate the screen of steel that the Germans were throwing at it. Wyatt and I descended Mount Maggiori, and the heat of the day made my combat suit a regular sauna. He had already radioed Landry to retire to Mount Rotondo positions with his men, who managed to get back in fairly good order under cover of smoke that our artillery was laying around San Pietro.

On the east side of Mount Rotondo, at its base, we encountered General Clark and an aide walking in full view of the enemy. Nearby under the cover of Rotondo's flank were camouflaged tanks of ours, and behind them we could hear the hollow sound of tank-destroyer guns. At that moment we began to receive artillery fire, and I dove under a tank hoping to God it would not be moved while I was there. Many men were killed in just such a position during the war since a tanker, in moving out from under fire, may spin the machine on one track and crush anyone lying under the vehicle. The day ended in a stinging defeat for our men, primarily because the army brass did not believe that the Germans were holding San Pietro so strongly, even though we had reported our sightings in detail. A short time later the Germans evacuated San Pietro presumably to maintain their timetable for falling back to Monte Cassino.

General Wilbur came to our CP in San Pietro one day a short time after we'd moved in and announced that one of our battalions would climb Mount Sammucro that night and come down east of the town of San Vittore to take the German defenders by surprise. He also said that I would go along with the battalion and report to him by telephone, hourly, as to the progress being made.

Only that day I had been on the lower slopes of Sammucro and had followed the line of a trail up over its peak with my eyes, trying to gauge the distance to the top. It was several miles, although on the old Italian maps we were using it seemed but a few hundred yards. I spoke up and said that I had made a personal reconnaissance of that area that morning. I pointed out that the map was incorrect and that there were heavy German fortifications near the top where the trail narrowed and ran between a cliff and a drop-off. I told him that we would not be able to reach the top in a one-night climb, much less fight our way through the fortifications and reach San Vittore to surprise its garrison.

I shall never forget his answer because it was a paraphrase of a statement made by a great statesman when an island-empire was threatened. Wilbur looked me in the eye, clinched his jaws together, and said, 'Doughty, this is the sweat and tears that save blood.' I couldn't help but remember that he had taught me military science at college. One of his first precepts was that a good officer always makes a PR (personal reconnaissance) before issuing orders in combat. Yet, here he was taking his data off a map. I simply answered, 'Yes, sir!'

The whole undertaking seemed doomed from the beginning. It rained as I have never seen it rain. Everything was delayed by a failure of supplies to reach us by burro on schedule. We stood beside the ghostly walls of blown-out houses on the slopes above San Pietro while rain trickled down our necks and soaked us to the marrow.

Wilbur had decreed that the usual, light battlefield telephone wire would not suffice for this night's work. He ordered regular telephone wire to be carried on very heavy reels up the mountain trail. This, of course, tired the signal crew early, and they soon fell behind the column of some 500 men that set out after 9 pm to scale Sammucro. Wilbur sat in a command tent among the olive trees south of San Pietro and awaited my reports. While the battalion climbed for 50 minutes each hour and took 10 minutes rest, I received no rest at all that night. I had to find my way back along the trail from the command group to the telephone set-up and tell the general where we were located. He showed some irritation when, after several hours, I told him we were less than one-third of the way up the slope. I had to put a poncho on the ground, take the telephone under it with me, and read a map by flashlight while I talked.

I reminded him that the map was out of scale and that the pathway was blocked in many areas by trees that the Germans had dropped as obstacles. I also reported to him that we were being watched by German outposts because we could hear muffled radios off to our left flank spitting out Morse code.

Our men were so tired that, at each rest break, they would simply lie down in the trail and go to sleep in the pouring rain. This made my job of retracing my steps much more difficult than it might otherwise have been.

It was nearly dawn when we reached the denuded, rocky slopes leading to the narrow trail where there were German fortifications. By that time I had notified General Wilbur that we had run out of telephone wire. He practically refused to believe me, suggesting that someone had conveniently lost most of the heavy reels. We had brought 10 miles of wire. I believe the total distance up that mountain by our circuitous route was 13 miles.

I was with the battalion commander and his combat staff as we approached the dangerous part of the trip. Suddenly, several green flares were visible against the sky. We hunkered down and sure enough several rounds of artillery landed on the slopes just above us. We fell flat and something whizzed by me that sounded like a bull-roarer – a whirling, deadly sound. It was either a shell fragment or a piece of rock sent spinning by one of the shells.

'What the hell are we supposed to do now?' the battalion CO asked. It was beginning to show light in the east, and there was no chance that we could take the German position, the approach to which was along a 3ft- wide path.

I said, 'Get out of here while we still can.'

'What about General Wilbur?' the operations officer asked.

'He's not here,' I said, 'and we're paid to make these decisions.'

'Right,' the battalion CO said. He called the company commanders up for a conference and told them to take the most direct route available back to San Pietro. 'Spread out,' he said, 'and get cracking before sun-up.'

'Watch for mines,' I cautioned. 'Especially in the olive grove just north of the town.'

It was just the beginning of a bad morning. Trying to get some of the men awake took what seemed like an eternity. Meanwhile, the German garrison had its wind up. Our position was fully known to them but they were waiting for us to walk onto the narrow ledge before letting us have it.

Some of the companies moved back along the trail and out of hearing in very short order. More flares went up and the command group froze in position. We heard dozens of artillery rounds screaming through the air and fell flat. Shells landed all around us and some men were hit. We were in a 'box barrage,' which means that guns were firing on four sides of an oblong, trying to knock us all out.

I took off, running toward a spur of rock that was visible against the skyline. Others followed me. As I heard shells whining, I dove to the rocky surface and rolled, expecting momentarily to feel myself hit. Rock and debris were falling everywhere but there was a sense of timing that came to me, reminiscent of the training at General Wilbur's School of Torture and Dirty Tricks in North Africa. I even yelled 'Up' after the shells fell, and 'Down' as more rained down on us. I sensed that the Germans were boxing in the trail and that if I veered left, I might get out of the 'box.'

I must have run and fallen fifty times before I finally realized that the shells were no longer falling near us. In that time I probably covered half a mile on slippery, loose rocks that were treacherous, even in daylight without the added spur of exploding shells to force a misstep.

I finally reached a shoulder of the mountain well to the south of the spot from which I'd started. I was surprised to find nearly a hundred men had followed me. They came tumbling over the edge of the shoulder past where I was sitting behind a huge boulder.

By this time the sun had come over the rim of the world. I looked up to my left to the topmost crest of the mountain to try to locate any enemy positions there from which we could expect trouble. While I was dressed in a heavily padded combat suit, my hands were bleeding from where I'd fallen on to the rocks so many times.

Someone said, 'You had a close one, Captain.' He pulled on my combat jacket and it fell almost in two at the back where some sharp object had slit it from my tail almost to my neck. I had not been aware of anything striking my clothing at any time.

I decided to move further down the mountain by way of a draw that zigzagged in our general direction toward the olive groves above San Pietro. We went single file, expecting momentarily to hear the sound of more shells seeking us out as the sun rose higher. Just as I was sure that we would attract attention, fog rose out of the valley to our right where the sun's rays lit the damp ground. The rain had stopped at sun-up. Great banks of mist rose all around us and if ever a prayer was answered, it was then.

Out of the fog came a lieutenant who was General Wilbur's aide. 'The general says you are to return to the CP,' he said to me.

'Just what I was planning on doing,' I responded. Very few people in combat like generals' aides, it seems; they appear to take on the aura, and quite often believe themselves imbued with, all the privileges of their superiors.

At the terraces outlining the olive grove a soldier who had been trained to spot and disarm mines led us step by step along the terrace walls, across the terraces and through the trees to the road near our CP. Two days later, several engineers were killed removing mines from those same terraces.

I began to realize by that time that my body was a mass of bruises. I hurt in every joint and my ribs were so sore I couldn't take a full breath. I climbed into an old German dugout where my striker had placed my bedroll and fell asleep.

Shortly someone shook me and said, 'General Wilbur wants to see you.' It hurt me to open my eyes.

I crawled out of the hole and eased down to the command tent where the battalion commander, whom I had last seen on the top of Sammucro, was talking with Wilbur and some other officers.

'Doughty,' Wilbur said, 'that was a good night's work!' I thought he was being sarcastic so I said nothing. 'Every officer I've talked with has sung your praises,' Wilbur went on. I still didn't believe he was sincere.

'They've been particularly complimentary of your coolness under fire,' Wilbur said. 'They have remarked that your voice settled them down all through the night as you gave calm, confident reports of your conversations with me. They also felt that your ability to make decisions is exemplary.'

I said, 'Thank you!' still waiting for the real Wilbur to show through. We had a few more words but I was just about out on my feet and excused myself as soon as I could do so.

I slept for nearly 20 hours in my dungeon and finally Pete, my striker, shook me and said, 'Capitan, Capitan are you OK?'

I thought I would die before I could struggle out of my bedroll. Every breath quivered and shook like a bowl of jelly and I hated to think that I'd have to walk more than two steps.

'There's a quartermaster shower truck up the road,' Pete said. I felt that even a shower was too much to ask of me, but I finally staggered out into the open.

At the shower truck Pete took one look at me and ran for a doctor. I was red, black, blue, scarlet, and old rose from broken blood vessels on my stomach, chest, legs and arms. The warm water on my body felt wonderful and slowly I began to think I might want to live. A doctor came along and gave me the usual prescription, 'Two aspirins and bed rest for a day.' I recovered very rapidly after a day or so.

A month later General Wilbur turned down a DSC that the battalion commander had recommended for me. 'We don't give medals for retrograde movements,' the general said, forgetting – I assumed – the 13-mile advance we'd made that night under murderous conditions.

Chapter 12

Monte Cassino

The one place in this world that I found to be Hell on Earth was on top of Monte Cassino in Italy. The abbey there was visible to us for miles as we fought our way, mountain by mountain, up the Mignano Valley to the Rapido River which races past the southern base of Monte Cassino.

We took San Pietro and San Vittore after heavy fighting. Winter was coming on fast and the Germans, with thousands of Italian civilians and others helping them, had constructed the Gustav Line running through Cassino and on out to the Tyrrhenian seashore. It was one of the toughest defensive positions of the whole war. In addition to severe mountain slopes, deep gullies and ravines, and fast rivers, there were literally millions of anti-tank and anti-personnel mines guarding all approaches to the positions the Germans had constructed for their guns and troops.

The Germans had brought to Cassino huge guns from the French Maginot Line, along the German border. I identified a French 240mm gun by a shell fragment that I found. In addition there were so-called 'Nebelwerfers,'[1] which our troops immediately named 'Necco Wafers,' designed to be fired electrically from six barrels and which were used to lay down smoke from very large shells that barely cracked open when they exploded on the ground. However, the Germans had learned to fire the guns manually since a number of gunners had been killed by shells, fired electrically, having overtaken other shells at the muzzle of the Nebelwerfer, causing fatal detonations there.

While the Nebelwerfers were not too effective, they made an eerie sound like a ghost in distress when they were propelled out of the six-barreled guns. They came whooping and screaming through the air by the thousands and, while we could get under cover and thereby avoid being hurt, the sound of their wild, coiling shrieks kept men's nerves on edge. There were several dozen regiments of these 'Necco Wafers,' and the concussive effects of their shells wore our troops down. Men in foxholes got very little sleep anyway and, when the smoke layers were belching, sleep vanished almost entirely – day and night, week in, week out. Once exhausted, men would sleep through the sounds of Hell.

We were pulled out of the front lines just after Christmas of 1943. I had to stay over a day from December 28–9 in order to give the new regimental officers coming into the lines all the information I had on German positions.

---

1. Translation: 'fog thrower.'

The new regiment was careless about its camouflage and vehicular movements so that I nearly got blown away by German shells just as I was leaving the CP near San Pietro. Fragments from one round struck my jeep as I was walking toward it on my way out. They blew a hole in the jeep body but didn't damage it enough to stop it running.

As I looked back from a mountain slope a few minutes later, I could see dozens of 105mm rounds falling in the olive grove I had just left. From a mountain pass near Venafro I could look toward Monte Cassino and see columns of smoke where German and American artillery were dueling each other. Almost immediately thereafter I ran a gauntlet where engineers had erected a sign reading, 'Next 500 yards subject to hostile artillery fire.'

We spent several days in Alife, Italy, high on a mountaintop where our regimental headquarters group slept in an old stone castle warmed only by braziers of burning coke, which cast little heat but lots of acrid smoke.

The GIs of our regiment were living in tents along the slopes of the mountain. It was almost more than one could bear to be able to get clean once more, after going practically bathless for a month, and to sleep at night without the dangers that lived at the front. Even so, the usual harassment by top brass began almost at once. We had to train recruits who were shipped to us to replace the men we had lost in battle. This meant working day and night in order to promote a smooth-running regiment.

On New Year's Day a gale blew, knocking down most of the regiment's tents and rain did the rest, disposing almost entirely of a turkey dinner that was to have been served that day. The soldiers were so accustomed to something happening to make life dreary that they complained very little, so long as no one was shooting at them.

We were receiving the usual rumors about going back to the front lines again, almost constantly, while we were in Alife. We heard of an end run being planned around the Gustav Line by sea to someplace south of Rome. We also heard that we would be called on to coordinate an attack across the Rapido River near Monte Cassino with the amphibious attack near Rome.

On January 9, 1944, we moved back to the front where our CP was located in the cave where I had seen the thousands of rats running wild at an earlier date. We relieved the 6th Armored Infantry, and I gathered that they had disposed of most of the stampeding rodents for we were not bothered by them for the one or two nights that we were there.

Up through the middle of the Mignano Valley were several lone peaks that rose from the valley floor like stepping stones toward Monte Cassino. First there was Mount Rotondo, beyond it Mount Porchia, and then Mount Trocchio, just across the Rapido River from Monte Cassino. The valley, near the road that ran through its center, was scourged and blackened by artillery barrages that had swept through it time after time from both sides. It was as barren-looking as the moon.

In addition to the main road in that area, we had a brand-new road that the Germans, unknowingly, had helped us build. As the enemy withdrew up the Italian peninsula, it destroyed the railroad tracks by a special train that dragged a heavy hook through the ties, breaking them in the center and then blowing up the rails every 50ft or so with dynamite. Our engineers simply put bulldozers to work shoving the debris to one side, and shortly we had a beautiful roadbed over which our trucks could supply us in good and bad weather.

We moved to a place behind Mount Porchia a day or so after we reached the front and started to get ready to attack Mount Trocchio to clear the way for crossing the Rapido River. I climbed the very steep side of Porchia away from enemy observation and found it a tough chore. German artillery fired at the crest of the mountain as I approached it. Something wet struck the back of my hand as one shell hit nearby and I found a piece of a man's brain stuck to my skin. German dead lay in windrows on the other side of the crest where I could see them as I looked through a gap in the rocks. German shells had chewed them to pieces as they lay there.

We were thrilled by the view we had of the German lines from Porchia but we were also shocked by the view they had of our positions from Cassino, whose abbey towered above us. We knew that if we were to cross the Rapido, we would have to have more than our share of luck to make it without appalling losses.

When we attacked Mount Trocchio, we practically fell on our faces for the Germans, anticipating our thrust, had pulled out and crossed to the north of the Rapido River to prepared positions along the Gustav Line. That occurred on January 15, 1944, and, at that time, we learned that the Allied landing south of Rome would take place on January 21 at the port of Anzio.

As usual, the top brass had backed into the situation. We were told that we would have to cross the Rapido River on January 21 regardless of the fact that we had to clear pathways through endless minefields just to get to the river. It was impossible to get ready for the crossing in the short time allotted to us.

We established our CP in an Italian farmhouse which proved to be a dangerous spot since Mount Trocchio, running at an angle to the front lines, did not protect us from enemy artillery and tank fire. I put an OP into a house on a small hill beside Mount Trocchio called Le Pieta. The I&R platoon had started to sandbag a cubbyhole near the roof when I got to the OP. I told them to finish the job, keeping in mind the lessons I had learned from the British brigadier, but warned them against using that cul-de-sac. Fortunately for all of us, we found a better spot from which to observe, nearer the ground but in the same building. A German self-propelled gun put a round into the cubbyhole almost as soon as the men had left it and the results were catastrophic, except that no one got hurt.

We spent a lot of time in the basement of that house, and during our fight to cross the Rapido River German heavy artillery tried to get us with delayed fuses. This meant that a shell would not burst when it hit the ground but would plow its way into the ground 5 or 6ft and then go off. The resulting explosions just outside the cellar walls would jar our systems. If one had entered the cellar, someone else would have had to write this story.

We sent patrols through the minefields each night and across the fast-moving waters of the Rapido River. 'Rapido' fairly obviously means 'rapid' in Italian, and the stream which had been contained by high-banked walls in our sector really was an obstacle with its speedy current. Men paddled rubber boats across the river and reconnoitered an area just west of a little town called San Angelo, where little opposition was reported.

While we were feeling out the hostile positions across the river east of San Angelo[2] and finding them extremely strong, engineers were constructing bridges (to be thrown across the river when we crossed), clearing mines, widening roads, and bringing up boats and all the material needed for a major operation of this kind.

The crossing site was to be an S-bend in the river opposite the strongest enemy positions. By striking there it was felt that we could put troops on both sides of the crossing point without having to cross the river to do so. Army manuals call for this treatment, but unfortunately all armies are aware of this fact so that those defending against a river crossing know where to block such a move. Because of the severe lesson we learned at the Rapido River we were saved from similar results later, particularly when we crossed the Moselle River in France in fall 1944.

The crossing of the river was a fiasco. The lanes cleared through minefields were too narrow. Engineers had marked their sides with white tape visible at night. However, the boats that the shock troops carried for the initial crossing were very wide, forcing those bearing them to step outside the tapes and onto mines. We lost hundreds of men on our side of the river.

From the OP I watched the hostile positions which were being shelled by our artillery and mortars. Even so, the German dugouts and trenches were so well shielded that their guns were fired continuously during our heavy bombardment. We fired some 35,000 rounds onto those positions while our troops made their way, in darkness, to the river.

Our OP received fire all the time during that operation. We heard machine-gun bullets rattling off the walls, mortar shells 'cramped' close by, and artillery dug deep holes all around us. No one was hurt! Several shells hit the house we were in, blowing wood and stone past us, but the deep-striking shells missed us.

At 3:30 am I received a call from Colonel Wyatt, then commanding our regiment, to go to the railroad station between Trocchio and La Pieta and to order all units not yet across the river to return to their areas on our side of the river. It was too late then to try to cross.

I took a couple of the I&R platoon boys with me and found that the area was foggy so that the German shells that began to fall in great numbers at that time

---

2. San Angelo is the site of a memorial to the 36th Infantry Division dedicated in 1984. The monument is an inscribed granite obelisk.

made it appear that we were walking through Hell, with swirling fog constantly lit up by shell flashes.

I finally reached the railroad and transmitted the colonel's orders. The area was under heavy fire, so we took shelter in the railroad station. It had already been hit several times and offered very little protection. There were holes though the wooden floor in several places and men had dug foxholes in those positions.

I got back to the CP behind Trocchio just in time to hear General Wilbur outline a plan to continue the attack at 2 pm that same day. Apparently one battalion, our 1st, had crossed the river but the 2nd and 3rd Battalions had run into unidentified minefields and because of delay had been unable to get their bridges across the river. We had no radio or telephone contact with the 1st Battalion so no one knew what had happened to it.

Later, because we realized that any attempt to cross the river in daylight was suicidal, General Wilbur changed the order to one calling for the further effort at 9 pm that night, even though General Geoffrey Keyes, the corps commander, was still insisting on a daylight crossing.

I returned immediately to the railroad station, which was a very hot spot under full German observation, and acted as liaison between the regimental CP and the units crossing the Rapido. The night was brutally cold despite the 'hot' shelling we were taking.

As morning broke, we were confronted with a stream of wounded men making their way to the rear areas as best they could through smoke, which we had laid on corps' orders along the river to blind enemy observation. Since the Germans had been able to see where our engineers had cleared minefields, because of the telltale white tape, they had registered their guns on those lanes. The result was that hundreds more of our men were killed and wounded while making the second trip to the river and before crossing.

I saw many officers, whom I had known for a couple of years and whom I liked, badly wounded. One of them appeared dead with gaping holes on both sides of his chest. I could not see that he was breathing and he had no pulse. (Imagine my shock and surprise when several months later I saw this same man looking into a store window in Rome. I could not believe he had lived. When we finally stopped beating each other on the back, he told me that a bullet had entered near his heart, struck his backbone and ricocheted out the right side of his chest. He had been given up for dead but had responded, somewhat, when his 'body' had been driven over a rough road in a jeep, and the medics had pulled him through.)

Word was sent from higher headquarters that troops must hold their positions regardless of cost. I sent Charlie Lane of the I&R platoon to the river to learn the status of the bridges that had been put across it. He came back through the smoke and reported a holocaust. The battalion that crossed the river was caught between barbed wire entanglements in front of the German positions and the river. They had dug in shoulder-to-shoulder, but their small area was swept by all kinds of fire and many were being killed or wounded with little hope of moving forward or backward.

We set up an aid station at the railroad site and because men were congregating there, established a first-aid emergency shuttle by jeep to clear the position.

We could hear the heavy thump of our machine guns across the river for most of the day. Then the news came that, despite orders to hold, one battalion of the 143rd Infantry had withdrawn its men from across the river. This left only our regimental troops there to receive the full brunt of hostile fire. The end was inevitable. A young lieutenant, soaking wet, came into the railroad station and said the remaining troops had been encircled by the Germans, who had moved against them under the cover of our smoke, and all our men except for about a dozen had been killed, wounded, or taken prisoner.

Because of the possibility of the Germans using our bridges to cross to our side of the river, I organized a strongpoint along the railroad with the I&R platoon and some stragglers. I also sent for reinforcements from the anti-tank company.

Meanwhile the engineers were standing by at the S-bend in the river with a Bailey bridge, which could support the weight of tanks. We stood on continuous alert against German counterattack until 3 am on January 23, which meant that I had been under fire constantly for well over 50 hours during which time I hadn't closed my eyes to sleep.

General Wilbur called this scrap 'The Battle of Guts,' and reporters flashed that message around the world. The trouble was that our guts were plastered all over the battlefield.

We were kept on constant alert for another crossing for the ensuing two weeks. At one moment the Germans called for a truce in order to remove the bodies of our dead soldiers. It was a strange occasion when, all shooting having stopped in an area 1,000yd wide, we stood beside German officers and enlisted men as they helped us clear the bodies from minefields and barbed wire. We ferried the dead in rubber boats back to our side of the Rapido for burial in a military cemetery. Shooting did not start again for several hours after the truce ended. During that period, also, two regiments on our right flank managed to cross the Rapido at a point which was much narrower than where we crossed and, with skillful use of tanks, blasted the Germans from a key hill. The Germans fell back to stronger positions on the Monte Cassino–Castellone ridge complex.

Finally, New Zealand troops relieved our regiment and, again, as S-2, I stayed over a day or so to give the newcomers full information on the enemy positions. The first night I beat their commanding officer in a game of chess.

Among the New Zealand troops were Maori officers. These are native tribesmen of New Zealand but their status is exactly equal to that of whites. My first contact with a Maori was on top of Mount Trocchio where I went with the brigade intelligence officer. There, lying on a huge rock looking just across the ridge line of Trocchio to the German positions on Cassino, was a dark-skinned man in an officer's uniform. He turned toward us and said in a real British accent, 'Looks a bit sticky, what?'

I rejoined the regimental headquarters in a town called Pastinella on the east flank of Mount Trocchio. Looking down on our position was German-held, snowcapped Mount Caira. From Pastinella we could look directly across the river to the town of Cassino, which was given a medieval expression by a castle in ruins and the great monastery high above it.

I set up an OP on the enemy side of Trocchio and fortunately walked to the position. Engineers later found the road leading to the OP to be peppered with anti-tank mines.

We were alerted to send our 2nd Battalion to the town of Caira across the river to a position behind other attacking regiments. I was sleeping at night in a destroyed building where one room, constructed of reinforced concrete, was fairly intact. In it was a huge stone oven on legs, under which Corporal Hobday of the I&R platoon slept. One night it rained and we soon found that our concrete hideaway leaked like a sieve.

On February 9, 1944, we received orders to move forward to positions on the flank of Monte Cassino and to join in an attack against that mountaintop with three other regiments. At that time some troops were fighting through the streets of Cassino and a gag made the rounds as follows: A sergeant of the 133rd Infantry when asked how the fighting was progressing in the town of Cassino said, 'We took a dining room and kitchen today and I understand that, presently, we have scouts in a bedroom.'

Fighting in a town is risky. Sometimes troops proceed from room to room by a process called 'mouseholing.' They dig a hole through a wall just big enough to lob a handgrenade through, and after the blast they plow through the wall, ready to take on anyone left alive. Trouble is, the defenders may lob a grenade through the mousehole first.

We split our headquarters group into a small echelon to go forward on to Monte Cassino and a larger one to remain in the town of Caira. At that moment since I was, of course, going forward, I started my descent into Hell by climbing a mountain.

There was snow on the ground as I stopped at the little town of Caira to get directions on climbing a trail up the northeast slope of Monte Cassino. The town was ruined by artillery fire with but one house standing two stories high while all others had been leveled. I advised the headquarters group to stay out of the one good house since it would become a target if a lot of activity was to be seen around it.

The headquarters commandant, however, said he would place sandbags on the outer side of a stairway that ran up the outside of the building to the second floor. He felt that this would prevent undue damage from shellfire but I disagreed since a shell coming through the roof could eliminate the headquarters group.

I left on foot and crossed several fields which had been ploughed by shellfire until they looked like honeycomb. Near the foot of the mountain I passed a first-aid station where wounded men were being treated by doctors and a chaplain was attending to some of the very badly wounded soldiers.

I started up a trail through thick woods and occasionally, as I climbed, I could see artillery pieces in position on the slopes with gun barrels pointed almost straight up in order to fire shells at German defenses on the top of Cassino and along Castellone Ridge.

As I climbed higher, the number of people I met on the trail thinned out. In one place a deep, narrow ravine running at right angles to the trail housed a mortar platoon and the hollow belching of the shells leaving their tubes made a lonely sound. A few seconds later I could hear the shells exploding high above me.

Finally I reached a small plateau where there was a house around which I saw a lot of activity. In the distance to my left I could see the mountain peaks of Trocchio, Porchia, and Rotondo marking the valley route by which we had approached this German stronghold. I asked at the house, which proved to be a regimental headquarters, where the headquarters was located of the regiment we were replacing. No one knew exactly but said that I would certainly encounter it if I kept on climbing.

This was the first indication I had, of many to come, that no one knew much about what was happening on Monte Cassino. While the responsibility for maintaining communications with lower echelons was on the higher headquarters, something about the fierce mountainside seemed to prevent such higher groups from doing their duty.

By this time I was within range of mortar fire and I could hear machine-gun bullets snapping overhead from time to time. I had climbed for about an hour and a half, and now I found the snow quite deep. Under it were the frozen bodies of men from many nations as well as horses and mules that had been killed by shellfire or by stepping on mines.

The trail grew narrower, and in some places engineers had cut stairs into the ground to help mules keep their footing in the icy going. In one such stairway I saw where a mule had slipped off the stairs and fallen on its side only to be blown to bits by a Teller mine that the Germans had buried beside the trail. Parts of the mule hung in frozen chunks in the surrounding trees. There were niches cut in the side of the mountain, here and there, where ammunition was stored.

As I reached a point just below the mountaintop, a mortar barrage from about 100 German guns hit the top of the ridge and in successive moves worked its way down the slope toward where I was standing. I realized that there was no place to hide, and a picture came into my mind at that moment that I had once seen on the front page of a newspaper. It showed a man in bathing trunks on one of the Hawaiian Islands looking up at a 100ft tidal wave that was about to swamp him. The caption read, 'One Second Before Death Struck.'

I knew it would do no good to run, so I just stood there and watched the creeping barrage. Just as quickly as it had started toward me, it reversed and swept back up the ridge. I had been saved by a whisker!

I moved on and suddenly came to a clearing and there in front of me was the great abbey of Monte Cassino. I dove back over a low ridge and registered my field glasses on the abbey. In one of the windows looking in my direction through field glasses was one of the enemy. I crawfished away from that spot, moving to my right and into the woods.

When I had traveled about a hundred yards, several rounds of shells struck where I had been when I watched through my glasses. I pushed on hoping there were no mines underfoot. I was no longer on a trail and the trees were fairly thick all around me.

As I passed a large stone outcropping I saw that it formed a cave by slanting up over an open space about 100ft wide and 50ft deep. In it were about thirty dead American soldiers. I could not imagine how they had been killed in that position except by hand grenades. A movement caught my eye in the woods ahead of me, so I knelt down behind a tree and waited to see who was there. I had my carbine ready in my hands in case the person coming toward me was a German.

I saw the shoulder patch of an American division, but I waited because this wasn't a sure sign that the man was friendly, since such patches were easily imitated. Just as I was about to hail him, the place turned into a blazing, crashing bit of real estate as a dozen or more mortar shells striking in the tree tops showered red-hot metal in all directions. I simply dropped flat and did a bit of praying. Again, I was just plain lucky, but as I got up and looked in the direction of the man I'd seen I saw him lying on his back. He was dead! I took his name from a dog tag to report his status to his regiment. He was a 1st lieutenant.

By this time it was beginning to get dark, and I was not happy about spending the night alone where German patrols could stumble on me. I thought I heard a voice but couldn't be sure where it was coming from. I listened and eased along through the trees until I could hear the language being spoken. It was a GI talking on a telephone. He was in a hole in the corner where two stone walls converged and over the hole there was a black tarpaulin to keep off the snow. I spoke to him and the first thing I saw was the muzzle of a .45 pistol. He poked his head out and said, 'Sorry, sir! Can't take any chances up here.' He was operating a switchboard for the regiment I was hunting. When I asked him where it was located, he pointed through the trees, and I could just make out the outline of a stone house about 100ft further on. The man was shivering in the cold as I started toward the house.

That house became the focal point of great activity for the next few days. Two regimental headquarters were located there. Only the basement and a lean-to room at one side could be used, as the Germans had knocked down the other rooms with mortar fire. At intervals of 3 seconds, day and night, 120mm mortar shells fell close to the house.

My first night, as I was trying to get some sleep, a shell landed just outside the entrance to our basement. Slowly, the whole back wall started to fall and great rocks crashed onto people sleeping on the floor, hurting some of them badly. Because Germans held the ground on three sides of us, our lights were visible to some of the enemy before we could extinguish them and put up tarpaulins to screen the hole where the wall had fallen. As a result we took much heavier shellings for most of that night. Many men became casualties.

We were given misinformation by the commanding officer of the regiment we relieved. He said that the Germans were located behind a stone wall from where they could roll hand grenades onto the American troops located downhill from the wall. We could not even get an attack started because of the casualties we were taking. Many of our troops were new and untested, having come to us as replacements after the losses we suffered on the Rapido River. Thrown into a maelstrom like that of Monte Cassino they were easy targets for seasoned German troops.

I was ordered by Colonel Wyatt to go forward to the top of the mountain one day when Ross Young, the regimental operations officer, claimed he had developed strained leg muscles. This was a very convenient way for him to avoid hazardous duty. I had had a sensing for several days that Colonel Wyatt was too uptight and incapable of using sound judgment. He ordered me to locate the forward battalions and to report their situation.

I took a young officer with me and as I left the cellar everyone shook hands with us as though they'd never see us again. We had to wait for a 120mm mortar shell to land and then run as fast as we could go, hoping to get out of the way of the next shell seconds later.

Once clear of the target area we climbed a steep slope, noting the shapes of dead men and mules under the snow all along the trail. We approached the rim of the mountain, and I sneaked up to have a look at the ground there. In the distance was the abbey and between us and some stone buildings that belonged to the abbey were upward sloping fields and stone walls.

The young officer asked to be let loose to go back to the regimental headquarters. I told him that we would both be safer if we kept together. I started up across the slope and almost immediately heard a bullet very close to my head. I dove into the snow, cradling a carbine across my arms, and crawled to a stone wall. The lieutenant crashed down beside me shortly thereafter. I motioned to him to crawl along the wall and to try to spot the sniper. He did and drew fire a second time. I joined him and he said he thought the gun had fired from a small clump of trees about a hundred yards away. We kept watch and suddenly saw movement halfway up one of the trees. Both of us fired several shots at the spot and apparently we got the sniper because there was no more activity from him. We had some 200 yards to go to a building toward which we had seen some telephone wire leading on top of the snow. Telephone wires were constantly out of commission due to shellfire. We felt that our battalion headquarters was in the building as had been reported earlier. However, we could not be certain that the enemy had not taken over. We approached the building, which looked like a small stone barn, from one side, running and falling, crawling and rolling to avoid offering any other snipers a good shot. Once I went down beside a mound in the snow and found myself looking into the face of a dead Goum, one of the French tribal soldiers from North Africa. My fall had dislodged the snow from his head and beard.

We were pretty well winded from the excitement and exertion of being hunted when I reached a corner of the barn. I looked around and saw a doorway about 10ft away. Since the door was on the enemy side, I took a minute or two to get my breath. Then I ran and as I slipped on an icy tract and fell, a machine gun cut a line across the doorway exactly where I'd have been had I not fallen. The lieutenant stayed under cover of the building while I crawled down a long hallway hoping that no more bullets would come my way. A man's head appeared at floor level through an open door. 'Down here,' he yelled and I slithered head-first past him and down some stairs, landing in a heap at the bottom.

We sent a man for the lieutenant to show him the back door to the battalion CP where I found a horrible situation. Nearly all of our men had been killed or wounded. We had but eighty-five men on position and for all practical purposes, we were defenseless. A major took me out behind the barn and along a trail through a ravine to a point from which I could see the German defensive position. Instead of a stone wall there was a line of what looked like concrete casemates with periscopes and embrasures from which the Germans could shoot their weapons with little risk to themselves.

I managed to reach Colonel Wyatt on the telephone to tell him the situation. He said, 'You've covered yourself with glory today, Doughty, and I'll see that you're recognized.' While I did not see what happened next, I learned later that he dropped the phone, called his striker and took off running down the trail. I never saw him again. An hour or two later as he climbed the outside stairway to the regimental rear headquarters in Caira, a shell burst through the sandbags, killing him and wounding Colonel Price, who was sitting in the room at the top of the stairs.

As the lieutenant and I approached the regimental CP from which we'd left several hours earlier, we could see a lot of activities by men carrying litters. A shell had struck the building while we were away and had wounded or killed everyone there. While I saw few of those men again, they had shaken my hand earlier because they felt I would not return from my mission to the top of Monte Cassino. Instead, I was untouched and they were the ones who were killed or injured. From then on, whenever I was assigned a dangerous task, I kept this memory in mind and said to myself, 'Straight ahead!'

Ross Young, who had developed the convenient case of strained leg muscles, was disliked by nearly everyone who knew him. He told me several days later that the colonel, who'd been killed, had said as he hung up the phone after talking with me, 'Remind me to put Doughty in for a DSC.' As we talked, Young offered to swap me a DSC if I would write him up for one, too, since we were the only two officers still functioning in the regimental headquarters. I declined his offer.

An unusual event occurred the day after I returned from the top of Monte Cassino. I was sitting in our cellar, which was cold and wet, when an enormous man came in. He was about 6ft 8in tall and a turban that he wore made him look a lot taller. He proved to be an Irish officer fighting in the Indian army. Soldiers under his command were Gurkhas. He had been sent up to learn what our situation was and when I told him, he decided that he had better leave for the foot of the mountain at once. He had been lost for hours on Castellone Ridge and in moving around had been shot at by both sides. It was late afternoon when he started back down the treacherous trail.

I had no idea when he might return and because of our dangerous predicament, I didn't dare to sleep. A medical officer gave me some pills to keep me awake, a fact that I later came to regret.

When one is in a dangerous locality many bodily functions slow down, particularly when there is little food to eat. In our discussions of such things as the need to go to the bathroom, it was generally understood that to go out for a BM (bowel movement) was worth a Silver Star and, in some cases, a DSC. There came a moment when, having hung on as long as I could, I knew I'd have to run the gauntlet of 120mm shells in order to go to the bathroom.

I lifted a blackout curtain and as I was about to run away from the house, a mortar shell struck at the base of a stone wall, not 10ft away, and propelled a boulder bigger than my head just past me, only inches away. The concussion of the explosion produced a strange effect in me. Everything around me turned orange and I had the taste of copper in my mouth. Even so, nature was twisting my arm; so, half-blinded, I ran along the trail for about 100yd. I found a niche between two intersecting stone walls and began to do what I had risked everything to do.

Without knowing, at first, what was happening I felt something cold at my throat and a hand reached for my dog tags and pulled them up toward my jacket collar. I had heard and seen nothing. As quickly as this inspection had started, it stopped and I heard nothing more. As I said later, 'If I hadn't been doing what I was doing, I sure would have when that hand fumbled for my dog tags.' The regimental chaplain heard my story and soon had spread it all over the 5th Army.

I prepared for the dash back to the cellar when I became aware of movement on the trail coming up the mountain. Against the flare of bursting shells I could see a line of turbans past a shoulder of rock and I could hear a swishing of feet in the snow. It was the Gurkhas! The Irish officer had done what few men would have been strong enough to do. He'd climbed Monte Cassino twice in 24 hours under fire.

Some of the Indian soldiers were killed by the mortar shells landing near our CP, so they spread out away from the building while I talked with their officer inside. He was white as a sheet from the exertion of his awful day. When I told him what had happened to me, he said that one of his flanking guards had apparently spotted me and had identified me by the shape of my dog tags, which were oval. German dog tags were round. He thought I was lucky to be alive. So did I.

I have no recollection of how I got off the mountain. I know I walked down with what was left of the regiment. Apparently, I reported in at the regimental rear headquarters and people didn't recognize me. I had not shaved for over a week and I had lost a lot of weight. I knew nothing until a moment arrived when

I could hear a constant hissing sound. I couldn't wake up enough to identify it and kept slipping in and out of consciousness. Finally, a voice said, 'How are you feeling?' It was the regimental chaplain. He told me I was in a tent near San Pietro where I'd been for 48 hours without moving. The hissing was a gasoline stove he'd had the cooks bring to the tent to keep me warm.

The tablets I'd taken to stay awake had finally let me down, and I had never felt so far from reality in my life. The chaplain had volunteered to drive me from Caira to San Pietro in daylight under hostile fire. All of which was lost on me for I have never been able to recall the trip from the top of Monte Cassino to Caira to San Pietro.

I had, I felt, been through all the Hell I'd ever need and the feeling came over me that if I could make it back from Monte Cassino, I could make the rest of the war in a walk. I didn't let this feeling lead me to take foolish chances. I simply knew that whatever happened, nothing would compare to the Cassino nightmare when our own division people, pretty obviously, gave us up for lost without doing much to try to help us.

A great stack of pancakes, floating in syrup, accompanied by six fresh eggs and half a gallon of coffee did wonders in restoring my physical and mental well-being. Who could ask for more of life after having walked a knife-edge for weeks?

I learned a few days later that my tall Irish friend had attacked the Germans' concrete positions, and his Gurkhas had fought so fiercely that the Germans withdrew. However, the Gurkhas lost most of their troops when a German counterattack retook the position, killing my Irish friend in the process. The Germans held that line until our planes bombed the abbey at the crest of Monte Cassino, an action that I observed.

A historical note: According to the *Fighting 36th Historical Quarterly*, Vol. VIII, No. 2, summer 1988, James G. Erickson (141st Infantry) reports:

> ... that the Rapido river crossing under the command of Gen. Mark Clark became known as 'the Rapido River Fiasco.' The US dead and missing was almost 1700 men. The German losses were negligible.
>
> In January 1946, after the war, the 36th Division Association passed a resolution calling the Rapido River Crossing 'one of the worst blunders of WW2' and demanded a congressional investigation.
>
> This resulted in hearings held by the Committee on Military Affairs during the second session of the 79th Congress between February 20 and March 18, 1946. It was inconclusive and hushed up.

In the fall 1987 (Vol. VII, No. 3) issue of the *Quarterly*, RKD wonders openly on whether the heavy losses at Cassino were necessary and cites a British book, *The Battles for Cassino* by E.D. Smith, as a good discussion of the strategic aspects of that part of the war.

Chapter 13

Out of the Lines

Once a division of infantry has been as badly mauled as ours had been in the vicinity of Monte Cassino, Italy, there is little to be done other than to remove it from the fighting front to where it can be brought up to strength and retrained.

I was sent to the rear on February 16, 1944, to establish a bivouac area to which the 141st Infantry Regiment could move when it was relieved from front-line duty. My party of fifty drew rations and water and in mid-afternoon of that day reached the little town of Pratella. There I took over the home of Dr. Manfredi Mancone since it was large enough to accommodate my group and still leave room for the doctor's family in one wing. The doctor was away, but I talked with his two daughters and a son in French.

We set about building roads which the engineers who were with me laid out for us in a short time. I felt that the area was not a good one for our purposes but was unable to change it at that time. Toward evening of that first day I returned to the Mancone home which was quite a mansion. It had a summer living room that was over 50ft long and 30ft feet wide. Constructed of stone, the house was much too large to heat in the wintertime so that, in effect, we were not putting the Mancones out of the portion of their home that they occupied in the winter.

Someone, I believe it was the Mancone boy, called me to say that his father was returning from having made a housecall on a patient who lived a long way off. I went to the door downstairs from my office and watched the doctor come hurrying up the road. He was a small man with a dedicated look about him. He also had a very professional air and yet was humble. He spoke French and we stood and talked in the dooryard.

Something made me look down into the light snowfall that had covered the ground the day before. In it I saw blood stains and realized that the doctor's feet had been cut and were bleeding through his shoes.

He had not complained but I insisted that he go to his rooms at once and get his feet attended to. He invited me into his home where I met his wife, who appeared frightened and tearful. She was working at a tile stove that burned wood and was cooking dinner for the family.

As we talked, I learned that the doctor had walked to his patient's home, some 30 miles away, simply to be with her when she died. He had had to cross an ice-filled river in a leaky boat and all-in-all had spent a miserable two days in the hope that he could alleviate suffering.

He told me that the Germans had taken all of his surgical tools and drugs when they had left the area. He was concerned, both for the civilians and our troops, that no epidemic outbreak occur, now that so many people were to be crowded into the vicinity of Pratella.

Nothing that I could say could keep the family from sharing their meal with me. When I sat down with all of them, I found a brazier at my feet with coke embers in it to keep my boot-clad feet warm. I immediately got up and placed the brazier at the feet of Mrs. Mancone who, by that time, was looking less frightened. After dinner I went to my room and returned with some shoes and civilian pajamas that were in my bedroll and for which I had no use. I also brought them some food, since we had managed to get both K and B rations for our use. K rations are terrible but contain nutritious food while B rations are fresh vegetables, meat, and fruit.

I turned over a truckload of K rations to the doctor when I learned that some of his younger patients were dying of malnutrition.

While we stayed in Pratella for just three weeks, I still think of Dr. Mancone as one of the finest men I ever met. He told me of his eighteen years of training and schooling before he could become a doctor. He had heard of the new wonder drugs that we had developed in the US and had read everything he could find on them, but he had never seen or used any of them.

One night I was awakened by screams and tore downstairs to the doctor's office where he had just opened a woman's arm without the use of anesthetics and with an ordinary knife for a scalpel. I had never seen a worse looking infection which the woman had tried to ignore until now, when she was threatened with the loss of her arm. I got hold of some sulfa powder and gave it to the doctor, who spread it on the infected arm. The woman was in unimaginable pain. Since we had no medics with us, there wasn't much else I could do.

However, the next day I made a trip to the outskirts of Naples and came back with medical supplies sufficient to outfit a full field hospital. I explained to the medical officer I talked with at army headquarters that our only physician was an Italian doctor whose supplies had been requisitioned by the Germans. Since I was not sure how long we'd be without medical assistance, I felt it important to equip Dr. Mancone to take care of our needs as well as those of the Italian people. He agreed.

Dr. Mancone practically wept when he saw what was in the huge chests I brought back. He spent the next 24 hours reading all of the instructions which I had to help him translate, but when he was through he had converted his home to a small hospital.

He was able to clear the infection from the woman's arm almost immediately and he could also take care of other surgery which had had to have been postponed pending receipt of anesthesia.

All of this paid off a few days later when, as sometimes happens, an American soldier killed himself. He apparently couldn't stand the release from tension that resulted when he left the front lines. I took the doctor with me to see the dead man and asked him to draw up a written report as to the cause of death. He wrote it out in Italian; together, we translated it to French and then I re-translated it to English. Higher headquarters commended us for the professionalism of the report. The Infantry School at Fort Benning cited us for using ingenuity in meeting unusual circumstances.

We left Pratella to move to Maddaloni near Casserta on March 5, 1944. Thereafter I received letters, some of which did not reach me until after the war moved on to France, in which Dr. Mancone accounted for the food and medical supplies in every detail. I corresponded with him for several years after the war but no longer know anything about him or his family.

In Maddaloni we took over a large Italian villa that had a central hall much like that in Dr. Mancone's home. An outside staircase with forty-eight steps led to this hall and in it, because we were now in a rest area, several troupes of actors and actresses put on shows for us. Among the entertainers were Jean Darling, formerly of the 'Our Gang' comedies, and Alfred Foye, Jr. Also a Valerie Jordan visited us and I remember dancing with her all one evening on the stone floor of our hall as part of her troupe played dance music.

In the same vicinity was the 64th General Hospital, which had been organized in Louisiana. It wasn't long before the staff of the hospital felt that it had a special relationship with the men and officers of the 36th Division. It wasn't only because the two units came from neighboring states, since by this time the personnel of both had changed considerably. It was just that we thought of each other as special people and went out of our way to ease the burdens of each other.

We set up an officer's club in a Maddaloni villa and held a dance there for the nurses of the 64th General Hospital. In turn the nurses had their own club to which we were invited from time to time.

We were in Maddaloni, training, for just a month. During that time I visited the opera house in Casserta where I talked with Irving Berlin. I also visited Pompeii and Naples and played on the floor with some little orphan girls in an orphanage near Pompeii. I managed to get some foodstuff to the nuns running the orphanage in a second trip I made there.

The sight of Vesuvius' slopes and surrounding areas was something to behold, what with smoldering lava trails flowing down the fluted crater and cinders blown over miles and miles of landscape.

On April 4, 1944, we moved once again – this time to Celzi near Avellino, inland from Naples. During the next few weeks it became evident that some of the staff of my regiment had been working behind the scenes to get out of a dangerous assignment. Several officers left for duty with 5th Army Headquarters. A week later I had a chance to go to Sorrento where Professor Corcione and his family gave Dr. Cunningham (who accompanied me) and me a warm welcome. I arranged to meet the professor in Avellino on April 19, 1944, when he went there to teach at the Instituto Magistrale.

In Celzi we took up serious training in terrain that compared to that part of Italy where we expected next to enter combat. It was mountainous, and immediately above the town was Mount St. Nicholie which I climbed on one occasion with a local Italian lawyer. He showed me an old monastery, the cellar of which was full of human skulls, in which he had hidden to evade capture by the Germans.

At Avellino the 3rd Canadian General Hospital had set up shop and we soon met Miss Roach, the matron, and several of the nurses who are called 'sisters' in Canadian parlance.

On April 15, 1944, I visited the officer's club at Avellino and had some drinks with several officers of the Royal 22nd 'Van Doos' regiment of Quebec. A Lieutenant Vincent, Captain Piccard, and Captain Parquette took me back to their headquarters and inducted me into the 'Van Doos' as an honorary member. We finished off the evening with a heavy-set sergeant fitting me to a regimental uniform and a beaver insignia which I still own.

I met Professor Corcione as I had planned, when he visited Avellino to teach, and with him called on an ancient priest, Dom Paulo, who lived in Avellino. The priest's home was one barren room, black with age, and equipped with a cot, two chairs, and a bureau on which were located three glass cases containing doll-like effigies of saints. There was also a stove.

Dom Paulo was striking looking with iron grey hair, a saintly look and a beautiful speaking voice. He invited us to join him in drinking some wine to friendship and allowed that this was a good use to make of a beverage normally reserved for Communion. He smiled as he said it.

I was also able to visit the Sanctuario de Monte Virgine that is visible on a towering mountainside overlooking Avellino. A Capuchin brotherhood runs the sanctuary and in summer the brothers climb the mountain, via the seven stations of the Cross, in order to spend the warm months in the sanctuary, which is cooled by winter snows packed deep in a crevice behind the buildings.

I met Father Garmello, head of the monastery, through the offices of Professor Corcione who took me, on another occasion, to see the monk at his quarters in Avellino.

Of all the beautiful places to be seen in Italy, the Sanctuario de Monte Virgine was the easiest for me to relate to because it did not overwhelm me as did St. Peter's when I later saw it in Rome. The approach to the mountain fastness that surrounds the sanctuary is up a winding, twisting road that leads to a stronghold that has guarded its special occupants since the fifteenth century AD. The sanctuary and all of the buildings that make up its ménage are reached through an archway in a wall. There were animals and poultry in the quadrangle, whose south side is open to a view that stays with me even now. It was springtime in Italy, and flowers and blossoming trees made a lasting impression on me as I looked down the ranges of mountains to the south.

The mosaic work of the sanctuary, whose roof stands 75ft above the floor, is unsurpassed in its artistry. As one approaches the altar, it becomes more beautiful in appearance with its wonderful designs and matching colors in marble. There are intricate designs in roses, greens, violets, blues, milky whites, and greys forming a cyclorama unmatched anywhere so far as I'm concerned.

On either side of the main vault are lesser but still large sections divided into separate chapels and places of worship. I have no responsive feeling for the side of Catholicism that prays to statues and effigies, and less for the macabre practice of preserving saintly bones and relics as special touchstones in communicating with God. There was one such relic in one room. It was a glass-enclosed mummy of a saint lying in almost powdery death. Pinned to her burial place were photographs of people, young and old, apparently committed to the care of the occupant.

It was freezing cold in the sanctuary due no doubt to the black encrusted snow lying at the rear of the building. I stopped a young, intelligent-looking monk and asked if he spoke French which he did. He took me in tow and guided me behind the scenes to the living quarters of the monks. I learned that he was called 'Père Charles.'

During our tour of the living areas, the monk pointed out a member of his order who was sitting at a desk in a library working on some hand-painted books. Most of the monks take a vow of silence, never speaking to anyone. This was such a man, according to Père Charles. The silent monk sat there, his face almost lost in a great mane of hair that fell over his shoulders and a beard that disappeared below the table top. A ray of light entered from one of the clerestory windows, high above, and lit up the rough texture of the robe he wore. He did not seem to move, but with head bent simply stared at the book in front of him. Beside his left hand, which was positioned on the table, were one or two other books.

According to Père Charles, the silent monk was over 90 years old, had joined the order many years before, and spent his time illuminating the pages of old books which meant, of course, that he painted colorful designs around each page. For all practical purposes here was a man reduced to the most fundamental aspects of living. Beside him on the desk were the only remaining vestiges of all that his life had meant. Shorn of all property, all family, all hopes of worldly possessions, his life was a symbol of an order that looks to the spiritual world for the only success it wishes to achieve.

While I had told Père Charles that I was not a Catholic he, nevertheless, showed me every courtesy and spent a long time uncovering some of the treasures of the sanctuary for me to see. In a drawing room were several solid-gold vases gifted to the monastery by King Umberto I of Italy. In the main reception hall was an iron cross bearing the figure of Christ. It was some 700 years old and had been given the order by Victor Emmanuel. Although rusted, it was delicately wrought and greatly prized by the monks.

In the reception hall, too, were paintings of four gentlemen who had spent their lives researching and writing of the life of Mary, the Virgin Mother, to whom the sanctuary is dedicated. Another painting, located in a small chapel where the monks gather for morning and evening prayers, was of ancient origin and unusual composition. Some 7ft high and 3ft wide, the 'canvas' is really of hewn wood where the marks of some ancient tool used to chip the surface flat are evident beneath the paint. It had been contributed to the monastery in the year 1500 by its founder, Father Guillermo. The head and halo of the main figure of the painting protruded from the rest of the composition, indicating that they had been carved in that position before they were finished with paint.

When Père Charles learned that I knew and liked Professor Corcione, he was delighted and he finally put his arm through mine and walked me to the main gate from which he left to attend vespers.

I returned to Celzi just in time to attend an evening meal given by the 1st Battalion at the home of a Signor La Doutis, where that battalion had its headquarters in Celzi. We had had a change of regimental commanders by that time. A Lieutenant Colonel John C.L. Adams had been in command for a short time when we were on the Rapido front and had brought the regiment back for retraining. However, Colonel John 'Jazz' Harmony arrived to take command and I learned for the first time that night, after we had become suitably mellowed with wine and good food, that Adams was giving Harmony a tough time, saying that the regimental staff wanted Adams to remain as CO.

Since this was not true, I made a point of telling Harmony as we sat on a stairway leading to his private quarters in Celzi, that Adams was too loud, too shallow, and too lewd for most of us. Harmony was happy to receive the news and we talked of regimental problems until almost dawn.

I revisited Naples to see the sights just after Vesuvius erupted and found the city sooty and smelling like phosphorus. I wore my best uniform for the first time since leaving the US and was accompanied by several officers of the staff. We found an officer's club in a marble-lined bank building and went in to get a drink. Everything was plush, as usual, for the rear echelon had no intention of roughing it if it could help it.

I was talking quietly with a couple of officers from the British navy when I heard a drunken voice say, 'Throw those goddamned roughians out of here.' I paid no attention to the voice and continued talking. Suddenly I felt my coat seized at the back followed by a ripping sound. I wheeled round and without even looking to see who had assaulted me, whipped a right hook to his jaw and knocked him over a long table that was full of canapés.

I realized, at once, that I was in trouble but felt that the provocation should prove a good defense. I had knocked a bird colonel into unconsciousness. However, second thoughts arrived very quickly and I dodged to the door where an MP started to block me off. I noticed a 3rd Division patch on one shoulder and said, 'If you're a fighting man instead of a rear-echelon punk, stand aside.' My coat was almost falling off me and I saw the MP's eyes shift to the sagging coat panels and then to the bird colonel still lying on the floor. 'Get goin'' he said and pretended to fall back as I brushed past him. The other officers from my regiment had taken pains to sneak out a back way.

Every effort was made, by bulletins and personal calls on the 36th, to locate the officer who had assaulted the assistant port commander of Naples. No one found me, and in the meantime I'd had an Italian woman resew my coat, knowing that tailors would be asked if they'd done the job.

After the war, during an ROA[1] convention, General Donald Adams and I were talking and when I learned that he'd been port commander of Naples, I asked him if they'd ever caught the man who KO'd his assistant. He looked at me with a calculated stare and said, 'Weren't you with the 36th Division?' I nodded. 'Guess that settles that,' he said. 'God, we looked all over hell for you.'

'Who said I did it, General?' I asked. He just shook his head and dropped the subject.

On May 5, 1944, just about one month after we had set up camp in Celzi, we decamped once more and took up lodgings along the coast in the vicinity of Qualiano, Italy, where I had received news of our 'son' Ann's birth. We were easing back toward the front again with this move, and to get us used to the idea, we lived in tents once more. The powdery soil of the area that had turned to sticky gumbo in the winter now became the bane of our existence. We lived, breathed, ate, and slept in a blanket of dust. After each ride in a jeep we would emerge looking fifteen years older because of newly developed grey hair and eyebrows.

On one occasion I revisited the 64th General Hospital at Maddaloni where, at a dance, I met a Lieutenant Mair whose father was in the British House of Lords. Mair had been in service since 1939 and had survived the rigors of many fighting fronts only to become 'shell-shocked' one night while looking at a war picture in which divebombing by German Stukas was so realistically portrayed that his nerves were shattered. Mair lived at 55 Hanover Gates Manor, Peyden Park, London, at that time and was scheduled to replace his father, in due course, in the House of Lords. He was of Scotch lineage, and we enjoyed swapping stories of the war all evening long. We promised to look each other up if we ever got to the other's bailiwick after the war. Unfortunately, on both occasions when I visited London after the war, I had misplaced my diary so that I no longer had these references to guide me.

On May 16, 1944, during a regimental review in which I shared honors on the reviewing stand with General Walker, General Robert I. Stack, Colonel Harmony, and Colonel Ives, General Walker praised the men of the regiment and told us that in his view the hardships endured by the Continental Army at Valley Forge were not as difficult as those we had suffered in the Italian mountains in wintertime. He went so far as to state that none of the historic infantry actions of all time compared with the frontal attack we had made across the Rapido River when the odds against survival were a thousand to one. He congratulated the men of the regiment for their great strength of character and courage in assaulting prepared positions in which the enemy gunners fought in comparative safety. As a result of our prowess, the general said, the 36th Division had been named as Army Reserve to be committed at a critical time in an upcoming operation of great importance. At times like that, when generals become overly generous with their praise, we had learned to start looking for cover somewhere because high praise was usually a forerunner to risky assignments. In this instance, we were not wrong.

---

1. Retired Officers of the Army, Reserve Officers Academy, or similar.

Chapter 14

The Haunt

A special note in my diary has prompted me to write about a Lieutenant Karam of Haverhill, Massachusetts, who was the 1st Battalion's intelligence officer of the 141st Infantry. On May 12, 1944, I inspected several camouflaged areas to see how the three battalions were progressing with this necessary training. Lieutenant Jamil Karam had an unusually good project set up over a wide area where he had also wired the sides of trails to keep men from widening them. He also had whole bivouac areas well concealed with nets and natural material to limit observation from the air.

We knew that while modern photographic techniques would disclose camouflaged sites, when bombing the human eye had to pick up those sites and a well-prepared cover-up might delay release of bombs just long enough to save a real pasting. Our next move was to be to a particularly sensitive area, and we had been alerted to improve our camouflage capabilities to thwart premature discovery of our presence as it would easily tip the hand of the 5th Army commander.

In order to tell Lieutenant Karam's story, however, I shall skip ahead to a time when, after landing in France, we were on the slopes of the Vosges Mountains in October 1944. My diary ran out just about the time I have in mind, so I'm forced to rely on memory alone.

We had our regimental headquarters in a church located in a small village somewhere on the slopes of the Vosges. The countryside was ablaze with fall colors, which I had an unusual opportunity to see from the air. I had, in effect, done the job of the division G-2 by flying along the front to determine the best means for defending our zone of responsibility. In the process, I had looked down just in time to see four shells from 105mm howitzers near the city of Bruyères rising toward our plane. I had never had the experience before of being in a position over guns where, to my consternation, I could actually see the shells coming toward us at a terrific rate of speed. The pilot did not know that a friendly artillery battery had changed position in the night and so flew directly over its new site.

The shells missed us but their passing shook the plane violently and the pilot, a Captain MacMurray, thinking that we were under attack by German planes, executed several evasive moves that left my stomach several thousand feet above where we passed between a number of trees with our wings in a vertical position. I pounded him on the back and told him I'd seen our battery firing. During our flight we watched an artillery duel in the vicinity of Belmont and observed the

German effort to blind our observation by laying smoke on Le Tholy. We also saw a German Nebelwerfer firing north of the US 45th Division's front.

My division was in a vulnerable position, trying to defend an L-shaped line that extended several miles beyond a normal division's defensive capacity. At the time my regiment was under the command of a colonel who, as far as we could learn, had been in charge of Ike's stenciling machines at SHAEF[1] and who apparently wished to have some combat time for the benefit of his career later.

I recall this colonel sitting like an oracle under a logged-over dugout on the wooded slopes of the Vosges, swearing that he would not leave that gloomy recess until one of our battalions was relieved after having been cut off by the Germans. This was a dramatic time in many ways and forms the heart of the story of Lieutenant Karam.

It started soon after we crossed the Moselle River. General Dahlquist, as quite often occurred, came to my regimental headquarters one day and told our colonel that our regiment was to attack along a line that would convert the L-shaped line to one that was U-shaped. This, fairly obviously, would trigger a drastic reaction by the defenders.

The colonel thought about it for quite a while and then sent for me at about 4 am and ordered me to see General Dahlquist, who was asleep in his trailer at division headquarters near Brayers. I was to tell the general that while we would attack as ordered, it would be essential to have other troops ready to commit to the fight in case we ran into the heavy opposition that I was certain would arise. I awoke the general and he said that he understood the colonel's concern but that the 442nd Infantry, formed of Japanese-Americans, had been attached to the 36th Division and was ready for instant commitment if need be.

With that we gathered the battalion and regimental staffs at the small village church to issue the operations order. It was getting cold at the time, and while we had oil-burning stoves in use, nevertheless we were glad to wear our heavy combat suits.

After the meeting Lieutenant Karam seemed to want to stick around to talk with me. As I recall it, my intelligence section was located inside the altar rail of the miniature church. Karam sat at my desk and suddenly blurted out something that I didn't quite understand. I asked him to repeat what he'd said.

'Haven't I done a good job?' he asked. I agreed that he had. 'Why haven't I received a medal, then?' he asked.

I was somewhat taken aback and said something to the effect that few people had been properly recognized for their contributions to the success of the regiment. I suggested that I'd be glad to discuss the matter with his battalion CO, whom I knew quite well.

'Okay, Major,' he said, 'but remember this: I expect to be killed tomorrow when we make that move against the German rear. If I don't have something to show my folks I've done all right, I'll haunt you for the rest of your life.' He

---

1. Supreme Headquarters, Allied Expeditionary Force.

laughed as he said it, but there was a real serious look in his black eyes. I told him he needed a rest, talking like that, and he agreed.

The attack took off as scheduled and, as anticipated, the Germans counterattacked but their timing was such that their attack cut the battalion command group off from the attacking companies, before those companies could take their final objectives.

The regimental combat command, including me, had moved to the trail juncture, where the colonel had had a ravine covered with heavy logs. I had objected to the location, since any road juncture is an artillery reference point. My objection was well-taken since the trees in that area looked like stunted bean poles once the Germans realized that we were located there and worked us over with artillery and self-propelled fire. However, the colonel was too new to the art of fighting to listen to seasoned veterans and simply sat out a rain of steel for days.

As I noted earlier, he sat under the logs with a candle or two for light and a blanket over his shoulders, refusing to leave while the battalion was so close to annihilation. The rest of us had to risk taking a shell fragment as we moved in or out of the underground chamber. At one time General Sandy Patch, another general commanding a corps, and General Dahlquist plus some of their respective staffs gathered in that dugout where one shell would have wreaked the kind of havoc both sides wished to avoid.

I was about my business of trying to learn how things were going. The little town of Biffontaine was located nearby, and I mention it solely because it was there that Joe Dine, commanding F Company of the 143rd Regiment, had such a tough time during this action.

Suddenly we got the news that the German countermove had caught the 1st Battalion staff in the open. The lieutenant colonel commanding had done everything possible to try to get through to his outfit, including commandeering a tank for the purpose, but without success.

Lieutenant Karam had been killed instantly.

This jarred me because he was the second man who had forecast the exact time of his own death.

The fight dragged on for days. The weather was so foul that airdrops of supplies and ammunition to the 1st Battalion were unsuccessful. As I recall it, at least one of our planes was downed in the effort. Medical supplies, finally, were packed in shells and successfully fired into the area where the battalion was encircled. Later, we were to learn that the Germans and Americans shared a waterhole under some tacit arrangement of the kind that can happen in combat.

The Japanese-Americans[2] eventually drove through the German forces to relieve the 'Lost Battalion' of the Second World War.

It is my recollection that Lieutenant Karam's parents received the evidence of their son's proficiency, but there is a haunting note to the whole incident, if it can be termed as such, that stays with me.

---

2. 442nd Regimental Combat Team (Nisei, also known as the Purple Heart Battalion).

Chapter 15

Breakout – Indian Style

Not long after our regimental review, the tempo of the war started to pick up for our division. On May 21, 1944, we moved to the 'Texas' area near the island of Nisidi from which we embarked for Anzio, the decision having been made to commit us, as Army Reserve, from that position in an effort to deliver Rome from the Germans.

We had moved in great secrecy since our whereabouts would, if known by the German commanders, tip the Allied hand as to the position from which a critical blow would be delivered. It was to preserve secrecy that we had undergone so much training in camouflage discipline and concealment. Even so, given the number of double agents operating in Italy, it would be the most fortuitous experience of our careers if we could make the move to the Anzio beachhead without discovery by our enemies.

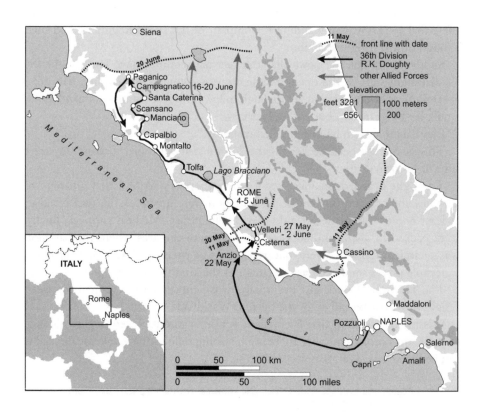

We moved by LSTs and I was assigned quarters in LST 210 moored along a quay from which, at an earlier date, we had conducted an amphibious feint to mislead the German High Command.

With me were several division headquarters staff members, a Captain Hotchkiss of Army Public Relations and Eric Sevareid, noted war correspondent whom I had not met before, although I had talked with such correspondents in the Mignano area as Ernie Pyle and Rex Packard and his wife.

I found Sevareid a very knowledgeable and unassuming man, polite and widely traveled in war sectors. We talked at considerable length, since we were keyed up for the upcoming voyage and the battle that everyone sensed was building to an early climax, now that our commitment had been made. A number of the group had never been to a fighting front and asked us what it would be like when we steamed into Anzio the next morning.

It was my view that there would be little excitement even though every portion of the beachhead was well within artillery range. Having been through the Rapido and Cassino fracases, it would take more than a shell or two to alert me. I pointed out that the Germans appeared to be having ammunition shortages and would probably not waste shells firing at port facilities, particularly where I was certain that smoke was being used by our troops to blind enemy observation.

It was with a certain amount of nostalgia that I left the Naples area for, while we had had some terrible experiences there and suffered in the cold of the mountains, nevertheless, I had come through battle after battle unscathed despite endless, or so it seemed, exposure to instant death.

Naples Bay, as we prepared to leave our quayside, was aflame in a sunset typical of the area and as we watched it, we blotted out the otherwise martial scene of the armada taking us northward to battle. I could make out some of the rooftops of Sorrento which had become so familiar to me because of my nearness to Professor Corcione's family and the quiet moments I had spent in their midst. I felt that I was leaving friendly shores en route to the unknown and yet it was also possible to believe that because the 36th Division in Army Reserve would, doubtless, swing the balance of power at a critical moment, it would thereby contribute significantly to shortening the war.

Before we turned in for the night I gave both Sevareid and Hotchkiss maps of the Anzio area, since they would need them in order to find their way around that battle zone. Hotchkiss and I talked until midnight and were awakened again at 4 am when the general quarters alarm awoke us, it being a standard operating procedure to be alert while at sea off Italy for an air raid at dawn.

Fog and mist cleared before we docked and we received our first glimpse of Anzio and Nettuno from a mile offshore. As I had suspected, smoke was being generated in great quantities about a mile inland and was most effectively blocking a view of the port facilities and coastal road net. I had breakfast with Padre Fenton of our regiment and we finished in time to watch the slow entry of our ship into its docking space. Our decks were awash with the paraphernalia of war. There were tanks with their camouflage paint jobs, jeeps, towed guns, soldiers' backpacks in great piles, rifles, blankets, and other impedimenta which distinguish an army's moves from those of civilians.

Overhead, thousands of swallows fluttered and sailed between the cables holding barrage balloons in place over the stern of each ship. Such balloons were one means of deterring strafing runs against the ships by hostile fighting planes. The warm sunshine and generally peaceful surroundings brought an unusual sense of security, offset – only in part – by the distant sounds of exploding shells and rising columns of smoke behind the bombed-out houses of Anzio.

We docked at 7:30 that morning, but I had to wait for quite a while until my jeep could be moved to the elevator for its descent to the lower deck from which it would be driven through the great mouth at the bow of the LST. During that wait I watched friendly planes, high above the circling swallows, move in formation until they peeled off and followed each other earthward toward the enemy installations that encircled the Allied beachhead. Only later, when we broke through the hostile zone, was it possible to see the havoc that our air force produced in the German defenses.

Once I was off the ship I had my driver take off for Nettuno and then further inland to a bivouac site which had been selected in advance because of the deep woods located there. It was at some distance from the front-line installations to assure maneuverability, should the Germans launch an attack to forestall the onslaught they must have sensed was building in the beachhead area.

We found some partially completed dugouts that other Allied forces had started to build but, for some reason, had not finished. They were improved on by our troops and very shortly thereafter became the headquarters of our division.

That afternoon we heard the order that would send the beachhead forces into an all-out effort to break the German defenses and open the road to Rome. Every effort was to be made to encircle German units and destroy or capture them as a means of forestalling any orderly retreat on their part to other prepared defensive positions.

May 23 was the target date and 6:30 am was H-hour with the capture of Cisterna in the center of the defensive line the initial objective of the attacking forces. At the same time, we were being kept informed of the progress of our forces south of us as they attacked the Gustav Line running through Cassino, thus putting Kesselring, the German army commander, in jeopardy of being caught in a pincer movement which, from the inception of the Anzio beachhead assault, had been General Clark's objective.

We were reminded that our last training period had been devoted to preparing an attack along a chain of mountains near Itri, Italy, an assignment that had been transferred to the 88th Division when we were named Army Reserve. We plotted the progress of the 88th as it fought from Minturno to Itri along the Arunci Mountain Ridge, the topography of which we had studied closely during our rehabilitation period after Cassino.

We also learned that being in Army Reserve called for flexibility beyond belief. We had to prepare for possible employment in any sector radiating out of Anzio from south through east to north. Some eleven alternative plans with appropriate map overlays and operations instructions were developed for standby use.

While awaiting orders that afternoon I was standing beside my jeep eating a sandwich that someone had prepared, when a sudden loud report overhead sent several of us to the ground, sandwiches and all. There was no further explosion, but there was the whirring of a large shell of some kind continuing on past our position. Finally, in the distance we heard a loud explosion. Someone said the shell sounded like an orange crate, with a trailer, moving sideways through the air.

I got on the phone to division headquarters and learned that we had just heard a booster shot that had sent one of Anzio-Annie's huge rounds on the last leg of its trajectory. The Germans had developed a timing device that would explode somewhere around the middle of the shell's trajectory to push it on down the road to maximum range. While such a gun is not very effective, it adds to the strain to know that a shell capable of wiping out a whole city block of buildings could drop in your lap without much warning.

I had all I could do to try to keep up with the hostile situation, what with the movement of German troops north toward us from the Cassino sector. I also was busy plotting known enemy positions on the arc that compressed the beachhead into a restricted area.

On May 23, I was up before daylight to stay abreast of events and to watch our bombers. However, a dense ground fog stopped the bombers cold. We had had some harassing long-range artillery fire in one area during the night but with slight damage except to our sleep.

Initial reports were to the effect that the 1st Armored Division of the US was being delayed by immense German minefields laid all around our defensive perimeter. Some units had made good progress, with the 45th Division, attacking on the left of the forward echelons, having reached its objective where it had cut the railroad tracks northwest of Cisterna. The 34th Division was hitting Cisterna head-on but had met very stiff resistance from heavy artillery and small-arms fire pouring from strongpoints in every house.

The Rangers, reinforced by elements of the Special Services Force on the right of the attacking formations, made excellent progress, initially, but became overextended and under pressure of a sharp counterattack had fallen back a considerable distance toward their original positions. One of our toughest tasks was to identify false rumors of all kinds and to squelch them. There was no doubt from the noise and confusion that a major battle was in progress.

The next day we were given the 36th Division's mission. We were to pass through the 34th Division when it reached a road running parallel to and southwest of the Teppia River. From there we would drive into the mountains to take Cori and the heights above it. However, my regiment was to be in division reserve or, if needed, in corps reserve. Previous plans were off the drawing board and ready for instant execution, since this was one of the alternatives for which we had prepared.

On May 25, official confirmation was received of previous rumors that the southern and beachhead forces had met somewhere south of Cisterna. In addition, the Canadian armor on the southern front was reported as moving up the Liri Valley and had reached the Melfa River, which they were preparing to cross. At that moment I was ordered forward to the division's advance CP to get the current situation and to report back to the regimental headquarters the location of the bivouac area to which we were about to move.

My driver and I took off in a jeep, glad to have the waiting over and to get in motion once more. The land was flat as a board but the fast-flowing generators were still pouring out great clouds of smoke to blind enemy observation along the front. I reached the division advance CP just as General Walker arrived there. Nothing had been learned of my regiment's move, although all other division elements were getting into position.

At 4:30pm I learned that our regiment would be in the attacking echelons while the 142nd Infantry would revert to the reserve position. This was SOP for the 142nd Infantry CO was adept at obtaining reserve status whenever heavy going could be anticipated.

My regiment was to move forward at once to a point northeast of Cisterna in the vicinity of a stream juncture. I noted that some shelling of our rendezvous point was going on at that moment and that the fight for Cisterna was continuing, house-by-house.

I telephoned the regiment to send an advance party to the designated area at once. On the way back to the regiment, I met that party and briefed its officers on the situation as I knew it. I warned them to be on the qui vive for booby traps and mines since the Germans had had all winter to plot our destruction.

I then proceeded to our regimental headquarters, where I gave Colonel Harmony a full report on all that had transpired. I led out with the I&R platoon to post its members as guides to assure us no loss of time or direction, and behind me came the regimental caravan of trucks, guns, and carriers with some troops riding while others slogged their way forward.

The attack had gone well and much of the defender's army had been killed, wounded, or captured. Small pockets of resistance were being encountered everywhere, but many of those surrendered after we hit them hard.

Because of German artillery fire on the main route toward our objective I was forced to swing wide and to take a circuitous route to our rallying point. Here I found a deserted German command post, which we took over after inspecting it for booby traps. It was dark when we reached the sandbagged house that had served some German unit as headquarters and searching each object for hidden wires and detonators took an enormous amount of time, since we had to shield our flashlights so that only a pinprick of light showed.

The Germans had dug two holes inside the building and covered them with heavy logs topped by large stones and earth to prevent penetration by artillery shells and bombs. They had also dug a hole through the back of the house for use as an emergency exit, and beneath this exit they had dug another large shelter. One more was located at the north side of the building. All such dugouts were straw-floored while roofs and sidewalls were lined with beautiful linens stolen from the Italian people.

It was evident to us that the occupants of this bastion had left hurriedly, for there were plates of unfinished food on the table and weapons were strewn everywhere together with suitcases of loot ready for transportation. All of these factors multiplied our work of inspection for booby traps. In fact, I got to bed in one of the deserted rooms at about 2 am and was up again at 4:30 am.

No counterattack occurred, giving further evidence of the overwhelming effect of our hammer blows on the German defenders who invariably counterattacked as a routine matter.

I was concerned about the possibility of an air attack against our position by the dwindling Luftwaffe. I felt that our concentrated location offered a rewarding target for an air force that had to make every bomb count. It was, therefore, welcome news when we received orders to move to a new bivouac area northwest of Cisterna on May 26. We had just completed our move to a wooded area when darkness arrived, and shortly thereafter, some fifty German bombers and fighters dropped flares nearby and proceeded to work over the positions we had just vacated. It was a strange sensation to be concealed in the woods while watching the planes bomb and strafe Cisterna. Nothing came even close to our new locality, and I fell asleep while the air attack was in progress.

The next day I went to division headquarters to receive the plan of attack about to be launched against the town of Velletri. While there I learned that, as of May 17, 1944, I had been promoted to major (!!). We moved the regimental CP to a heavily indented streambed and, at night, moved again to the vicinity of Castel Ginnetti, arriving in time to observe another German air raid on a nearby position. There was a deep wine cellar at hand which could be used as a shelter if we received close attention from the Luftwaffe.

During that phase of the war some idiot had decided that there should be an exchange of duties between the various services so that while some of our dog-faces, as we called them, went to the US Army Air Force to see how they lived, certain airmen came to our regiment to get a taste of life among the foxholes. I always felt that this was a rotten way to prove anything, particularly to airmen who had had little or no training on how to survive combat on the ground.

However, one such airman had taken to the life of an infantryman as a natural-born doughboy. While most of the fly-boys crept into a foxhole and never left it even for bodily functions, this particular sergeant was eager to go patrolling with one of our battalion's patrols. The situation in the vicinity of Velletri was chaotic, and while the G-2 of army was cautioning about heavy concentrations of enemy forces in Velletri and other towns, no one could be sure – least of all the German commanders – as to who was where and in what numbers. German communications had been shattered and prisoners that were taken by our 1st

Battalion were badly shaken and ignorant of any future plans. They had been told to stand and die.

In any event, I received a telephone call from one of our battalion S-2s, whose identity is not established in my diary or in my memory. He had had a report from the sergeant of the air force that there was a huge gap in the German lines. Apparently, the sergeant had gone on patrol, had taken command when the patrol leader was killed and had stayed out for two days and nights moving for several miles to the east of Velletri.

I have no way of knowing now whether or not this report influenced a decision by General Walker to execute a daring move to get behind Velletri and cut off the German retreat. I have a sense that the report was critical to the decision.

While we were moving toward Velletri, slowly, our progress was hindered by the dense vineyards of the area that concealed self-propelled guns of the German units, making every move dangerous. On one occasion I was in direct radio contact with a Sergeant Kelly of our I&R platoon. It was May 27 and Kelly had moved out beyond our front lines and was in a house from which he could see fifty or more Germans digging into a delaying position. Kelly called artillery fire down onto his own position in order to break up the German defenders. We didn't see Kelly for a couple of days thereafter and had about given him up when he came walking in, having collected some macabre momentos of his one-man sortie.

But this vignette of life among the vineyards of Italy anticipates my story by a few days. On May 27, the decision had been made to infiltrate the 142nd and 143rd Infantry Regiments past Velletri and to move them, Indian-file at night, to the crown of a ridge called Colli Laziali, where they would block the escape route of the German defenders.

This move, which could be hazardous if caught amidships while the regiments were strung out on a mountainside, was to be accompanied by an attack against Velletri by my regiment to hold the German troops in place. Our own position was rendered fairly difficult by the fact that we were to attack with three battalions abreast leaving, so far as we could determine, absolutely no reserve in the 5th Army for any untoward event. Our 1st Battalion was to be on the left, driving directly into Velletri from the east, our 3rd Battalion was to be in the center, attacking from the northeast, while our 2nd Battalion had the mission of moving north around Velletri close-in, in order to cut the route of withdrawal.

On May 28, 1944, we moved our CP to a tremendous wine cellar located some 5 miles from our last position. Some of our units were relieved by the 36th Engineers who then moved into our CP with us, there being plenty of room since extensive tunnels and vaults radiated in all directions from the central cellar. Our electricians, using captured German wire, set up electric lights for us in our subterranean hideout. We ate outdoors, however, beneath a grape arbor where honeysuckle and orange trees also grew and gave the place a heavenly aroma. We managed to stay there for two or three days only, and moved again on May 31 to a riskier location on a hilltop where we hung perpendicular camouflage nets to try to conceal the activity around our headquarters. Here we found a deep wine cellar with a stairway cut into the earth and leading to more of the tunnels where wine could be stored. There was no sign of supporting timbers in most of these cellars and the chip-marks of excavating tools could be seen and felt everywhere. Something about the soil, when exposed to air, produced a stone-like surface that apparently was most stable.

During the night of May 31 our two sister regiments had infiltrated according to plan and had seized the heights above Velletri. It then became the task of my regiment to force the issue by driving into Velletri. We moved our CP on June 1 to a schoolhouse near the main road to Velletri, approaching it from the east. Our bold maneuver began to pay huge dividends as prisoners by the hundreds started to reach our stockades. Interrogators assigned to my regiment and under my control worked over some 200 PWs that night, but the glut was so great that we finally had to ship the prisoners directly to the division PW cages in Cisterna.

By that time we had become expert at gauging the possibilities of breaking prisoners' natural desire to withhold information. By looking at a group we could almost automatically select the ones most likely to break under conditions existing at the front. Even so, we took nothing for granted in case our automatic selection of easy marks was wrong.

German officers, of course, were the most troublesome, but some of them thought they could delude us with false answers. This was a mistake since, once they began to talk at all, they soon could be led to the edge of a trap because we always interspersed among our questions some to which we already had the answers. We also employed the technique of putting on a show of knowledge, learned at Duera, Algeria, wherein we would state certain facts as though we were positive of their validity, merely wishing for corroboration of some that we were not sure of. Often the flick of an eye, or an involuntary motion of the head or mouth would give us our signal.

However, in the vicinity of Velletri it was fairly evident early in the game that the prisoners knew little or nothing of future plans, having been surprised by the speed and massiveness of our attack. For that reason I could not complain of direct shipment of PWs to the division cages, although, for the greater part of the war, I raised hell if anyone tried to circumvent our headquarters with prisoners taken by our troops. I had learned early on that the nearer one lived to the front, the more persuasive one could be in getting valuable information, since one's neck depended almost entirely on the effectiveness of one's interrogations.

The Germans taken prisoner were the sorriest examples of soldiers I'd ever seen. They were crumby, dirty, smelly creatures, so worn out and tired from the pummeling we'd given them that they looked like sleepwalkers.

While our own men were fatigued and dirty, morale – as is true in all victories – was as high as the surrounding hills. No one had slept more than an hour or two at a time for over a week. There was a sensing that the 36th Division was now taking vengeance for the terrible beating it had received at the Rapido River, where the odds of survival in a frontal attack across a dangerous river had been a thousand to one. Now that we were on even grounds, man-to-man and out in the open, no one was about to stop us. That was the undercurrent that kept men's feet moving when their brains were begging for release.

Our regiment took 600 to 700 prisoners of 1,000 captured by the division at Velletri and in the surrounding areas.

On June 2, 1944, I went into Velletri to supervise the disposition of some 200 German prisoners who were herded there in a square near the middle of town. Some German self-propelled guns were firing into the town from the slopes of hills to the north. These prisoners had actually left Velletri in an attempt to escape to Rome only to find the trap had been closed by our other regiments. Demoralization extended to their officers. As the shellfire increased, I marched the prisoners to a point east of town and told them, through one of their officers who spoke English well, that should their artillery register on our present position, I would move them into a deep draw nearby for their own protection. A couple of rounds straddled our site and, as I had instructed earlier, their officers marched them into the ravine. They were soon in the lowest point of the ravine while I stood on the rim in my jeep with a 50-caliber machine gun aimed at them. I had but three other men with me to control the herd of prisoners. I let them know through their interpreter that we wanted no movement of any kind. Hands were to be kept in sight and any attempt to escape would be met with machine-gun fire. Most of them went to sleep at once.

The day wore on and the shadows were beginning to worry me for I had no idea when a quartermaster company of trucks would arrive to take the captives off my hands. It finally arrived, having been lost for several hours, and the prisoners were jammed aboard. I think that it was typical of the German reaction that one prisoner, having been asleep in a thicket, woke up just as the last truck was leaving and ran, yelling at the top of his voice not to be left behind. They pulled him over the tailgate as the truck gained speed.

I finally reached the regimental CP in Velletri and despite all of the conditioning I had received to death and destruction, was aghast at one sight I saw in a yard behind our headquarters. The house had been a German CP and had been used, apparently, by the equivalent of our graves registration units. Piled 15ft high in a conical mass were the arms, legs, heads, hands, and torsos of German dead that had been picked up on the battlefield. Many of the human remnants had been bleached as though they had lain beneath snow or in the sun for months. Pieces of clothing and equipment were still draped on these relics of the battlefield.

I walked past the pile to an outhouse that had been a greenhouse and behind a door stumbled over another German cadaver. There were several more around the building, evidence of a sharp fight before our men captured the place.

I sat on a stump in that yard to eat a box dinner that had been awaiting my return to the CP. Other men were there, too, eating more of the dried-out sandwiches that had been prepared, it seemed, several days earlier. As I watched, I saw an enlisted man hold a sandwich between his lips while he reached into the pile of flesh and bones to retrieve a belt buckle he'd seen there. Then he went on eating, having cut the buckle from a belt with a bowie knife. It probably says something about what combat does to one's sense of propriety when I indicate that I was hungry and ate my meal washed down with Italian wine without much more thought of the lives represented by the ghoulish collection of men's anatomies.

While General Walker, in his diary published after the war, touted the brilliance of his maneuver in taking Velletri, I have never seen any authoritative critique of the battle that found infiltration of an enemy position by Indian file anything but an invitation to disaster. My own view is that it was a plan that took into consideration the hopeless tangle of German communications and troop movements and turned out lucky.

Chapter 16

Eternal Open City

There was no question, once we forced the volcanic hills above Velletri, that Rome would soon be liberated. It had been declared an 'open city' by the Germans and by our side as a means of preserving the wonderful art and architecture of the ages. However, that did not mean that we could shoulder arms and walk into it. Very skillful delaying actions by the Germans tested us well. Significantly we began to take prisoners dressed in the blue uniforms of the Luftwaffe. These men had been grounded by a lack of planes and had been thrown into the infantry, willy-nilly.

I interrogated some of them from the 20th Luftwaffe Division and found their morale lower than a snake's heel. They had been rushed into battle in daylight and had been cut to pieces, first, by our air force and then by our artillery, of which they were deathly afraid.

We set up our CP on June 3, 1944, in a small house located on a steep mountainside against which German artillerymen registered their weapons by use of airbursts high above us. This had been a German staging area at one time or another, and the countryside was replete with dugouts screened from aerial view by trees. It was a relief to climb into a relatively safe hole and to get a night's sleep after the turmoil of the preceding week.

Our 1st Battalion took the town of Nemi, enabling us to set up a headquarters there in a beautiful, modern villa overlooking Lago di Nemi. We had space enough for every section of the headquarters, and life was made easier through use of polished Italian desks.

The next day we set out by trucks in convoy to break our way to Rome. Everyone had his wind up to be the first to enter that great city. I went forward to a road junction where I could hear considerable shelling and rifle fire being exchanged. We were at the town of Marino near the head of Lago Albano and not far from Lago Gondolfo, where the Pope has his summer residence, which we could see in the distance. It appeared as a great mass of architecture superimposed on terraces descending to the lakeside.

Strong resistance kept us from pressing forward, and the German commander of that blocking force pulled one of the slickest maneuvers of the war, taking advantage of a tactical error on the part of two of our battalions.

General Robert Stack, assistant division commander, took command of the situation at the roadblock at Marino and sent two battalions in a double envelopment of the town. Progress was slow, but finally they were in position to close the pincers on the defenders. The German commander, at the critical moment, massed his troops in a column of fours and marched them down the main street and out of the trap. Each of our two battalion COs, having failed to maintain radio or other contact, thought the parading troops belonged to the other's unit. As a result no one fired at the German column.

That day our artillery took under fire one of our own units that had found a weak spot in the German position and had taken off in trucks to reach the outskirts of Rome, only to be blasted with our own 105mm shells.

Our 2nd Battalion plunged ahead in vehicles led by our I&R platoon and claimed the honor of being the first Allied troops to cross the Tiber River on the morning of June 5, 1944. I traversed the Appian Way that afternoon and finally found our CP in an open field beside an ancient Roman aqueduct that, in the fading light of sunset, looked bleak and worn where it abutted the Appian Way. We continued that night to a moving picture production center in the southern outposts of Rome and, because the situation was developing rapidly, moved once more to the outskirts of Rome itself where I fell asleep in my jeep on a bridge over the Tiber, waking at dawn. It was something of a rude awakening to learn that we had been sitting on top of some aerial bombs that had been used to mine the bridge, and that only the grace of God had kept us from being blown sky-high. We were glad to move out of danger and into the city of Rome.

It would be impossible to describe accurately the reaction of the Roman populace to our entry. To say that we were greeted as conquering heroes would not only be a cliché but it wouldn't begin to state the animation of men, women and children as they rushed into the streets by the millions in all stages of undress. They shrieked and cried and yowled. They jammed around our vehicles, and a beautiful girl in a kimono jumped into my lap and kissed me when my driver stopped for fear of running over the wildly exultant Italians. Then she drew back and said something like 'Barbarossa' which I took to mean that my three-day beard had hurt her face. Anyway, she hugged me and screamed something to her friends who also jumped on the jeep to the great delight of the two GIs riding in the back. Men proffered bottles of wine and jumped and yelled like kids at the beach. We moved slowly forward after I deposited the girl in my lap back into the road and stood up to try to see the vehicle ahead of me.

Great bells were ringing everywhere and the atmosphere was electric. I kept an eye out for signs of hostile resistance but deep inside Rome none came. There were many Italian partisans running around armed to the teeth and bringing to justice German prisoners caught hiding in the various buildings as well as Italians who had aided the Germans.

Because of the jam, our convoy finally took a wrong turn and ended up in a cul-de-sac. Another division's column also reached the same point at the same time and we were at a dead stop. There was a small square at our blocking point which I proceeded to clear of all civilians while Colonel Harmony went back to reconnoiter a new route. General Stack entered the picture about that time and indicated an alternate route around the Vatican. In the meantime, being old stagers, we brewed up some coffee in the small square and ate some more of the leathery sandwiches, which seemed to survive all kinds of contretemps to show up as appetite depressants whenever it came time to eat.

We managed to turn our vehicles and to gain access to the new route. Even so, progress was slow and in one area a man addressed me in French and offered me some delicious wine. His name was Count Pietro Mataloni, and I had occasion to see him again later in his home in Rome and after the war to receive a letter from him through the Italian Consulate in New York.

Our early morning route had brought us close to the Colosseum, and I found it hard to believe that here at last was one of the great edifices of history. Some of the neighboring famous arches like that of Constantine had sandbags around them all the way to the top and, of course, were not the things of beauty I've since seen them to be.

As we passed St. Peter's we could hear the thump of artillery shells in the distance. Everywhere, as we moved ahead, thousands of men, women, and children applauded and ran along beside us to throw flowers to us. We began to be concerned, as we wound our way through the hills, that a lot of our well-wishers would be slaughtered at the northern gateways to Rome. It never seemed to occur to the crowds that shells aimed at us could injure and kill them. They only wanted to stay with us, calling out the warmest kinds of greetings and identifying relatives of theirs in the US.

At one point, as I traversed a sunken portion of the road just short of our objective, we encountered mortar fire and the only refuge I could find in that trap was under a Sherman tank that had halted there for some reason.

Our troops knocked out the mortar position and enabled us to move into a defensive position guarding the northern approaches to the Eternal City.

We set up a CP in two gatehouses of a very large hospital located there. I climbed into a cot that my striker put up and slept for 15 hours without moving, judging from how my body ached when I was awakened by boys from my section who briefed me on new plans and new objectives to be set in motion at once.

It was now June 6, 1944 and we were assigned the task of pushing the Germans hard as they retreated up the Italian peninsula. While we were fatigued to no end, we still knew that dipping down for reserve strength at such a critical time would save lives and energies by preventing the fleeing Germans from establishing strong defenses on an organized basis.

The 88th Division, directly on our right flank, was to move east of Lago di Bracciano while we would move west of it. Both columns would be supported by combat commands of the 1st Armored Division or by separate available tank units in the area.

My job was to scout the road over which both divisions would move in the initial stages of their northward march. I took the boys of the I&R platoon, on whose skill the regiment had always relied to keep it out of trouble at such times, and started out. As we approached Highway 2, I found it completely lined with hundreds of vehicles. Everything was in good order with an open lane for traffic that might have to move up or down the road but German shelling was interdicting a road junction several miles ahead. We could hear the crashing of heavy artillery.

I pushed ahead with the I&R vehicles, of which there were about a half a dozen filled with members of the platoon. At various intervals I dropped off a vehicle and crew to act as radio relay stations to regimental headquarters since radios often acted strangely in the hills, and signals could not be heard from points well within their range. We tested reception on each leg of the journey so that, as signals faded, we knew it was time to insert another relay. As we neared the contested road junction I talked with a tank commander by standing on his tank's broad rump while he stuck his head up through the turret. He told me that both German infantry and artillery were involved in holding this critical juncture. We were receiving some near-misses, too, at the time.

I reported the state of affairs to Colonel Harmony and a general of the 88th Division and set out with more of the I&R platoon to find a route around the roadblock. We used a railroad bed to bypass the obstruction, and I went on ahead with one of the I&R crews in a single jeep.

It was a strange feeling being out in the open like that between two armies. We took precautions as we moved and always stopped the jeep at right angles to the road so as to turn in either direction as the situation might require. We approached a group of houses on a ridge that stood out against a fairly high hill behind the houses. I had a sergeant and a private reconnoiter the houses on foot. I saw them enter one of the houses and a minute or so later, one of them waved furiously at me from an upstairs window. I ran, crouching low, to the house, and raced up a stairway where the sergeant warned me to be quiet.

He led me to a window at the back of the house that gave onto a view I seldom saw during all of my combat experiences. In a deep valley behind the house was a scene of huge horses being hitched to cannon by German artillerymen, many of whom were stripped to the waist with red suspenders glistening in the sunlight. Some horses were plunging hard and upsetting the artillery pieces. Others were racing up the other side of the valley with blond German soldiers, many of them of extraordinary size, holding long reins and running beside the horses to try to direct them. Here, then, was the enemy, vulnerable and racing away unscathed. I got on the radio and through relays reached the division artillery, but because someone had put a line on a map and said, 'Shoot only west of that line,' our artillery was unable to bring down fire on the German artillery that had been delaying our advance all morning.

When we first saw the German artillery, it was less than 500 feet downhill from our observation post. We watched it go plunging and rearing up the valley for about half a mile before it disappeared over a hill. The sergeant and I had a few things to say to each other about redtape in the army.

The road north of Rome was strewn with more debris than I had ever seen on a battlefield. Vehicles of every description lined the roadway where our air force had bombed and strafed them. There were bodies of men and animals everywhere from where our artillery had caught them in the open. The Germans, at last, were beginning to learn what some of their opponents had learned early in the war when German might was unmatched. They now knew fear and what it felt like to be hunted down and destroyed in the way they had set the example. The stench in our noses, as we passed their dead, must have been with the retreating army constantly.

I made contact with troops on our right flank and reported back to Colonel Harmony what I had learned about the German troop dispositions ahead of us. I stated that we could bypass the immediate resistance and continue the march toward the port of Civitavecchia on the west coast of Italy.

We made our way around the strongpoint but almost immediately thereafter found a bridge blown out, effectively stopping our vehicles until engineers could throw another span across a deep-running river. At that moment, it became evident that we were 'running off' our maps. Colonel Harmony ordered me back to Rome to get more maps that our division engineers were in process of duplicating from captured German and Italian maps. When I arrived at division headquarters in a beautiful mansion in Rome, I learned that my regiment was about to be given a mission different from the one it was in the process of accomplishing. It would require our stopping short of our original objective toward which our men were marching beyond the blown-out bridge.

The 142nd Infantry Regiment was to pass through us at a designated road junction, and it was up to me to get the word to Colonel Harmony. By this time it was pitch-black and the idea of driving 40 miles or more under blackout conditions, and particularly where our troops had bypassed centers of resistance, was not appealing. I had had a good meal at division headquarters and once again had noted that, for all practical purposes, anyone fighting a war at division level or higher isn't confronted with much danger or discomfort.

I had a couple of hundred copies of new maps with me when I left under a rising moon and nearly lost them together with my life when, in rounding a curve and going at a pretty good speed, we ran into a cable stretched across the road where a tank retriever was trying to recover a tank that had gone over on its side down an embankment. We had a vertical bar in front of the jeep designed to cut cables that Germans often rigged to decapitate us during night drives. It didn't cut the retriever's cable but it sure stopped us short. After cussing out the blockhead who had failed to warn oncoming traffic of the cable, I got going again.

Colonel Harmony had gone on by foot, after wading through the stream where the bridge was destroyed, and was somewhere up ahead at the headquarters of Combat Command B, a tank unit supporting our advance. I took some of the maps and waded across the river, finding it necessary to brace myself against the current at one point. The maps suffered considerably.

Troops were walking on each side of the road in complete silence, their hard breathing attesting to their fatigue. They stopped for a 10-minute break and sprawled dead-to-the-world in the roadway. I stumbled over several of them in the dark and they never quivered. I made my way across two more streams and after a 6-mile hike caught up with Harmony and Red Lehman, one of our battalion commanders. I gave them the new instructions from division and as luck would have it, an armored car hove up in front of us at that moment, its driver having found a place to ford the rivers we had waded.

We commandeered the car and clambered aboard, only too glad to get off our aching and blistered feet. Our progress was slow, as we had to pass between the plodding troops, and the wide beam of the armored car gave many a man a bruise as we blundered on in the dark.

We made it to the critical road junction in the nick of time to stop the column there and to order it into bivouac on the spot. Harmony and I then rode the armored car back to CCB's headquarters and from there hiked the last 6 miles to our CP located on the immediate Rome side of the blown-out bridge. We were grateful for the chance to roll up in a blanket on the floor of a partially burned-out, and still smoldering, house for a couple of hours of sleep.

The next morning we found that engineers had constructed bypasses at bridge sites and had also removed mines through which we had been cavorting the night before. We moved the regimental CP to a position forward of the area where our battalions were in bivouac and then spent the rest of the day quietly in a broad field surrounded by the hills and mountains that form the usual background of Italy.

One incident occurred that showed up a phony American officer for the big nothing he was. One of our battalion officers told me of a wounded German hiding in a house near our headquarters. I took Sergeant Kelly of the I&R platoon and went looking for the casualty.

As we approached the house in question we heard two pistol shots ring out several hundred yards away where we could see a man's figure gesticulating and firing as he walked up a slope toward some underbrush. As we caught up with the figure, I saw it was a lieutenant colonel brandishing his weapon at a poor, disheveled, badly wounded German soldier. Both of the German's arms were in bloody slings and he very obviously had only been trying to find a way to surrender. The American officer was full of bluster and bravado, among other things, and I pegged him for a louse as soon as I saw the look in his eye and heard him bragging to a small group of men of the tough job he'd had taking the PW.

I told him to cut out the crap and stand aside since we had been apprised of the wounded German's presence in our area earlier that day and that I was taking him to my headquarters at once for tactical interrogation. The would-be captor gave me a lot of guff about the artillery needing to interrogate the prisoner, too. I pointed out to him that the artillery was still in Rome, that I was reporting the taking of the German to Colonel Harmony, and if there was to be any question of priority of interrogation, he could take it up with Harmony.

My main interest was humane, since tactical intelligence at that stage of the game was a nonentity under the circumstances and the man was in obvious pain. I turned the German over to medical channels after checking his scanty knowledge of German plans.

Our bivouac was located at a point just south of Lake Bracciano that was hidden from view by intervening hills. As we awaited further orders we learned that our original mission of capturing the port of Civitavecchia had been accomplished by the 34th Division, moving practically unopposed up the coastline from the Anzio beachhead.

As a result we moved out of the bivouac by truck in the afternoon of June 7, 1944, and followed in trace of the 142nd Infantry Regiment. As usual the I&R platoon led the way and reported resistance at Manziana, but this was reduced by the 142nd before we reached the town. We passed through the 142nd at that point and headed for Tolfa, which we were to take that night. Although the road was narrow, hilly, and partially demolished in places, we arrived at Tolfa at two in the morning without having encountered hostile action anywhere.

Many Italian people were in the streets to greet us on our arrival at Tolfa, and someone gave me a bottle of good wine as we moved past. I trailed our column to a point southwest of a town called Allumiere where we were scheduled to rest for a day. I rolled up on the ground on an open hillside at 4 am and managed to sleep unmolested for 5 hours, which was as good as having had a vacation, or so it seemed.

From our hillside we could see artillery bursts north of us where a large valley was split by several small ridges. Other troops were now bedeviling the German retreat while we licked our wounds and tried to catch up on our sleep that had been intermittent and troubled since May 27, some eleven days earlier, during which time we had broken the bonds of Anzio, swarmed through the hills to Rome, taken over that great city, and slashed at the enemy's rearguards without pause.[1]

---

1. Other major events took place during this time. The Allied Normandy invasion on June 6, 1944 resulted later in the liberation of Paris by those forces on August 25, 1944.

Chapter 17

Ambush

While we had a couple of days surcease from combat, nevertheless, we followed closely behind the 361st Infantry Regiment which had been attached for operations to the 36th Division. We reached the town of Montalto on June 9, after several very dusty detours caused by enemy action en route. The Germans were really racing northward and while there was some anti-tank mining by their rear guard, it was sporadic and therefore that much more dangerous.

As I checked the route ahead, I could see possibilities for some nasty ambushes in defiles where mountains jammed the roadway. At Montalto, we took over a fascisti's home, which was a beautiful, spacious dwelling set amid lovely gardens and lawns. Partisani had liquidated the fascist leader that morning. We stayed one night, as it turned out, but we slept in clean beds with sheets and pillowcases for a change from dirty sleeping bags.

On June 10 my regiment was ordered to relieve the 361st Infantry at a spot where it was held up by hostile action near Staz. di Capalbio. I went on ahead with the I&R platoon and caught up with the 361st as it began to deploy under fairly heavy artillery fire. The outlook a mile or so ahead caused me a lot of concern as I stood under a small bridge with the regimental commander who was fairly new to combat. I suggested to him that he was moving into a bottleneck where Monte Palpi came to a juncture with Laguna di Arbitello. I also asked him if he had patrolled the low-lying ridge off to his right flank, since it formed one side of the funnel that was about to compress his space and make him and his men a really rewarding artillery and mortar target. After the months of combat I'd put under my belt, I could sense danger in the situation that was completely lost on him. At least, there was nothing to indicate that he was about to probe that dangerous right flank.

I asked him if he objected to my checking out the ridge line in question and he told me to go right ahead. I felt sorry for the men of his regiment who were progressing across an open field that ran parallel to our route to the north, as though they were at Fort Henning Infantry School. One squad would run and drop, followed by another, while machine-gun crews struggled with their weapons to keep up and mortar crews wrestled heavy base plates as they displaced forward, too close to the infantry.

From the look of the artillery airbursts from hostile guns, I felt certain that a large unit was sighting in target areas for a real pasting when the trap was sprung.

I took three jeep-loads of I&R platoon men and posted the others to direct the 141st Infantry Regiment to the 361st's headquarters. It was a hot day without a cloud in the sky and yet there was an ominous feeling about the countryside.

As we reached a road junction where the left fork led off to the ridge where I suspected trouble lay, we opened the interval between our vehicles. I rode in the middle of three jeeps and as I watched a yard that we were passing, I caught a glimpse of a man's back as he scuttled away from us behind a stone wall. We stopped and chased after him, catching him in a small shed behind his house. One of our men spoke Italian fluently, and we soon learned that the Italian farmer had run because he anticipated a lot of shooting the minute we rounded the next curve up the road. He had seen several truck-loads of German soldiers pulling field pieces past his home that morning on their way toward Capalbio.

He told us of a trail that led through small trees and underbrush to the ridgeline not far ahead of where we were located. We hid the jeeps behind the Italian's home and took off on foot with carbines at the ready. The sun baked us as we began to sweat with the exertion and excitement, for I was certain that we were on the trail of real trouble.

Sergeant Kelly, like an old war-dog, was leading the patrol and he suddenly held up his hand and sank to one knee. All of us did the same and I released the safety catch on my carbine. Kelly motioned us to stay still, and he crawled slowly out of sight through a small grove of trees toward the road. The buzzing of insects seemed extraordinarily loud, and prickly heat broke out on my chest as the moments passed. We were in a vulnerable position with no cover in case we were discovered.

Kelly reappeared and crawled to where I was kneeling. 'There's a big 88 mm cannon in position on a curve in the road,' he whispered. 'The crew is sitting around smoking and talking, and there's a lookout down the road toward where we left the jeeps.'

We crawled to the left of the trail about twenty-five paces and then got up and sneaked along toward the ridge until, once again, Kelly signaled a halt. I crawled up to where he was waiting, and from there I could hear the sounds of digging on both sides of our position. We were in the middle of an outpost line screened by underbrush. We parted some bushes to our front and the sight was chilling. I could count twenty or more field artillery pieces being dug into position just behind the crest of the ridge that we were on. Some were already in place and as we watched, one crew serviced its weapon and fired a shell that burst in the air near the bridge where we had talked with the 361st Infantry Regiment CO that morning.

I heard a movement and on looking around, found that Kelly had disappeared. The other men and I retreated very carefully, crawling for the most part and keeping low when we rose from the ground. I had seen all I needed to and knew that I had to get to our regimental CO with the news. If our regiment took over from the 361st in the position we had left that morning, it would be well into the

General Wilbur receiving the Medal of Honor from President Franklin Roosevelt. General G.S. Patton at right, General G.C. Marshall standing at left. (*Photograph by Mason, H.A. (Lieutenant) – http://media.iwm.org.uk/iwm/mediaLib//467/media-467301/large.jpg; this is photograph A 14059 from the collections of the Imperial War Museums, Public Domain, https://commons.wikimedia.org/w/index.php?curid=39594146*)

After the Salerno beach invasion American casualties were buried by German burial parties as the front line shifted back and forth. The author describes the red-uniformed German men who cleaned the battlefield of cadavers. The Allies were under orders not to shoot them.

The 141st moves on to Naples after the Salerno beachhead is secured.

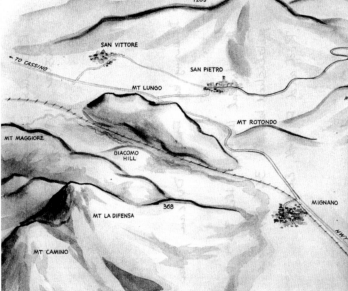

The San Pietro area; painting by Frank Duncan (War Department artist) and published in *A pictorial History of the 36th Division*. This image is clipped, thus the following are noteworthy: 1. The mountain at the top is Mount Sammucro (elev. 1205m); 2. The road off to the top right from San Pietro leads to Venafro; 3. The mountain at center right edge is Mount Cessima; and 4. The highway to the north of Mount Lungo is Highway 6. The caption notes that the German Winter Line stretched across the Mignano Gap. Key defenses were located on Mounts Camino, Maggiore, Lungo, and Sammucro, as well as in San Pietro. The failure of this line moved defenses to the Rapido River and Cassino.

View from Mount Trocchio across the Rapido River valley toward the abbey. From *LIFE* magazine: '*They stopped us at Cassino*' (*Life*, Vol. 16, No. 15, April 10, 1944).

Monte Cassino. The bombing mission on the morning of February 15, 1944, involved 142 B-17 heavy bombers followed by 47 B-25 and 40 B-26 medium bombers. In all, they dropped 1,150 tons of high explosives and incendiary bombs on the abbey. The abbey fell on May 17, 1944. (*Deutsches Bundesarchiv (German Federal Archive), Bild 146-2005-0004*)

Camp at Pratella, Italy.

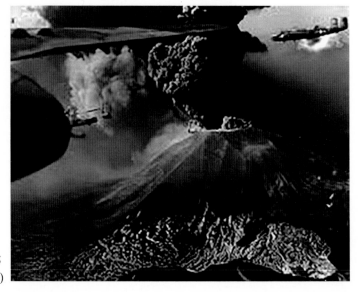

A major eruption of Mount Vesuvius occurred between March 18–23, 1944. The airplanes are American B–25 bombers. (*National Archives*)

The author in Pratella, February 1944.

FOXHOLE GERMAN

In this advanced stage of the war, many a sensible Kraut would rather give himself up than continue fighting. There are situations where a word or two in HIS OWN LANGUAGE may convince him that he can safely surrender — and so stop shooting at you. A cornered German will sometimes listen to reason — if he can understand.

Keep this and study the German phrases. Foxhole German may help you, but remember not all Krauts are reasonable.

FOXHOLE GERMAN

English	German
Hands up, Soldier	HEN-da hoe, LANN-ser
Call it quits, Soldier	Mock SHLOOS, LANN-ser
Drop your gun	Ga-VARE, HINN-lay-gen
Come here, Soldier	Come Here, LANN-ser
Come out, Soldier	Come RAH-oos, LANN-ser
Halt	Hahlt
Don't move	SHTILL-shtayn
Slowly	LAHNG-sahm
Quickly	SHNELL

Speak clearly. Accent capitalized syllables as in: vic-TOR-ious. Pronounce "G" as in: GET, and SH as in SHOOT.

Handouts to American soldiers to master 'fox hole German.' Front and back of the same card.

Le Boulay (France) September 1944. Standing third, fourth, and fifth from left: Steele, McGrath, and Doughty.

Toll gate at Schweigen with Texas state flag. Note the swastika on the right-hand side of the tower.

Major General J.E. Dahlquist (left, 2 stars) and a captured member of the Volksturm Wehrmacht, a civilian army of conscripts to fight the 'last' battle, March 1945. An armband distinguished them from regular army, although uniforms were similar. Note the 36th Division 'T-patch' on the military police (MP) helmets. (*US Army photo*)

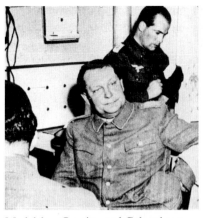

Medal-less Goering and Colonel von Brauchitsch after capture by the 36th Division. From an article entitled 'Nuremburg [*sic*] Prologue' by R.K. Doughty published in the *Consumer Credit Leader*, March 1974.

General Stack (right) and Goering (second from right), probably on May 8, 1945.

Hermann Goering (center) talks with Major General Dahlquist, Commander of the 36th Division (left), and Brigadier General Robert I. Stack, Assistant Commander (right), after his arrest in the Grand Hotel at Kitzbühel, May 9, 1945. (*United States Holocaust Memorial Museum, courtesy of Joseph Eaton. Photo No. 509950*)

The landing monument at Le Dramont during the installation celebration.

Le Dramont after the festivities. From an old postcard in the author's scrapbook. Note the T-patch signs.

R.K. Doughty in the late 1970s when he wrote this memoir.

trap and could get badly mauled. We reached the house where we had parked our vehicles and the men conjectured that Kelly was up to some more of his tricks. He often took off alone and returned only after playing some particularly heinous trick on German troops.

Sure enough, in about 5 minutes and just as I was about to leave to get the word to Colonel Harmony, Kelly showed up with a prisoner. The PW was chortling and dancing like a maniac, and Kelly was holding his hand over the man's mouth as he booted him along with his knee toward where we were standing. It soon became evident that this was no ordinary prisoner. He had an oriental cast of face and was absolutely delighted to be taken prisoner. From his pay-book we learned that he was of Turkestanian origin and had been captured by the Germans near Stalingrad. Given the choice of fighting and eating or not fighting and starving to death, he had chosen to fight – until, it seemed, he could be captured.

We drove back the way we had come, the time then being late afternoon. I found the 36th Division Artillery set up in position to fire and gave them the results of my own observations. Never in the war, before or after, had I obtained such reliable data on enemy dispositions. Our artillery took the enemy guns under fire and simultaneously set up a roadblock along the road we had taken to the ridge line in order to prevent a surprise attack on our flank and to warn others not to take that route.

I stopped at the 36th Division CP, gave several staff officers there the results of my patrolling, and looked over a captured German map which showed that the area I had observed was to be defended and held as long as possible.

I had a difficult time, as darkness fell, making it forward to the 141st Regiment CP which, as luck would have it, was beneath the bridge where I had talked with the 361st Infantry CO that morning. Trucks, artillery, and tanks were lined up along the route and I had to double the line, darting in and out as oncoming traffic blocked my way.

I found the regimental officers and others of our combat team listening to the last part of an operating instruction that would be put into effect that night. I stopped Colonel Harmony and told him my story, including the fact that I had just come from division where the command group had ordered me to get to the regiment with the new information, since it would have a serious impact on our plans.

Colonel Harmony had seldom issued combat instructions under wartime conditions and was uncharacteristically stiff-necked about changing anything. I pointed out that his plan envisaged that no enemy resistance would be encountered and that the plan to put the artillery up front from where it could support the next day's attack for a maximum distance was dangerous under the circumstances. As I described the enemy positions I had seen, the artillery battalion CO spoke up and said that in his view it was foolhardy to go on with the artillery displaced forward where it could be caught in an ambush and added that since I had had considerable action under fire, it was insane to ignore my report.

I could not understand Harmony's insistence on going forward, particularly as artillery fire was beginning to hit our convoy all along the road.

It was a monumental mistake but we proceeded with the original plan. Communications were only partially intact, and our situation required more time than we had in order to move in a direction other than forward. At least, that seemed to be the basis on which we acted. I had a very deep-seated resentment at the cavalier way in which my report was dismissed or, at least, not taken into consideration. I warned the I&R platoon to put in relay radio stations on the route back to division, thus disposing of most of its men where they had a chance to escape when the trap I knew existed was sprung.

I went forward a few hundred yards with Colonel Harmony and the regimental combat command. We took over a big Italian farmhouse and yard that straddled the road in full view of enemy observation from the right flank. Our artillery and tank destroyers moved forward of that position and the rumbling of their heavy trucks made our CP rattle.

After daylight the next morning all hell broke loose as the German guns I had seen and many others from a more northerly position took us under fire from the flank and front. As expected by me, all room for maneuver was cut off by the narrowing bottleneck of the mountains. Toward midmorning several tank destroyers came barreling back from the front and nearly ran Colonel Harmony and me down as we dashed out to stop them from going further back.

Heavy shelling was going on everywhere and our CP was hit several times and finally caught fire, which we managed to extinguish. Wounded were being evacuated by ambulance from our CP and a church near it. A Captain Herbert Eitt and I were finally the only ones left on duty as Colonel Harmony took off with several enlisted men to learn what had happened to our troops. Several 105mm howitzers pulled back from the front and set up nearby to work over the ridgeline I had scouted. Communications were not good with our division CP even though we had an armored car backed up to our door with a powerful radio in it, which we used for contact with our forward elements.

Our position was, generally, in open flat country astride the main highway on which German gunfire took a mounting toll. The Germans had actually held most of their fire until they saw our advance units starting to move forward that morning, when they opened up with all barrels flaming.

Colonel Harmony, meanwhile, had caught up with the 2nd Battalion and had directed it to attack the ridgeline where I had seen the hostile positions. He also directed the 3rd Battalion to move up to reinforce the actions of our 1st Battalion deep in the bottleneck. General Stack, assistant division commander, arrived at our CP at about that time and indicated that the 361st Infantry Regiment was being committed to a fight against the ridge, rolling it up from the south. The main effort now would be to do what I had advocated the night before to Colonel Harmony: dislodge the enemy from his dug-in positions on the ridge near Capalbio.

General Stack ordered me to get in touch with Colonel Harmony and have him report at once to division headquarters. As the general left, we received some thirty-nine mortar rounds on and around our CP. Several men were wounded, including our artillery liaison officer as he stood just outside our door. He came into the operations room for first-aid with blood pulsing out of a gaping wound in his arm. We put a tourniquet on it and turned him over to an ambulance crew who happened by at that time.

My telephone rang and for several moments I was caught up in one of those direful events that can happen in warfare. A voice said, 'This is the 1st Battalion telephone line. We're surrounded and most of my men are dead. I'm afraid I'll have to surrender.' I could hear the sounds from several German machine pistols over the phone. I tried to calm the officer at the other end of the line and to get some idea of where he was located. However, his situation was so dangerous that he could only blurt out partial impressions of what was going on. I finally learned that he was the new communications officer of the 2nd Battalion and had been in charge of a party laying wire to the 1st Battalion when he was surrounded by German troops just as he reached the 1st Battalion's main telephone line back to our regimental CP. Two of his party were dead and two wounded but were fighting back with side arms. I kept him on the line and sent two groups of men along the wire line to try to rescue the small band. It was too late, of course, and even as I listened I heard shouting and more shots and then the phone went dead. Our rescue parties reported back that they had found four dead GIs at the spot I'd sent them to but the lieutenant had disappeared – probably as a prisoner. I have always had a warm spot in my heart for a young officer who put up a game fight, as an untried and untested replacement. I hoped he had survived and would one day return home.

One of the groups I dispatched to the rescue of the wire-laying party was led by a sergeant from our regimental headquarters. He was young in age but old as the hills in warfare. He even looked grizzled with a long drooping moustache and sad eyes. He was wearing around his neck a very large leather case containing a set of field glasses. When he assembled his squad together to tell them of their mission, he turned to me and said something like the following: 'Sir, I prize these sea-glasses more'n anything I own. I'm entrusting them to you while I'm gone. They're night-vision lenses and are used by the German navy.'

I took the heavy burden, wondering where he'd found it, and put it on my field desk. Later I opened the case and found that the glasses contained large blue lenses. It was a job to hold such heavy glasses still without resting them on something. I never did have a chance to try them out at night for the sergeant returned in an hour or so and claimed his prized possession. He only shook his head when I asked him how things had gone.

Our attack against the ridge line produced a number of prisoners, once our battalions got in gear. Many of the PWs were replicas of the one we'd taken. We soon identified the 162nd Turkoman Division and learned that most of its troops were simply looking for a way to surrender when their German officers and non-coms weren't looking. It was a long, long day with our CP catching its share of attention from artillery and mortars.

On June 12 we were relieved by the 361st Infantry which, with two of our battalions, had finally dislodged the ambushing units from the ridge at Capalbio. Again, my regiment had taken an unnecessary beating because of questionable leadership.

I took with me from the ruins of the farmhouse where we had been trapped a small ceramic motto that hangs in my study today. It reads 'Salute e cortesia all'ospite gradito in casa mia.' Roughly translated it means, 'Health and courtesy to all invited guests in my home.' We had found nothing but death and destruction there, but then we hadn't been invited guests.

Chapter 18

Task Force D for 'Doughty'

W̲e moved after dark on June 12, 1944, to our rear CP where I subsided into a comatose state, or so it seemed, for many hours. We were located in a fine campsite beside a small lake situated behind ocean sand dunes. The next day we simply sat around recovering from our last mauling. Very heavy explosions north of us told of German demolitions being conducted prior to the defenders moving backward to other positions.

I was called on to make a reconnaissance of a route from Montalto, several miles behind our campsite, to Canino but before we could saddle up the I&R platoon for the job, it was cancelled as our only 3rd Battalion was assigned to work with part of a task force there. The rest of our regiment, to include regimental headquarters, was assigned to another part of the task force under a General Ramey.

Before that took place, though, I had been awakened during the night of June 12–13 by Colonel Harmony, who had just returned from division headquarters. I can't remember ever having seen a man reduced to a lower status than he seemed to occupy at that moment. He only hinted at some of the things said to him by the division CG and his assistant. He apologized to me for not having taken more cognizance of the serious matters I had reported, as he was giving out the regiment's plan of action on the evening of June 10, 1944. He also offered me any job I wanted in the regiment.

I told him I was trained for intelligence operations and would prefer to continue in that capacity. It was perhaps 3 in the morning when Harmony first routed me out. We went outside to talk and walked around the shore of the lake until sun-up. I did my best to cheer him up even though I made clear that there would seldom, if ever, come a time in the future when I could give him as clear a picture of hostile dispositions as I had offered on the night in question.

We never again mentioned that night's discussion even though I have seen Colonel, now Major General, Harmony several times since the war ended. While I do not know for sure, I believe he was put on probation by the CG which, to a professional soldier, must have been a degrading experience. I was never asked by anyone from division headquarters if I had given Harmony the report of German weapons on our right flank. I'm sure that he acknowledged that fact without making any attempt to do otherwise. Certainly, our artillery commander who had plugged for a change of plan must have recounted the whole story too, for he had lost at least one field piece, knocked out at a roadblock at the very deep end of the bottleneck.

June 14 found us moving again. We went, initially, to Manciano and from there to Scansano where, as was too often the case, we were delayed by a bridge having been blown up by Italian partisans in their great zeal to punish the Germans.

I went forward to the blown-out bridge with guides and assisted in controlling the column's movement. The 117th Recon. Troop, assigned to our task force, took the delaying force of Germans under fire and drove them out of Scansano before we got there.

We moved into the largest municipal building and learned that it had been a fascist headquarters, as attested by its comparative luxury. Partisans were roaming the countryside in that vicinity, many of them as horsemen riding sleek animals liberated from fascisti and raiding German stragglers and Italians who had earned their hatred.

We received some SP fire that evening but there was little if any damage, leading us to conclude that such shelling was largely unobserved and therefore erratic. Prisoners of the Turkestan variety were coming in from time to time, but they were of little value to us since they were not well versed in German and we had no one who knew their language. Having made 50 rough miles that day, it was good to get a real night's sleep.

The next day we were ordered forward to Santa Caterina, which we would occupy together with Roccalbegna and Vallerona. The reconnaissance troop, fanning out ahead of our column, radioed back that it was being greatly delayed by German mines that had been dug in across the roadways. Later, when the mines were cleared sufficiently to permit our passage, I saw some of the huge artillery horses, like those I'd seen at the outskirts of Rome, blown to bits from having stepped on the German minefield. This showed a lack of coordination among German units that attested to our ability to keep things chaotic for them. We also took two German prisoners who, having been badly wounded, were left in the vicinity of the minefield, no doubt for their own benefit, since we could get them to medical facilities more quickly than could the Germans, whose lines of communication were being systematically destroyed by our air force.

We encountered stout resistance at Santa Caterina, which lay below an extensive ridge line from which the Germans could see our every move while our view of their defenses was limited. When our column was shelled, we pulled off the road to cook supper during which time we watched tanks and infantry move forward to drive the Germans out. We stayed that night in a sprawling farmhouse of such strange proportions that a crazy-quilt impression of rooms and hallways still persists in my mind. It was taken under fire by German artillery that night and I finally ended up on my cot in the cellar, which was dank and musty.

On June 16, 1944, we entered Santa Caterina and had just established our CP when we were ordered to move again. I sent the I&R platoon to reconnoiter the route out of Vallerona to Cana and across country to Campagnatico. This was essential as a sideslip to the west in order to bring us back within a newly established corps boundary. As a result, the French Colonial Expeditionary Force was to be responsible for a wider zone adjacent to our right flank.

We moved through Cana in the afternoon but found that the route was impassable, except for jeeps and even they and their occupants were severely tested by the roadway. Since 2.5-ton trucks carrying soldiers had to be rerouted, troops went forward on foot once more.

I rode on ahead in my jeep and met some Italian partisans who gave me specific descriptions of German defensive installations in Pianetti and Cinigiano. Major O'Brien, who went with me, thought it silly to believe such sources of information and laughed at what he termed was a mutual misunderstanding between me and the Italians. While this smacked of his predecessor's attitude, O'Brien soon became a believer when we ran into the first German machine-gun position exactly where our partisani had said it was located. All other data later proved correct, too.

I got more information about the German dispositions from the leading team of our I&R platoon and set up an OP from which we could see Germans digging in, while specialists laid mines around their defenses.

When Colonel Harmony arrived at our vantage point, I could brief him quickly as a basis for the disposition of our troops. We set up our CP near a blown-out bridge initially and then moved to a small brick house whose owners were living in a cave at the rear of their property. A third move that night took us to a large, comfortable Italian farmhouse where I commandeered a double bed for 5 hours' sleep.

The next morning we opened fire on German positions with tanks and artillery while our infantry moved out to take several hills. By this time the flight of the German army had slowed down as it moved to positions that had been fairly well prepared after Rome fell. We received heavy artillery fire that stopped our attack in place. Our CP was set up on a mobile basis along a country lane and later we moved forward, carefully avoiding the minefields we had seen the Germans install. As I was passing the minefield, a barrage was laid down near it and the going was hairy for a few minutes. All manner of fragments composed of steel, stone, and turf whizzed past me, but I told my driver to go like hell toward a ravine whose security we reached without damage to us or our vehicle. However, our trailer had bounced high, wide, and handsomely, spilling our belongings over a considerable patch of meadow. We recovered our property after the infantry dislodged the delaying party.

We stayed in the ravine until dark when we pushed on once again to cross a high ridge and to descend, by complex trails, to a valley through which ran the Ombrone River. There we took over an ancestral home of an ex-cavalry man of the Italian armed forces. He was a very correct person in all that he said and did and was happy, he said, to turn over his home except for one room where he and his daughters slept, more for the girls' safety than for his. Heavy shelling struck near our CP that night but even so, we managed to get a few hours sleep there. Chasing a retreating enemy is a debilitating procedure, even though the joy of defeating him makes up for the sweat, blood, tears, and blistered feet otherwise engendered by such an operation.

Colonel Harmony had joined our 1st Battalion, which was attacking Campagnatico. The rest of our headquarters group sat around in the large kitchen of our CP and talked of an incident that had occurred that afternoon as we were being shelled near the minefield. As my driver had gunned the jeep toward the ravine where we took shelter, I had looked back along our route. The guard who had been posted on the road to warn traffic of a minefield laid across its width had run for cover so that a jeep following mine at several hundred yards interval was not directed off the road into a meadow bypass. It, of course, struck a Teller mine and a Captain Barnett, riding with Major Lehman, was killed instantly. Lehman was badly wounded and was out of action for a long time. It was the first and only time that I witnessed such a mishap and I could scarcely believe the force of the exploding mine. It threw the bodies of the two men at least 30ft into the air in addition to making scrap of their vehicle.

The next day, June 18, 1944, found us fighting a determined and well-placed defense of Campagnatico. German tanks, artillery, and infantry were thrown into the battle. At the same time I observed a lot of activity on Monte Cucco, several miles off to our right flank, and reported to General Ramey that it appeared to be some sort of ambush in process of preparation. Toward evening we took the town of Campagnatico and moved our CP forward by echelon.

I was sitting at the side of a road in my jeep when a jeep bearing the single star of a brigadier general pulled up beside me. It was General Ramey. I reported to him and he said, 'Doughty, you are hereby appointed commander of Task Force D for "Doughty."' I was too surprised to say anything. 'Your mission,' the general said, 'is to guard the right flank of this task force and the Fifth Army.' He swirled a grease pencil in a circle around a mountain shown on a map which he handed me and said, 'Take your force to that point and prepare a 360 degree defense. The French Colonial Expeditionary Force will be advised of your location and will make contact with you in a day or two.' With that we saluted, and he took off in a burst of speed for the forward areas.

It was but a few moments before a company of infantry, a platoon of engineers, a battalion plus one battery of artillery, a company of tanks, a cannon company from the 141st Infantry Regiment, and the I&R platoon reported to my position. I also had B Troop of the 91st Reconnaissance Squadron attached to my force. We made quite a lengthy column as we struck off east of Campagnatico to the mountain I'd been given as an objective.

While I had been very active in handling the regimental problems in battle, it was, I found, quite another thing to be the commanding officer, a situation that was not made easier by the fact that several unit commanders outranked me. However, these were old hands at the game of war and only one real problem arose after I took charge and in a council of war disposed our troops, as night fell, on our objective, which was clear of Germans. It was wild country, sparsely settled and forested so that observation was restricted and forced us to establish a network of OPs in a vast circle some 6 miles in diameter, with radio relays open at all times to warn of hostile activity.

The thing I did not like was that we were directly beneath Monte Cucco where I had observed, at long range, a lot of German activity. I spent the first night inspecting our outposts by jeep and on foot over a strange road net. I moved the artillery during the night to a position nearer the center of our area of responsibility where it could be better protected by infantry. However, I realized at once that I had insufficient infantry for proper protection of our all-around perimeter and radioed for reinforcements before midnight. C Company of my regiment was dispatched to our position and arrived at daylight on June 19.

One problem that could have been serious arose when I found, during the first night, that our tank company CO had moved his unit back toward our main body without having notified me. His excuse, when I jerked him out of bed by the collar at 2 am, was that he had felt the need to refuel. This, of course, was a court-martial offense but because I had been actively checking all dispositions and had caught this one act of insubordination in time to prevent real trouble, I simply rode herd on him without letup after I led him and his tanks back through the black night when we were really vulnerable to hostile infantry attack. I had him report hourly to me, personally, with a map overlay showing any change of position of his tanks. By noon of the 19th we had our position as well locked-in as possible, given the circumstances of limited troops and a 27,000yd perimeter to defend.

The I&R platoon and the recon troop boys were reporting continued signs of enemy troop movements on Monte Cucco. Some 200 to 400 troops were estimated to be digging in on ground that dominated our position. I went to a forward position and ordered artillery and tank fire on Cucco. Our first salvos flushed out two troop carriers from a position halfway up the mountain. As they moved uphill, tank fire caught them squarely and left them in flames. We kept up our fire on targets of opportunity and on likely defensive zones all day, scaling some 3,000 rounds into the rugged flanks of the mountain. Thereafter, patrols discovered that the German units had pulled out. We took more Turkestan prisoners during that day's shelling since, in the confusion, they had managed to evade their German officers and non-coms to surrender to our outposts.

After this first real action the whole situation, in our vicinity, settled down to a fairly humdrum existence. One unusual event occurred on or about June 20, 1944, when I received a report from C Company near the base of Mount Cucco that about 300 horsemen were observed near the east flank of the mountain. They were in civilian clothes, so far as could be seen, but they appeared ready to come into our forward positions.

I rode a jeep to the area and arrived just as the horsemen, led by someone on a white horse, came charging toward us. I was watching through field glasses and saw that the leader was in an American uniform. They were armed but held their rifles high over their heads. We had telephone communication established with all units so that I could control any firing that might be required. I cautioned everyone to hold their fire. The horsemen stopped short of our defensive perimeter, and the leader came forward with hands empty and shouting in

English, 'Don't shoot. I'm a GI.' While this could be a ruse, I believed him and signaled him to come to where I was standing outside an OP. He was an air force sergeant, of Italian origin, he said, and had escaped from a PW camp after his airplane had been shot down and he'd parachuted to earth. He'd been on the rampage for two months or more.

We had his fellow partisans come in to our defensive zone and on to our CP where I questioned the sergeant at length. It had been his unit, under his supervision and with dynamite stolen from the Germans, that had destroyed the bridge at Scansano the week before. It was evident that the sergeant had never had it so good, as the saying went. He had a bandanna around his head and several weapons were on his person, including a long stick with a lead ball at the end of its handle that British commandos used in their raids at night. This he carried strapped to his right leg.

We furnished food for the partisan group and then, just as the sergeant indicated he had to get back to his headquarters in the hills, I informed him that he was not free to go. I had a number of men standing around the room of the home where we had set up our CP and had warned them to be ready for trouble with the sergeant. The sergeant looked at me with eyes showing so much hurt that I took pains to tell him all of the reasons why I could not, under military regulations, permit him to return to the leadership of a renegade band.

First of all, under regulations as an escaped PW he had to be evacuated through channels for de-briefing, since he may have had important information for the air force.

Secondly, he could be taken prisoner again and not only suffer penalty for having escaped once but might be persuaded to give German intelligence important information with respect to my troops.

Thirdly, his uncoordinated attacks on German positions had already served to hinder our advance more than they had deterred the Germans, as witness the bridge at Scansano. He had boasted of that episode and was struck dumb when I told him that if he hadn't blown the bridge the Germans, no doubt, would have.

Fourth, his assumption of command of a band of marauders could put the seal of US approval on acts of personal vengeance that, from many reports we'd received to date, had already been performed by his group. He denied this but quickly admitted that he couldn't be sure of the facts concerning some cases where the partisans had hung Italians accused of collaborating with the Germans. I pointed out to him that since Germany and Italy had been partners in the Axis, few Italians could escape punishment for collaboration, if accused, under such circumstances.

There was no doubt in my mind but that the sergeant was smitten with his role among the Italians that smacked of a cross between Robin Hood and Attila the Hun. He was a big, well-muscled man, full of dash and verve and a natural leader. While I was talking with the sergeant, men of the Task Force D headquarters and I&R platoon, particularly those who spoke Italian, were quietly circulating among the partisani outside. On one pretext or another they had all weapons placed in one part of a separate barn while the partisani ate their meal.

The sergeant finally looked at me and with the deepest kind of despair in his voice, said that he had a sweetheart back at his headquarters and that he just couldn't leave her as he was planning to marry her. I told him to write her a letter setting forth the fact that I could not let him return to her under army regulations but that he would return for her as soon as possible.

We went out to the yard where the partisan band and their horses made a striking scene. The animals were beautifully bred specimens, most of which had been taken from fascists by the band of guerrillas. The sergeant then told the partisans, with all good grace, that the commandante – meaning me – had apprised him of certain regulations that he, himself, had not fully comprehended and that he was unable to return with them.

In fairness to all concerned, no one made any sudden moves toward the place where guns were stored. The sergeant had faced the facts squarely and in doing so had thrown off the mask of swashbuckler that he'd worn with such abandon when he first came on the scene. There were some real emotional scenes, though, as the partisans, individually, said goodbye to their leader. I returned their weapons to them and when I said they could go back to their old stamping grounds, they decided that without the sergeant, they would do better to ride to an area behind our advancing troops and call off the game of harassing the Germans from the rear. The sergeant in the meantime, having given the letter to one of his Italian friends to deliver to his waiting paramour, had started for our main body in a jeep surrounded by four I&R platoon men. The last I ever saw of the Italian horsemen was when they cantered off down the road the sergeant had taken, without fanfare and leaderless.

Later, the I&R escort reported back that the sergeant had stated that he'd never go back on his word 'to a guy' that had taken the time to explain why the guerrilla action was a mistake. He had been reconciled to his new status by the time they delivered him to the division CP somewhere along the main axis of advance of the Fifth Army.

General Ramey was in touch with me several times during the performance of our task force's mission and when, on June 22, 1944, TF D for 'Doughty' was dissolved, he thanked me for a 'bang-up' job. I had a feeling of satisfied emptiness as I returned to my regiment. At no time, however, had I seen or heard of the French force that was supposed to catch up with my task force of 1,500 men.

Chapter 19

Invasion Preparations

On July 20, 1944, Colonel Harmony called me to his trailer and told me that I would have to take over the duties of Captain Wilmer Schroebel who was the transport quartermaster of the regiment. It seemed that Schroebel had cracked under the strain and was in the hospital with what was diagnosed as brain fever.[1] I had had a similar experience with Schroebel in North Africa when the loading of our regiment for the Salerno invasion had bogged down.

Harmony said that the loading for the Southern France invasion had to be carried out exactly as scheduled because the landing craft were already listed for transport to the Pacific combat zone at a specified time.

I agreed to undertake the assignment provided that I could have all the assistance I might need, not only to maintain liaison with affected units but to prepare diagrams of ships' spaces below and above decks. Time was running short, even then, and I not only had to load our regiment but also all assigned and attached units other than the two regiments that made up our reinforced division. To make matters worse, we moved to the Qualiano area north of Naples right in the middle of our planning. We called the new area the 'Dust Bowl' since the soil that forms gumbo in wet weather becomes a fine dust in summer. Each truck or jeep that rolled through that area brought down a pall of dust on everything we touched.

Before we moved I spent 54 hours, straight, lining up a staff, checking all operations orders to learn the nature of the attack we would make and double-checking all plans that Schroebel had made to date. It is difficult to conceive but, in his reliance on a slide rule, Schroebel appeared to have loaded ships cubically – one truck on top of another. As a result, division and army had been notified that we did not need all of the shipping assigned to us. I changed that in a hurry and put artists to work developing schematic diagrams of every ship, its carrying spaces on deck, and templates to scale of our vehicles, weapons, and other paraphernalia of any bulk.

I remember checking out troop lists with colored pencils, ticking off names and serial numbers of every man within my sphere of influence – nearly 10,000 of them. I also checked every vehicle identification number and in doing so not only discovered innumerable errors but, amazingly enough, I found that a number of units that allegedly had engaged in our Salerno landing and were now scheduled

---

1. PTSD (post-traumatic stress disorder) today.

to go into Southern France hadn't ever been mobilized in the US. Some of these were barrage balloon outfits.

When we moved into the 'Dust Bowl,' I had a huge tent erected and in it put up on high easels, which I could see from a central vantage point, the diagrams of our thirty-two ships, their names, the units assigned to them, and the numbers of vehicles, weapons, and general cargo that would be loaded on them.

The division staff, as usual, was inept in just about all phases of planning the invasion. Arbitrary changes and thoughtless decisions multiplied the difficulties of my job. I had dozens of officers waiting, outside of the command tent where all of the multitudinous problems of putting armed forces ashore on a defended beach were being solved, to carry messages to their units in order to coordinate changes as they occurred. It was during this time that Captain Joe Dine of Worcester, Massachusetts heard me talking and knew from my accent that I was another New Englander. We didn't meet until later but have been friends since that time.

To make matters worse, Ross Young, who had inveigled his way out of a court martial and into a division assignment, was the division transport quartermaster. I shall never forget the moment when he called and in his infuriating manner announced that we had loaded the wrong ships for the assault echelon against Southern France. It seemed almost impossible to believe that such a thing had occurred but it had, and it stemmed from early inaccuracies that I had no way of checking until it was too late. By that time, however, I had everything else under control and could find a moment now and then to anticipate possible foul-ups and have an answer ready for them.

Later, one battalion of our regiment had already started loading its equipment and vehicles on a ship in Naples Harbor when its commanding officer came to me and said that he had been told to unload. This would have set back the whole operation for days. I told him to leave things where they were and to continue loading, but to mark on each vehicle in chalk the unit designation of the outfit that would use the vehicles. In the same way the vehicles of the other unit involved would be marked with his unit designation. Later we would affect a swap, once the landing area was secured. This worked out perfectly and kept our schedule moving on time.

But to return to Young's bombshell. His news nearly panicked everyone concerned. He had, of course, notified the division CG of this contretemps before calling me. I suddenly realized that the only damage done to date was the preparation of rosters showing, in eighteen copies, the name, address, and serial number of every man being loaded into the respective ships. I told Colonel Harmony to put out the word to delay loading, which was to begin in earnest that afternoon, while I affected a thirty-two-way shuffle of boat names so that we could merely paste over each leading copy of the troop lists the correct ship designation.

I sat there at my central desk while people around me seemed to stop breathing and with a chart of ships' names in front of me – the sixteen we had planned to load for D-day and the sixteen that were to follow a week later and which we had shown as assault ships – proceeded to make the shift.

To complicate the matter still further, one of our ships was to take our 1st Battalion into a separate landing area, where it could scramble up the Rastel D'Agay, a promontory overlooking the whole landing scene, and seize German observation before artillery could be registered on our troops.

I knew which ships would take the assault units to their dropping areas and which units would land left and right of our zone of action. Starting with the first ship we had planned to load, I changed its name for the name of the correct ship and held the name of the first ship aside until, by following this process logically, I could insert it into its correct position as the changeover came into focus. It took about a half-hour, and when the last name fell into place I looked up and gave Colonel Harmony the high sign. His eyes watered and I soon had the AG's[2] men typing new headings for the lists that they had slaved to produce and which they thought had gone for nothing.

From then on things moved with increasing momentum and I felt that I had contributed to a situation for which I had had no formal training as a transport quartermaster, for whom schools were run in the states and in North Africa.

All during this time I had managed to fit into a schedule that permitted me no more than 4 hours sleep a night meetings with the French liaison officers. They were in direct radio contact with French underground operators with whom they were acquainted and had produced some of the very best combat intelligence of the war. They knew the locations of casemates along the coast where we were to land, how many German soldiers were assigned to each, morale factors, status of supplies, and all of the things that permitted us to direct our attack against occupied strongholds while ignoring seemingly strong positions where 'guns' were made of wood and which were not manned.

They also knew that some German army headquarters had been infiltrated by French underground agents and that, at critical moments, these agents would take control of communications and add chaos to mayhem as we closed in on German positions.

The night before we were to board ship off the Amalfi Drive, I was on my way to my tent that Pete, my Mexican striker, had put up in the middle of a vineyard when we moved to Qualiano, and as I passed a squad tent nearby I heard voices I recognized, talking about the imminent invasion. They were most pessimistic and one voice said something to the effect that it would send its 'last letter' to its wife.

I walked in to where the regimental doctors were having a squirt or two of alcohol alleviated by canned grapefruit juice – a favorite drink among the medics – and gave them hell for such pessimism. I realized as we talked that they knew

---

2. Adjutant General: The chief administrative officer of a major military unit, such as a division, corps, or army. This officer is normally subordinated to the unit chief of staff, and is known as the G-1.

little of what I had learned simply because I had had no time to put out much more than the intelligence section of the operating instructions that would not be opened by them until we were at sea.

They had, of course, been impressed with Hitler's propaganda about Fortress Europa and had no idea that we would make a safe landing. I told them that only third-rate troops occupied the coastline where we would strike. I couldn't give them specifics, even then, of French reports for fear of a leak that could be reported to German authorities in time to change dispositions as we then knew them.

Before I left I bet each of them $100 that we would effect a clean breakthrough and race up through the lower Alps to meet the other armies then closing on Paris. This brightened their outlook considerably and as a result of the conversation, I was prompted to make two more moves that night before I retired – a circumstance that never occurred since I was awake and moving for the rest of the night.

First, I set Corporal Hobday of my section to work developing acetate overlays of our landing area on which every road junction, terrain feature, and bridge was given a number or a letter. Completed in seven copies, I was to give one to each of four I&R squads, keep one and, as it happened, give one to General Dahlquist after we had landed at Le Dramont, France. Through use of these identifying marks, a reconnaissance squad could radio its position in the clear, and anyone lacking an overlay would be ignorant of that position. I felt that we should be prepared for rapid advance, based on my knowledge of the situation, and that a coded group of maps would keep us immediately informed of all progress by our reconnaissance elements.

It took me some time to prepare the original overlay but, once done, the work could be carried on by the section personnel using Indian ink on the acetate to sharply define each feature.

As I worked, I suddenly realized that while it was forbidden to carry ammunition in any quantity on board troopships, nevertheless, it would be essential for Colonel Bird's ship to carry more than a normal supply in order to assure the accomplishment of his mission. It took until morning to set this operation into motion, since no one else had thought of the need to make resupply available to Bird from his own ship.

I was pretty well worn out by the time I went aboard a Landing Craft Infantry in Pozzuoli. I can't recall all of the details but I believe that we sailed from Pozzuoli to a rendezvous area in Salerno Bay at the base of the Amalfi Peninsula, where we stayed overnight.

It was a strange feeling to be leaving Italy where so much had occurred, so many lives lost and bodies mutilated, so many friends gone and I found myself harking back to the episodes I had experienced from the moment I had landed on the fortified beach at Salerno until the night of our departure. It was difficult to realize that I had gone through battle after battle, often exposed to direct gunfire, mines, and bombs and had come out without a scar.

In some ways, even though we had undergone trials seldom equaled in the annals of warfare, it was frightening to be heading away from the Italian scene to one unknown and untrusted. The setting around us was one of serenity and peacefulness with vestigial remains of ancient castles and edifices showing dimly against the evening skyline, disturbed only by guarded lights and blinking orders from military signal towers dispelling the illusion of tranquility.

Chapter 20

Southern France Invasion

On August 12, 1944, we received the long-awaited order to sail to Corsica, leaving early in the day. The sight of that armada brought a sensation of overwhelming might as, once again, craft of all kinds spread from horizon to horizon. As we rounded the western end of the Amalfi Peninsula, the Isle of Capri came into full view, looming in the distance as a rugged peak or series of peaks and domes whose brownish tones were relieved here and there by mottled green patches of shrubs and trees clinging to pinnacles much as lichen spreads over rocks. As we approached, the island appeared to be divided by a rough cleft, one-third the distance back from the landward cape, which ended high above the water where a cluster of houses stood.

I Faraglioni, the rock formation at the south end of Capri, took form as we drew nearer. They looked like two great thumbs opposing three slender pinnacles of varying height, occupying a rough circle and in one instance pierced by an archway through which the morning sun streamed.

In the far distance of a bright morning Mount Vesuvius loomed out of fog lying at its base. I could only count it a good omen that, unlike my entry to Italy at night against elemental shades of red and black, my exit was accompanied by brilliant sunlight and the blue of the Bay of Naples. We all expressed the hope that France would be as good, to those of us who had lived to reach it, as Italy had been.

The next day we passed through the straits between Sardinia and Corsica still in giant convoy. That day, too, another armada of larger ships passed between our two flotillas heading for the same drop zone but on a different course. Sid Feder of the UPI had elected to come with my regiment to learn what an invasion was like, firsthand. He told me that the division staff had recommended that he go ashore with me since I was an experienced officer and would help keep him out of trouble. It was another of those anomalies of wartime that Sid and I sat in an anti-aircraft turret on board our ship and watched the scene unfold in warm sunlight much as one might on a vacation cruise.

Our quarters were crowded but we had a small deck outside of them which was covered by an awning, where we could also sit and talk while watching the sea and half-hidden shore areas. A Sergeant Kahn, correspondent for *Stars and Stripes*, was also with us and joined in sessions of bridge on the open deck. He also had elected to join an invasion for firsthand reporting, having seen some front-line action in Italy.

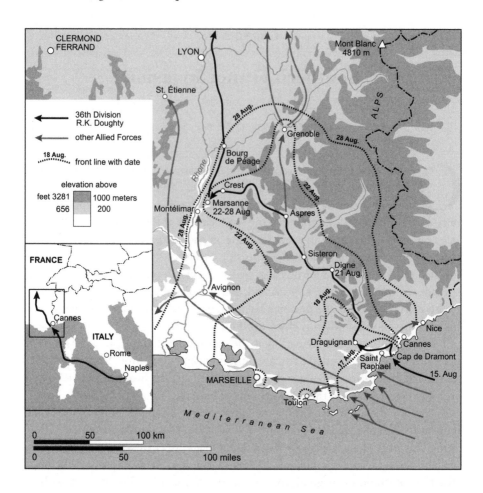

In order to reach the harbor at Ajaccio[1], we were piloted through devious channels in minefields that protected that port. Once behind these barriers we anchored, two abreast, to await the signal that would culminate in another attack on a defended hostile shore.

While our study of the defenses of the Southern France shore had shown possibilities of a very strongly held position by German troops, our underground sources, referred to earlier, had prompted the conclusion that hostile manpower was not of the highest caliber. We could not, of course, afford to underestimate the enemy, since even poor troops, behind casemates, can pull triggers quite effectively. It was also significant that all during our planning phase of the operation we had received daily aerial photographs showing that the Germans were constantly improving their defenses, particularly in our proposed landing area. Reserve troops were known to exist in areas from which they could quickly reinforce front-line units, once our striking point was identified. All in all we

---

1. Ajaccio is on the French island of Corsica. The island was under the control of Italy which had by this time switched to the Allied side.

were prepared for a rough landing followed, as usual, by a strong German counterattack aimed at preventing our lodgment on the French coast.

At Ajaccio, aware that our position must have been made known to German defenders, we remained on guard for air attack. Some of our men swam from the boats; while ashore we could observe members of the air corps, encamped at Ajaccio, swimming at a beach reserved in peacetime for high society. As things worked out, we were not molested in any way while we lazed around. No question as to our ability to hit and stay in France was raised by anyone within my hearing and the relaxed atmosphere, after the six-months drive to prepare for invasion, was most welcome.

August 14, 1944, brought a rise in tension as word was passed from ship to ship to lay a course northwest to the French Riviera. We left Ajaccio at 3:45 pm and men fell to work, for the last of many such efforts, checking equipment, cleaning weapons, re-rolling packs, writing last-minute letters to loved ones, and psyching themselves up, once more, for battle. Faces turned a little grimmer but, in general, the sense was one of relief to be getting on with it, at long last.

Strangely enough, I slept well that night and at dawn was up and gathering my gear together for the last vulnerable mile by small boat to shore. The air became charged with powerful currents as we looked out at great warships, their guns bristling from every turret, cruisers and destroyers and large cargo vessels, all in position for the imminent assault. We moved through them at flank speed to our dropping area where small boats would take us to shore.

Now the adrenalin began to run as we swept forward into fighting positions, knowing that shortly all hell would break loose and the day would bring another milestone in the history of a long war. I remember a ghostly quality to the whole scene just before the sun rose high enough to burn off the fog clinging to the water. We could not see shore. Our position lay just off the Côte d'Azur near Cannes, France. While the lack of visibility screened us from hostile view at a critical moment, we couldn't help but wonder if, later, when we needed supporting naval fires, the fog and mist would harm us.

Fully expecting an air attack in the drop zone we cleared for action, with all unnecessary equipment out of sight and guns of all calibers ready for instant use. What had been a cruise ship, en route from Salerno to Southern France, now took on the look of a grim, grey warrior.

As the sun's glow grew steadily brighter, the moment approached when the huge naval preparation would start, signaling the opening of our assault. Overhead, clouds with scarcely an opening through them were our next source of concern, for we had laid on some special bombing missions against selected casemates that would call for bombardiers' ability to see their targets near the small town of Le Dramont, France.

I stood on deck looking off to starboard when, suddenly, I saw a great rolling ball of red flame and black smoke belch into the mist, followed seconds later by the sounds of a great shell whispering its way overhead and then the crashing roar of a 15in naval gun. Almost immediately the whole scene was one of red and black as gun after gun hurled shells landward. The noise was deafening, and men held their mouths open to ease the shattering effect upon their eardrums. On occasion the smoke ejected from a gun's barrel formed a giant ring that hurtled into the gloom and was lost.

Everything on our ship quivered and danced under the concussion. No one could doubt, among our forces or those ashore, that the invasion was under way. This was it! Once more we were heading into danger and uncertainty until we could signal the invasion command group that we were in France to stay.

As the day grew brighter, we could hear above the roar of naval gunfire a heavy continuous droning sound and realized that our planes were now overhead. Through an opening I could see light striking off several flights of planes as they streaked for target areas. There were hundreds of planes, as opposed to the few that accompanied the landing at Salerno, for we had learned that the time to hit the enemy hard was during the run of small boats to shore. If the sound meant anything, it was that German troops were taking a fearful mauling.

Right on schedule we heard and felt the jarring sounds of thousands of bombs hitting home, or so we hoped, for we could not see their effect from where we stood. It was a solid sensation to realize that all of these preparatory fires and bombings were designed to help us get ashore as intact as humanly possible. Even so, we knew that in the final analysis only the doughboys of our invasion fleet could seize and hold a bridgehead and, as we prepared to face that foreign shore, tensions grew and men became quiet.

It was my job to go ashore in a smaller craft called an LCVP (Landing Craft Vehicle and Personnel) with the rest of the combat command group of the 141st Infantry Regiment. We learned later that through some misunderstanding our craft had been sent to the wrong ship. As things stood, we knew we could not wait too long if we were to control the landing effort, so we embarked on an LCT, a different landing craft from the one with which we had practiced at Salerno during the dry run of this invasion.

The forward echelon of the command group, of which I was a member, went first taking with us the correspondents and several French guides who had joined us at the last minute in Italy. It was broad daylight as we clambered into the smaller boat and waved 'so long' to the crew members of our ship. Officers and men of our regiment, still on board ship, wished us luck and, veterans that we were, we all yelled 'See you later' as we gathered speed and started into the mists.

We hadn't gone very far before we were hailed by a naval officer in a control boat. When he learned that we were in the wrong boat, he ordered us to stand fast until our assigned coxswain showed up with the correct craft. This became the hardest part of the whole landing maneuver, for by this time the fog was sucking upward under the sun's heat and parts of the shoreline became visible. We felt like sitting ducks on a millpond, but the navy had charge until we hit the beach and we simply waited. Strangely enough, there were no sounds of shooting ashore and the Luftwaffe never showed up. It was becoming quieter now as troops neared landing beaches and naval fires lifted to inland targets.

In a relatively short time the control boat, which had swung into action after halting us, came back leading our boat and crew. We transferred over the sides of our two craft and shortly were on the way to shore, alone in the LCVP. Normally we would have been part of a wave of several boats. While we had waited we had been able to see several large LCTs equipped as rocket ships bore into the shore ahead of our troop waves.

As we watched the LCTs, we could see them fire test patterns of rockets to probe for the shoreline. The rockets apparently were all of the same limited firing range so that the only way to deepen their effect was to fire them one bank at a time while the LCT ran at a good speed directly for shore. In this way the rockets would form a searching pattern inland commensurate with the distance traveled by the LCTs between firings. Once the shoreline was within range, the ships fired thousands of rockets, arching out with flaming tails, and landing with terrific impact on the shore and subsequently to areas well inland before the rocketeers broke off their attack.

The concussive effect of these rockets was brutal, and adding to the noise level were the explosions caused when rockets detonated mines on the beach, tearing great holes in the shoreline. Anyone caught in a barrage like that, whether under cover or not, was likely to become a casualty, as we learned shortly after we had landed.

I had spent a lot of time studying aerial photographs of the beach taken with an oblique view of the area as well as from directly overhead. Becoming familiar with every indentation of the coastline and every up-thrusting peak from all angles was the best insurance we had for knowing where we were at critical moments.

What we hadn't anticipated, however, was the unusual reddish color of the rocks in that portion of the Riviera. We were looking, it seemed, through rose-colored glasses and the panorama was gay and cheerful except for the man-made clouds of black, grey, and white smoke spiraling up from many sectors.

The Cap du Dramont dominated the immediate vicinity of Green Beach where I was to land, while behind a fairly large cove called the Rade d'Agay, rose the steep-sided prominence called Rastel d'Agay – Colonel Bird's objective upon which we knew existed German OPs. The navy had fired smoke shells into the Rade d'Agay, blinding any defenders located there.

Off the coast of the Cap du Dramont lay a small island called Île d'Or on which was situated a lighthouse and which we were practically certain contained a machine-gun nest, judging from an analysis made by photo interpreters some weeks before our landing.

We had to pass close to Île d'Or in order to avoid minefields and as we neared it, I was very much on the alert since we had decided not to divert any part of our force to the island and the chances were good that this might be the source of our first opposition. I remember tasting salt on my lips from spray thrown into the LCVP as its blunt bow hit an occasional large wave. Posted along our route were two more control boats located to warn landing craft away from sea mines off the Rade d'Agay.

Naval fire, by that time, had lifted to the commanding heights behind the landing beach and as we had anticipated, had started several forest fires, the smoke and flames of which added to the scenes of destruction. As we moved closer to shore we could see our artillery pieces being transported in the large amphibious vehicles called DUKWs and, of course, referred to by all and sundry as 'Ducks.' The artillery would be carried by these swimming trucks directly to firing positions and from then on would be supplied by the same vehicles running from shore to ship and back again until ammunition dumps could be established ashore.

From our position we could see two long lines of Ducks, one on either flank, sitting very low in the water. This, with the protruding muzzles of guns set up to fire if need be, gave them the appearance of gigantic waterfowl.

When Sid Feder had first told me that he was coming ashore with me, I had taken pains to warn him of the dangers. Among other things I had said that the most important thing he could do, once our landing craft hit shore, was to get off the beach in the fastest way possible. No matter when we landed or the conditions of observation, German guns would have been pre-sited and data obtained to guarantee sweeping the beach with heavy fire. I also told him that when the forward ramp of the LCVP crashed down, I'd be up and running full blast and nothing would interfere with my crossing the beach except being hit.

As we passed the Île d'Or, we took cover below the gunwales of the landing craft as partial, if paltry, protection against flying bullets and shell fragments, should they come our way. At this juncture we heard the first sounds of small arms fire on shore as German machine guns and pistols, with their high rate of fire, were undergirded by the slower but deadlier aimed fire of our infantry rifles and the deliberate chugging of our machine guns.

Three German artillery shells shrilled their way over us and blew up on the water several hundred yards seaward of my position. Just as we recovered from ducking low, our keel scraped bottom and the coxswain gunned the motor driving the bow well up onto the beach. The ramp went down with a crash, and I hit the beach with the first wave off the boat.

The impression that stays with me was one of rocks everywhere, large craters half-filled with water, and in the background, abrupt faces of stone where the beach had been quarried for years. Unlike my last landing at Salerno when I'd had to shrug off my equipment and swim, I got but one foot wet as I jumped for shore. I had known all along that the one sure route off the beach lay to the right rear and had told Feder to move in that direction.

Keeping a sharp lookout for mines and taut wires that might suggest a booby trap, I sprinted across the stony surface bearing right and skirting obstacles and deep craters. I was carrying quite a lot of gear and remember stripping a waterproof cover off my pistol as I ran. I had spotted a house lying at the rear of the beach near an overhead railroad bridge and made for it, watching all the while for possible German uniforms and helmets. Even though our troops had passed this way earlier, it was always possible for some Germans to escape detection in the darkness and await the arrival of the command group and artillery.

I noted that some small-arms fire was coming from our right flank where the Cap du Dramont joined the mainland. But straight ahead and to our left there was no sound of close-in fighting. Instead I could see our troops swarming all over the hillsides unopposed by anyone. In passing some casemates, I realized just how lucky we'd been to have the French underground working on our side. The casemates were still unfinished, and it was evident that the German high command had either written off the possibility of our attacking over a relatively narrow beach or had had to give priority to other more vulnerable defenses in the hope that they'd have time to complete these later.

As part of our orientation on the assault landing, we'd been told that the French populace had been evacuated from the shoreline to points several miles inland. If this had been true earlier, we soon found out that the evacuees were back home again and eagerly awaiting our arrival. Many of them, however, were almost in a state of shock from the bombing, naval fire, and rocket barrages.

I ran up to the house I'd spotted as the one we'd pre-picked for our initial command post and found it heavily sandbagged and barricaded, having served as a German forward CP. We set up temporary offices consisting mainly of telephone communications and radio sets, and shortly thereafter German prisoners of war arrived by the hundreds. Many of them were bleeding from the nose, eyes, and ears from our bombardment and there was no fight left in them.

Some long-range artillery, located in the vicinity of Saint-Raphaël off to the west of us, began to fire unobserved and therefore ineffectual concentrations onto the beach area and at a railroad bridge near our CP. It was of passing interest to note that, despite differences of opinion resulting from attempts to interpret aerial photographs of the beach where we had landed, there was no exit from the shore except by way of one cut at the right rear of the beach over which a railroad ran. I had studied the stereo-pairs for hours and had concluded that the left side of the beach was nothing but a barrier over which no vehicles could pass. This proved true and, again, we were in luck for later I went to the bridge over the nearby cut and saw, in precise bundles, aerial bombs already in place and wired for detonation, but unexploded. Engineers were at work disarming the bombs and making safe the one route over which 18,000 men, their weapons, and vehicles passed to form a beachhead for the 36th Division whose other attacking echelons were repulsed before they could reach the shore.

Chapter 21

Breakthrough

As I had thought possible when others did not, we slammed into the German defenders in overwhelming strength and drove through them almost at once. It's true that the 142nd Infantry Regiment tried a delayed landing at Saint-Raphaël where there is a beautiful beach, but because it was heavily mined and bristling with underwater obstacles that could penetrate a boat's hull and sink it, the landing was cancelled.

It wasn't long after I landed that General John Dahlquist, the division commanding general, came into Green Beach and dashed up to our CP. We talked a bit and I told him of my plan to send the I&R platoon out as far as it could go, reporting back every 15 minutes as to its progress. He and I went up a slope toward the little town of Le Dramont and, as we approached it, some mortar fire was laid down fairly close to our position.

The general was quite excited over his first amphibious operation and for a few moments, when the shells exploded, was glad to take refuge with me inside a garage where, instead of hydraulic lifts, there were pits for getting at the underside of automobiles. I told the general that I didn't like wearing a helmet because it muffled the sounds of approaching shells and made it difficult to determine where they were about to land. He agreed, so we both shucked our helmets, putting them in a nearby jeep and put on our overseas caps. When I looked at him a few minutes later, after he had tried without success to radio the command ship to divert the 142nd landing craft to Green Beach, his cap was on sideways.

The 143rd Infantry was to follow in our trace as soon as we had landed. The general took off in the direction of sounds of firing near Saint-Raphaël, and I went up a roadway toward a small inn. I was standing below a ridge that ran parallel to the beach and inland from my location. Later on I had occasion to wonder about the fortunes of war, for I was in the gun sights of some 200 German soldiers dug in on that ridge but who never fired a shot during the whole landing operation.

I could hear sounds of battle on Rastel d'Agay where Colonel Bird's battalion was fighting after having landed on Blue Beach. It was about noontime when I stood there watching the 1st Battalion shoot its way up Rastel d'Agay. By that time we had taken all of our initial objectives and were awaiting further orders. Troops were digging in along a predetermined perimeter that would not be secure until the 1st Battalion took its objective. We expected the usual hard-headed German counterattack at any time but as things worked out, it never struck us.

We took some 800 prisoners that first day, thanks mainly to Bird's attack on the right flank of the beachhead. By this time thousands of men from the 143rd Infantry were piling across Green Beach and fanning out, to our left, to take Saint-Raphaël from the flank and rear, if possible.

About that time Sid Feder, typewriter and all, caught up with me. He said he'd had a bad time since he'd fallen into a crater on the beach and didn't dare move out of it because of the wires and mines he could see all around its perimeter. We had a good laugh over that and from then on, I couldn't move anywhere but that he was on my heels. I never heard how he finally extricated himself from his predicament.

We were talking outside the little inn I'd approached earlier, and Sid said he thought he'd find a place to set up his 'office' – that being his typewriter. Bird had taken Rastel d'Agay and our troops were ready to move out. As I stood under some trees I felt a hand on my shoulder and turned to look into the face of a German officer. Behind him were some 200 men all armed and all dangerous-looking. The officer spoke in English with a British accent and said he would like to surrender his unit to me.

It took me about 3 seconds to realize that if our troops spotted this contingent of armed Germans, we'd be in for trouble. I told the officer to line his men up and to stack arms right where they were. He appreciated the speed of my decision for he told me he'd awaited this chance to quit all morning.

In a minute or at most two, I walked the Germans away from their weapons to a road junction where I turned them over to two MPs with instructions to evacuate them to the beach and to a PW ship as soon as possible. The German officer who was of dark complexion with a bristling moustache smiled as he saluted me and said, 'We could have killed you when you were watching your troops on the mountain across the bay.' I smiled and returned his salute and walked away. What was there to say?

At about that time General Dahlquist came to the inn and called for his reconnaissance troop commander. Dahlquist still had my map overlay that I had given him in the garage at Le Dramont when I'd said I was ready to send the I&R platoon out as far as it could go.

The captain commanding the division recon troop showed up and had to admit ignominiously that his recon vehicles were not in the assault ships but would come in the next week. Dahlquist raised hell and I jumped in and said, 'General, we can use a number of the Recon troopers with our I&R platoon, which is here and ready to go.' We loaded our I&R jeeps with extra men and provisions and sent them out with instructions to move boldly but with deliberate speed to give us a report every 15 minutes on their progress and enemy sightings. I had heard a report just before we left Italy that the Recon Troop was not planning to take its vehicles with it on the landing and while I could scarcely credit such news, nevertheless, I was ready to fill the breach. Our jeeps in any event were better adapted for use in the hilly, forested country of the Riviera than were the heavily armored reconnaissance vehicles.

Our CP was about to move to the east toward Cannes and into the hills for better radio contact with our forward echelons when anti-aircraft guns started their rapid-fire crescendos. This was late afternoon and occurred after hundreds of our own planes droned overhead, many of them towing one or two gliders. As the airborne troops were dropped by parachute and glider, the returning planes formed a second and lower column in what appeared to be an endless parade of air power. I later talked with a battalion CO of our regiment, who had been assigned to the First Airborne Task Force as liaison officer, and he told me of the impressive sight he'd seen when thousands of different colored parachutes opened and floated quickly to earth. He had gone in by glider and had been injured when landing, as the Germans had built small pylons of rocks and trees beneath grape arbors to obstruct such landings.

The German air raid on our landing site comprised but two large bombers that moved deliberately over our position in a hailstorm of bullets and shells. I never understood how they got through the flak but they did. Suddenly one of them discharged what appeared to be a radio-controlled bomb, for its trajectory changed radically in mid-flight and it struck a ship that was unloading at the shoreline. Huge clouds of black smoke rose almost immediately from the target area, and we had to take cover from the falling shell fragments of our own ack-ack.

By that time the 142nd Infantry had gotten ashore and were in position to relieve the units holding down the left flank of my regiment. This gave the 141st Infantry an opportunity to wheel to the right toward Cannes, on which it moved in three columns to establish the easternmost limits of the beachhead.

Sid Feder and Sergeant Kahn of *Stars and Stripes* rode with me in my jeep, and we soon caught up with the leading elements of the regiment in the middle of a heavily forested area.

I had been keeping track of the progress of the I&R platoon squads through radio signals showing their positions as they fanned out. The acetate overlays worked well so that I was immediately aware of the localities involved as soon as the men identified them on our overlay. I'm sure that the coordinating effect I undertook that day led Sid Feder to write a story naming me as one of the leaders of a successful landing operation, a story that hit the US press and brought reporters to my mother's home in Walpole to get more background information on me.

We worked our way toward Cannes by way of the rugged hills, stopping in a field overnight and very much on the alert against a shift in the wind which could bring forest fires into our zone. I stretched out on my sleeping roll on the ground behind a jeep, as did Feder and Kahn.

The next morning was not rendered memorable with a cold K ration breakfast. We were in the middle of a governmental reservation filled with many rugged pinnacles and hills. Roads were gravel-topped and along their flanks were many markers describing the views, particularly those to seaward, although, in the landward direction we could occasionally make out the serpentine tracings of the old Napoleonic Highway.

During the night our 2nd Battalion had gained its objective along the Cannes–Fréjus road while our 1st Battalion, in pushing eastward along a ridge that paralleled the coast, had run into, and reduced, many knots of resistance, all of which had been time-consuming. However, the 1st Battalion had taken over a thousand prisoners in two days. The 2nd Battalion, helped by the I&R platoon reconnaissance, had also had great success in intercepting a convoy and other traffic, passing both ways along the Cannes–Fréjus road. It had knocked out most of the vehicles with machine-gun and mortar fire, there being no artillery or other heavier weapons in position to assist them.

As daylight arrived we made our way through the tangled hills overlooking the Cannes–Fréjus road, to two woodsmen's houses where we set up our CP. From there I went with several members of the I&R platoon to establish an OP but we were taken under fire, since Germans on other heights could see our movement and adjust fire on us. We received artillery, mortar, and tank fire but eventually we found a position that we could approach without being seen and from there could observe much of the action taking place around us.

We held that position for two or three days and then moved on, only to learn sometime later that a German battalion headquarters had been located in a deep ravine but a few hundred feet from our CP. Again, we might have been ambushed at any time by hostile troops who chose, instead, to surrender when opportunity arose, without firing a shot. Even though I had driven past the mouth of the ravine several times, I had never noticed any signs of occupation in that vicinity. However, on one occasion, as I sat at my field desk in a window of the house where our CP had been established, I had had a sensation of someone watching me. I chanced to spot a man's figure on a high cliff and the flash of sunlight on what must have been binoculars. I sent some of our men to try to capture the lone sentinel, but the patrol got lost on the way to the pinnacle and the man escaped.

On August 17, 1944, we took over the area occupied until then by the 143rd Infantry, spreading our troops to hold both territories. This meant that our area of responsibility occupied a front that was 30,000yd long, behind which there were few if any good lateral roads to assist us in maneuvering, should we be hit on one flank or the other. The risk, however, was calculated to be a minor one under the circumstances, in which the heat was on the German army to move northward as soon as possible since General Patton was already narrowing its escape route in his dash toward Germany.

One of the unaccountable incidents that thread their way through a massive upheaval, like a world war, occurred at about this point in the invasion. We suddenly picked up a radio transmission, as our communications men scanned the several channels open to us. It was a wounded British paratrooper who, apparently, had landed on a hilltop overlooking one of the enemy's main supply routes. He called himself 'Wounded Paratrooper No. 3' and also had a code name of 'Cigarette.' While we were in touch with him, he gave us excellent reports on German positions occupied by infantry and tanks. As a result, we brought heavy artillery fire directly down onto gun emplacements, foxholes, and tank positions that the Germans had every right to believe were not under our observation.

On August 19, we attacked Callian as a means of rescuing a number of paratroopers under siege in that area who held out, gamely, against heavy odds. While we enabled many to escape the German trap, we never did learn the identity of 'Cigarette.'

In communicating with this wounded paratrooper, we had to work through our 2nd Battalion, whose radio operators were the only ones who could pick up his transmissions. Such were the vagaries of radio waves among the mountains of that area. We were also able to relay messages to army headquarters to arrange for re-supply of the paratroopers through air-drops and thus enable them to hold out until we could reach them.

We were ordered to move our CP northwest to a point above Saint-Raphaël. In doing so, we passed through the center of that lovely town and wound our way through the hills. Unfortunately, the buildings of Saint-Raphaël had taken a real pasting from our bombers. We could also see, as we passed along an esplanade near the shore, the concentration of underwater obstacles that had blocked entry to that harbor.

It was easy to see why the Riviera is such a popular resort area. The coastline is heavily indented. Tropical and subtropical trees and shrubs beautify the estates and pastel-colored villas that line the shore and roadways for miles. People were friendly and helpful even though they knew we had done most of the damage to their properties. They flocked into the streets and pretty girls hugged and kissed us as they ran alongside our barely crawling jeeps and trucks.

There were dead horses, dead German soldiers, overturned vehicles, and guns, ammunition, and equipment strewn all around the streets and roadways. The smell of death permeated the air of Saint-Raphaël as the sun grew hotter. French people were busily burying the dead and doing their best to return to normalcy even as we entered the town.

Several miles north of Saint-Raphaël we arrived at a large red farmhouse of modern and utilitarian construction, which we used as a CP. As though it were a gift from the gods, there was a hot shower awaiting us and after having lived in our clothes for several days we were happy to get clean and change uniforms.

We felt that we were within range of German artillery in our exposed position but even though there were Germans in the not-too-distant hills, we were not fired upon during the two days that we were there.

We attacked Callian, as I've noted earlier, on August 19, 1944. During the attack I went forward to watch the progress of our troops from a hilltop. Fighting was a pretty nasty business of house-to-house combat with Germans on top floors throwing grenades at our troops. We took the town and brought back some 200 PWs. That night I slept in a small town on the rough floor of an old mill and, the next morning, climbed down out of the hills to join the regiment again at Draguignan. This was our assembly area where we gathered preparatory to initiating the long trek to nail the German army before it could fall back to prepared positions along the German border.

As a means of learning more about the situation, at best difficult to keep up with, I dropped by the 36th Division headquarters at Draguignan where the G-2, Frank Reese, briefed me. In the vicinity of the division CP and for miles around it, were the smashed frameworks of gliders by the score. Caught in trees, too, were parachutes with dead paratroopers still suspended in them. These poor devils had been shot before they could reach the ground. However, those paratroopers that had landed had captured a German general and killed or captured his entire staff.

Later I learned that this was the most successful air-drop mounted during the war, which made me glad that I had not seen others. Even so, the Southern France Invasion was well launched and the German defenders were running before us as fast as they could go.

Before I left that area, I received data from some French civilians out of Grasse that German troops were concentrating near that city. Because the paratroopers were to take over our position to free us for the northward chase, I went to Saint-Raphaël where General Frederick called me in to report my findings. He was a very pleasant, thin but strong-bodied man who listened intently to what I had to say and then, turning to his G-2, said, 'Why in blazes can't we get intelligence reports like Major Doughty has just given us?' I bowed out since it was somewhat embarrassing to have events turn to personalities in my presence.

Chapter 22

Hot Pursuit

On August 21, my regiment left Draguignan, France, to follow the well-marked trail of a task force that had been put together somewhat hastily by Army under the command of a General Butler. The breakthrough that I had anticipated had occurred, and Butler's fast-moving force of infantry, artillery, and tanks was snapping at the heels of the retreating Germans and exploiting the confusion.

Much of the confusion had been caused by the FFI[1] in accordance with long-laid plans, some of which had come to my attention when we were in Italy. It appeared that the French underground had so successfully infiltrated the German communications network that, at a crucial moment, it had sent false information to the German headquarters in command of all defenses in that area of France. Having cut the German telephone lines between Draguignan and a city called Digne [60 miles to the north] in the lower Alps, the FFI had sent misleading data over its own lines into that headquarters.

As a result, the German general and his staff, having been told that Allied troops were just entering Draguignan when, in fact, Task Force Butler was on the outskirts of Digne, were captured intact and the town taken with only token resistance. In addition 500 German soldiers who had formed the garrison of Digne were also captured. Eight of our tanks and armored cars raced into Digne on the day it fell and captured the general, who was taking a leisurely bath. Being caught with his pants off must have contributed to the lowest morale in that part of France. The surprise was so overwhelming that all of the German defenders quit without returning fire.

When my regiment reached Digne everything was under control. We took over the Ermitage Hotel which had been headquarters for the German army. I recall looking around the hotel upstairs and finding it littered with eiderdown where our men, in searching out German skulkers, had bayoneted pillows and mattresses.

Local gendarmes reported to me, and I went with them through various buildings of the town looking for important documents, maps, stragglers, and minefields, finding a number of each but always warned ahead of time of their whereabouts by FFI who were everywhere with their skeletonized machine pistols, knives, and hand grenades.

---

1. Forces Françaises de l'Intérieur.

The FFI had taken some prisoners and had confined them in a former German concentration camp. Among the prisoners was one mealy-mouthed German sergeant who, he said, had once lived in Cairo, Egypt. He tried to tell me of his sorrow at having to fight the Americans again. I laid into him pretty strongly and assured him that, so far as most Americans were concerned, we'd do our best to see to it that Germany never again would be allowed to rearm, now that it had been responsible for two world wars.

Strangely enough, some of the French people of Digne wanted me to arrange for the sergeant to be let off easily. It seems that he had treated some of their fellow citizens well, saving their lives when orders had been issued to have them shot. I told the FFI that he would be treated as any other prisoner of war and would be evacuated through channels to a PW camp, probably in the US. This was better than he deserved and at the same time gave him the protection of the Geneva Convention, as little as most of the enemy deserved such protection. I found many German soldiers and officers completely obsequious and servile when the shoe was on the other foot.

August 22, 1944, proved to be one of the wildest days of the war for me, even though it started out innocuously enough. Having borne the brunt of the fighting along the shoreline, the 141st Infantry was in division reserve. As such, it was ordered to make an administrative move north so as to keep the division's various elements within reasonable distance of each other. I had had a wonderful night's sleep in the Ermitage Hotel, which our men had cleaned up in the hope that we might stay there for some rest. We'd reveled in clean sheets, soft beds, and electric lights after weeks of dirt and candlelight at night. However, the morning brought news of our next move.

Colonel Harmony, my regimental CO, and I went to division headquarters at Sisteron, several miles north of Digne. We had just walked into the office of the chief of staff when General Truscott, the corps commander, entered and in a rather terse conversation learned that 'Skip' Vincent, the chief of staff, had not acted on orders that Truscott had given him the day before. 'Since when have a corps commander's orders been something to forget?' Truscott shouted when Vincent, in the most ignominious way, had said that he had forgotten to transmit Truscott's orders. Truscott struck the chief's desk with a riding crop. We learned later that the division G-3 had received the order and had forgotten to tell anyone about it, so that the chief of staff had taken the blame on his own shoulders.

We stood there while Truscott, pointing to a wall map with his crop, said, 'Montélimar and the high ground north of it are the most important pieces of ground in the whole of Southern France. If we get there we trap the whole German army retreating north up the Rhône Valley. Fifteen hours, delay, since I issued the order, will mean all the difference between our walking into it or fighting like hell to get it – but get it we will!'

Fur began to fly in all directions shortly thereafter. Our regiment, of course, was named to race for Montélimar to seize the key ground. The fact that the regiment was moving administratively and not tactically meant that our job would be twice as hard to perform.

In the meantime, while we were listening to General Truscott, General Dahlquist, having been misinformed as to who held Montélimar, had flown there in one of the division's artillery spotting planes, only to receive heavy German anti-aircraft fire. He was lucky to get out alive. He landed at the division CP just as I was about to move out with the I&R platoon on a cross-country, mountainous run toward an unknown objective somewhere in the Rhône Valley, 55miles away. As I left, the general was grounding a convoy of trucks in order to have vehicles enough to move our 2nd Battalion to Montélimar without further delay. Colonel Harmony had already started for Crest, but I was delayed a few moments while I radioed Lieutenant Colonel Matchelott, another officer commissioned by General of the Armies Pershing, whom I had met at Fort Leavenworth and who was the executive officer of the 141st Infantry. I briefed him on the new developments and told him what might develop to delay movement of the regiment's rear echelon.

The speed of our race through that mountainous area still remains a blur in my mind. We had no way of knowing whether German troops had found their way east to set up roadblocks that would cut us down as we sailed around corners as fast as our vehicles would take us. We drove from Aspres to Saint-Dié to Crest, where I arrived in early afternoon. Just outside Livron I met Colonel Harmony again. While that town had been shown on overlays as the headquarters of Task Force Butler, again, our information was erroneous, for the Germans held it.

I shall always be glad that I had studied French, for I saw a group of FFI squatting around a small fire beside the road and stopped to ask what they knew of German dispositions. They said that a German anti-tank gun was located just around the next curve in the road, not too distant from where we were talking.

In the group was a US colonel named Clyde Steele, who was to figure strongly in the fortunes of my regiment during the next few weeks. Once we had all the information that the Maquis could give us, Colonel Harmony headed south to reconnoiter the terrain near Condillac, from where he hoped to jump off to attack Montélimar.

I set up I&R platoon guides from Crest to Marsanne and then returned to the FFI roadblock, where a couple of Frenchmen took me to a nearby house for fried eggs, salad, bread, and wine. It was my first meal of the day and I put away a lot of food to the satisfaction of the woman who, poor as she was, pressed me to eat more. Later I returned to Crest to await the arrival of the first units of our regiment. It was my job to brief their officers on our mission and to tell them the places to which they would move their troops in carrying out their assignments.

Our 3rd Battalion was still in Digne some 60 miles away, our 1st was somewhere on the road from Digne to Crest and the 2nd was expected to arrive at Crest momentarily. While waiting I went to a small cafe and ordered some wine, which I drank surrounded by some of the local people who clustered around and shook my hand. They expressed their thanks in the self-conscious manner of country people but with great sincerity.

While I sat in the cafe a little old woman named Mme. Vve[2] Clement Nivon came to me and said that her son, George Nivon of 4654 Nob Hill Drive, Los Angeles, was a professor at 'Le College Occidental' and that she would appreciate my writing to tell him that she was safe and well, as were other members of her family. I took her card and while several months elapsed before I could find an opportunity to do so, I finally delivered her message. I never received an acknowledgment.

Hans Wagner, regimental PW interpreter and interrogator, came along then accompanied by a fine-looking Alsatian woman he had met in the town, and the three of us sat on a tiled terrace and drank some champagne that the proprietor made available to us.

In the meantime, I had set up a roadblock at the entrance to the town where I planned to meet Lieutenant Colonel Bird of the 1st Battalion to give him his orders. I returned to that post and found more of the townspeople there talking to the I&R men and giving them fruit and vegetables. By the time darkness fell, Bird had not shown up and since I could not know when he'd arrive, I rolled up in a blanket and stretched out on the gravel driveway of a filling station while my men took turns standing guard.

Bird finally arrived at 4 am having been greatly delayed by driving blackout in tangled terrain and narrow roads. I gave him a rundown by flashlight of the location of friendly and hostile troops and told him where he was to move his battalion in preparation for the attack on Montélimar. His battalion did not show up until 6 am.

Wagner, an officer named Shamburger, and I had breakfast in a nearby French home that morning, where fine china and silverware added to the pleasure of another home-cooked meal. We started for Condillac at once, arriving at an old schoolhouse, long ago condemned, according to a sign in French, as unsafe, where we found our regimental CP.

This was now August 23 and we were already getting an impression of what we were up against. The 2nd Battalion had been ordered to attack Montélimar as soon as possible after daylight. This was our first mistake; high ground overlooking the town should have been our first objective because its capture would dictate who held Montélimar.

When we arrived at our CP we found that reports had already been received of infantry and armored attacks hitting our front-line troops at daybreak. It was obvious to us that the Germans would fight like tigers to keep us from cutting their only escape route east of the Rhône River. The western slopes of the Rhône Valley were extremely unhealthy places for German troops since the FFI were there by the tens of thousands, attacking at night in swift but bloody raids, setting

---

2. Short for *veuve*, widow in French.

up roadblocks and ambushes and, in general, bedeviling the Germans in every way they could devise while avoiding head-on battles.

The Germans we took prisoner in the next few days indicated that they would prefer to fight a well-trained, formal enemy than to face the bushwhackers of the French underground, who showed them no mercy.

When our 2nd Battalion moved on Montélimar, it ran into very heavy opposition from infantry, tanks, SP guns, and supporting weapons, all located in good defensive positions. A full day's fight found our troops unable to penetrate the German positions. In the meantime, our 1st Battalion had moved north of La Coucourde to try to establish a roadblock on the main Rhône Valley road at that point while taking the high ground overlooking the escape route from the east. This was a long ridge rising to three salient peaks, any one of which would have required a full regiment to capture from determined defenders.

I was busy by that time interrogating prisoners of war. In a short time we had identified the 198th German Infantry Division as well as the 11th Panzer Division, one of Germany's finest armored units still left in fighting condition. I also learned the identity of another German division which was located south of our position, and of a battalion of flying students who had been en route to Germany when we cut them off with our delayed flanking movement. Everything else that could be identified seemed to be small units, remnants of larger organizations that had been destroyed in the initial assault against southern France.

We could hear sounds of very heavy fighting emanating from the site where our 1st Battalion was attempting to take the heights north of La Coucourde. Reports from that battalion's headquarters confirmed that fact, while reports from our 2nd Battalion were few and far between, being limited to occasional radio signals. Shortly, we lost all contact and they appeared to be in danger of being cut off by the German attackers. Later the next day, observers reported that German tanks and infantry had infiltrated past the 2nd Battalion's position during the second night and that we could no longer maintain any contact with that battalion.

The situation was turning grim, for we were beset from three sides by strong German forces trying to extricate themselves from a trap while simultaneously we were trying to attack to take the key ground for cutting off the German retreat to the north. We had all available units committed to battle with nothing left for maneuvering around German forces. Our 3rd Battalion was still somewhere on the road from Digne, a situation that had developed when all available transportation had been employed to carry our 1st and 2nd Battalions to the Montélimar area in an attempt to overcome the odds placed against us when the division staff had failed to transmit the corps CG's orders. I never learned whether the defaulting officer was court-martialed for such a serious lapse but he should have been, for the delay cost us in casualties.

In the meantime, a steady stream of traffic was moving north along the Rhône Valley road that we were trying to wedge shut. The fact that we slowed down and at times completely stopped that flow attested to the determination and fighting skill of our regiment under unusually difficult circumstances.

Our 3rd Battalion finally arrived and after several changes in the tactical situation, particularly one German armored thrust from the north that threatened to overrun our position, it attacked to the south of the 1st Battalion to try to take the ridge dominating the Rhône Valley highway. Sharp fighting took place all that day and if we had not had seven battalions of field artillery, including some Long Toms, we might have been wiped out by tank and infantry charges, pushed with tremendous vigor by the German troops. However, artillery blunted each such attack and turned it back. During this time we were awaiting reinforcements from the rest of our division, some of whose units had penetrated well to the north and would, therefore, take days to reorganize for a return southward to our battleground. In the meantime there was a sense that another debacle was about to occur, which would have been par for the course followed to date by the 141st Regiment.

We later captured a document which, when translated, proved to be the order of the 198th German Division CG to attack us that day, August 24, 1944, reinforced by a number of Tiger tanks of the 11th Panzer Division. We stood off three regiments with our one regiment and our artillery, recently equipped with proximity fuses that produced air-bursts just over the heads of attacking infantry. They were deadly in their effect.

The road network in this hilly and mountainous area was baffling both to us and to the Germans. It was a labyrinth of small country roads twisting and turning in all directions. Our force was too small to establish a block on all roadways so that no matter how we positioned ourselves, German forces could infiltrate past us.

On one occasion we were warned to be ready to fight off a coordinated infantry and armored attack coming at us from the south. Since we were already locked in a life-and-death struggle with forces hitting us from the west and north, there seemed little chance that we would be able to turn to meet the new threat without exposing our flanks and rear to real danger.

Fortunately, a portion of the 143rd Regiment arrived with more artillery in time to allow us to make dispositions toward the threatened southern front, although this meant vacating the hard-won ridge position which we had finally secured and from which we were decimating the German columns on the Rhône Valley road.

Our morale was not improved when, the next day, we were ordered to retake the ridge we'd evacuated. It was due only to the skill of our 2nd Battalion commander, Lieutenant Colonel Critchfield, that we had successfully extricated ourselves from that position in time to meet the threatened attack on our southern flank.

At about this time our regimental CP became the focus of a lot of shelling due, no doubt, to the amount of activity around it where messengers from all directions were converging. Once we began to receive fire from three directions, we moved out to a position close to the town of Marsanne, where we took over a large farmhouse and barn. It was on a forward slope in full view of enemy observers, and it overlooked a spur valley leading to Marsanne from Montélimar. While we should have been a target for even more artillery fire than we had received at the condemned schoolhouse, I had camouflage nets erected vertically, screening the approaches to the farmhouse.

Behind us at a distance of about 500yd a deep ravine was located. I figured its approaches were screened by low-lying ridges from the enemy's observation. It was a good risk. I thought that the Germans would not shell such an obvious target as the farmhouse, even though they could see vehicles turning toward it. Instead I hoped they would fire at the ravine, which they did.

One or two shells, just for luck, were dropped near enough to the farmhouse to blow out several windows with their concussion, but in general we were left alone. Our vehicles were parked in a sandpit about 100ft past the farmhouse but out of range of the shellfire directed on the ravine, and screened from observation on the route from the farmhouse to their location.

We were, once again, ordered to put a physical block across the main road over which the German army was running for home. Colonel Harmony personally led the fight that finally blocked all passage along the Rhône Valley road. However, German reaction was immediate and overwhelming as their tanks and strong infantry units threw our men out of the blocking site. We already knew that we were stretched too thinly to blockade the retreating Germans but, since they were being pushed from the south by the rest of the 7th US Army, our efforts were delaying them long enough for heavy casualties to be inflicted on them by the pursuers.

The Germans continued to hold La Coucourde and the dominant terrain nearby and when, later, a much larger blocking force than the one we mounted tried to reassert the roadblock, it failed to do so.

Our efforts, however, and our constant cannonading of the retreating enemy troops forced the Germans to flow around the blocking site in order to find a different escape route through the hills which, by this time, the 36th Division as a whole was defending.

The day came when something had to give. The Germans put on an infantry-armor attack that looked like something I had witnessed at the Infantry School at Fort Benning. I had a grandstand seat in the farmyard where our CP was situated. Screened by some shrubs, I could look down to the south across a clear valley that rose at right angles to the Rhône Valley.

Suddenly eighteen Mark IV German tanks, followed by five or six of the newer Mark Vs, debouched from a tree-lined ravine and headed toward my position. Behind them came wave after wave of German infantry in their grey uniforms. Everyone in our division was standing to arms ready for the onslaught. I was listening in on a telephone network that connected all of our artillery and heavy weapons units and which was under the supervision of the general commanding our division artillery.

In front of me, hidden from sight with its long-barreled gun screened by camouflage nets and shrubbery, was a TD half-track and crew tracking one of the lead tanks that was slowly moving toward us but which was still half a mile away. 'Steady' came the general's voice over the network. 'Do not fire until I give you the signal. Hold It, Hold it!' Then the single word 'Fire!'

The ensuing cannonading was scarcely believable. Before the dust blocked my view I heard the TD's hollow sound as its 3in naval gun cut loose and clobbered a tank at 1,200yd. The tank seemed to lift off its tracks as the ammunition inside detonated in a number of explosions that went on for several minutes. As the tank burned brightly, it could be seen even through the dust and smoke of battle.

At the same time all of our artillery fired a 'TOT,' as it was called, a 'Time on Target.' This meant that firing had been so coordinated by the Fire Direction Center that, though the shells left the guns of the various batteries at different intervals, they arrived simultaneously at the target area. Almost immediately the whole valley, with its thousands of advancing German infantry, was blocked from view by clouds of dust that rose as shell fragments struck everywhere. Just before that happened, though, I saw several tanks take direct hits from artillery and TDs which stopped them cold!

Most of our artillery and all of our infantry weapons were directed at the infantry, which was being decimated by airbursts produced by our proximity fuses. These fuses, as shells neared their targets, were triggered by proximity to the ground or any object in their way. In bursting 40ft in the air, they would rain down thousands of fragments that would hit men even though they were in foxholes. Because they could be triggered by airplanes, our artillery could not use them when firing past our spotter planes.

Through rifts in the smoke and dust I could see many German troops lying still on the ground. Front-line observers using the artillery network could be heard directing fire onto targets, and even though the Germans regrouped and attacked time after time, our heavy fire knocked them back with extremely heavy losses. It was such an awe-inspiring scene that I, momentarily, forgot that my position was vulnerable – a bullet or stray shell could easily penetrate the bushes through which I was looking.

I was very much concerned about our position, since both flanks of the division were flapping in the breeze. It seemed to me that, while the Germans were hitting us head-on in a frontal attack, they must also have sent other units to find and turn our flank. This would have been catastrophic and could have annihilated our units caught in between German grindstones.

It so happened that on the night before this grand-slam attack by the German army, I had talked with the commanding officer of the FFI in that area. A French lieutenant, whom I had befriended when he broke through to our lines from Lyons, where he had awaited a chance to get out from under German control and back into the war, had taken me to the FFI headquarters in a secluded valley. The lieutenant's name was Giraud de la Garde. It was not until the war ended that I learned that 'Zero,' as he had asked us to call him, was a real, live duke and count in French royalty and had won the Croix de Guerre in earlier fighting before the Germans knocked France out of the war. (In 1979, de la Garde was a marquis, not a count.)

He had escaped German authorities at Lyons by riding his bicycle out of the city while wearing his French officer's uniform under his civilian clothing. As he pedaled south toward the sounds of firing, where we were trying to blockade the main route, he had been arrested and thrown into jail as a curfew violater. He told me that he had almost panicked when taken to jail because, had his uniform been discovered by the Germans, he'd have been shot out of hand. He kept cool and shortly remembered that, as an air-raid warden appointed by the Germans, he was authorized to be out after curfew. He called the jailer, produced his pass and in a great show of bluster conned his way back to the street. Without his bicycle he had to hoof it and upon nearing the battlefield had been taken under fire by both the Germans and our troops, who suspected anyone coming into our lines from any direction. He told me that he had lain in a ditch that was half-full of water until, under cover of darkness, he had infiltrated through our lines and reported to my regimental CP.

I was the only one who could really communicate with him, and when I saw the condition of his uniform I immediately had him outfitted with clean uniform to which he could affix his French insignia. I also showed him where he could get a shower and something to eat. I never knew anyone to be more grateful for even the smallest attention paid him.

He was a Saint-Cyr[3] graduate and a highly qualified officer, and we grew to be great friends before he left us at the German border some months later. His knowledge of French terrain, political affiliations, and FFI locations was invaluable to our operations.

Before taking me to the local FFI commandant, he warned me about another French underground organization called the FTP of which I had never heard. It was named the Francs-Tireurs et Partisans and was communistic in its orientation.

The FFI commander was using a *nom de guerre*.[4] He was a French priest named Father Fraise, and long after the war he came to visit us in Mamaroneck. We had never really seen each other, as it was full dark when I met him along a road behind our lines. However, he remembered my comprehension of his problems and the need for his followers to avoid formal warfare when we discussed the manner in which the FFI could assist us.

We agreed that he would extend our flanks by posting his men as observers and warning us of the approach of any hostile forces from the rear or flanks. Strangely enough, Father Fraise had been a Saint-Cyr graduate too and was a fully qualified officer even though, belatedly, he had turned to the priesthood, forsaking the military until the Germans occupied France.

---

3. French military academy.
4. Wartime alias name.

Under his command were some 8,000 Maquis who could, through judicious placement of outposts and observation posts, extend our flanks for miles. Because of this safeguard I was not as much concerned about a surprise flanking attack as I might, otherwise, have been.

The division headquarters had been set up south of our zone of responsibility and while I didn't know about it at the time, that headquarters was partially overrun by the organized German attack that I had witnessed from behind the shrubbery at our farmhouse. It is still a puzzle to me that the Germans, normally good tacticians, had failed to try an outflanking move to knock us out.

I believe it was because of the heat they were taking from the 7th Army divisions to their south, which produced enough panic to influence their choice of a frontal attack against a veteran division.

That the division headquarters was nearly overrun caused a lot of hilarity among the lower units because it was our view that most of the division staff was scared witless (or words to that effect) whenever a shell exploded within 5 miles of their location.

Our artillery, having repulsed the strong German move to oust us, shifted its fires onto the main escape route. Our 8in Long Toms, with an effective range of 8 miles, were firing with deadly effect upon the massed convoys trying to surge past our position. For 16 miles up and down the Rhône Valley road, the real meaning of carnage became clear.

Thousands of vehicles, hundreds of great horses that drew German artillery, tanks, troop carriers, staff cars, SP guns, and cannon were strewn together with thousands of dead men along that route. It appeared as though our air force had caught a gigantic convoy in the open and destroyed it. Actually, we had requested the air force to avoid our sector simply because, in the early going, we had received some close-in bombing assistance most of which caused casualties in our own ranks. It was too difficult to control bombing when targets were close to our lines.

By the time the battle ended on August 29, 1944, we were still in position and some 4,000 German dead were still lying where they fell. The stench of dead animals and corpses of men was almost unbearable, for the summer sun soon decomposed all flesh.

We had also taken thousands of prisoners, among whom was one German general who, due to the complexities of the road network through the hills, drove up to our lines and was proceeding merrily on his way when a roadblock, alerted to his passage by front-line observers, captured him. He was the first officer I saw who had an outsized German Luger pistol, which was carried in a wooden holster at his side. The holster could be fitted to the pistol's grip to convert it to a shoulder-firing weapon. He had made a move to go for his pistol when stopped, and a GI had simply hit him in the head with a rifle butt, effectively stopping any further resistance. Later, when under interrogation, the general complained to me about his treatment. I told him that the only mistake the GI had made was to spare his life and that so far as I was concerned, he should have been killed.

During this fight the artillery supporting our division had expended some 75,000 rounds of all calibers. The enemy suffered 11,000 casualties. Some 1,500 vehicles were destroyed, and the artillery of 2 divisions was wiped out. In addition, the Germans lost three 380mm railroad guns. In short, at La Coucourde the German 19th Army was effectively destroyed. This was fairly well demonstrated by the fact that little or no German resistance was encountered thereafter until we reached the Vosges[5] foothills beyond the Moselle River.

---

5. Vosges: pronounced 'Vooj' – long 'o' and both 's' are silent.

Chapter 23

'Strategic' Tactics

In the last moments of the battle at Montélimar, Colonel Harmony was badly wounded while conducting an attack against the German forces guarding the main Rhône Valley route. While Lieutenant Colonel Critchfield was designated acting regimental CO, he was almost immediately relieved by General Dahlquist, under circumstances where Dahlquist was anxious to make up for the bonehead play made by the division staff when it 'forgot' the corps commander's orders.

Critchfield had come to the barn near Marsanne, where our headquarters was located, and upon talking with General Dahlquist on the telephone had demurred when the general ordered him to move out, at once, to follow and harass the retreating Germans. I heard Critchfield say that it would take two days before he could get the regiment out of its widespread defensive position and in shape to attack. He pointed out that the fighting had been almost constant for a week and the troops were exhausted, since no one had slept more than an hour or two out of each day.

The general, apparently, let loose with every kind of excoriation which Colonel Clyde Steele, standing near him, overheard. At this juncture in the war, all of the bully boys who had clung close to the Pentagon began to sweat for fear that their future careers would suffer if they didn't establish some kind of combat record. With Patton streaking across France and our army closing to the north, after successful lodgment in Southern France, it looked like the 'glory road' to Berlin was opening. In fact, we named the so-called 'War Department Observers' the 'Glory Road Boys' as they descended on us from light planes as we pushed toward the Vosges Mountains. Every day would find half a dozen colonels looking over the field, secretly picking a slot for themselves but discreetly maintaining their special designations as 'observers' just in case the going got too hot for them. Once a man has laid back out of reach of danger, any effort he makes thereafter to take on the guise of a fighter fools no one who has been in the thick of the battle. 'Phoney' is the word that described all of the latecomers. They disappeared the first moment that any resistance was met.

Colonel Steele was designated regimental CO of the 141st Infantry and the results were nothing short of weird. We first saw him in that capacity in the late afternoon of the day that General Dahlquist relieved Critchfield of command. Steele came on like gangbusters and, sure enough, he wore a pearl-handled revolver in his holster. We were assembled in a room when he strode in and announced in a loud voice that he understood 'this regiment is yellow!'

His gaze dropped first as all of us who had seen over a year of front-line combat at that moment glared at him. No man ever got off to a worse start. It was obvious that Dahlquist, in a burst of spleen at being frustrated by Critchfield, had said something about our being yellow.

The more Steele talked, the worse his position became. Shortly he was running out of words. We received him in deadly silence and when he finally ended up, lamely, with a statement that no outfit he'd ever been with had failed to improve under his leadership, Critchfield said 'Is that all, sir?' and, without awaiting a response, walked out. I turned on my heel and went out to the barn where our regimental sections were housed to take care of some housekeeping details.

That night, after chow, which was served late, I received a call to see Steele in his quarters. The runner who came for me said he would take me to him. I was in the farmhouse at the time. We went out through the dark night and into the barn. By this time there was no shelling going on from either side.

The runner lifted a trapdoor in the barn floor, which I had never seen before, and we went down a ladder to the basement. In the center of the dirt floor was a cemented square in which was a steel plate. It was hinged and stood open. I looked down into a vault where Steele had had his bunk made up some 8 or 10ft below the basement floor level. It smelled of cabbage and I gathered that it was a cold cellar where the farmer had stored his winter vegetables.

Steele sat on his cot and motioned me to come down. I told him that I'd prefer to stay where I was, and I'm sure that my tone of voice jolted him.

'Say, feller,' he said, 'I just wanted you to know that General Dahlquist especially told me that you were an outstanding officer and that I could rely on you.' He was in a bad position, of course, having to strain his neck looking up at me.

'Did he also tell you,' I asked 'that I was yellow?'

'Of course not,' Steele said. 'He obviously didn't mean that when he said it. He was just hot under the collar.'

I said, 'Colonel Steele, you made one hell of a blunder repeating something like that when you knew it was said under the strain of battle. And, by the way, if you're looking for any of us during the night, we'll be at ground level where we've spent the war during the last year.'

I knew my shot struck home because of the bleak look that crossed his face. I, in fact, had as much as said he was yellow and he knew it. I left without another word and climbed up out of the stench of cabbages and old beets.

The next morning Steele tried to act buoyant and after breakfast mounted his jeep and said something like, 'Let's go.' His driver took off in a cloud of dust but returned a few minutes later to give Steele a chance to ask where everyone was. The regiment was still in the process of gathering itself together. Furthermore, since there weren't enough vehicles to transport all of the troops of an infantry regiment, the old 'Tally ho!' of the armor which, as I remember, was Steele's component, doesn't mean much.

Eventually we got on the road again, moving north toward Germany. We headed toward Bourg de Péage, a fairly large French town which we found burning in many areas when we reached it. Steele knew very little about infantry capabilities, and we were constantly trying to teach him something about space and time requirements. His muddled approach was almost as great a handicap to our operations as was the planning of the division staff. While General Dahlquist, eventually, proved himself one of the finest front-line generals of the US army, he was green at that time so far as concerned battle conditions, even though he had been in the army for many years.

The division staff, so far as I was concerned, reflected in large part a group of men whose loyalty to a National Guard unit in peacetime was being repaid with promotions they little deserved. Its members were seldom, if ever, seen as far forward as regimental headquarters and much of its planning was seldom attained and when hitches developed in the execution of plans, the division's only response was an arbitrary insistence that the lower echelons adapt to the golden rules of the division staff so that if, later, question arose as to the efficacy of basic plans, the situation could be treated as confused due, of course, to the incapacity of the regiments and other units to follow orders.

While General Dahlquist had been in the G-1 section of SHAEF before he took command of the 36th Division, he was, apparently, satisfied with the G-1 staff of the division even though when I took it over toward the end of the war, I found it lacking in every regard. Officers were busy writing up awards and decorations and thus living in commodious safety while strength reports were either missing altogether or were so outdated as to be useless. Understrength regiments were being ordered to do battle as though they were at full complement.

No one from the G-1 section came to regiments and battalions to check the accuracy of reports until I instituted that procedure as SOP. Even the awards and decorations aspects were being short-circuited since, lacking a special team to investigate possible heroic actions, few men would advocate their own heroism. The exceptions, in a number of instances, received high honors under circumstances where doubt existed as to whether the heroism had, in fact, occurred.

Courts martial were being conducted on a basis that, finally, had to be resolved by having many findings set aside because of prejudice to the defendants.

Military government operations were neglected, and I found certain members of that section attempting to curry favor with high-ranking officers by scavenging, inside Germany, for cigars, wines, and liquors, instead of doing their duty.

Even when officers were appointed to high staff positions, under circumstances where they had never been members of the National Guard unit earlier, the fallacy was clearly outlined that a member of the West Point Protective Association, as we called the professional members, could take any high-ranking job and perform better in it than any other officer. In short, it was evident to many of us that the division performed well in spite of the division staff. Regiments, where the bleeding and dying were done, more often than not took poorly conceived plans and made them work by the personal attention of their staffs at every phase of operations.

General Dahlquist had a rare turn of mind for a member of the regular establishment, albeit not a West Pointer. He told me very frankly after the war, one evening as we were riding a cab down 5th Avenue in New York en route to a 36th Division reunion, that he had not been able to bring himself to downgrade members of his staff even when he knew they were inefficient. He acknowledged that he had leaned on me as a source of intelligence material when I was S-2 of the 141st Infantry Regiment and said he could not account to himself for not having promoted me to the G-2 slot. Nor had he given his G-2 anything but the highest rating during the war!

Getting back to Colonel Steele's tenure as regimental CO, the regiment on that first day moved past Valence, ran into token resistance at Chabeuil, and then raced on to Bourg de Péage, which was also called Romain. We set up our regimental CP in a beautiful chateau where the furnishings were fit for a museum. Colonel Steele called the staff together for what he called a 'war council' and right away the illusions of grandeur that marked his administration began.

We were sitting around a beautiful large table in one of the chateau's great rooms when Steele foisted upon us two civilians, a Mr. Esve and a Mrs. Evans, whom he had found somewhere along the roadside. While I later found that Esve had earlier made himself available to the division G-2's office for whatever tasks they might have for him, I had never heard of him and I immediately objected to the presence of any civilian at one of our conferences.

Steele later advised us, as we sat awaiting orders, that he intended to use both Esve and Mrs. Evans in the counterintelligence work of the regiment. I stated that I was responsible for counterintelligence work in the regiment and that under no circumstances would I stand still for the use of 'spies,' particularly when they were people who had made themselves instantly available to Steele without benefit of a security clearance.

I pointed out that Esve was a contrived name and probably stood for the initials 'S' and 'V.' When Steele said he had met Esve earlier and had referred him to the division staff, I still demurred on the grounds that I had received no notice of any clearance as I would have in the ordinary course of events. I had asked Esve for his credentials before any discussion of our plans was had, and under questioning Esve had admitted that he was using a spurious name and that he had no evidence as to his membership in any organized resistance group.

I kept remembering that I had gone to a resistance headquarters near Marsanne with 'Zero' de la Garde only to find that it was of the FTP persuasion. The colonel in charge of the group had attempted to bargain with us on the basis that he would help us fight the Germans only if we would permit his forces to take all the weapons and ammunition left on the battlefield once the fighting ended. De la Garde and I had walked out of the headquarters without coming to any agreement with the FTP. 'Zero' had been oriented on the aims of the FTP and stated that the only reason they wanted the weapons and ammunition was to help the Russians at the end of the war if the other Allies failed to stop at a place mutually agreed upon with Russia.

As Esve showed an immediate interest in our plans and those of the other 7th Army units on our flanks, I warned him in no uncertain terms to get out or I'd put him under arrest. Just as he was about to leave, Steele came in with Mrs. Evans. He had found her pedaling a bicycle along the road, he said. She introduced herself as a former English girl who had married a French Jew, the manufacturer of silk hosiery. Even though she had two children at home she wanted to accompany us to assist, by what appeared to be a very amateurish kind of espionage, in ridding France of Germans. She hoped to ride her bicycle ahead of our column and report back by radio whenever she met German resistance. I told Steele, who thought her idea a brainstorm, that even if we permitted her to accompany us and ride on ahead, the Germans would shoot her down the minute they spotted her radio mast.

I asked Mrs. Evans for her identity card, and she handed me one with a profile view. I knew instantly that it was a forgery for only full-face photos were permitted for use on such cards. I asked her if she had shown it to German inspectors and she said she had on several occasions when she had traveled extensively throughout France during the occupation.

I then asked her for her true identity and she acknowledged that the card was a forgery when I told her that no profile pictures could be used for identification purposes. She, then, produced a British passport alleging that she had always maintained her English citizenship. I had the distinct impression that she was willing to admit the false identity card as a ploy designed to cast an aura of validity on what I assumed was a fake passport, and I told her and Steele so.

In order to get on with the important work of deciding the next day's operations, I asked both civilians to leave the room and to get on home. Steele objected so I took him aside and told him of an incident I had observed that morning in the town of Chabeuil, where Mrs. Evans said she lived.

We had been stopped outside Chabeuil momentarily and while we waited in our vehicles, a GI came along and told me he had seen a French civilian use a telephone that was located under a woodpile behind a nearby farmhouse. I checked with a local FFI officer, who knew neither of the existence of the telephone nor why it was secreted. He set out at once to learn more about it. I also pointed out to Steele that Esve had told me that he was acting as a lone wolf who, six weeks earlier, had come south from Paris to organize espionage teams. It occurred to me that the telephone could have been part of the Esve network but that it could also be used to transmit information to the Germans.

Later on I learned through 'Zero' that a high-tension wire had been used to transmit telephone messages from the hidden instrument and that a masterful job had been done tapping in and concealing the wires. All in all there was enough evidence in the false identities and the possibility that the two civilians were playing a double game of espionage to warrant placing them under arrest.

Nothing I said had any effect on Steele. He stood me at ease finally and said that the two volunteers would sit in on our deliberations. All of this went on while tired officers awaited word on the next day's activities. Steele also said he'd run the regiment in any manner that suited him and warned me to object no more.

I stood up and said that so long as I was S-2 I would run the intelligence operations and that if he didn't like the way I did it he could relieve me at once. In the meantime, I had not yet reported to the regimental officers a change of plan for the following day which I had received from the division staff.

I waited for the meeting to break up and then persuaded Mrs. Evans to go home or face the results of an immediate investigation of her background by our CIC unit. It was raining, and I finally got her to return home by vehicle with her bicycle riding with her.

Ten minutes later Steele climbed all over me for disobeying his orders. I challenged him to court-martial me and told him I'd make a monkey of him for his day's work. He sent a stooge named Axelrod, a French lieutenant he'd brought along with him, to retrieve Mrs. Evans.

While Axelrod was gone I prepared a report to our CIC unit with copies to corps and army G-2s setting forth the circumstances of Steele's establishment of an espionage center at regimental level and other facts I had uncovered relative to false identities.

In the meantime Esve had obtained what he thought was our whole plan of action. He could hardly wait to get moving toward Grenoble, our purported objective, and he dusted around getting spare bidons of gasoline for his trip.

After he'd gone I called Frank Reese, division G-2, and asked him what he knew about Esve. He said he had first met him in Grenoble but that Esve had left there for Valence with the 143rd Infantry Regiment where the 143rd had made an abortive attack. This hardly set my mind at ease. In any event I was certain that if Esve were a double agent, anything he'd gotten from me would only confuse the enemy. I called the CIC operatives at division headquarters after Esve left and demanded an investigation of both Esve and Evans. I told them that Esve had gone to Grenoble but that Mrs. Evans would be traveling with our headquarters, having left her home and children in Chabeuil. The CIC boys were up to their ears in checking suspicious circumstances but admitted they'd never heard anything like the mare's nest we were building.

Early the next morning the CIC agents called on me at my office and having confirmed the data I had already given them took off like bloodhounds on a hot scent. I was not to see them again for ten days, at the end of which time they came to our headquarters which, of course, had moved in the interim. They were pleased to inform me that they had corralled Esve in Grenoble with $196,000 in francs on his person which he could not account for. Neither could he account for his activities or whereabouts during the six days the CIC had hunted him down. I never did learn what happened to Esve, for the best I could get out of the CIC men when I asked were sly looks and head shakes and the statement that the Deuxième Bureau of the French army had 'taken care' of him. I never saw or heard of Esve again.

My own impression, unchanged over the years, was that he was a member of the FTP and was purchasing guns and ammunition for that organization at a price. Both he and Mrs. Evans were opportunists and probably thought they could buy weapons from our GIs, particularly German arms which our boys took as souvenirs.

In the meantime, while the CIC tracked Esve to his Grenoble hideout, Mrs. Evans was moving with our headquarters, sitting in on our deliberations, and going on a few 'shopping' expeditions during which I tried to have her trailed by some of our personnel. She, however, was either clever enough to avoid them or they were sidetracked by other pursuits like finding wine, women, and song. I called division headquarters on a number of occasions to protest her presence and was told that steps were being taken to get her out of our hair. The fact that we were moving rapidly forward each day accounted for most of the lag in loosening her grip on our regimental CO.

The executive officer of our regiment at that time was a Lieutenant Colonel McGrath who wore a handlebar mustache which bristled when his dander was up. While Mrs. Evans accompanied us, his moustache stood at 'high port' most of the time. I took it on myself to disparage everything that la Evans did and purposely fed her false data on a number of occasions. When I asked her how she could abandon her children and husband as she had done, she simply said that her husband was somewhere in France serving with an underground unit against the Germans. No response was evoked as to the status of her children except that 'a friend' was taking care of them.

I put the hook into Steele at every opportunity and furthermore warned him that I had already notified intelligence sections as far back as army as to his 'spy' operation. When he asked why he hadn't seen such communications, I read him pertinent regulations governing the freedom of intelligence echelons to communicate with each other without interference. His knowledge of army administration was weaker than his grasp of infantry tactics. There wasn't much doubt in the minds of most regimental officers as to why Steele insisted on Mrs. Evans' presence in our headquarters.

We moved from one chateau to another on our trek northward and Mrs. Evans always took the best available room. There could be little doubt that, because of her presence we lived better than might otherwise have been the case. However, on the other side of the equation was the fact that, on many occasions while Steele was eliciting ohs and aahs from her as he murmured to her during meals, tired line officers were kept waiting for meetings scheduled each evening after dinner.

I had taken most of the regiment's senior officers aside to tell them that the CIC was working on her case and that, sooner or later, we'd get rid of her. I also told them not to trust her in any way and to establish positive controls against giving her vital information at any time. In derision and as an example of Texas wit, these same officers passed the word that Mrs. Evans was one of 'Doughty's undercover agents,' always to the tune of guffaws!

Steele, as a matter of backing his ploy of using Mrs. Evans as a forward observer, had an artillery liaison officer at our headquarters instruct her on the art of adjusting artillery fire. His absolute lack of combat experience permitted him to hallucinate in this manner, never thinking of German reaction to a woman on a bicycle carrying a radio transmitter. What little resistance we encountered was dispersed almost at once by a couple of infantry squads outflanking small roadblocks.

Steele thought of himself as marching to more distant, lordlier drums than any heard by ordinary men. He had a 'big shot' complex that came into sharp focus whenever any higher ranking officer was present. On one occasion when General Dahlquist rode up in a jeep to determine what had delayed our column, Steele jumped up onto a half-track and with all the sangfroid of a John Wayne fired a hundred or more 50-caliber machine-gun rounds at what everyone present knew at first sight was a scarecrow set up in a garden some 50ft off the road. His act endangered the lives of men who, having dispersed the members of a roadblock well beyond the scarecrow, were removing the material forming the block. I'm sure that the frame of mind that could influence a man, who had hung back out of the war until its end seemed imminent, to call veterans 'yellow,' could also convince itself that such men would fall for a show of bravado that, normally, could be expected of an 8-year-old boy.

Dahlquist only appeared puzzled by the grandstanding Steele had put on for his benefit. I'm sure it never occurred to the general that Steele was showing a 'fighting' spirit and a 'dauntless' attitude with his puerile act. The fact that Steele had repaired to a bomb-proof shelter his first night with us was but the first sign of many to follow that he was extraordinarily gun-shy. We had seen enough of such characters during the war to know that the longer they had managed to escape the combat zone the more their gun-shyness became exaggerated to the point where they could hardly be contained inside their own skins when a shell went off nearby. We had also learned to adapt to such men knowing that it would be but a short time before they found a way out of danger. It just took a little longer in Steele's case, probably because he'd never 'had it so good,' as the boys used to say.

As the days went by and I had heard nothing from the CIC, busy – as it later proved – nailing Esve in Grenoble, I decided I'd have to handle the case of Mrs. Evans personally. It was a day or so after I'd learned, inadvertently, about her motivation and possibly something else about Colonel Steele.

We were forced to make a wide detour, through some of the lushest countryside I'd ever seen, because the Germans had blown out a bridge across a wide river. There were great herds of dairy cows on all sides of us belly deep in grass, and wherever we passed through small villages people rushed out to present us with flowers and chunks of fresh butter wrapped in cloth. De la Garde told me that this plethora of dairy products in one part of France and none in other sections was part of the German plan to divide France into factions that hated each other, thus making it easier to control the country. No butter was permitted to be shipped north to Paris, it seems, so that much of it was used in the countryside we were crossing to grease axles on farm carts.

I took the I&R platoon to scout the detour by leapfrogging our vehicles in a pattern whereby the lead jeep would move out to a predesignated position and there, positioned to move forward or back at a moment's notice, would maintain watch while the next vehicle, on signal that all was well, would roar past that position and take up a similar stance at another predesignated spot. If there were suspicious-looking areas near the predesignated localities, men would move on foot to probe them and then signal the 'all clear' or other appropriate news.

It was getting on toward fall at the time, and the September days were some of the prettiest we saw in the war. It seemed a shame to defile them with more killing. On the day of our wide detour, we approached a great farm with many buildings set on rolling hillsides. Through the meadows a fast-moving stream, wide enough to reflect its surroundings, was crossed by a rustic bridge. Through barn doors could be seen haymows filling all lofts and along the stream were hundreds of sleek-looking cows, a herd of goats, and some sheep. Pigs squealed in enclosures nearby as I drove my jeep into a barnyard.

I called to a hulking man with a straw-colored moustache, who appeared to be the owner as he stood in the farmhouse door and watched us approach. Both he and a woman who was looking over his shoulder came out to see me. They seemed glad to find someone who spoke their language, but there was a definite impression that they were on guard about something as they stood there quietly talking with me.

When I asked the farmer if there were any Germans around, he answered in the negative but, since I was watching his wife's face, I was instantly aware that she was frightened and almost spoke up as though to disagree with him. I needed nothing more to confirm what I had sensed as we talked. Beyond the farm at the end of a long upgrade of meadows stood a dense forest. Our lead jeep was positioned some 500yd ahead of mine and about halfway to the wooded tract.

I had my driver move slowly forward while I signaled the men in the lead to halt in place. As we pulled abreast of the jeep, I cautioned the men not to look anywhere but at me and to move slowly when we finally left the spot. While we talked I had a radio operator signal the lead vehicles of our regimental column telling them to follow another route forward, somewhere east of the one we were on, for I had a sense that we were already in trouble. I had sent part of the I&R platoon to scout out the easterly route earlier in the day.

Our parley in the open field was of course conducted with our vehicles standing at right angles to the road ready to go in either direction. At just about that time, several rounds of self-propelled gunfire barely missed our jeeps, which catapulted back toward the farm within seconds. It was a wild ride and I expected to be wounded or killed any second. A small declivity helped us reach an area behind a barn which, together with the farmhouse, was then receiving artillery concentrations. It was obvious that German troops had witnessed the discussion I'd had with the farmer and had assumed that I'd been warned of their presence.

We couldn't do much against artillery fire so stayed undercover in the cellar of the barn. I estimated at the time that we were under attack by a regimental combat team and radioed that information back to the regimental command group. We kept a sharp lookout against infiltrating skirmishers who might surround and take us prisoners, if they didn't kill or wound us.

The men of the I&R platoon were the best fighters I'd ever seen, taking chances when the mission required it, but cool under fire. Their jobs were always dangerous, consisting of patrolling, running observation posts, and generally doing whatever was necessary to keep enemy activity properly portrayed to the regimental CO. I worked the whole war to keep them from being subverted to straight infantry tasks, a problem I had to solve with each new CO, most of whom had to learn that a highly trained, dependable group of experts was not to be expended uselessly.

Nerve was the key to the I&R platoon's operations. Nerve to patrol at night behind enemy lines. Nerve to go out front and draw fire while keeping casualties to a minimum. Nerve to stand and report what they were seeing and hearing in a steady, objective manner without resort to exaggeration.

When possible I kept the I&R platoon in safe areas so that they could get enough rest to maintain their functions. Then, when emergencies arose, they were ready and willing to move and to produce results that often meant the difference between success and failure of the regiment's, and possibly, the division's mission. They were proficient in the use of all weapons to include captured foreign arms. They knew infantry tactics and could envisage hostile use of terrain so as to know where to expect defensive positions, minefields, routes of access, routes of supply, armored approaches, and all of the myriad aspects of importance to armies in the field.

We finally realized, as the barn and farmhouse burst into flames, that we were going to run a gauntlet to escape. It was nearly dark at that time and we had not seen or heard any hostile troops near our position. The farmer and his wife and some farmworkers had long ago crawled away from our position, where they had gathered when there was a lull in the shooting. I knew that German supplies of all kinds were running low and that artillery ammunition was in very short supply along our zone of advance due to the devastation of German logistical support by our air force.

Before it was too dark, we took off back along the road we had come on and hoped that no German troops had had a chance to mine the roadway. We carried loaded sandbags on the floors of our vehicles in the hope that, if we struck a mine, anywhere, we might be spared some of the explosive force of it. After a half-hour's run I felt that we were clear, which proved to be the case.

It was a black night by the time we reached the secondary route over which we had learned, through radio signal, that our regiment had passed without difficulty. It took a long time to find our new CP, and I finally crawled into a room of a house where a sentry had told me my section was located. It was about 3 am at that time, and I was tired enough just to lie on the floor in my padded combat suit and go to sleep.

Several hours later, I was awaked by people whispering. I sensed that it was daylight even though I didn't open my eyes. Suddenly I realized that Colonel Steele and Mrs. Evans were talking and there was someone stirring in a room beyond where I lay. There was a rattle of spoons and cups on saucers, and I gathered that breakfast was being served to them. Colonel Steele whispered to someone who came tiptoeing in, 'Don't wake him.' I was pretty obviously in the wrong place, but I pretended to be fast asleep and I didn't really want to move because the effects of sleeping on a wooden floor were stiff joints and sore muscles. I dozed along and I was pleased that everyone was so considerate of me. 'Major Doughty did a good job of keeping us out of trouble yesterday,' I heard the colonel whisper, and if Mrs. Evans responded, it was with a motion of the head for I heard nothing.

Then Colonel Steele said something that has puzzled me ever since. 'I don't eat ham either,' he said in a low tone. Mrs. Evans said something to the effect that she was glad to know that bit of intelligence concerning his eating habits. I have only the conclusion that ran through my mind at the time, namely that this had something to do with religious scruples but I never did find out.

While I was busy pretending to be asleep, I fell off into deep slumber and when I woke up several hours later I was alone in the room. We were resting in that vicinity for a day or so, which resulted in the first good sleep I'd had in weeks.

When we resumed our march to the Vosges, I rigged a deal whereby Steele was called up to one of the battalions while Mrs. Evans rode in his jeep. Prior to that she had been hiding out, in a manner of speaking, in a truck near the end of our column. I had learned from someone in the G-2 section of division headquarters that General Dahlquist had ordered Mrs. Evans' removal from our ménage. On the day that Mrs. Evans rode Steele's jeep, the general saw her along the road and it hacked at his butt to see her in the colonel's jeep as though in command.

Rather than cause any commotion, Dahlquist instituted an inquiry as to why Mrs. Evans was still with us, once he returned to the division CP. That afternoon we reached a beautiful chateau and just before the evening meal, Steele called me upstairs to where he and Mrs. Evans had been talking for a long time. He told me that, henceforward, 'Zero' de la Garde, a properly accredited liaison officer from the French army, would report all FFI data to Mrs. Evans so that she could 'screen' the information and transmit to him only what she thought valid. I raised hell in spades and stormed downstairs to where the battalion officers were awaiting orders.

At that juncture, and before I could submit my resignation to division, as I had told Steele I would do, General Robert I. Stack, assistant division commander, walked in. He was one of the grossest people I ever knew and in characteristic manner ordered Mrs. Evans to go home at once. I had sent another report to division headquarters that day after seeing General Dahlquist observe her riding the colonel's jeep. In that report, I had said that my next appeal would be to army G-2.

In the ensuing conversation with Steele, he had the consummate nerve to tell me that I should have been more forceful in convincing him that his actions in 'employing' Mrs. Evans were not consonant with army regulations. There were fifteen or twenty officers present who heard me say, 'Colonel Steele, I did everything but shoot you and I doubt that you've heard the last of this yet.' He was the type of professional soldier I despise. Blind to his own shortcomings with a vengeance, a braggart, a con artist, and one who tried to evade responsibility when he goofed off. Furthermore, he tried to prove himself possessed of a vivid imagination by finding some unorthodox way of accomplishing a mission, as witness the use of spies. He was a conniving slob, as well, who thought that his real use of Mrs. Evans was completely camouflaged by her alleged capacity to act as an observer for us. It was apparent to me that he had reached the grade of colonel by using every shortcut available and would go on giving short weight until someone was bright enough to call his bluff. I was also convinced that by use of fancy footwork, Steele had often concealed the fact that his basic military education was lacking in many fundamental ways.

The officers who had been waiting Steele's presence for his daily 'war council' (devised by him I'm sure as a handy gadget against the day when we might hit stiff resistance and all the risks would then fall on the battalion officers to make their way back to regiment instead of Steele's taking the risk of going forward) applauded when they learned that Mrs. Evans had been thrown out of the regiment.

All in all Steele was a fine example of an officer completely detached from reality, setting his own rules while endeavoring to keep people around him off-balance as a means of maintaining his superior position. The only reason he took all the guff I handed him was his fear of Dahlquist's anger if Steele tried to brass his way by retaining Mrs. Evans and sacking me. I would have preferred charges against him had that occurred.

It just so happened that Mrs. Evans chose to evade General Dahlquist's order by asking de la Garde to requisition a vehicle for her so that she could follow us. 'Zero,' of course, told me of her plan and I put her under arrest. Steele, I'm sure, had suggested this possibility to Mrs. Evans but, as soon as he had left our CP where General Stack had issued his summary order, I sent Mrs. Evans on her way south.

Our next CP was located some miles north in a girls' school still occupied, in fact, by young ladies. Steele started to give me some more of his crap when I got there, and I teed off on him in the strongest terms I'd had yet used. While I could not prove that Mrs. Evans was responsible, nevertheless the inference was very strong that she could easily have made contact with German troops while we were at our last CP.

We had been moving through a strongly nationalistic region where FFI depredations had been conducted on a fearsome scale against the Germans, resulting in much damage to German plans and morale. Mrs. Evans had sat in on our councils, as Steele had insisted she do, and knew there were no other units behind us. When we had orders to move forward again she'd gone 'shopping,' and while my men had trailed her, they'd also lost her. That night a sizeable detachment of German troops had, apparently, moved out around our flank and had sacked and burned a village that had been a center of resistance.

I recited this plus some fairly pungent remarks to the effect that if my disobedience of his illegal orders were to be tested, he'd look fine in the eyes of his fellow West Pointers for having connived with Mrs. Evans to disobey the proper orders of his commanding general. I told him that, so far as I was concerned, he'd already earned a court martial. I'm sure he had already alerted his mentors in the Pentagon to be ready to pull the string still attached to him and get him out of a sticky situation. It wasn't too long after we met firm resistance that he was gone.

Chapter 24

The Moselle River Crossing

German resistance, once again, was stiffening as we approached the Vosges Mountains. However, there was always the chance that German troops could be diverted from the Rhône Valley route to attack our rear, inasmuch as the 36th Division had pulled out far ahead of the remainder of the 7th Army on a route running parallel to the Rhône.

I convinced Steele that it would be sensible to patrol back along the route we had advanced on, to check certain river crossings to be sure that our rear was fairly secure. I briefed the members of the I&R platoon, personally, and warned them to take no undue chances, particularly where the area to be probed appeared to be free of Germans.

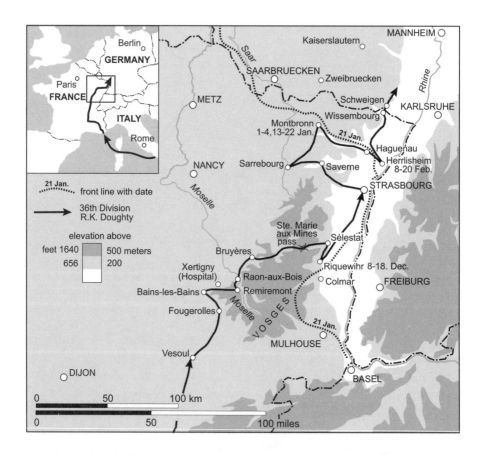

One of the most intelligent men of the platoon, a man of German extraction, uncharacteristically became excited about the mission. He had earlier refused to go to Officers' Candidate School, saying that he was happy as a non-com (non-commissioned officer). I asked him, as we stood in the dark amid the platoon's jeeps, checking map positions by flashlight, why he was so nervous, and he said he didn't know but felt that it would be good to be away from the combat zone for a few days. I cautioned him, pointedly, to take no chances whatsoever since this was the type of mission that could prove dangerous simply because it appeared to be so routine. He agreed that he would proceed with caution.

Several jeeps were to participate in the patrol, which would take about a week to complete, in order to set up radio relay stations to permit direct communications between the patrol leaders and our regimental CP.

No untoward activity was observed by the patrol as it faded back along our earlier trail. We received daily reports of critical areas and were assured that the river crossings had been destroyed in those sites where, should German armor succeed in crossing, our supply line could be severed.

Then came the news that I had tried to guard against. The bright young non-com had gone out to inspect a bridge site at Marsanne, the place from which our latest trek north, under Steele, had started. Apparently, he had walked across an open area secure in the thought that, having come this far with no German sightings, it was highly unlikely that any German forces would be in position so far south. The rest of the squad that had gone to Marsanne with him told me later that they had already observed the position well enough to know that the bridge was blown out and impassable. A civilian tried to warn our men, at the last moment, of a German machine-gun emplacement there and had actually saved some of them from being machine-gunned along with the man who was killed. The news of his death, so seemingly unnecessary under the circumstances, dampened the morale of everyone who knew the facts.

After the war I wrote this man's mother and, while I never indicated to her the circumstances of his death, I was able to put together a very long scenario, tying together a whole series of photographs he had sent home of places he'd been and comrades he'd served with. She wrote to thank me and told me that she had never seen the lad again from the day he'd left home on the West Coast to join the army. She and her daughters were grateful for the light I had been able to throw on his activities in the States, North Africa, Italy, and France.

Shortly after the I&R platoon returned with the body of their friend, a special service was conducted for his burial by the regimental chaplain. At that time, too, I returned to Romain with 'Zero' de la Garde to check on some stories, in general circulation, of Vichy 'Milice' who had collaborated with the Germans and who were being hunted down like dogs by the French FFI. We visited the small village which had been so brutalized by the Germans who had slipped around our flank to do the job. All boys and men from age 14 to 60 had been rounded up by the Germans and killed out-of-hand during that night of terror.

Some idea of the depth of hatred that existed between French people of that region and the Boche was made clear to me while we were in the town. Three of the hated 'Milice' had been caught by the FFI just before we arrived. They were tied to stakes set up outside the town hall and we witnessed their execution by firing squad. Women held their babies high above their shoulders to see the *coup de grâce* rendered by a French officer after each man had sagged against a stake. The coldest feeling stayed with me for days occasioned by the women's screams of joy at the moment of death. I felt that the entire scene was an obscenity best carried out away from the eyes of children.

Sometime during this period we stayed at the Chateau de Moncley, a particularly lovely edifice where the Countess de la Garde, no relative of 'Zero's,' gave us a warm reception. I remember sleeping in a blue bedroom beneath eiderdown blankets after having had a bath in a tub where I could soak for an hour.

At another chateau, whose location has long since been forgotten, de la Garde set up a dinner for the regimental staff who were to be honored by an old French army officer. We sat in a baronial banquet hall replete with mementos of other wars and were each given about a thimbleful of one of the rarest and oldest wines in existence. The old French colonel toasted us as liberators and said he'd saved his last bottle of the wine for the day his homeland was once again free.

Another episode, out of chronology but brought to mind as part of the kaleidoscope of that area, concerned the liberation of Lyons (September 3, 1944). I was on a hill overlooking Lyons just at dusk. Our engineers were replacing planks in a dam across a river that was to be our route of access to the north, all other bridges having been destroyed by the Germans as they fell back.

There was no shooting near us, and a number of jeeps were drawn up along the roadside as FFI members showed our engineers where the people of the area had hidden the bridge planking. I walked up to one jeep and was surprised to see Colonel John Cabot Lodge sitting in it. He was assigned to the VI Corps as I recall it and was making sure that the bridge we'd found was capable of bearing up under the weight of tanks.

As we stood there, the heavens were suddenly turned pink and the sound of very heavy explosions came rumbling from the direction of Lyons.

'There go the bridges,' Colonel Lodge said. It was a dangerously beautiful sight as groups of aerial bombs, used as mines, were detonated at several bridge sites down in the valley. When the destruction ended it was dark, and 'Zero,' who was with me, suggested that we go to a nearby railroad station where, in his scouting around, he'd found a fairly clean restaurant.

We had a good meal and for dessert the chef brought out some cheese of the countryside, 'fromage du pays.' 'Zero' took one look at it and unloaded some fast French invectives on the chef. There, in the middle of the cheese, sat one of the largest maggots I'd ever seen. With great aplomb the chef simply leaned over the counter and snapped the maggot with a broad fingernail. It sailed off into the station somewhere, and we ate the cheese with French bread and wine, pronouncing the whole meal 'très bon.'

As we ran north, one day seemed to follow another with very little difference in the pattern of fighting. Roadblocks, hastily established by the fleeing Germans, prisoners from scattered groups giving evidence of the lack of cohesion in the enemy ranks (one day's catch of twenty-three prisoners turned up twenty-two different organizations), and supply problems were part of the daily routine. We were running supplies with our own trucks for hundreds of miles, necessitating double crews to handle the driving which in some cases took the men back to the original beachhead on the Riviera.

We were aware, through PW interrogation, that the Germans were trying to slow us down long enough to permit their famed Speer (after Albert Speer, the Nazi architect turned war materiel chief) Organization to construct defenses along the Vosges Mountain flanks. We fought a sharp battle at Vesoul. I heard the sounds of firing and went forward on foot to our OP where I could use my field glasses to look into a valley in which heavy concentrations of our shells were exploding. Suddenly, the view turned black in front of my eyes and the ensuing explosion rocked me. Under magnification, I had the sense that the explosion was much nearer to me than proved to be the case and I threw myself down an embankment cut into the hillside where I had been lying in the grass to avoid detection by the enemy.

As I resumed looking through my field glasses, I saw some 200 German soldiers riding bicycles rather leisurely down the main road beyond the bridge which, I gathered, they had just destroyed.

A mortar was firing from a ravine just to my right and the observer, seeing the cyclists, directed heavy fire on them. I saw a number of them go down and lie still while the rest of the group sped away, pedaling like maniacs. We were delayed until after dark while the engineers put a Bailey bridge across the river blocking our advance. As I passed the spot where the Germans had been killed, it was sickening to feel the jeep wheels ride up over bicycles and bodies. We could not stop to clear the road as the Germans had put in another roadblock a little further on and were shelling the area as we rode through.

We pulled up at a farmhouse, ready to stay the night, while one of our battalions prepared to drive out the defenders of the roadblock at first light. Even when it seemed safe enough, the I&R platoon had been cautioned never to take cover or sleep in a confined area. I have the impression, still, that they breached the rule that night because of the loss of one of their best men at Marsanne. They found a barn full of new-mown hay and sacked out in a group. One SP round struck the roof during the night and killed or wounded several of the platoon members. Morale was never quite as high, thereafter, as it had been prior to that cataclysm. Somehow the men seemed to believe that their luck was gone when they buried one of their non-coms. Basically, I kept reminding them that, in both instances, they had breached safety rules and that, while they had been phenomenally lucky to have had so few casualties in the past, they could still perform like the aces they were if they would pull up their socks and do things right.

Our route led through famous old watering places as we drew near the Vosges foothills. We took Fougerolles and then Luxeuil Les Bains, Bains-les-Bains (which we later adopted as a division rest camp, naming its five hotels for our Congressional Medal of Honor winners), Plombières Les Bains, and others.

Resistance against our forward movement was becoming stronger with each day. Intelligence sources showed that German reinforcements had come in from east of the Rhine to bolster the defenders blocking our advance and, inevitably, slowing down our earlier rapid forward movement. Ahead of us lay the Moselle River and since we had already fought 'The Battle of Guts' at the Rapido River in Italy, we weren't looking forward with any great joy to forcing another river crossing against prepared positions.

When high brass pays particular attention to an infantry unit like the 141st Infantry Regiment, the antennae of the officer complement of that unit are apt to become highly sensitized. There's something about special attention, especially if it is accompanied by earnest inquiries into the welfare and esprit of the unit, that warns the veteran of dire things to come.

We encountered another of many such moments in the vicinity of Fougerolles, France, when General 'Sandy' Patch visited our regiment and had dinner with its staff one evening. He was quite solicitous of our welfare and right away we knew we'd been 'picked' for the Moselle Crossing, in capital letters. Sure enough, before the meal was over, General Patch started the old shibboleths rolling about the trust and honor about to be placed on our most capable shoulders. He said, among other things, that a breach had been opened in the German defenses in front of us and that our regiment had been elected to enter the breach and close on the Moselle River, prepared to cross it at the first opportunity to do so. I have a recollection that good old redoubtable Steele, who had, so far, had a hard tussle with a scarecrow, thanked General Patch for the wonderful opportunity to prove our mettle, or some such garbage.

The next day we cut west from Fougerolles, to sidestep a heavily blocked area, and set out through the breach to Remiremont and from there to a small town called Raon-aux-Bois, which we reached on September 20, 1944. I immediately sent out patrols through a heavily wooded slope to the top of a ridge west of the Moselle, from which we could look into the Moselle Valley. I accompanied the patrols in an effort to preserve the element of surprise by cutting down all radio signals and by guarding against being observed by the Germans, who could be seen digging in defensive positions all along the river's edge and back into the hinterland.

It was a strange feeling to lie concealed in heavy woods and, once again, to see the enemy using shovels, picks, and axes as they worked inside a cemetery wall, completely oblivious to our presence. We were some miles away, but through our field glasses we could see the sweat standing out on workers' shoulders and bare backs. I was careful to shield the lenses of my field glasses to prevent a telling flash of light from showing our presence.

I took off my helmet and crawled out onto a promontory from which I could see up and down the river for some distance. From this vantage point I could determine that the main defensive positions were sited to prevent a crossing at an S-bend, similar to the one where our regiment was decimated on the Rapido River. The bend was where the river divided the town of Eloyes.

My regiment, of course, was alone behind the German front lines but enemy communications were so poor at this juncture in the war that, unless we gave away our position by some foolish action, the chances were good that the Germans along the river would learn of our presence only when we opened fire on them.

When I returned that evening to Raon-aux-Bois, I learned that we had been ordered to cross the river that night. It seemed to many that this was pushing our luck but I pointed out to the headquarters group that the quicker we moved, the greater chance for surprise, an essential element to a successful attack of this nature, and, to those who remembered the precipitate haste of our Rapido Crossing, I noted that the rest of our division was in a position to prevent heavy reinforcement of the positions opposing us, by attacking Remiremont in strength.

My estimate of the enemy strength, which I tried to be objective about, was that some 400 to 500 Germans occupied the defenses along our portion of the river. Steele remonstrated at this as too great a number, more, I believe, to calm his own fears than to oppose me. I doubt that he had taken a good look in any event. My estimate was thought to be too low by some of the patrols that had approached Eloyes. I stated that I had not been able to see past the houses on the fringes of that town but thought that the heaviest defenses of all were at the S-bend in Eloyes.

At this point Steele started to outline a plan of attack that would duplicate the fiasco at the Rapido River. 'We'll cross at the re-entrant,' Steele said, as though reading it right out of the book; 'Like hell we will,' I said, and all of the veterans of the Italian campaign shouted agreement. Steele was taken aback but now that we were faced with real serious battle conditions, all of his bravado was gone. He even seemed smaller in stature as we sat in the little town hall of Raon-aux-Bois planning our attack.

Fortunately an FFI member, a fairly young man, had reached Raon-aux-Bois that afternoon from Eloyes. How he knew we were at Raon-aux-Bois has always been a matter of conjecture. My personal belief is that the mayor of Raon-aux-Bois had telephoned Eloyes, where he had a pregnant daughter whose time was at hand.

The mayor, one R.M. Gribelin, was a former French naval officer and a tougher, braver man never lived. His contribution to our effort made the difference between success and failure.

In any event, the young FFI member told 'Zero' de la Garde of an underwater weir or dam that was but lightly defended, if it was defended at all. When the question arose as to whether or not we could locate its position in the darkness, Mr. Gribelin volunteered – at age 70 – to guide our leading elements to it through the mountains and forests at night.

In order to distract the Germans and to pin down defenders on a wide front, we ordered our 2nd Battalion under Critchfield to attack Eloyes as a feint. He was to put on a lot of firepower and some maneuvers in effecting this part of our plan. Since crossing at a re-entrant appears to be conventional wisdom in all armies, defending against such a move becomes SOP. Therefore, we wanted the Germans to believe that we were ready to fall into that trap again. Experience at the Rapido, learned the hard way, stood us in good stead on the Moselle Crossing.

Our 1st and 3rd Battalions were to cross at the weir by wading and, to the extent possible, maintaining secrecy until well established on the far side. The 1st Battalion, through the efforts of the old mayor, reached the crossing site exactly as planned despite the fact that the night was one of the blackest I'd ever experienced, made worse by a heavy ground fog.

The 3rd Battalion lost contact with the rear guard of the 1st Battalion and, as a result, reached the river a long way from the ford, with the result that it suffered heavy casualties when it tried to cross there. It was driven back with much damage to men and materials.

An engineer, accompanying the 1st Battalion, swam the river and anchored a heavy rope to a tree on the far side. With the aid of this 'handrail' the battalion, once again assuming a tactical disposition frowned on by good military doctrine, crossed in Indian file, reminiscent of the breakout from Anzio several months earlier.

In the meantime, the 2nd Battalion took that part of Eloyes located on our side of the river and accomplished its mission of tying down defenders at the S-bend. In the morning the 143rd Infantry followed in our tracks to expand the bridgehead, established by our first battalion, sufficiently to permit the engineers to build a bridge at the site of the ford near Saint-Nabord.

It rained during that day and the approaches to the bridge became a quagmire as vehicles of all kinds churned their way to the far side of the river.

The 143rd Infantry turned left and attacked and took that portion of Eloyes situated on the German side of the river. The 141st Infantry, as soon as it could gather its scattered battalions into a cohesive unit, moved right along the riverbank and helped dislodge the enemy from Remiremont. By September 28, 1944, the bridgehead across the Moselle was deemed secure even though the Germans, now completely aware of how Germany's fate was being sealed by encroaching armies, were taking desperate steps to reinforce the Vosges defenders. The 36th Division had cleared the way for the 3rd and 45th Divisions to cross and expand the bridgehead. In doing so, it had used to advantage much battle lore its men and officers had amassed in the long trek from Salerno, via Rome and Grosetto, to Southern France, the Lower Alps, Rhône Valley, and points north.

Because we were in the Forest of Fossard once we crossed the Moselle River, we were confronted with some unusual conditions. The forest was thick with trees and dense with underbrush, providing a beautiful ambiance for ninety members of a German sniper school, whose training we had disrupted, to earn their degrees in sniping. The confusion caused by relatively few men shooting from cover and running, to shoot again, was hard to believe. No one was safe anywhere, it seemed. On one occasion I had looked out of the second-story window of a house where our headquarters was located and had just about fallen out of my hide when a bullet ploughed into the window frame, showering me with splinters and drawing blood from my lip, for which I refused to accept a Purple Heart.

This was the first of several occasions when, technically, I suppose, I could have been awarded a Purple Heart. However, I adamantly refused for two good reasons to become the recipient of a medal that was awarded men who, for example, lost arms and legs or had other serious damage done to their bodies. The first was that I couldn't stomach men who were 'sweating' every medal they could obtain by hook or crook. Many of them by crook! We'd had some bad examples in our regimental headquarters, starting with the landing at Salerno when members of the 'Old Buddies' Club' wrote each other up for Silver Stars under circumstances in which, if such medals were merited, then every man in the regiment had earned one twice over, simply by going ashore.

Secondly, and in warfare there is no accounting for such reactions, I was sure that if I took a Purple Heart medal for a minor abrasion, something would later happen to me in a big way to warrant such an award. Call it superstition if you will.

In any event, *Time* magazine and *Stars and Stripes* reporters interviewed me on September 29, 1944, when I told them of the snipers' harassing our every move and of our need to hunt them down, individually, and put them out of action. The terrain was so tangled that two of our own units mixed it up with each other for hours, one day, until someone with presence of mind asked both for the coordinates of their respective positions and found them firing at each other.

While still fighting to enlarge the bridgehead to a secure position we learned that Colonel Steele had been 'withdrawn' from front-line action. I can only speculate on how he arranged this but by that time the 'Glory Road' had turned to 'Sloggers Alley' and all of the 'glory boys' disappeared, exactly as we had known they would. The last communication I received from Steele was from the George Cinq Hotel in Paris. This occurred when we stood on the borders of Germany preparing for the 'last mile' across the Rhine and on to the Bunker in Berlin. He wrote as though he and I were old buddies, a much-abused attitude that had apparently stood him in good stead during his career. He apparently was in charge of the hotel, a very fitting job for a West Pointer, and planned to take a ride south through that portion of France we'd fought over. I had no doubt this was to promote some grandiose scheme whereby all and sundry would be given an opportunity to thank their lord and savior for his gallantry in liberating them. He asked me to send word by our supply trucks to Mme. de la Garde at the Chateau de Moncley, telling her that he would be calling on her during his tour. How he could imagine that at that late date in the war we would be supplying ourselves from the Riviera, instead of from nearby quartermaster and ordnance dumps escapes me completely. Furthermore, how he could imagine that I would do anything to forward the pursuits of an officer who, instead of fighting as he had been trained at public expense to do, was engaged in seeking his own pleasures, while our regimental personnel faced death every day, is just another measure of the sound of the drums he was marching to, oblivious to the contempt I felt for him both as a person and as an officer. I tore up his note.

When our newest regimental CO arrived we were ensconced in an old stone barracks that the French army had used for many years. It was a cavernous, cold place and, while we could heat some of its smaller rooms, the main armory was bitterly cold.

The newcomer, one Colonel Carl E. Lundquist, was fresh from SHAEF headquarters and he promoted an air of mystery about his past activities at that exalted place, right from the outset of his tour with the regiment. He was kindly enough, but there was something lacking in his psyche that had us all guessing. He also appeared to be one of the 'Glory Road Boys.'

He told me, personally, that whenever he had left SHAEF, while it was located in England, he was 'shadowed' by CIC men even when he had gone to Scotland on 'holidays.' This was, of course, the usual persiflage that such characters put out by way of camouflaging their lack of combat experience. What they didn't seem to understand was that we didn't give a damn one way or the other. It had been our experience that we were better off not to have at the front anyone who, for whatever reason, had been absent from it for most of the war.

Furthermore, it did not seem to occur to such wandering minstrels that while they had been on 'holidays,' as he had put it, we'd been fighting our way from hell to breakfast. I finally learned from division headquarters that Lundquist had been part of SHAEF's adjutant general's department more or less in charge of mimeographs! Of course, in that capacity he had been privy to much top-secret material and probably was 'shadowed,' as he said, wherever he went to prevent possible leakage of important matters.

In any event, it was difficult to understand how such experience qualified him to command a combat regiment. My first real contact with him came when he directed me to take him to an OP in the Forest of Fossard where our I&R boys were watching for hostile action to include snipers. We left the old French barracks and, as I recall it, proceeded on foot through the dense woods accompanied by a couple of riflemen.

There was nothing to be seen from the promontory where a squad of men kept watch over a valley in which thousands of enemy troops could have been hidden without danger of being observed.

I was suddenly made aware that someone was sick and on looking to the rear of the camouflaged position saw Lundquist vomiting beside a trail. On the way back, he suggested that his breakfast had not set well and that he would appreciate it if I would not mention his queasiness. 'Colonel,' I said, 'everyone's scared at the front and it doesn't get any better all the time.' He didn't bother to counter the 'scared' part, which raised him in my estimation several points. What had scared him, I'm sure, was that from the OP we had been able to look upward to the peaks of the Vosges Mountains where the Schlucht and Sainte-Marie-aux-Mines passes could be seen. Rumors had been flying for days that these were our next targets.

Chapter 25

The 'Lost Battalion'

S hortly after my sortie to the OP, from which the peaks of the Vosges Mountains could be seen, I had occasion to interrogate a German general who had been bagged by our regiment. By that time in the war I had participated in the questioning of thousands of German prisoners. Certain techniques, based on the effective advice of the British major at the NATOUSA Intelligence School, had been worked into a scenario that seldom failed to produce results.

I suspect it is only natural, when exposed to danger at every turn, to limit one's outlook to the factors which increase or decrease that danger. I know that most infantrymen were concerned primarily with that wedge of the front that angled out from their two eyes to a distance measured by the range of hostile guns that could bear on them.

My own outlook was scarcely wider or longer range than that, except that my responsibility was to keep our regimental command group aware of hostile capabilities along our immediate front. Anything that improved or cut into those capabilities was of concern to me as I prepared intelligence reports daily for use by regimental and division officers. We wanted to know the state of morale among troops opposing us, the status of their supplies of all kinds, the possibility of reinforcement, normal eating hours (so that we could harass the chow lines), supply routes, new weapons in the offing, battle experience, commanding officers, gun emplacements, supporting weapons to include armor, tactical plans, and on into a full range of activities. My wedge of the front was enlarged by the regimental stance and the need to assess conditions affecting our operations.

When we captured a number of prisoners at any one time it was not difficult to spot the 'easy marks,' provided that the capturing group obeyed instructions and kept the prisoners from standing easy until after we had interrogated them at our regimental headquarters. Early in the war, green troops often gave PWs cigarettes and food as soon as the latter were captured, thus easing their minds as to their eventual disposition. We did not stand for prisoners being abused except as the exigencies of any situation caused us to exert unusual psychological pressures on them, but we aimed to capitalize on the German propaganda that promised German soldiers that death was preferable to capture. Quite often prisoners would take for granted that they were going to be shot by us and would ask if they could write letters to their families first, or simply beg for mercy.

It was dirty pool in many ways, but quite often requests to write families would be denied in a brusque manner and since the prisoners would have jumped to the conclusion that we were about to shoot them, the simple denial as to letter-writing would reinforce their beliefs that their futures were short.

Careful interrogation, while maintaining the tensions created by such an atmosphere, would seldom fail to produce results of benefit to our regiment and highly injurious to the enemy.

One part of our technique would call for a US officer-interrogator, assigned to our regiment to interview a prisoner while a huge sergeant stood by in case of trouble. I would stand out of sight, but within hearing distance, and at an opportune time I would stride in, as belligerent as a wild bull, and berate the interrogator, who would call out 'Achtung' and jump to his feet as though frightened of me. If the prisoner failed to scramble to his feet, assuming that he was seated, as was usually the case, the sergeant would help him in no uncertain manner.

On the day that we handled the general, the interrogator was acting somewhat obsequiously, as we had agreed he would, when I walked into the large stone-walled barracks hall in which were located a desk and two chairs. The atmosphere was icy and our breathing vaporized as we spoke.

I slammed up to the desk and the interrogator jumped up shouting 'Achtung' as always, but the general sat where he was, looking me up and down for the few seconds it took the sergeant to jump to the chair and eject its occupant onto the floor. The look in the general's eye changed very quickly from arrogance to, what best can be described as, uncertainty.

I knew that the general could understand English, as he had answered some of the questions in that language. I sailed into the interrogator in my best parody of a Prussian martinet, accusing him of mollycoddling Germans and letting them walk all over him. I asked him why he had given the prisoner a cigarette before I'd had a chance to conduct the questioning and, in general, laid it on thick.

While such playacting has always sounded hokey, it worked more often than not with troops who had been trained in an atmosphere full of bluster and rigid formality. During such tirades I quite often accused the interrogator of wasting time asking prisoners questions to which we already knew the answers. In a way, this was backing into the technique known as 'show of knowledge,' aimed at convincing prisoners that, if we knew so much already, little harm would come of telling us more. Quite often in parading our knowledge of hostile activities, we would include items of which we were not sure and would have them confirmed by the prisoner, directly or by implication.

The general had some difficulty getting to his feet because of his girth which was well cinched in by a heavy Sam Browne belt. By this time I was fairly boiling with anger! I nodded at the sergeant, who was standing behind the general, and almost immediately the high-billed cap that added inches to the man's apparent height, went sailing across the hall. Underneath that handsome headpiece was a bald pate that seemed to lessen the austerity of the officer. I yelled at the general, telling him that I was damned sick and tired of German officers calling on the Geneva Conventions (which he had done) to save their own hides when, to my certain knowledge, they had never refrained from torturing our soldiers when interrogating them after capture.

He started to remonstrate by raising his hands toward me and I pushed him down into the chair with considerable vehemence. His feet flipped up as he landed and a look of pain crossed his face. I told him I wanted one question, and one question alone, answered and with no more quibbling.

'How many troops did you have under your command when you were captured?' I asked. His silence was punctuated by the sound of a Sam Browne belt being removed from the general by the sergeant. This resulted in a vast sinking of the general's paunch. Repetition of the one question followed by silence brought similar divestiture of boots, tunic, breeches, shirt, underwear, and socks.

It was, then, but a matter of moments before the general answered. In fact, he went on and on as he stood first on one foot and then the other, shaking and shivering in the icebox of a barracks. I inquired into any information he had as to reserves available to him, having emphasized to him that the Allied armies would soon penetrate Germany and crush it absolutely. It would be, I told him, to Germany's advantage to get the slaughter over with as soon as possible.

He was fairly well advised of the state of affairs to his immediate rear and as far back as the Rhine River. He gave me to understand that the defensive positions along the flank of the Vosges Mountains were not ready for occupation yet and that he had been warned to hold the Moselle River position for a month longer. He acknowledged that the penetration of the German front by my regiment had come as a complete surprise and our crossing of the river by wading had caught them unawares.

'Usually,' he said, 'you Americans attack with artillery and jeeps, but you fooled us this time.'

When he was permitted to dress again, it became apparent that his arrogance returned with each article of clothing that he donned until, having again cinched in his flab with the Sam Browne, he jutted his chin toward me and said he would protest 'to higher authority' about such mistreatment of a general officer of the Third Reich. I simply asked him if he thought his word would be better than mine, under the circumstances. I never heard of him again, once we sent him back through channels to the higher authorities he was seeking.

However, a few days later, General Dahlquist dropped by to see how we were faring and, as usual, stopped to question me about hostile dispositions and capabilities. I asked him if he'd had a chance to talk with the German general my regiment had captured and he said he hadn't, nor had he received any dope from his G-2 section. I had been busy in the interim and while I had sent back data as to hostile strength reported by the German officer to be some 3,500 of all ranks, I hadn't felt that the business of Vosges defenses and reserves was sufficiently definitive to warrant reporting.

General Dahlquist then mentioned that he was having trouble with some of the thinking of corps and army headquarters, some of whose officers had served in the First World War. It seems that they were possessed of the mentality of that era which had considered the Vosges an impenetrable barrier. He mentioned that in the First World War the flank had been contained in the vicinity of the city of Saint-Dié, and army personnel were now talking of holing up at about that same spot for the winter.

I said something to the following effect, 'Hell, General, if what the German general told me is true, we could get through the Vosges in three days and close into the Rhine River.' I went on to relate that the Vosges defenses, according to the general and other sources, were nowhere near completion; that our air force was knocking out the limited reserves the Germans had as fast as they appeared; and that German morale appeared to be dropping out of sight. Then I added, 'Are we prepared to cut around the Vosges passes, carrying our provisions and ammo on our backs?' I told him that the Germans expected us to drive our jeeps up the limited roadways where they had established solid roadblocks of trees standing on end in ditches. If we did, the German general felt that we would be bogged down for the winter, and since he had been ordered to destroy all habitations and supplies forward of German defenses, we'd be forced into facing a perilous winter on the mountain flanks.

Several days later General Dahlquist dropped by again and said, 'Doughty, I told the corps and army commanders about your three-day deal for crossing the Vosges and they think you've been here too long.' He laughed as he said it and then added that he was strongly in favor of my view, as opposed to the supine attitude dictated by the exigencies of the First World War. He also said that he had ordered up enough A-frames for the attacking battalions to back-carry their supplies for an extended period.

At about that time our division was augmented by the attachment of the 442nd Regimental Combat Team comprising Japanese-Americans – the Nisei – whom we were proud to have with us. Their 100th Battalion had worked near us in the Monte Cassino area of Italy and had earned tremendous recognition for their daring tactics and staunchness under grueling conditions.

It was at this juncture that a particularly poignant event occurred, which I covered earlier in Chapter 14 of these memoirs and which involved Lieutenant Karam's premonition of his own death.

The first real combat to which our new colonel was exposed arose when General Dahlquist, having taken the city of Bruyères, was ordered to extend the division's front to protect the corps' right flank while other corps troops attacked toward Saint-Dié. In order to do this, our regiment would have to attack, striking at the German rear areas from one leg of an L-shaped division front, in effect making a U-shaped front which would, if successful, force the Germans to withdraw to escape encirclement. Colonel Lundquist had almost suffered a recessive personality when he received his instructions to mount the critical attack aimed at knocking out the German troops in front of us. He could be heard muttering to himself about an 'impossible situation' and occasionally he was observed shaking his head for all to see. A good commander seldom shows such a negative attitude, but mimeograph machines are probably not susceptible to contagious fear and buckling courage.

In any event, I was summoned by a messenger at about 4 am on the morning of the projected attack, and I reported to Colonel Lundquist. He had aged considerably and much of the mystique of the high-level operator seemed to have disappeared as he told me of a mission he wanted me to perform. We sat in a room of a small house at the edge of a heavily wooded slope of the Vosges foothills and had a cup of coffee as he outlined a message I was to take to General Dahlquist. It became evident to me that Lundquist had no faith at all that the regiment would succeed in its latest mission and that, like all second-raters, he was 'covering his ass,' as the saying went. I was to tell General Dahlquist, among a number of other things, that while Lundquist was prepared to attack in the direction ordered by Dahlquist, he could not take responsibility for the results since he expected strong German reaction and once our 1st Battalion was committed to the fight, he, Lundquist, had no troops with which to maneuver since the rest of our regiment was strained to the limit by holding an excessively long front.

Lundquist also told me that he had ordered an engineer platoon to bridge over a deep gully, well into the woods, for the forward regimental CP and that I was to report there on returning from Bruyères where the division CP was situated. He also said that I was the only officer he could 'trust' to deliver the message and, by implication at least, survive any storm that might be occasioned by Lundquist's temerity in raising the issue.

I looked at him for a long half-minute and very nearly told him that I was sure that Dahlquist was aware of the risks involved and had ordered the attack to break the German line so that we could cross the Vosges Mountains before winter set in. I refrained, however, for I never saw a bleaker look on anyone's face in the flickering light of a candle that only added to the shadows around the colonel's eyes. His nerves, I felt, were strung out to the limit.

However, I asked him to show me on a map where the forward echelon would be located, and he pointed to a trail junction at the top of a ridge. 'Jesus Christ,' I said, 'Colonel, you're putting us right on an artillery registration point.' He looked sicker then, but said he'd already had the engineers working at building his 'dugout' since earlier in the previous evening.

I took off for Bruyères in dense blackness, accompanied by my driver and a couple of riflemen from the I&R platoon. It was eerie going under blackout conditions, and the sun was throwing its first rays over the horizon before I finally reached division headquarters. An MP showed me where General Dahlquist's trailer was parked and I pounded on its door. An orderly peered out at me and started to caution me to be quiet, but I pushed up a couple of stairs past him and found General Dahlquist, pajama-clad, sitting up in bed.

'Good morning, General,' I said, saluting him, 'sorry to break in on you at this hour but Colonel Lundquist has sent an urgent message by me and wants an answer as soon as I can get back.'

The general got up and put on a robe, for the trailer was cold, and then, with a quizzical look in his eye said, 'Hasn't got cold feet, has he?'

'He's nervous and edgy,' I said and then proceeded to tell the general the gist of Lundquist's observations.

'Tell him that he's got nothing to fear,' the general finally said. 'I've got the 442nd Infantry as part of the division and will have it alerted to move when your attack takes off.' We sort of sized each other up as though not wishing to say what we were both thinking about Lundquist, and then Dahlquist smiled and said, 'I'll see you up on the hill.' I told him where the forward echelon would be located and saw him frown as he also spotted the trail junction and thought about what would happen as soon as any activity around the 'dugout' was spotted by hostile observers. 'Lousy position' he said as I highballed him and swung down out of the rear of the trailer to where the general's orderly had brought coffee for my men. They'd also extracted a canteen cupful for me, and I was glad to feel its warmth as we sat there for the few moments it took to drink it.

When I returned to the regiment, I learned that Colonel Lundquist was at the forward CP and expected me to get there at once. I put on a heavy battle uniform for warmth, slung a bedroll into the jeep, and took off. I left the S-2 section where it was since I figured that any 'dugout' would be cramped at best.

Engineers were building a new road up through the woods, following an old dirt road for the most part. We were held up at one point and I could hear the sounds of battle as our First Battalion was heavily engaged almost immediately after it moved toward the enemy's vitals. I talked with an engineer captain I recognized and he came to the jeep, face black with soot and soil, teeth shining white against the dirt. 'Good to see you,' he said as we shook hands. 'Heavy fight just ahead,' he added.

'What's the "dugout" I hear you guys built?' I asked.

He looked at me and shook his head. 'You've got a hot one in Lundquist,' he said. 'Back to the First World War in a hurry. First "dugout" I've heard of in this war.'

He described the work the engineers had done in decking over a fairly sizeable ravine that surface water had dug through the years down the opposite flank of the hill we were standing on. Several layers of trees, some of them 50ft long, had been placed over the top of the ravine for 30 or 40ft feet down the slope, and more had been added at each end to block off all access to the space beneath, which did not permit a normal man to stand erect once inside. Some work had been done to the interior to square off the floor and walls, but all in all it was makeshift and primitive.

'How about a direct hit on it by heavy artillery.' I asked.

'Not likely,' he responded. 'Too many trees around it, but it's a hot spot already because some SPs have already taken it under fire.' I wondered how the Germans had learned of its existence so soon and thought that a patrol, watching at night, could have reported the work of the engineers in roofing over a sizeable space.

I waved goodbye to my friend, who looked as though he hadn't slept for a week, and my driver shifted to four-wheel drive as we skirted a bulldozer and started a precipitous climb toward the top of the hill.

I had the jeep pull off to a small parking area just before we reached the crown of the hill and went ahead on foot. I could see the log roof of the 'dugout' as I reached the crest and spotted a man crawling out of a small hole near the upper end of the ravine. It was the regimental S-3 and when he saw me, he sent a thumbs-down signal to indicate things were not going well. He disappeared along a trail through the underbrush to what, I later learned, was a latrine built behind the crest of the ridge.

I eased down into the 'dugout' and found a number of officers and enlisted men sitting about, while the colonel spoke on the field phone. I heard him say, 'That's a damned shame!' and hang up.

'What did the general say?' he asked me as he motioned me to sit down on a stool beside him. I told him what General Dahlquist had said and Lundquist said, 'Better get him on the horn, now. Bird's battalion headquarters has been cut off from the rest of the battalion by a German counterattack coming in from both sides, and Lieutenant Karam was killed. Bird tried his best to rejoin his outfit – even commandeered a tank – but couldn't make it. That was him on the phone just now. He's coming in here shortly.'

I told the colonel that it would be well to await news of the 1st Battalion's position and status before calling Dahlquist. 'Hell, the battalion's cut off just as I knew it would be,' he said.

Lieutenant Colonel Bird slid down into the dugout at about that time and the look on his face was heartrending. 'Goddamn it!' he said. 'I lost my battalion' and tears streaked his face. Men spoke to him in easy tones trying to calm him down, while Bird spoke of the ferocity of the counterattack and the volume of automatic fire that had torn his headquarters apart.

Someone called 'Attention!' and we looked up to see General Dahlquist kneeling at the entranceway. He took the news calmly and after cheering Bird up, left to get back to his radio to call division headquarters. Telephone lines had been blasted out of service by German artillery fire that was just beginning to increase in volume in our vicinity.

We spent a cold night in our First World War 'dugout,' helped a bit by a hot meal that carrying parties brought forward in marmite cans that kept the food warm. It was an eerie sight to see Colonel Lundquist sitting, wrapped in a blanket to include his head, with one candle on a field table before him. He said he planned to stay right there until the 1st Battalion was rescued. We later referred to him as the 'Oracle of Delphi.'

I rolled up on the ground and got several hours' sleep before shelling of our area brought me out of deep slumber. The day wore on with each of us, including Lundquist, running the gauntlet to relieve ourselves behind the crest of the hill. It became evident that the 1st Battalion was indeed 'The Lost Battalion' of the Second World War. Radio contact was made through a Lieutenant Erwin

Blonder, a forward observer of the 131st Field Artillery who had been cut off with the infantry when the German counterattack was sprung. By this time it was October 24, 1944, the attack having been initiated on October 23. While the remaining two battalions of the 141st Infantry had been cut loose to assist the 1st Battalion, their efforts to do so were strongly opposed and shortly the entire regiment was pinned by superior defensive forces.

On October 25 and 26 the Nisei regiment was committed to force a passage to the lost battalion while the 2nd and 3rd Battalions of the 141st Infantry put pressure on the hostile forces in front of them. Artillery fire wasn't too effective because of the density of the forests in that area.

The 1st Battalion meanwhile had been lying doggo so that it wasn't until after several days had passed that the Germans became aware of its predicament. From then on the battalion fought for its life. It was later learned that both the American and German troops involved in that siege had obtained water from the same waterhole.

Finally on October 30, 1944, after beating off heavy German counterattacks the Nisei broke through and rescued 211 survivors who had withstood a 10-day siege. The Germans lost heavily in the balance, a factor that did much to prompt the decision to force the Vosges Mountain passes instead of putting in another winter on their western approaches.

In order to try to support the lost battalion, unusual efforts were made to supply them with D rations and first-aid packets loaded into big shells and fired into the battalion area. This, however, did not work very well as the shells either buried themselves too deeply into the ground or hit trees and exploded, scattering their contents in all directions.

P-47 fighter bombers of the XII TAC (Tactical Air Command) were used to drop supplies at sites marked with men's underwear, white linings of parkas, and map sheets, set out in a long strip. Smoke grenades were also tied to bent saplings so that, as planes neared the site, the saplings could be released to pull pins from the grenades just as they reached tree-top level for quick spotting by the flyers. The first air drop missed the landing area by a hundred yards and supplies went to the enemy.

Subsequently, however, both the food-laden shells and the belly tanks of medical supplies and rations and radio batteries hit the target area simultaneously. Men who had had to pull in their belts for several days to allay hunger pains finally got a meal.

The resupply effort, however, had fully awakened the Germans to the real situation regarding the battalion. The result was a heavy cannonading of the battalion's position followed by a ground attack that, fortunately, struck where Lieutenant Marty Higgins, A Company commander and temporary leader of the hapless battalion, had had prepared the strongest defenses with heavy machine guns.

While ammunition had to be rationed, gunners were more effective than they might otherwise have been, and by sharpshooting laid the Germans out in windrows. The German casualties until then had been light, since the hostile infantrymen had been lying in covered foxholes that protected them from tree-bursts. Outside of their foxholes, the onrushing enemy troops were slaughtered by shellfire called down on them by Lieutenant Blonder. Several hundred bodies were found later in one pile where the German graves registration officers had placed them, preparatory to burial.

At the end of that period of fighting, the average number of men in my regiment's rifle companies was 83, down from 200. The 111th Combat Engineer Battalion, reinforced with another company from the 232nd Engineers, was as responsible for the success of this hard-fought operation as any other element of the forces involved in it. It built and maintained a 7½-mile mountain road, under hazardous conditions, into a major supply route that, at its height, bore the traffic of four infantry regiments, three tank companies, a company of anti-aircraft artillery and a medical evacuation unit. Three angle dozers were destroyed by enemy artillery fire and two operators were wounded, a third killed. In all, the engineers suffered fifty-seven casualties. There was no doubt in anyone's mind who saw the action that the serious losses taken by the German forces during this battle contributed to their ultimate failure to hold the Vosges Mountains. The 'Lost Battalion' of the Second World War, in effect, contributed significantly to the German 'Lost Cause,' since the effort to rescue the battalion redoubled our impact upon the hostile forces and, in the end, our morale soared while German morale, finally, went down the tube.

Chapter 26

Breaching the Vosges Mountains

Early in November 1944 a general offensive was opened all along the Allied line aimed at driving the Germans back across the Rhine River and slamming the door forever on Hitler's ambition to conquer the world. VI Corps, of which the 36th Division was a part, faced the high Vosges barrier. Our division, tired out from ninety-eight consecutive days of combat, was given the mission of defending the corps-army right flank and of taking over ground captured by a fresh division, the 103rd, about to be committed to the breaching of the Saverne Gap along with the newly reconstituted 3rd Division.

Throughout the time we'd spent fighting from the shore on the Riviera to the Vosges Mountains, German construction units had been building a defensive position along the Meurthe River, designed to be used as a winter line. On our side of that line all shelter had been destroyed by demolition or fire in the hopes of bogging us down and decreasing our will to go on to gain the unconditional surrender of Germany. We had no intention of falling in with such a plan.

Our division reached the Meurthe River at St. Léonard on November 19, 1944, and the next day one of our regiments crossed at St. Léonard and Anould. On November 23 my regiment assisted in producing a breakthrough of the German defenses at Le Chipol and La Croix-aux-Mines. So much for our resting and cleaning up after others! So much, too, for the German winter line! The losses suffered by hostile forces around Bruyères prevented their manning the line sufficiently well to stop us.

The Sainte-Marie-aux-Mines Pass was breached on my 35th birthday, November 25, 1944, by troops that scaled the precipitous slopes carrying their supplies on their backs, exactly as General Dahlquist had envisaged they would when we had talked, after my interrogation of the captured German general. They had no supporting artillery with them and no vehicles and, again, the German defenders were taken by complete surprise. Our troops came at them from the rear of the German prepared positions just at sun-up, and the pass fell with scarcely a firefight. So much, then, for First World War attitudes toward the impregnability of the Vosges Mountains. We took more than 2,200 prisoners.

Later, I recalled the German general's contribution to our effort as I drove past some formidable roadblocks the Germans had constructed across the road leading to the Sainte-Marie-aux-Mines pass. Tree trunks, placed vertically into trenches, formed a palisade 15ft high. These were defended by minefields, artillery, and automatic fire plus booby-trapped abatis.

German resistance stiffened almost at once as reserves were rushed up the eastern slopes of the Vosges from the Rhineland in an effort to block our further passage of the line, which the German High Command had felt it could hold indefinitely.

On November 28, 1944, Koenigsbourg Castle fell to our forces and from that imposing structure, high on a promontory, we had a dazzling view of the entire Alsace Plain, the Rhine River, and the Black Forest inside Germany.

In this general area and at about this time I participated in a discomfiting vignette that has stayed with me, almost as poignantly as on the day it occurred.

We were headquartered in a small French schoolhouse on the south side of which was a fairly large and comfortable farmhouse we'd taken over for billeting purposes. It was getting colder each day as winter came on, so that we had had oil-burning stoves set up in the schoolhouse, which had a main room sufficiently large to house most of our operating sections and several smaller rooms for supplies, mess, and the like.

On a day when two German planes had flown low over us and strafed the building, we were talking in the main schoolroom, wondering whether we should move the headquarters that night to avoid a possible bombing the next morning. All at once the door from the yard opened and there stood Colonel Harmony, all smiles. We greeted him with great enthusiasm and yet, while it appeared that he was about to resume command of the regiment, I knew on good authority that it wasn't true. As soon as I could, I maneuvered him into a smaller room where I had my section installed and asked, 'Didn't you get my letter, Colonel?'

He looked at me with a completely blank face and said, 'What letter?'

'I sent you a letter,' I said, 'in care of the Naples hospital where you were recuperating within a week of the time you were wounded at Montélimar.'

He shook his head and said, 'I never received it!'

I asked him if he'd been to division headquarters before arriving at our CP and he shook his head, 'Nope! Came right here. I'm AWOL from the hospital. Bummed my way by ship and truck all the way from Naples! It's great to be back.'

I hated to tell him but I said, 'General Stack told me you were permanently relieved of command of the regiment just as soon as you left. I wrote this to you but didn't name him. I simply said, "The person over whose grave we may, one day, cross swords says you won't be back."' (We had agreed on one occasion, when Stack was acting his usual obnoxious self, that we'd enjoy pissing on his grave, one day.)

Harmony's face went absolutely dead. 'God! I can't believe it,' he said. 'This regiment means everything to me. If I can't fight it, then I'm opting out of combat. My wounds aren't healed and I'll go back to Italy.'

He stayed the night and as we ate dinner, Colonel Lundquist tried hard to impart the aura of a well-respected leader who had replaced in the minds of regimental personnel anyone who might, previously, have held that position.

He had no way of knowing that Harmony knew exactly how we felt about our 'leader.'

Colonel Harmony left the next day and I saw him again, only after the war ended, at his home in San Francisco, although I heard of him both when he was a military attaché in Rome and Yugoslavia and when he had a heart attack in Korea. We have exchanged Christmas cards ever since, and Ellie has visited his home with me. He retired as a major general. He did tell me on one occasion when I saw him at his home that he, finally, received my letter – months after the war ended!

After Koenigsbourg Castle fell we learned that friendly forces just north of us had won through to Strasbourg. On November 30, 1944, the 36th Division broke through the Vosges and descended onto the plains beyond which lay the Rhine River. As usual, no one had managed to keep up with our progress so that we were out front with both flanks exposed.

Our breakthrough caused the German High Command to order reinforcements to move in daylight to try to block us. Anticipating heavy losses, the Germans nevertheless had to take the chance in order to meet our challenge. Their losses to our air force and artillery were appalling.

Our next objective, the city of Sélestat, fell on schedule and, on December 4, 1944, was securely held by our troops. At that time, due to open flanks, the division occupied a sector some 35miles wide and my regiment had extended itself to defend 21 miles of that front.

Because I have speeded up the events leading to our breach of the Vosges Mountain passes, to stress the relatively short time it took to dispose of that obstacle, I shall now retrace my steps to cover certain events that occurred during that period which bore on my own career.

Just after I had interrogated the German general at the French army barracks, a French civilian was brought to my regimental headquarters. I talked with him and learned that he was a French air force reservist who had led a group of guerrillas from the Vosges hinterland. He lived in Corcieux, a small town which had been the subject of savage attacks by the German troops of that area because of the underground terrorism that seemed to emanate from Corcieux.

The man called himself Leclerc, a name commonly employed as an alias by many French Maquis. We called him the 'one-man army.' I never met anyone who could be so cheerful and almost debonair about slaughtering Germans. His blue eyes would flash and gold caps on his teeth would emphasize his pleasure as he told of blowing up convoys of German troops and freight trains, bridges, and power stations.

When I first saw him he looked enormous due to his having worn a heavy overcoat, fastened by a broad leather belt into which he had thrust at least ten German 'potato-masher' hand-grenades, knives, bayonets, three pistols, and bullet pouches. He had a German Walser rifle slung over one shoulder and a German machine-pistol (a Schmeiser) over the other. He had binoculars around his neck and a stiletto in his right boottop.

Leclerc was a stocky, fairly short but broad-shouldered man, powerful as a bull. His civilian job, during the war, had been to drive a truck throughout the Vosges and Rhineland, and this had given him a great opportunity to select targets for attention by the underground. If France had had more men like Leclerc, Germany would have been stopped when Hitler remilitarized the Rhineland!

I asked 'Zero' to clear Leclerc with French army officials for service with our regiment, for his intimate knowledge of the whole area was priceless. We had him outfitted in some of our uniforms to include helmet, khaki trousers and shirts, windbreaker and overcoat, boots, and the whole works. He was glad to put aside the German firearms since ammunition was in short supply. However, in addition to an American carbine he carried a German pistol, a 45 caliber sub-machine gun, a dozen pineapple grenades, bayonet, knife, and stiletto. He stayed with the I&R platoon, who liked his attitude and his willingness to patrol with them.

For a number of days when we were in the vicinity of the Meurthe River, I had the feeling that we were in an increasingly dangerous position. Stormy weather had grounded all reconnaissance flights and German front-line troops were reacting savagely to our patrols. Operating blindly always generates uneasiness and, finally, I asked Leclerc if he knew of any French civilians who would risk passing through the German lines at night with radios on their backs in order to report on German activities.

He was back within 3 hours with six woodsmen who knew every nook and cranny of the area and who were aching to get into action again. They'd served with Leclerc on some of his more memorable sorties from the underground. I set them to work with some of our radio operators and Leclerc, supervised by 'Zero,' learning the use of our radio equipment.

In the interim, I had the staff of my intelligence section drawing up a special code in French terms designed to expedite reports of hostile formations and activities. A single word would translate into a complete sentence identifying weapons, armor, infantry, artillery, as the case might be. A map with a special overlay, much like the one I'd used at the landing on the Riviera, could be used to describe the location of the reported findings.

Once we were sure the men could handle the radios and knew the importance of maintaining security on the air through use of the code, a matter that took three or four days as I recall it, we set out to pass them through our lines at night. Just before this occurred, we had taken over some territory on our left flank from the 45th US Division. I went with the group and, after alerting our troops to the fact that we were going to be moving around in front of the lines, we set out through the darkness.

Suddenly, as I was moving behind one of the woodsmen, while several others followed in our footsteps, there was a loud explosion behind me. I heard someone shout and froze in my tracks. One of the Frenchmen had stepped on an anti-personnel mine.

There is no worse feeling, probably, in warfare than that occasioned when one finds himself in a minefield. To make it worse, I learned later that this minefield had been planted by the 45th Division, with no advice to us of its existence when we'd taken over the position.

For a horrible moment we all stood there; no sound of movement reached me. Then I called to 'Zero' who was near the casualty and told him to retrace his steps and for all men to follow closely in each other's footprints, so far as could be accomplished under tough conditions. We managed to return to the outpost line of our battalion, where men had been alerted by the explosion, which they'd taken to be a shell. The man who'd stepped on the mine was dead. Miraculously, no one else was touched by flying debris.

Two nights later, after being assured by the 45th Division CG that there were no more minefields in our area, so far as concerned any put in place by his units, we repeated the nighttime infiltration and I whispered, 'Bonne Chance' to the men as they moved silently toward the German positions.

Although I returned to our CP with 'Zero' after regaining our lines, I couldn't settle down. We had set up a radio relay system from the front line OPs to our headquarters and had equipped our men on the observation posts with copies of the code. However, I felt that we should be where we could get the first transmission directly, in case it became necessary to clarify a situation.

'Zero' and I, therefore, took our gear by jeep to a forward OP on a high hill overlooking the Plain of Corcieux. While there were hills in all directions ascending to the main Vosges system, a fairly extensive plain – in the middle of which stood a sizeable, tree-covered hill – surrounded Corcieux.

We spent the night talking with I&R platoon boys who were on duty at the OP. It was a long night but such were the pressures of the situation that no one could sleep. We hadn't a glimmer of German dispositions or movements for the last two weeks.

At dawn we gnawed on some hard chocolate and ate a 'dog biscuit,' washed down with a bottle of wine someone produced. Quickly, the stillness was shattered by a French voice on the frequency we'd assigned the woodsmen, giving a recognition signal followed by a torrent of words – not one of which was in code! Without interfering we plotted a hundred gun positions as we employed the overlay, a copy of which the Frenchman was using to show locations. All of the artillery being identified by the excited voice was located on the hill in the center of the Corcieux Plain. This meant but one thing; the Germans were about ready for a counteroffensive which, if it struck our overextended position, could produce a breakthrough. With their artillery pieces displaced forward to the furthest point of their lines, they were in a position to maintain the momentum of an attack by firing constantly without the need to displace forward during the attack.

I signaled 'Zero' to break in on the French woodsman and order him to move from his position, since I felt sure the Germans were already zeroing in on his position with their electronic gear. Just then, another voice cut in from a different location further to the rear of the German sector and described armor, self-propelled guns, and infantry.

I got on the telephone at that juncture and sent the only 'Flash' message I used during the war. 'Flash' was the highest priority available and took precedence over all other calls. I called army and, in turn, the G-2 there called Army Group. In the meantime, as the word spread through the different message centers that 'Doughty's got something hotter'n hell,' the drag on the line became so great that I could scarcely hear Army and Army Group. I yelled for everyone to get the hell off the line and General Dahlquist's calm voice came over clearly, 'I'll send the air liaison officer right up,' he said and hung up.

Army Group diverted planes carrying incendiary bombs scheduled initially for a less-important mission and told us to stand by to direct them onto the target. The planes were to arrive in something like 25 minutes. Within 15 minutes the air liaison officer from division headquarters was led to our position and from his jeep made contact by radio with the air strike leader.

Shortly thereafter we heard the plane motors and saw a flight of twelve planes moving at a fairly high altitude toward us. It was a bright day for a change, and we could see everything clearly as the planes peeled off and screamed down toward the hill in the center of the Corcieux Plain. We saw bombs drop as the planes swooped back to higher elevations and German anti-aircraft fire went into action, peppering the sky with shell bursts and tracers.

In the next few minutes we found ourselves shouting and yelling, as the incendiaries set fire to the whole back end of the hill in the Plain. Horses, mad with fear, plunged out of the underbrush - their bodies on fire. Some pulled cannon, bouncing and crashing around, while others were dragging men at the end of long halters - men whose clothing was in flames. The hill looked like a colony of ants – all afire – as men, animals, and vehicles broke from shelter, only to run into well-aimed artillery fire that division and corps artillery poured on them.

The Germans, under the cover of bad weather in much the same manner as occurred later at the Ardennes, had gambled on launching a surprise attack from a position which, if discovered, would lay them open to stunning losses. They lost, but we were lucky!

I learned later that the French government had honored the woodsmen who had served as our eyes and ears at a critical time. That government also honored me, later, with a Croix de Guerre with gold star, a decoration earned only in combat.

Sometime during the Vosges Mountain phase of our combat experiences, while we were still in the schoolhouse where Colonel Harmony rejoined the regiment for a night, we had an unusual prisoner in the shape of a German colonel who was a medical officer. He was a handsome man standing well over 6ft tall and with the approved Aryan look – blond hair and blue eyes. His uniform was immaculate.

He was brought in toward dusk on a day that had seen little action. It occurred to me, more or less in passing, that it might be a good idea to let people like the doctor know pretty much what we thought of the Germans under the Hitler regime. We interrogated him in the kitchen of the farmhouse across the road from the schoolhouse, since I was there eating dinner when he was brought in. I sat at the kitchen table and the only light we had was a Coleman lantern that hissed and sputtered a lot. The doctor's 'soldbuch' (pay-book) showed considerable data regarding his education and experience as a surgeon.

As soon as we started, he interjected that since he was a non-combatant he could not, legally, be held as a prisoner. He'd received some of his education in Great Britain and spoke English perfectly. I laughed at his pretended naïvety and told him that there would be a great deal of work for him to do in prison camps since our forces, by that time, had taken prisoners by the hundreds of thousands, many of them wounded.

We talked in generalities and I avoided questions bearing on the tactical situation since I was certain he would not answer them but even more certain that he knew little of the subject.

I finally said to him, 'Tell me, Colonel, as a medical expert just how is the German soldier a "Superman?" Your propaganda machines keep turning out stories about your superior qualities. Apparently no one has thought to tell Herr Göbbels that anyone can look superior when using tanks and planes against horses and men, as you so nobly did in Poland. But what are you doing these days, now that Göring's promise of immunity from bombing by the Allies has proved as empty as most of your leader's promises?'

He bridled somewhat at the slurs but kept himself under firm control. 'You Americans are lucky that the Russians are holding so many of our divisions on the Eastern Front.'

'We're not lucky at all, Colonel,' I answered. 'Your leaders are simply addlepated and silly. They chose the odds and elected to fight on two fronts. I can bring you the dumbest of our American soldiers who'll tell you, without hesitation, that only fools fight on two fronts, simultaneously.'

I could see that I was getting to him, a result I intended to achieve if it took all night!

'You're evading the question I put to you earlier,' I said. 'You Germans have believed your own propaganda for such a long time that you've lost touch with reality. As a matter of fact, most of you are too cowardly to dispute the great Hitler. He tells you that you are a superior, a "pure?" race and you believe him. Now, as a medical technician, wherein are you superior? If you take your pants down, are you better equipped than, let's say, the average Englishman or American? Tell me, how are you able to prove that you are a super race?'

He batted his eyes and looked daggers at me but my .45 pistol on the table had a quieting effect on him. He may have guessed that the pistol was part of my technique. He could not have guessed that, under similar circumstances behind Mount Luongo, Italy, a German paratrooper captured on Monte Cassino had made a desperate attempt to grab the pistol. He'd been brought in after fighting like a wildcat to kill his captors. I sat in a command tent partially dug into the flank of the mountain and further fortified by sandbags piled higher than its roof on all sides, with a small space left to permit entry down three steps. He was the toughest German soldier I encountered in the war. Highly trained and motivated in the Hitler Youth program, he was a fighting machine intent on giving his life if need be but extracting payment for it every inch of the way.

He had finally been knocked out after all attempts to keep him quiet and tractable at the front had failed. His hands were manacled behind him and as I watched him I could see that any movement of his arms brought a suppressed grimace to his face.

I finally got up from the field desk where I was sitting and walked behind him, as the big sergeant I kept on hand at such times moved in from the doorway to be nearer in case of trouble. I found that the man's wrists were pinioned with barbed wire and were so swollen that the wire was deeply imbedded in the flesh. I had the interrogator tell the prisoner that we would remove the wire if he would simply give his word to behave himself. The man nodded his assent and the sergeant managed to cut the wire without further damage. I had a medic come in and dress the wounds inflicted by the barbs.

Shortly thereafter we resumed the interrogation with the prisoner chafing his wrists to restore circulation. As the interrogator worked to get answers, none of which were forthcoming, the prisoner very casually shifted his position to more direct alignment with the desk where I was sitting. I was watching him like a hawk and as he prepared himself to leap forward, I brought my knees to the desk's under-surface and when the man sprang for the gun I crashed the desk up under his chin with my hands and legs, rising at the same time to send him sprawling toward the far end of the tent, where the sergeant knocked him out cold.

This was the kind of human being, I'm sure, that met the parameters of Hitler's 'superman' prototype. In goading him to do what I felt sure he would try, having heard of the difficulties encountered in capturing him, I felt no compunction at all at the price I made him pay.

I gave the German doctor most of the story of the captured paratrooper and said, 'I assume that such a man would meet all specifications set down by your leader, wouldn't he, doctor?' He answered with a resounding 'Jawohl,' and his look was one of admiration for the paratrooper and contempt for me.

'You feel that such a man represents the best in Germany today?' I asked.

'Certainly, any soldier of Hitler should refuse to give information of value to the enemy and should do anything to inflict harm on all of Germany's enemies,' the doctor said.

'Oh, but Colonel,' I said, 'I didn't say he gave us no information. When he was revived, he was still in the command tent where he made his try for my gun. Beside him we had positioned one of the Goums of the French colonial army who had been lent to us by the French for such purposes. The paratrooper took one look at the tribesman and all of his bravado left him. The interrogator told the prisoner that the Goum would take him back to the Goums' encampment for further interrogation and the paratrooper caved in.'

'You had no right to threaten him with such barbarous treatment,' the colonel yelled, as though he could stop something now long past.

'The main point, Colonel,' I said, 'seems to have escaped you. We simply took advantage of one of the many weaknesses we've observed in your military training. You've taught your men to regard us as fools, particularly us Americans. Hitler has referred to us as an inferior race – more to inflate his own superiority, I assume, than to establish a sociological theory. Your paratrooper really thought I'd left a loaded gun where he could grab it. Much as you've thought tonight, Herr Colonel. Here take the gun.' I shoved it toward him but he recoiled and the thought crossed my mind that he felt I was baiting him, so as to work him over if he made the try.

'As I told you,' he said, 'I am a non-combatant.'

'Too bad,' I responded as I took the pistol and released the clip to expose the nose of a cartridge. 'It's fully loaded.' The interrogator smiled as did the sergeant. 'I wouldn't want you to think that we aren't somewhat flexible in our handling of prisoners. I knew you wouldn't go for the gun, for I'm sure you tried to get yourself captured. Otherwise, how did a surgeon from a rear-echelon hospital manage to get near enough to the front to be taken while wearing a spotless uniform?'

I looked straight into the man's eyes and felt I'd hit more closely home than I had thought when I first made the statement.

'The nearer we get to Germany,' I added, 'the more rats leave your sinking ship.'

The colonel's face had turned pale and he finally lost his temper.

'You Americans are fools,' he shouted. 'Damned fools! You think you can defeat Germany on her own soil?'

'Easily, Colonel,' I said. 'The Rhine is just over the hill from here, and we can put patrols across it any time we please.'

He stood up and I motioned the sergeant back when the latter took a purposeful step forward.

'You will see,' the doctor shouted leaning down to stare into my face, just inches away. 'Father Rhine will protect Germany and you will never cross into Germany. Hitler's secret weapon is almost ready and Himmler told us, just yesterday, that we have only to hold where we are before we slaughter all of you.'

By this time, the doctor was panting and almost frothing in his effort to overwhelm me. What he didn't know in his excitement was that he had given me a key to the importance with which Germany considered the Vosges barrier. 'Himmler told us, just yesterday' had come out in the heat of the moment and yet it was a clear indication that a top Nazi was in the vicinity, a fact that we later established as true. I kept this fact uppermost in my mind and later, when assessing hostile moves, interpreted intelligence reports far differently than did my opposite numbers in higher and safer echelons.

'Don't excite yourself,' I said, as I stood up. 'I just wanted you to know, since you have a good chance of returning to Germany after the war, that we don't think you Germans are a super race at all. More likely you have what can only be described as a national inferiority complex from having taken so long to become a modern state. A little more modesty on your part would seem to be in order, too, since you've just told me who's in charge of this front. Many thanks.'

The look on his face was such a mixture of defiance and misery that I had all I could do to keep from laughing. 'I'll see you,' I said, 'after Father Rhine's done his best to stop us. As you go down the road tonight keep a sharp lookout for the boats we've brought up from the coast of France. You know, the ones that helped us breach "Festung Europa," another of your propaganda shibboleths.' I walked across to the CP while the I&R boys hustled the colonel to the division PW cage.

Another development arising in that general area in November, specifically near the city of Gérardmer, has remained with me as a funny event tinged with a potential for disaster. We were awaiting the advent of a new colonel since Colonel Lundquist had gone the way of many others, back to the rear areas, never to be heard of by us again. A Colonel Charles Owens was to take over the regiment and, as I recall it, had served with General Dahlquist in the US.

Lieutenant Colonel Donald McGrath, the regimental exec., was temporarily in charge as we slogged our way through the hills and forests of the area. There came a day when I received word by telephone from the division G-3 section that our regiment was to fall back to a position some 3 miles to the right rear of where we were located. I did my best to pin down the reason but received what can only be considered a half-assed response. It appeared, said one of the assistant G-3s, that we were going into reserve.

I gave the word to Colonel McGrath, who sent an advance party from the regimental headquarters company to reconnoiter the area. We alerted the battalions, none of which were in active combat at the time, and at sundown we pulled out and took up our new position. It was the first time in weeks that we were off the fighting front and we felt release from strain.

The regimental headquarters was established in a house that the Germans had prepared as a headquarters by sandbagging it all around up to a height of 6ft and shoring up its sides with long beams braced against the house and against heavy stakes driven into the ground. Not 50ft away was a railroad crossing and a small gatekeeper's shed that protected the crossing guard in inclement weather.

It was dark by the time I reached the CP but I immediately called in engineers to check for booby traps. It seemed to me that leaving the house ready for safe occupancy was the German way of inviting us into a pile of trouble. We found several hundred bottles of wine in the basement but careful search located no mines or booby traps.

We had a late dinner in the kitchen of the house and demolished several bottles of wine, the consuming of much of which put McGrath about six sheets into the wind. He finally stumbled off to his billet in a nearby house, much of which had been destroyed.

At about 4 am the telephone wakened me from my cot nearby and I answered only to learn that General Stack was on his way to our regiment to inspect our defenses against the anticipated flanking attack the division was expecting at dawn! No one had bothered to tell us that we were in a tactical situation and that our mission was defense against counterattack. I asked the basis for the expected thrust against us and was told the G-2 section of the division had put it together. I felt relieved at hearing this for it would have been the first time the section had put anything together correctly, if its estimate proved true.

I called three battalion COs and told them to get cracking at digging in defensive positions against possible attack from our right flank. I also told them that General Stack was en route to our position and that we'd better make some dirt fly.

Next, I set out to find Colonel McGrath in a black, black pre-dawn. I nearly broke my leg falling into a foxhole someone had thoughtfully dug near the entrance to his billet. I finally located him upstairs in a huge old bed with a tester atop it. He was fully dressed, boots and all, and was snoring loudly. No matter how I shook him and yelled, he only muttered something and refused to come out of his comatose state. A bucket of water from a nearby washstand did the trick though, and he came up fighting mad. However, the word that Stack was coming to inspect our defenses struck just the right note with him. I led him to our CP where a quart of black coffee brought a near smile to his face, which was still adorned with the handlebar moustache.

Dawn came but, as I had suspected – no attack materialized. I had felt that the Germans were not strong enough to counterattack and since they were in comparatively comfortable quarters, there was little reason for them to swap them for our miserable situation.

General Stack arrived and found a few things wrong, as a matter of course. That we had a defensive position at all was due basically to the fact that a veteran outfit never moves to a new area without digging in. While some positions had been changed after I heard that Stack was coming to visit us, in order to meet the reported threat from our right flank, our battalions had spent most of the night preparing strongpoints and defensive lines in depth.

Later, after Stack left, I observed a flurry of action at the gatekeeper's small hut and walked over to see what was happening. Three engineers had ripped up some floorboards inside the shack and there, piled in a triangular heap, were ten 500lb bombs wired to a detonator that had been ticking away for nearly a month. It appeared that there were several hours to doomsday still left on the clock when an engineer cut a wire and stopped its infernal ticking. All along I had known that our 'safe' CP was an invitation to disaster but hadn't looked far enough away for the diabolical *pièce de résistance* that would have put us out of combat. Typical of that method of creating serious threats to our existence were several others brought to our attention by local inhabitants. In one area along a roadway, running through a defile, the Germans had dug a hole in the center of the road some 50ft deep and in it had placed some twenty 500lb bombs wired to be detonated sometime within a month of the time they were put in place. Had this bomb-mine gone off, our sole supply line would have been blocked for days.

However, local residents in secret had observed the installation of the bombs and despite the re-paving of the road for several hundred feet in either direction from the potential crater, had marked the exact location of the explosives so that, accepting the hazard of immediate immolation, engineers had dug to them and rendered the bombs harmless.

In another instance, German soldiers had dug several tons of coal out of a hotel basement, fixed a heavy enough charge on the floor to destroy the hotel and then shoveled the coal back over the lethal pile. We were told of the destructive mechanism in time to disarm it and enjoy the relative comfort of the hotel. All in all, the dirty work of the Germans brought them very little tactical advantage but caused our engineers endless hours of super-hazardous duty, to their everlasting credit.

Chapter 27

The Rhineland

On December 4, 1944, orders were issued attaching the 36th Division to the II French Corps commanded by General de Goisiard de Montsabert. The remainder of the Seventh Army was to concentrate its efforts to the north of Strasbourg in order to force the defenses of the Maginot and Siegfried Lines before the Germans could man them to optimum effect.

The First French Army, delayed by high and rugged terrain in the Vosges, together with the 36th Division, was to clear the so-called 'Colmar Pocket.' Just prior to this juncture, one of our regiments had captured the city of Ribeauville. Roads had been blocked by huge felled trees, called 'abatis,' the removal of which was slow and hazardous.

I have vivid memories of watching engineer companies working to clear one area where trees were piled in tangled masses. It was just about sunset when we were halted by guards and told to stand clear. We pulled our vehicles back a safe distance while a tank retriever crew hitched a cable to a key tree in the middle of the pile and then pulled it loose to the tune of several very heavy explosions that threw debris all around us. Booby traps often consisted of anti-personnel mines which in turn were connected to Teller mines containing 21 pounds of dynamite. A man triggering the smaller mine could be blown to smithereens by the detonation of the anti-tank mines. In the gloaming, the flashes of the several detonations accompanying the removal of the abatis were like the final pyrotechnics of a July 4 celebration.

Colonel Owens, not long with the regiment, was wounded by mines on December 5, 1944. He was a quiet man, not given to demonstrative speech or action at any time and possessed of a slow smile that matched his speech. His one quirk appeared to be the need to wash his mop of white hair with a bluing rinse that made it appear purplish once he had completed his toilette, which he managed to accomplish behind locked doors.

By December 6 the 36th Division had cleared its sector of the Vosges as a prelude to an attack involving the crossing of the Ill River. Just prior to that date my regiment was relieved by the 5th Combat Command of the 4th French Armored Division and five units of Moroccan Goums. We moved north to rejoin the rest of the division.

The division front ran from Sélestat on the north to Guémar and Ostheim, then to Mittelwihr and Hill 351 south of Riquewihr. Our right flank for all practical purposes was open, since only the 36th Recon Troop was available to screen it against surprise attack and its strength was inadequate for the distances and type of terrain involved. The French were unable to close in on our flank.

Just as the division was about to attack east, from the vicinity of Ribeauville toward Neuf Brisach near the Rhine River, winter rains caused the Ill River to overflow its banks, turning the entire Alsace Plain into a great morass, impassable by vehicles.

This necessitated a change of plan whereby our division would wheel to the right and attack in the direction of Colmar along the eastern base of the Vosges foothills. In order to accomplish the change of direction it was necessary to put back the date of our attack to December 15.

It seemed that at every critical juncture involving the 36th Division something intervened to shift the burden onto the 141st Infantry. Some of us were privy to the machinations of one of the regimental commanders who always managed to 'suck' out of dangerous assignments. He bragged a lot about his own expertise and that of his regiment, but when it came to grappling head-on with the enemy – for example, in amphibious operations – he would manage to fulfill the floating reserve assignment.

At the Rapido River, he drew another reserve assignment. He was the only one of the regimental COs who would find some excuse to be at division headquarters when vital planning was afoot and in one way or another would convince the general of the need to keep his force intact against possible failure of either of the other two regiments to take their objectives.

To make matters worse, the men assigned to write the division history, by going to Washington DC, before the war ended in order to gain access to official Signal Corps photographs for that purpose, came in large part from that regiment. As a result, it goes without saying, that the history contains a badly biased slant in favor of the 142nd Infantry which, for my money, was the poorest of the three.

A case in point will illustrate the kind of tactics employed by the 142nd Infantry as related to me by a captain who occupied a cot next to me at an evacuation hospital when I was sent back with a strep throat. First, though, the background on my illness will set the stage.

I realized one day that my throat, which had been sore for days, was closing to the point where I could no longer swallow. Instead I began to drool, even though I felt strong enough to carry on. We were then engaged in the Vosges, fighting somewhere in the vicinity of Remiremont.

Our medics took me in hand and when they looked at my throat, tagged me for immediate evacuation. This means they literally attached a tag to my uniform as though I were a piece of luggage and sent me posthaste to an ambulance pick-up area for a long ride back to the 27th Evacuation Hospital at Xertigny, France. I remonstrated as well as I could with my breath being nearly cut off due to the swelling on both sides of my throat, but the chief doctor told me that my case was very serious in that my temperature was normal in spite of the heavy infection in my throat.

I rode in the back of an ambulance, which contained three litter cases of men who had been severely wounded in combat. All were heavily sedated but as the ambulance, whose suspension was the worst I'd ever encountered, bounced and wove along the torn up roads of rural France, they would moan and groan as though the mauling they were receiving had penetrated their unconscious state.

Sometime in early morning we reached the hospital which, of course, was brightly lit by flood lamps to show the large red crosses on the roofs of the tents that formed long wards where overworked nurses showed the strain on their faces and their stoop-shouldered walking was symptomatic of the burden of lifting heavy men all day long. A number of doctors met several ambulances that rolled into a receiving courtyard with mine and read our tags. A colonel, blood-spattered and tired to the point of death, took me by the arm and said for all to hear, 'This man, first!!'

I was relieved, although surprised to receive such immediate attention, particularly where a man lying at my feet on a litter had a blood-soaked bandage around a stump of his right leg where a schuh-mine[1] had crippled him for life. The surgeon propelled me through an admissions tent, saying over his shoulder to an orderly sitting at a desk, 'No time for formalities. See me later.'

My ears, by that time, were hurting worse than my throat and every attempt I made to spit out mucous made me sweat. The doctor sat me in a chair in an operating room and said, 'This is going to hurt like hell but do your best not to swallow the stuff. You have two large pus sacs, one on each side of your throat. I'll lance one and after you've cleared the crap from it, we'll do the other, okay?' I could only nod, figuring that I might faint, for the first time in my life.

He positioned a light behind his head that made my eyes film over and holding my chin said, 'Open!' I could feel my chin shake as I tried to open my mouth. 'Further!' he commanded. I could feel the pain down to my fingertips as I forced my lips further apart. He stuck something between my teeth deep inside my mouth that forced my jaws still further apart. I was sitting astride a chair with its back toward the doctor so that I could hang onto its top.

I think I shut my eyes at that point for I suddenly felt a searing pain on the right side of my throat and I gagged horribly. 'Spit it out,' he yelled and clapped me on the back while holding a basin to my mouth. Strangely enough, I had the sensation that life had suddenly turned easier for me – I could breathe better and the ache in my right ear seemed to disappear. I did my best to follow directions and managed to clear the bulk of the effluence without too much difficulty, although I could feel blood seeping down through my esophagus.

'You okay?' the doctor asked.

'Fine!' I said and he shook his head.

'I'll bet,' he ejaculated.

'No, really,' I said, 'I feel ten years younger.'

---

1. A German anti-personnel mine contained in a wooden box. Literally a shoe-mine.

The same procedure produced similar results on the left side of my throat and I felt as though the weight of the world had lifted from my shoulders. Then, something happened that sent me reeling and gasping and fighting for breath. Without telling me what he was about to do, and probably at the end of his endurance, the doctor – his hand trembling – put something into my throat. It was a powder, I think sulfa, that caught me as I was breathing in and sent me into a paroxysm of coughing and gagging that brought me to my knees on the tent floor. I spit up gobs of blood and really thought my last moments had arrived, what with trying to get some air through the dust that had penetrated my lungs.

Other doctors came running to help as the colonel went to the door and barked something at them. Later he told me he was afraid I'd hemorrhage through the open wounds to the point where he might have to take drastic action to stop the bleeding.

'Try not to cough,' he yelled at me, staring into my eyes from a position on his knees opposite me. That was like telling the wind to stop blowing. I did everything I could to control the violent tickling, but each time I held my breath I felt I would pass out. Finally, I caught my first full breath and felt that I'd probably live. I was trembling from head to foot with the awful experience of feeling smothered. My head was wet with perspiration and I had sweat through my shirt.

A second doctor was holding my head to try to slow down the awful gagging and another, I realized, was rubbing my back in a circular motion between my shoulder blades. I finally began to regain my composure and realized that I was no longer swallowing blood.

'Sorry about that,' the colonel said. I simply waved a hand at him in a sign of dismissal of the whole mess. I got up, with help, and was led away to a ward where some 200 men were lying quietly. A nurse came along as I sat on a cot that was assigned to me.

'Out of that uniform,' she said, dangling a hospital Johnny in my face. 'I'll take your clothes and store them for you.'

'No way!' I said. 'I'll be leaving here tomorrow or the next day.'

'You sure will,' she said. 'You're scheduled to go home.'

I damned near fell over when she made the most improbable announcement I'd ever heard.

'I'm what?' I yelled, hoarsely. 'You're going home,' she repeated. 'No one could be normal who had the infection you had without carrying a high temperature. The orders are being cut now to send you back to a general hospital for observation.'

If there was anything that any of us didn't want during the war, it was to be relieved from duty with a trusted outfit and put up for grabs by second-rate organizations.

I was feeling well enough to get on my feet where I towered over the nurse. 'I don't want to make your job tougher,' I said, 'but there's no way in the world

I'm going to a general hospital. I'm a remarkably strong and healthy man and I'm returning to the 36th Division right now, if I have to.' My throat ached with the effort.

I walked out of the ward and found my way to a mess tent where, fortunately, the colonel who had operated on me was sitting having coffee with a couple of nurses. All three looked so jaded I almost decided to put off the confrontation until the next morning.

'What are you doing out of bed?' the colonel growled as he focused on me.

'Look, Colonel,' I said, 'I just want to forestall any attempt to send me back to a general hospital and possibly from there to the states. I hate to take your time now but I'm absolutely set on returning to my outfit.'

He cocked his head to one side and said, 'Look, Major. You're under my orders now. No need of any heroics.'

'Jesus, colonel,' I expostulated, 'let me give you the GI's view of such things. I'm with an outfit now that's been through hell and back and I trust it to keep on acquitting itself well, no matter what the assignment. You cut me loose now and I'm apt to be grabbed by some lousy Johnny-come-lately division that's been kept in the states because it can't be trusted in combat.'

'You don't want to go home?' the colonel asked.

'It's not a question of going home,' I said, 'and you know it. Even if I did get home, I'd be liable for duty against Japan in thirty days. You don't know this man's army as well as I do.'

'I'm tired now,' the colonel said as he got up. 'See me in the morning. I'll stop any paperwork until we thrash this out.'

'Thanks very much,' I said and saluted him. His response was a sloppy slap of the fingers in the air.

The nurse from my ward came in and slumped at a table resting her head on a plate. 'I think I'm dying,' she said. I sat down beside her and found that she was asleep. Her breathing was stertorous and her fingers twitched.

An orderly came up and said to me, 'Help me carry her. We've had a terrible two days and I don't think she's slept at all.'

We carried her out of the mess tent across an uneven plot of ground to a squad tent where we put her on her cot and covered her with a blanket.

'Thanks, sir,' the orderly said and saluted me.

'Good night,' I answered. While my throat was tender, I had the euphoric feeling that the worst was over and that my main need was to get something to eat. By that time the dawn was beginning to show and several cooks were in the mess hall.

'What'll you have?' a voice asked. It was a fat cook looking at me through hair that curled across his eyes.

'I can't swallow anything hard,' I said. 'Got any ice cream?'

'Sure have,' he responded and in a short time I was slurping down, but not easily, a mound of vanilla ice cream.

When I returned to my cot, another nurse tried to get me to turn in my clothing.

'Listen, Lieutenant,' I said, pulling rank, 'I've been all through this with everyone from the colonel on down. Now, I'll get into my own pajamas but under no circumstances are my clothes to leave this spot under my cot. Got it?'

'Okay, Major, okay,' she said. 'Jesus, we get 'em all!' she snapped as she brushed past me and started reading charts.

I slept for about an hour when I was awakened to have my temperature taken by the nurse who had let me know what she thought of me.

'Feeling better?' she asked.

'I'd feel a lot better if I could sleep for maybe another hour,' I said after she had removed the thermometer from under my tongue.

'Go back to sleep. You can't eat anything today anyway,' she said.

'I've already eaten something,' I responded, 'and by God, I'm still hungry so, if you don't mind, I'll go get breakfast.'

I got up and dressed in my uniform while the nurse clucked her tongue and talked to herself under her breath.

I returned to the staff mess tent and was told it was off limits to patients. 'Says who?' I asked, and pushed on in.

'Says me!' said a smooth-looking major wearing the caduceus of the Medical Corps.

'Where's the colonel?' I asked.

'In bed,' old smoothie responded.

'Look, Major,' I said, 'the nurse in my ward says I can't have any food. I'm starving and about 2 hours ago I had some ice cream. Suppose I could have some more?'

'Let me look at your throat,' he said. We went to an operating tent where he looked into my throat and shook his head at the scars showing where the lance had cut me. 'Man, you're lucky,' he said.

'How so?' I asked.

'If you'd swallowed all that stuff, you'd have been a sick man,' he said.

While I was at it, I thought I'd be certain that no more moves had been made to evacuate me to the rear.

'Major,' I said, 'were you in on the talk I had with the colonel earlier this morning?'

'He briefed me,' the major said, 'before he sacked out. He thinks you're playing to the gallery.'

'That's a real crock of crap,' I responded. 'I will not be sent to the rear and you can put all of your army regulations in your ear,' I added as he started to remonstrate with me. 'My pulse is strong, my temperature is normal, and the only thing wrong with me is the fact that I've had damned little to eat in the last week.'

'We've stopped the presses,' he said and then, as he clapped me on the shoulder he added, 'What the hell is wrong with you infantrymen? Here we give you a good "out" from the war and you act like we were the enemy.'

'You're worse than the enemy,' I cut in. 'At least we know what to expect from him, but you bastards have no idea of the misery you can cost us by trying to get us relieved from our assignments. Maybe I'm superstitious but I have the deepest conviction that I'll make it to the end of the war if I stay with the division, and I know I won't make it if I'm cut loose.'

We talked for another few minutes, during which time I got him to admit that the lack of a fever didn't necessarily connote a serious condition. I went back to my cot and just as I was about to fall off to sleep, a hand clasped my shoulder and a voice said, 'You from the 36th?'

I looked up at a fairly young, good-looking man who stood about 6ft 2in height and who was dressed in regulation hospital garb. I sat up and said, 'Yeah. You?' In the next 2 hours I learned that the man was a captain in the 142nd Infantry. He had finally become so sickened by the con game played by the regimental CO that he had made his move to get out. He'd had a spur on his heel for many years and after completing a 'dirty' assignment, as he labeled it, he complained about the spur even though it was not bothering him.

He swore by all that was holy that he had been part of a team that had been sent all over the countryside searching for German cadavers under circumstances where General Dahlquist had laid into the regimental CO for failing to press the fight before Remiremont. The bodies were brought to the 142nd front and then General Dahlquist was given a guided tour of 'hostile positions' that had been 'overcome' by the regiment in a 'tough' battle. This so matched my own impressions of the officer in question that I had not the slightest doubt that the ruse had been conducted exactly as described to me by the disgruntled captain.

Since I had left word with the I&R platoon to send a jeep with my mail to the Evacuation Hospital the day following my exit from the regiment, I woke up after a couple of hours' sleep, following my discussion of the Remiremont ruse with the 142nd captain, to find Corporal Hobday of the S-2 section there. He had my mail and a very large box of cookies, all in fine condition, that my mother had sent to me.

I told Hobday that while the commanding officer of the hospital was intent on sending me back to a general hospital and 'out' of the war, I was going to leave the evacuation hospital in two more days. I asked him to drop by the AG's office at division to be sure to head off any attempt to replace me and to tell Colonel Steele I'd be back in a couple of days. I also directed Hobday to return in two days, ready to transport me back to the regiment.

Later, I passed the cookies out to the men of the ward who were well enough to eat them. Many of the wounded lay comatose all the time I was there, being fed intravenously and a heavy burden for the nurses and orderlies. I managed to make myself useful by helping turn some of the fearfully wounded men while their sheets were changed. On some the smell of putrefaction was sickening even though with modern medicines, the likelihood of their dying was diminished over past wars.

The nurses were happy enough to have some help and since I was showing absolutely no bad after-effects of the strep throat, no one saw fit to tie me down to the routines established for real casualties.

I asked to see the colonel on the day I planned to leave for the front. I hadn't caught a glimpse of him in the interim and was given to understand that he was resting after having operated for 36 hours – a stint that had ended when he finished with me. He saw me at lunchtime which I ate with the staff, it being understood that there wasn't much sense in trying to feed me in bed.

'Still adamant?' he asked. He looked like a different man.

'No question about it, colonel,' I said. 'I've got to get back to my regiment. We were on the verge of a breakthrough when I left and I've got a lot of work to do.'

He asked me the nature of my job and I told him I was out front a lot what with the open warfare we'd experienced since the landing in Southern France.

'You really want to return to that kind of a job?' he asked.

'You bet,' I answered, 'and since you think I'm playing to the gallery, forget it. With or without your approval I'm going back.'

'You'll be AWOL,' he said.

'Ever hear of anyone being prosecuted for escaping to the front?' I asked.

'Well, we'll see,' he finally said. 'Stick around for another week or so and we'll take another look at your situation.'

'Goodbye, Colonel,' I said and stuck out my hand. I'd seen Hobday outside the mess tent. 'Come see me sometime.'

He shook hands, looking dubious, and I walked out of the tent, got in my jeep, having seen Hobday put my musette bag in it, and took off for the regiment. Three days later the division AG called to tell me that the medical colonel had listed me as AWOL from the hospital.

'Sue me!' I said and hung up. That was the last I heard of the charge.

Getting back to the situation near Colmar, the 141st Infantry, as usual, was given the mission of defending the right flank of the division sector. German reaction to our bold move into the Rhineland became stronger. Probing thrusts, feeling out our defenses, began on December 7, 1944, anniversary of the day that, in President Roosevelt's terms, would 'live in infamy.'

I had ridden into the old walled town of Riquewihr one noon, just in time to be greeted by an artillery concentration that nearly got me. I rolled out of my jeep, my driver close behind me, and down about fifteen stone stairs to a basement door. It was unlocked and we entered to sweat out the noon-hour greetings from the German artillery located in Colmar. That basement was to become the CP of my regiment for quite a long time. It was a commercial wine cellar and in looking around it with a flashlight, I found some diamond-shaped wine bottle stickers labeled 'S. S. Pierce Company, Brookline, Massachusetts.' Somehow, I knew we were in the right place.

Along one wall of the basement, which was about 50ft feet long, sat three huge tuns of wine, up on staging. Each one was large enough so that, as we found later, five soldiers could actually live in it. We later uncovered a German espionage group that had hidden in such a vat and was bringing artillery fire down on us with greater accuracy than we felt possible under ordinary circumstances. This led to a search that uncovered the asp in our bosom, so to speak.

Also in the Riquewihr wine cellar were some large wooden tubs of sauerkraut fermenting and exuding offensive odors. General Stack was commanding the regiment at the time, since Col. Owens had been injured by a mine explosion. We radioed our position to the regimental headquarters once the artillery shelling let up and soon were joined by the full headquarters complement. While most of our sections could be accommodated in the cellar, the depth and superstructure of which gave us a lot of protection from shelling, several sections and units spread out around the town. Vineyards surrounded the town on gentle hills that sloped upward to a ridgeline south of the town that overlooked Colmar. The countryside where the front lines were located was tangled with false crests and heavy woods.

At one time during the combat that soon erupted our troops were back-to-back with German troops and so confused was the terrain that neither knew the other was there. Supply lines to these positions were routed from opposite flanks so that the rear echelons of both armies were not aware of the anomalous position.

On December 11, 1944, I had been out to a battalion position overlooking Colmar and had established an OP there with I&R platoon men. Among them was Charlie Lane, a tall, handsome private first-class who hailed from Houston, Texas, and who had been through some very tough combat with me, particularly at Salerno and the Rapido River in Italy. Lane was the senior man on the OP from the point of view of service and had with him at least one new recruit. I charged Lane with giving me reports of vehicular traffic at night, as well as other enemy action observed or heard. The German position was outlined to me by the men who had been observing for our Second Battalion.

That night, after I had written an intelligence report noting that of all the capabilities open to the Germans the most serious was the envelopment of our right flank by a reinforced German division, I woke up realizing that one vital gap existed in our observation posts. If enemy troops struck around our right flank, we had no one in position near our headquarters to observe their coming until too late.

I got up from my cot behind one of the large wine vats and told the OD that I was going to a nearby church where the I&R platoon and the Frenchman Leclerc were holed up. I stumbled around in the darkness outside and was challenged a half-dozen times before I finally reached the church.

A Sergeant Haas was asleep in the basement when I entered and flashed a light around on twenty or thirty forms lying there. I woke him and told him I wanted an OP established in the church steeple. 'We were thinking of putting one there tomorrow,' he said.

'Tonight,' I stated. 'Right now!' He shook three or four men awake and we went up through the church, shielding our flashlights to allow only a pinprick of light between our fingers.

Below the belfry we found a fragile-looking ladder rising 30ft feet straight up through the tower. A heavy bell was suspended over the opening we squeezed through. It was cold in the bell enclosure, but we set up a telephone, radio, and telescope before I left. I could hear the men griping about the need to set up an OP at night, as I left the church loft and returned to the street. I called up to them to report to me by telephone at least once every 15 minutes at sun-up and later.

Charlie Lane got me on the radio as I reached the CP. 'Major,' he said, 'German vehicles are coming into the position from the east and with little noise. They're leaving on a one-way traffic scheme, to the west, and moving fast and light.'

'Good work, Lane,' I said. I was convinced from having seen the topography that the Germans were bringing materiel and men in by coasting downhill and leaving fast on an uphill exit. I called division and reported this fact to a sleepy sergeant. 'Get the G-2 out of bed,' I said, 'and tell him that we're expecting a flank attack at daybreak.'

In the whole war I never had hit the enemy plan so smack on the nose, as events proved. The G-2 called me back a half hour later and asked what the hell was the matter with me.

'Afraid you'll lose a little sleep?' I asked. 'You'd better alert General Dahlquist to a report I've just received from a front-line OP. The Germans are reinforcing this sector very heavily. I estimate a full new division has been brought in tonight.'

'Doughty,' the G-2 said, exasperation clear in every tone, 'You're the only one who figures reinforcement all the way from here to Army Group.'

'You're all wrong, as usual,' I replied. 'I sleep where I can hear Germans and therefore I make it my job to know what they're doing. I'm making a journal entry that at 3:30 am I've alerted you to an upcoming attack. You take it from there.'

Just as dawn cast its first faint light, I took some men of the section and went to the church where I had a phone set up on a sound-power basis directly to the bell tower from the main floor.

'See anything yet?' I spoke into the phone.

'Nuthin', Major,' Haas answered.

'Watch carefully along the slope to our right,' I admonished. Our whole regiment was on its toes awaiting the outbreak of a firefight. At sun-up people began to look at me as though I'd been at the front too long.

Haas called, 'Guess you had it – hold it! Jesus Christ, the whole goddamn German army's coming down that slope! I'm calling artillery.' I could hear him on another telephone giving a registration point to the fire direction center. 'Don't bother to register,' he yelled. 'Fire for effect!'

At about that time, all hell broke loose. We heard a flight of shells go over and from the sound of the detonations, German troops were at our front door.

'Major,' Haas said into the sound-power phone, 'this is a strange-looking group. Must be 800 of them coming down the slope in columns of twos. They've got big packs on their backs. Makes them look huge – Christ!' I could hear the bell clang as someone from the Kraut skirmishers had fired a burst at the belfry. 'Take that, you bastard,' Haas yelled, and I heard the bursts of a .45 caliber sub-machine gun over the phone.

Outside a window of the room where I was sitting there was a sudden exchange of gunfire and as I looked at the window, I saw a German potato-masher grenade strike the window frame and bounce back. 'Down,' I yelled, and everyone in the room crashed to the floor as the grenade burst, throwing glass all over the room. A soldier leaned out the space where the window had been and fired a long burst at someone below. 'Got him!' he yelled.

So much was happening that it was impossible to get a clear picture of events. Haas was yelling like a banshee to the artillery fire direction center. 'Comb that whole ridge,' he yelled. 'They're starting to break and run. Burn those tubes, baby, we got good huntin' today!'

At this juncture, a couple of GIs from the regimental headquarters company brought in a fairly young Jerry prisoner. He appeared to be a sergeant. I took him outside the room into a hallway and ordered the interrogator to find out where the German reserve was located. It was my view that the German attack had been laid on hastily and that, as a result, everyone in it had to have been privy to all of its aspects.

The German sergeant shook his head when asked to give the location of the reserve. I thrust the interrogator to one side, grabbed the man by his jacket, and pulled him close to me. 'Ask him once more.' I said to the interrogator, 'and tell him he's a dead man if he won't talk.'

The German started to shake his head again when the question was repeated and I smashed the bridge of his nose with my .45 pistol butt. He went down like a pole-axed steer and I put a map under his nose, still holding him by the jacket.

'Tell him to put his finger on the map showing the reserve location,' I said. The prisoner's blood was falling on the map as he traced a ridgeline with the index finger of his right hand, stopping it at a cluster of contour lines that connoted a deep ravine in a position that would have been a logical point to hold troops until a breakthrough could be exploited.

'Haas,' I yelled into the sound-power phone, after bounding into the room where my section was set up. 'Yeah, Major,' he replied, 'What's up?'

'Get division artillery and tell them to lift their fires to these coordinates.' I gave him the location the German had shown me. 'Tell them the German reserve force of some 900 to 1,000 men is there. Can you see the location from your position?'

'Sure can,' he answered. I heard him call the artillery and shortly thereafter flight after flight poured into the ravine. 'Nice shooting,' Haas yelled.

While the Germans pressed their attack for well over 2 hours, our defenses were solid and we stopped the onslaught but only after it had run off one of our front-line battalions and had spiked an artillery piece well on the way to the division CP.

Later, after we had sorted out what had happened, I found that Charlie Lane had hung onto his OP position even though the battalion around him had fallen back. In doing so, he had saved the position so that the Germans were unable to hold it or pass through it. Charlie was killed but only after he had been responsible for the deaths of fifty or more German soldiers who lay in windrows in front of his dug-in OP. I later talked with the recruit, who was the only one to come back unscathed, and he said he'd never seen anyone so cool under fire as Lane had been. Apparently, Lane had taken deliberate aim at individual enemy troops and had killed them as fast as they could approach his position. I put him in for a DSC. A Medal of Honor would have been more appropriate.

General Dahlquist, having been alerted by the division G-2 to a possible attack against our position, had been caught by hostile fire en route to our CP and had had to lie doggo in the cellar of a house while the battle went on all around him. His aide-de-camp managed to tie into a telephone line to our CP, and in that way the general was kept aware of what was transpiring.

We also learned that the unit that struck us was a graduating class of German non-commissioned officers about to be commissioned as officers and whose final exam, so to speak, was this battle. As a provisional unit, it had had difficulty finding its way through the wooded hills and therefore had set back the attack plan some 2 hours. Otherwise, they would have been at our throats before daylight.

Strangely enough, the only telephone line back to artillery ran through a 4.2 chemical mortar[2] position that the Germans had overrun in the first 10 minutes of the attack. However, they hadn't thought to cut the line and the artillery saved the day for us. Nothing was ever heard of the provisional unit again. Its reserve had been caught in a cul-de-sac by well-aimed artillery fire and had been cut to pieces.

We learned during the day, too, that our entire front had been taken under attack at critical areas, simultaneously, and while we had little if anything in reserve, we fought like hardened veterans, a fact attested to in a German field order captured later, and held firm, extracting heavy casualties from the German forces.

It also came to light later that the attacking echelons comprised the remnants of three German divisions plus the seven battalions of officer candidates who had collided with my regiment. In charge of the whole operation was Reichsführer Heinrich Himmler.

We had been hearing rumors that we would soon be taken out of the line for a rest, having then been in combat for 122 consecutive days. While we could not be spared to go into a rear area for rehabilitation and rest, we were told that we

---

2. A 4.2in mortar with a range of 500 to 4,000m capable of shooting chemical smoke shells as well as high-explosive shells.

would swap places with the 3rd Division, which was garrisoning Strasbourg, a relatively quiet area.

In order to give the 3rd Division a more defensible zone it was decided to bring its 30th RCT (Regimental Combat Team) into our sector to attack Kaysersberg and a hill south of it, but on December 17 a German counterattack retook the hill and part of the town. On the night of December 16 I was called to General Stack's trailer, where he had gone to get some sleep. As I approached the area I could hear a number of French voices speaking just outside the trailer. I found General Montsabert there, accompanied by his staff. I had been called to translate.

General Stack was in his underwear and somewhat the worse for wear from liquor. His trailer was hot from an oil heater and, in general, he presented a sorry picture. I introduced myself to Montsabert and some of his men and asked what I could do for them.

General Montsabert was, then, our commanding officer but Stack's attitude was testy and impatient and he asked me what the hell the Frenchman wanted. I told him that we were under Montsabert's command in case he'd forgotten it.

The French officers pointed out that they had been given the assignment by 6th Army Group to attack Kientzheim in the morning with a detachment of the 5th Combat Command of the 4th French Armored Division. However, in order to accomplish their mission, they would require a battalion of infantry from our regiment to go in with them and defend them from counterattack.

There was some national pride involved in this situation for our own armored forces had stated that they could not take their tanks down such precipitous slopes without the risk of turning them over. The French, who were using the same Sherman tanks, had said that they would make the attack over the treacherous terrain.

General Montsabert, recognizing some of the nuances of the situation, apologized to Stack for the intrusion but outside the trailer spoke quite severely to me, saying that he would hold me personally responsible for having our troops at the IP (Initial Point) from which the attack would take off at daybreak. I spent the night seeing to it that the 2nd Battalion was in position as ordered. With little or no preparation, the attack took place and the French, in a great burst of hell-for-leather coursing down the hill with guidons flying, retook Kientzheim. After mopping up the town and spending the night there, the same task force moved against Kaysersberg and bottled up the German forces fighting the 30th Regimental Combat Team. Again, the city was retaken together with the terrain south of it. Later that night our 2nd Battalion and the French armor moved into still another town south of Kientzheim. They formed a good ad hoc fighting team.

On December 19, 1944, my regiment, minus the 2nd Battalion, motored to Strasbourg. By December 22 the two divisions had changed places. As of December 25, 1944 the 36th Division had spent 133 successive days in combat, had taken 19,751 prisoners between the Riviera and Strasbourg, and had killed or wounded an even greater number of the enemy. In that time, it had made its second landing on a defended shore, helped defeat the German 19th Army at Montélimar, crossed the Moselle River and the Vosges Mountains, and had successfully prevented a German counteroffensive and breakthrough just before the Ardennes Offensive began.[3]

3. The last major German counteroffensive was what Americans called the Battle of the Bulge (December 16, 1944–January 25, 1945).

Chapter 28

Another Winter at the Front

Our stay in Strasbourg was for less than a week, but it gave us a far better Christmas than we'd spent a year earlier in the San Pietro area of Italy. During that time, however, a number of things arose that still stand out in my mind.

The first occurred a couple of days before Christmas when I rode to a point near the Rhine River and then hiked into a tunnel that led to the interior of an old French fortress standing on the riverbank. It was a labyrinth of tunnels and as I proceeded deeper into the structure, most of which lay below ground level, I heard men's voices singing Christmas carols.

At a cross tunnel, I turned right and came upon a small group of men, detailed to man the fortress, holding a church service in the presence of one of our division chaplains. A man from our I&R platoon came up to me and asked if I'd like to join him in an OP that looked out across the Rhine.

We walked quite a distance, passing sleeping quarters, kitchen, and mess hall and finally came to a ladder that climbed a couple of stories to a steel turret from which I could look through a slot to the east bank of the Rhine. It was quite a sensation, at last, to see the enemy's own land a few hundred feet away. The river was in spate and racing past the base of the fort. The opposite shore was a solid line of steel-reinforced cement casemates with an occasional opening to admit access to the river. In front of one of these openings a short pier had been built out into the river. I immediately thought that it probably was used by Germans to swing boats by rope across the river, thus obviating the sound of motors or oars when patrols came calling.

I asked if there had been any signs of patrolling to our side of the river by the Germans and received a negative response. One of the men, who had been on observation duty for several days, said that it seemed as though one man was detailed by the Germans to light fires in the casemates since, every morning, smoke showed first in one casemate followed by more from each casemate down the line at about 5-minute intervals.

'They shoot at us only if we shoot at them,' a young lieutenant from one of our battalions said to me as I descended from the turret. 'I guess they're using the place as a rest camp, just like we are,' he continued.

When I got back to regimental headquarters I found a message to the effect that we were to take German prisoners to ascertain whether the enemy had changed the garrison of the casemates opposing us.

That night I had ten trucks move to a point near the fortress I'd visited, where crews unloaded lumber, crates, and other items and then reloaded them, making as much noise as possible. From there the trucks would traverse a circular route out of earshot of the river and come back to the off-loading area again to repeat the performance. During the night they made several trips and lots of noise. It was supposed to sound like the preparation of an effort to cross the river in some manner.

Simultaneously, working under cover of darkness, we'd had several anti-aircraft searchlights installed along the fortress wall where we could light up the river as needed. These, however, were camouflaged against observation.

Nothing occurred the next day during daylight, but that night toward midnight men posted outside the fort heard faint sounds on the river and signaled the fort's command group. Sure enough two boats approached the western shore and as men stood to get out of them, the anti-aircraft lights went on to disclose some twenty German soldiers about to land. A sharp fight ensued during which three prisoners were taken. The rest of the patrol was killed or believed drowned. We never knew just what happened to them since the lights were soon put out of action by machine-gun fire from across the river. Both boats were sunk almost at once.

Our ruse had worked well, and we were able to report that the identities of our prisoners' units were the same as had been reported for months, although I raised the possibility that the Germans might have concealed new troop units by outfitting them with the identities of earlier units.

At about this same time I made my first contact with 'T-Force.' I had driven to an old factory close to the Rhine where our I&R platoon had established an OP on the top floor of the building, some four stories above ground level. We had to exercise the greatest of care in moving about the building which had many windows on all sides. I went up an enclosed staircase to the fourth floor and from the entry to that floor crawled to a window where three men were watching the opposite side of the Rhine through field glasses.

Almost immediately I heard a commotion at the stairway from which I had just crawled. A corporal came slithering toward me where I was using a power scope to look into Germany. 'Better come out to the stairs with me, Major,' he said. 'There's the damnedest looking crew you ever saw. Could be Krauts.'

We crawled across the factory floor to the stairs where, sitting at various levels I saw six men dressed in makeshift uniforms comprising US, British, French, and other garbs. 'Who are you?' I asked of a man who wore a heavily waxed and pointed moustache that extended for several inches on either side of his nose.

'T-Force,' he responded. 'What does that mean?' I wanted to know.

'Top Secret,' he said. I told the corporal to take the weapons from each man and said 'Top-Secret or not, you have no right to come into a tactical situation and expose our positions without some word from higher authority authorizing your visit.'

I ordered the motley crew to the basement where I put a guard over them and then called regimental headquarters to ask what the men were doing in our regimental area. Since no one at regiment knew what 'T-Force' meant or what its mission was, I called the division G-2. He knew nothing of the mission of the group, and I told him we'd hold them under guard until we had clearance. 'Move it man!' I said. 'We're exposed as hell out here.'

In about 6 hours we had the clearance sought. Someone had goofed in not clearing the mission in advance. The Germans, no doubt alerted by having seen activity at the factory, lobbed in a few artillery shells to make things interesting.

Subsequently, I learned that 'T-Force' comprised scientific fellows from Allied nations who not only were not military in any way but took special pains to be unmilitary even though a uniform of sorts was their best means of recognition. These men followed attacking infantry closely when target areas were believed to contain scientific undertakings which might, if brought to fruition, influence the course of the war.

In Strasbourg the task force was looking for two-man submarines, some of which had already been sighted at various intervals in the war, and also for heavy-water manufacture or use. While I didn't know it at the time, this was my first contact with anyone concerned with any aspect of the atom bomb.

I returned to our CP, which was opulent in that it had been a duke's former home which the Germans had taken over for use as an air force college. It had a very large entry hall giving onto a ballroom plus some forty or fifty rooms. On Christmas Eve 1944, hundreds of Alsatians dressed in national costume and including some beautiful children – who did a traditional dance – put on a party for us in the ballroom. It was a heart-warming experience despite the fact that we were well within range of guns from across the river.

We supplied many items of food that people of that region hadn't seen or tasted for years. Coffee, bread, sugar, turkey and all the fixin's, plus candies for the children that made it seem almost like Christmas Eve at home. I remember wondering as the evening passed whether this would be my last Christmas away from home and family. Such thoughts, worn out from running the gamut for so long, were but fleeting reminders of a way of life almost forgotten in the labyrinth of war.

We were relieved that afternoon by the 42nd (Rainbow) Division from New York. Possessed of a fighting history in the First World War, the division appeared to be a long way off the mark in the Second World War. While it could not be held responsible for lacking equipment, which it did in nearly every important category – such as field telephones and artillery pieces, nevertheless we felt that its appearance so late in the war betokened a lack of confidence by high military authorities in its fighting capabilities. Events proved us right by the time the war ended. As a matter of fact, we received proof that night, for several of our men were shot and killed by men of the 42nd during the period it took to affect the relief.

We had made it clear to the officers of the regiment taking our place on the line that there were no Germans on our side of the river. And yet sentries shot some of our men without challenging them, the strongest kind of indication that the troops involved were of poor caliber. We were glad to get out of the area more because of the 'friendly' troops than the Germans.

The division was ordered to Sarrebourg some 50 miles to the rear through the Saverne Gap. At about that same time the German attack through the Ardennes had hit its high-water mark as of December 24, 1944. In an effort to relieve the pinch that Patton and others had put on the shoulders of the breakthrough, the Germans – on January 1, 1945 – attacked the center of the 7th Army's sector at the town of Bitche, from which they hoped to strike for the Saverne Gap and box in the entire VI Corps while threatening to retake all of Alsace.

While we were at Sarrebourg, which lasted something less than a week even though the US chief of staff – General George C. Marshall – had ordered us into a long period of rest and rehabilitation, I received word through G-2 channels that the Germans had trained some of their soldiers to pose as Americans, wearing GI uniforms, talking US slang, driving US jeeps captured during the war. They were to raise hell with our rear areas and lines of communication by changing road signs, blowing up bridges, and capturing or killing high-ranking Allied officers, to include Ike Eisenhower. This outlook had thrown some of the newer outfits entering combat in our general vicinity into even spookier attitudes than might normally have been the case.

On our way back to Sarrebourg we had been passed by some of the latecomers who, more or less, jeered at us, saying that they would now prosecute the war and give us a few lessons in the process. We could only feel sorry for people who knew so little about warfare that they could treat it as a college football game. We also had the gut feeling that we'd have to bail them out before too long, for they were really wet behind the ears!

Sure as shooting, on New Year's Eve we got the word that we were to proceed to Montbronn in the Saar Palatinate in order to reinforce some of the new divisions who had come under severe attack that day. It was freezing cold and snowing, and to make matters about as bad as could occur, many of our officers were in the south of France on R and R.

Colonel McGrath, regimental exec., and I were the only regimental field-grade officers present. We took off in late afternoon, riding with windshields lowered and covered with canvass, as was our habit when driving to an active front. The battalions were stretched out for miles on hilly, icy roads and the going was slow, cold, and rough.

En route we saw the first signs of panic we'd ever encountered during the war. Vehicles, artillery pieces, and tanks had slid off the slippery roads and were left behind by their crews. A group of MPs at a road juncture was panicky when I stopped and asked them what the hell had happened.

'We're expecting a German paratroop drop tonight,' one of them said through clenched teeth. His whole body shook with fear and cold.

'That's not even sensible,' I said to him as Colonel McGrath got out of his jeep, his moustache – in the small flare of a covered flashlight – showing small icicles at each end.

'What's that about a paratroop drop?' he demanded. Several of the MPs spoke at once but we quieted them down.

'Look,' I said, 'we're heading for Montbronn. Do you know who's there?'

'The 100th Division is supposed to be there,' a sergeant answered. I didn't like the answer and asked him why he said it that way.

'I seen a bunch of them going through here earlier tonight, and they had no weapons,' he answered.

'Get hold of yourselves,' McGrath said, 'and stop this talk about paratroopers. No one will fly or drop in this storm.'

We went on with our tires squeaking in the deeper snow, feeling that we were heading into real trouble with no one to help us. Before reaching Montbronn we sent an I&R squad ahead down a long ridge to the town located in a valley and almost in the heart of the old French Maginot Line. The squad returned in a few minutes and said they'd found the CG of the 100th Division and his G-2 in a store in Montbronn.

We eased down the hill and into the store where we heard the most incredible story, put together by the G-2, that I'd ever had brought to my attention. A German prisoner had been taken the day before. He had told the G-2 that before the war he had trained with his tank unit in that area. I pointed out that we were within the French lines that pre-existed the war. Therefore, the story was a phoney to begin with. But, it seemed that somehow the word had gotten out that a German tank attack could be expected the next morning, which was almost on us.

'Why would you believe that tanks could operate in these hills and mountains with their restricted road nets?' I asked.

'We're having reports from flanking units, as well as our own that enemy pistol signals are almost incessant,' he said.

'What does that prove?' I asked. 'Have you heard or seen any armor anywhere?'

'A couple of SPs[1] showed up at dusk last night,' he answered.

The CG of the 100th was almost in tears after talking with McGrath, who took me to a corner of the store and said, 'The 100th Division has taken off for the rear.'

'What?' I almost shouted. 'How many men are here in Montbronn?' I turned and asked the general.

The G-2 answered, 'Just our drivers and us.'

McGrath and I got busy. We brought the battalion commanders in and posted them to various sections of the Maginot defenses that formed the reserve areas of the main line, then in German hands. We held the key defenses to the only road net traversing the zone with two battalions and kept one battalion in reserve.

---

1. Probably self-propelled gun vehicles.

It was dawn before we were ready, and I was dead tired. I had my striker set up a cot at the rear of the store in a separate storage area and went to sleep. In the meantime the last vestige of the 100th Division had disappeared into the night.

Patrols from our regiment had been sent out in all directions but had made no contact of any kind. We were once again in the position of being in the open with unprotected flanks necessitating a 360-degree defensive position.

McGrath got word off to the division headquarters by messenger detailing our position. We later learned that our other two regiments, sooner or later, were sent on widely separate assignments because a whole US corps had pulled out of position, with corps headquarters retreating almost all the way back to Paris. In effect, some 90 miles of front extending to the Rhine River were now the main responsibility of the 36th Division. Panic had thinned the front to one hardened division. Unfortunately, our division could no longer act as a cohesive unit because of the distances involved, and General Dahlquist was out of a command for a short time.

I had slept about an hour when we started to receive messages of 'purple flares,' which normally signaled armored action. On top of those, however, came reports of green, red, white, pink, and blue flares arching up all along the front. I talked with a battalion CO named Ciccolella. He'd gone out with a squad of men and knocked out three SPs that had started to move up a road toward his battalion's position. We heard sounds of small-arms fire, then, and a lot of mortars.

McGrath got on the telephone and suddenly he said, 'You're kidding!'

He turned to me with the weirdest look on his face and said, 'You know who we're fighting?'

Before I could answer, he said, 'Deaf-mutes! That's why they're using pistol signals!'

It was stunning to learn that Germany's manpower problems had descended to such depths. We took several hundred prisoners, some of whom wrote out answers to our questions. It was evident that they had known of the panic in the new American units and had been ordered to take territory without fighting as our units fell back.

One of their non-coms wrote, 'If we'd known that the 36th Division was here, we would have gone back to Germany.'

While the division history, obviously written carelessly at this point, speaks in terms of a 'heavy attack against the 141st Infantry,' my own reaction – at the time and now – remains the same; it was a shame to kill such cripples. We had no trouble taking most of them prisoner, which spoke reams about the units that had retreated.

While the other regiments of the division did back up the 141st Infantry after January 3, 1945, their assignments were limited to action by one regimental combat team at a time and they were forbidden by army orders to stir up a fight by taking direct action.

Basically, the position shortly developed into one whereby the 141st Infantry simply held the line while elements of the two remaining regiments of the 36th

Division, together with the 111th Engineers, prepared a secondary position several miles to the rear. This was done, it appears, in order to remove a bulge from the Allied lines occasioned by the 36th Division's having held its position, while greener troops fell back. With the advent of winter it was evident that a period for building up our forces for the final thrust into Germany would be required. A safer position for this operation was thought to be behind the Moder River, running past Haguenau, Bischwiller, and Drusenheim into the Rhine where the switch position was built.

The 142nd Infantry was moved west to the XXI Corps to back the line at Saarbruecken while a relief of the 103rd Division was affected in the period January 13–18.

In the meantime the Germans were harassing the 7th Army's right flank by armored thrusts at the VI Corps' positions north of Haguenau. Simultaneously, in early January, a sizeable force of German troops had been ferried across the Rhine and had seized a bridgehead at Gambsheim, just north of Strasbourg. Efforts to retake this position had proved futile and as reinforcements crossed the Rhine, the threat to Strasbourg became critical.

On January 12, 1945, the 12th Armored Division, one of the latecomers, attacked Gambsheim but was thrown back with heavy losses, occasioned, as I later learned, when inspecting the area, by careless outposting of their defensive perimeter at night. An army survey team found that many of the casualties had been caused by German infiltrators dropping grenades into the turrets of tanks after dark.

The 79th Division, on a front east and north of Haguenau, was also under constant attack and was weakening under the pressure. To correct this dangerous situation, the 36th Division, less the 141st Infantry, was ordered to Haguenau with the 142nd moving from Saarbrucken to Haguenau, a distance of some 80 miles.

The 143rd was ordered to relieve the 12th Armored Division which suffered a breakthrough by German armor just as the relief occurred. All forces rallied to form a defensive line along a small stream running southwest from Rohrwiller, and the next day the entire VI Corps line was re-established along the pre-constructed Moder River defensive zone.

On January 20, 1945, the Germans put pressure on the Kurtzenhausen salient, which formed the center of the 36th Division's front. Twenty German tanks, followed by infantry, participated in the assault that was thrown back by TDs and artillery with heavy German losses.

While, allegedly, the 141st Infantry was attached to the 100th Division during the time the enemy threatened to retake Strasbourg, the fact of the matter was that it took us several days to locate the fighting elements of that division. They were found several miles to the rear, sitting in the cellars of houses and, in effect, incapable of fighting.

We, however, got them back to the front-line positions where we sat, all German action against our defenses having ceased. The presence of our seasoned troops had the desired effect of firming the spines of the newcomers, none of whom thought of the war as a game anymore.

A story, out of which I got one of the major kicks of the war, could be found in our experiences with the green troops. It seems that one of the divisions that had given way before the German attack on January 1, 1945, was one that General Dahlquist had trained in the US before joining us. While I can't be sure of its number, I believe it was the 79th Division. In any event, during some of our earlier battles under Dahlquist, he could often be heard to say, 'The 79th could handle this situation better than the 36th.'

A little of that kind of crap can go a long way, particularly when the ideal unit had yet to see battle! It was more than some of the Texans could stand when they learned that Dahlquist's earlier division had not acquitted itself well under fire. So they awaited a moment when they could raise the issue. It took a while and didn't occur until after I had joined the division staff, as Assistant G-1. One evening while we were all sitting around the general's mess, General Dahlquist was talking in his fairly quiet way about the 36th Division's exploits during the war, and bragging to some degree about its fighting qualities.

'Just one thing, General,' a voice spoke up, with a heavy Texas drawl, 'I reckon we still ain't as good as the old 79th, at that.'

General Dahlquist looked up in surprise half-expecting, it seemed, a serious charge against the 36th. 'How's that?' he asked.

'Why, General,' the voice said, 'shucks, we ain't learned yet how to about-face and advance like the old 79th.' The general had the good grace to join in the laughter that exploded around the table. We never heard another comparison of the 36th with any other division from Dahlquist, except one where all other fighting units took second place.

On January 20, 1945, when the division joined in the VI Corps move to the Moder River line some miles to the rear, I was one of the last to leave Montbronn, where I'd had a close brush with death one night. I had continued to sleep in the storage room of the store where we'd first opened our headquarters. One morning I woke with the taste of old plaster dust in my mouth. It took me a few moments to realize what had happened. On looking up toward the ceiling over my pillow I saw the nose of a shell that had penetrated the wall but failed to explode.

Later ordnance men removed the shell and found it filled with sand after they had tried to detonate it. I could thank some nameless soul, probably from the Skoda works in Czechoslovakia, for that minor miracle.

While we were at Montbronn, too, a new military order, established by typical wags who help keep morale high in difficult situations, was formed. Naturally, it was called 'The Sons of Bitche' for a nearby town, central to our zone of action. Our insignia was a small circular red patch to be sewn on our sleeves and known as 'The Drop of Blood.' Whenever anyone mentioned the town of Bitche, wearers of the insignia would twist the patch between thumb and forefinger and moan a little as though no words could express the extent of the suffering endured in that hellhole.

When I left Montbronn, I called Bennett, my driver, from the I&R platoon billet and noticed that he staggered a bit as he walked to the jeep.

'You been drinking?' I asked.

'Nawsir,' he replied. ' ... Well, maybe I had one snifter.'

He seemed all right and I was anxious to get out of the town for it was now defenseless and we'd had word that German troops were moving in, as our front-line troops pulled out.

We started up the long incline northwest of the town and as we rose higher, I thought I could see track-laying equipment moving in the shadows around the town. I realized that we were silhouetted against the snow and skyline and momentarily expected to be taken under fire. By this time we were moving along the tree-lined road at a good clip. I was having difficulty seeing some of the nearby trees because a recent storm had plastered the near side of them with snow that blended with the surrounding ground cover.

Suddenly, I knew we were going to crash into a particularly well camouflaged tree and as I yelled, a shell burst off to our left and the jeep crashed into the tree.

Sometime later, my wrists felt as though they were freezing and I could hear someone swearing. I found myself some distance from the jeep, crawling on my hands and knees in deep snow and realized that the cursing was coming from my own mouth.

My right leg appeared to have been broken from where it had smashed into the jeep dashboard before I was thrown clear. I was dragging it behind me as I lurched through the snow. The two men in the jeep with me were superficially hurt. Bennett, if he'd been drunk, was cold sober and Hobday, sitting in the back seat, had struck his head against the iron roof support and was bleeding from a scalp wound.

The thought went through my mind that we were in a dangerous position and liable to be captured. I staggered to my feet and hopped through the snow to the jeep. Both men had been knocked out but were recovering slowly.

'Bennett,' I said. 'You bastard. You were drunk.'

'Yessir,' he said, 'but I ain't now.'

Because the regiment had a rule that any driver involved in a careless accident would be shipped to a front-line unit to walk with the infantry, I told Bennett that we would blame the accident on the shell that had landed near us. 'Well, sir,' Bennett said, 'that's right, sir! They's a hole through the engine compartment and the right tire is blowed. That's why we hit the tree.'

By this time it was dark and we could hear nothing coming up the hill from Montbronn. Just as we had decided to start walking, with me between the two men, we saw the blackout lamps of a truck coming toward us from the west. The outline was of a 2.5-ton truck that looked like one of ours. As the truck slowly moved toward us, we held pistols and carbines ready. 'Hey you,' a voice yelled, 'this the way to Rondo?'

Those were the finest words we'd heard in years. Rondo was the code name of my regiment. 'Yep,' Bennett called, 'come on over.'

The truck slid to a stop near us and we could see the division lettering on its bumper. On the side was the word 'Night-hawk.' In it were two drivers who had been moving supplies from a distant rear dump and who had not heard that the division had withdrawn to the Moder River line.

'Look,' Hobday said, 'we gotta get out of here right now.' We told the men our story and soon we had backed up to a turn-around and were headed toward our lines again, having left the jeep where it lay.

We reached the 100th Division CP within a relatively short time where I decided we'd stay until we could learn more of the situation. I had no way to let my regiment know where I was or what had happened to me. As a result, I was carried on the roster as 'Missing in Action' for several days, during which time my status was reported back to the US but fortunately did not come to the attention of anyone in my family. At the twenty-five-year reunion of my high-school class in 1952, Jay Vose, formerly Jay Barrett, told me that she had seen a report in a newspaper in South Carolina that I was missing.

Doctors at the 100th Division worked on my knee, which had swollen to more than twice its normal size, and told me that I'd have to go to a general hospital in Saverne the following day in order to have it X-rayed. We stayed that night in a farmhouse where a large porch had been converted to an aid station. When I woke up in the morning I found that one of the doctors had pinned a purple heart on my pillow. I called him in and returned the medal, despite the fact that he assured me that some of his people were getting purple hearts for 'hangnails.' I told him that we had different standards in the 36th.

I was driven to Saverne by someone from the 100th Division, while Hobday and Bennett went back to the regiment with the truck drivers to report on what had occurred to delay us. At a general hospital one of the doctors, after attending to my X-ray needs, took me to a window to point out where a shell from an Anzio-Annie, the large railroad guns employed by the Germans, had landed. A whole city block had been razed by the explosion the night before.

'Get me out of here, Doc,' I said. 'Hell, I'm going up to the front where it's quieter. A guy could get hurt here.'

I was released at about noontime and was later picked up by a jeep from the regiment, which took me back, carrying two canes, to my headquarters where I received a fine welcome home. My leg, though not broken, caused me a great deal of pain, which subsided over a week's time when I could finally walk quite well with only one cane.

Chapter 29

Watch on the Rhine

There came a day when Colonel Owens asked me what the S-2's job was in the regiment. I told him I was the enemy's agent in the camp and stood ready to give him a picture of hostile capabilities whenever he needed it. I gained the impression that he thought I should be out patrolling or manning an OP.

'Do you have a different view of my job?' I asked.

'How can you know what's going on from here?' he returned.

'There's nothing going on, Colonel,' I responded. 'If there were, I have four OPs with wires to this headquarters which would be busy. I've had patrols going out each night to the Moder River to check the battalion listening posts. The land is flooded and there is little or nothing going on in either the German or American camps.'

'We always had the S-2 out front on our maneuvers,' the colonel stated.

'Then you had an S-2 that didn't know what was happening, Colonel,' I stated, having been through this kind of juvenile questioning before by a series of officers whose total experience in handling the 'enemy' had been on maneuvers or command post exercises (CPXs).

The next day he roused me quite early to accompany him to a battalion then in process of affecting a limited attack in the vicinity of Herrlesheim. We approached the battalion CP, which was set up along a lane, and the colonel asked where he could find the battalion CO, a West Point major.

'He's in his tent sleeping, sir,' a cook said.

'Where's his tent?' the colonel inquired in a quiet tone.

'Yonder,' said the cook. We went over to the tent and roused the officer in question.

'Good morning, Colonel,' he said as he rubbed his eyes and stretched.

'Good morning,' the colonel responded. 'What's happening?'

'Damned if I know,' the major replied. 'Guess everything's going all right. The battalion took off at 4 am?'

'Why aren't you with them?' the colonel asked.

'I was up most of the night, sir,' the major responded, his voice reflecting a change of attitude, going wary as he stopped rubbing his eyes and started to put on a shirt.

'You are relieved of command,' Colonel Owens said and turned and walked away. We went through some thick underbrush and woods and came to a canal, where we found the battalion more or less lying around. No sounds of battle had occurred while we were in the area.

'Where are your officers?' the colonel inquired.

'They're in a gully up there about a hundred yards,' a sergeant responded. 'They're checking on the engineers who're gonna put a bridge across the canal.'

'What's the story on the Germans?' the colonel asked.

'They're over there, all right,' the sergeant said, 'but they're waitin' for us to cross.'

We found the officers in the gully talking with an engineer captain. All stood and saluted as Colonel Owens and I approached.

'What's the delay?' the colonel asked.

'Bailey bridge coming up, sir,' the engineer said. 'We're going to have trouble getting it over that ditch unless someone can clear the enemy away from the immediate vicinity of the crossing site.'

We heard the sound of tracked vehicles coming up a road behind us and saw a tank retriever rigged to hold a Bailey bridge by cables in front of its nose. It snorted past us and the engineer captain said, 'Boy, that's a new one. They'll put that bridge in position without anyone getting hurt.'

Hostile mortar and SP fire opened up as the bridge appeared at the edge of the canal. We took cover in a couple of foxholes that had been dug by earlier occupants of the area. Four tanks came along nose-to-tail and followed in the trace of the tank retriever.

I had a map with me showing hostile installations and also the disposition of tanks of the 12th Armored Division that had been knocked out on the other side of the canal. I crawled over to the colonel, who was talking with a tank commander, and showed them both the probable defensive system across the canal.

'If we can get your tanks over the bridge,' the colonel said to the armored officer, 'the infantry will follow right on your tails and protect you from close-in attack.'

Shortly the bridge was in position and the lead tank nosed up to it, while the tank retriever pulled back out of direct line of fire. It had received a lot of small-arms fire during the installation of the bridge.

Slowly the first tank made its way across the canal and took up a firing position to the right side of the bridge. In about 10 minutes the four tanks were on the far bank and infantrymen were infiltrating across the bridge, two at a time, as the tanks butted their way through the underbrush and small trees, firing machine guns and cannons as they went.

German gunfire ceased almost at once and shortly, the colonel and I dashed across the bridge. We could see a large field through the bushes as we moved further away from the canal, and dotted around it, almost in the fashion of pioneer Conestoga wagons forming a defensive circle, were the burned-out tanks of the 12th Armored Division. At a house on the east side of the field I saw a couple of GIs beckoning to me to join them. We went into the basement of what was left of the house and found eight men, six enlisted men and two officers, where they had fallen at the foot of the stairs. All had been machine-gunned. It was a sad sight giving proof, it seemed to me, of what happens to inexperienced organizations that fail to take necessary precautions at night when thrust into a dangerous situation. A later inquiry into the losses taken by the armored division was conducted, but I never learned what conclusions were reached.

We, subsequently, took over the area around Herrlisheim and set up our headquarters near an old railroad station. It was flat land in that area abutting the Rhine River and in the distance, to the northeast, we could see German soldiers atop a water tank held aloft by a steel framework. It offered them such a good view of all our movements that I felt we should knock it down. Artillery was ineffectual, and while a TD tried to knock out the steel supports, it drew so much artillery fire in response that its crew backed away.

I finally called on army to bomb the water tank. Colonel McGrath and I decided to go to the garret of the house where we were billeted in order to observe the bombing run. We had just had breakfast and then, on learning that the flight was on its way, we climbed to the attic where we could remove several ceramic tiles in order to poke our heads through the hole between tile supports. The supports were built in such a way as to require inserting our heads while looking southeast and then turning them to thrust our chins over the support for a look to the northeast.

Two fighter planes made the attack, and we watched the first one drop wing bombs close to the water tank. Smoke and dust blocked our view and the wind carried the cloud toward our position. It was with some consternation, therefore, that I saw the second plane emerge from the curtain of dust and smoke heading directly for our position, while one bomb, whose releasing mechanism had failed, swung by its tail from the rack beneath the plane's wings.

In my rush to get out of harm's way I forgot to turn my head and nearly broke my neck trying to extricate my jaw from the encroaching support. Simultaneously, I could see the side of McGrath's face as he, too, did what came naturally and tried to recede into the attic the hard way. His moustache stood at high port as his cheeks ballooned out in his extreme rush to withdraw. At about that moment, while our heads were held as in vises, the bomb cut loose, sailed over us and went off with tremendous force in an adjacent field. We simply stood there, two heads on a roof, and laughed at the lugubrious sight that near-panic had caused. We only had to look at each other for weeks thereafter to start another round of guffawing, and the tale we told of our predicament got better and better as time went on.

One day, the interrogator called me on the telephone from another building near the railroad station and said he had a prisoner who had turned himself in the night before. I told him I'd be right over, work having slacked off a bit, since I wanted to see for myself if the man was as worthless as the report I'd received indicated.

When I got to the interrogation room, the prisoner was sitting beside a desk, smoking a cigarette and talking in a friendly way with the interrogator. I asked, through the interpreter, what the prisoner's job had been. He told me he'd transported ammunition between an ammo dump and gun positions near the water tank we had tried to bomb out of existence. My first sizing-up of the prisoner had given me the impression of a keen intellect and a topnotch military man, far more capable than the private-first class insignia on his uniform indicated.

I produced some aerial photos of the town where the prisoner had been located when he gave himself up. I'd received them that morning from division and had already studied them with a magnifying glass. I asked the prisoner to trace his route from the ammo dump to the gun site and as he did so, his finger hesitated for just the fraction of a second at a point where a bridge had been bombed out the previous evening. It was a dead giveaway since he had correctly read the photograph, a feat not usual with ordinary privates.

I changed the entire atmosphere in a second's notice by accusing the man of having come in under false pretenses. I told him, always through the interpreter but in a deadly serious manner, that I knew that he was an officer and probably a high-ranking one at that. The interpreter, by this time, began to suspect that he had been conned by the prisoner and he went into a ringing denunciation of a man who would hide his rank in order to surrender.

It didn't take too long to discover that the man was an engineer colonel and that his job had been to supervise the laying of minefields. Hundreds of thousands of mines were being planted all along the front to forestall the spring attack that everyone knew was coming. But, and this was a surprise, the mines were of a new variety, hard to detect, since they were constructed of glass for the most part. A small element of the detonator was made of metal but it would create so little reaction in a mine detector that it would probably not be considered worth investigating.

I felt we had a major discovery here but decided to keep it quiet for just long enough to verify his statement. I told him that we were going to test his veracity since we had little cause to believe anything he said. I indicated that I would keep him, incommunicado, at the regimental level, until we had checked out everything he had told us. The implication was fairly broad that he could disappear without a trace, if we found his story another lie.

I sat him down at a table and had him draw to scale a replica of the minefield in front of us. At that time, too, we had been using a new invention called a sniper-scope to observe hostile action at night. Employing ultra-violet rays, the scope cast a beam that could be seen through special lenses sufficiently clearly to permit sniping at night. Through it we could also observe patrols coming through the hostile minefields at night. We could also watch surrenderees who, having been worked on by psychological warfare teams operating loudspeakers at night in our vicinity, sought to surrender.

I asked the German colonel to show me how patrols knew where to walk and how the lanes through minefields were varied from day to day, for that purpose. He readily complied with all of these requests and, that night, we verified most of what he had said even to the point of obtaining one of the mines exactly where he'd said one could be found. Parts of the minefield near our lines had been planted with the old steel Teller mines to throw off discovery of the newer, more deadly mines.

While our unit, when it came time to penetrate the minefield during the general spring offensive, was located further west, the French forces who had taken over from us suffered no losses to the glass mines but, instead, surprised the Germans by having removed many of them in advance of the attack. The result, of course, was an overwhelming onslaught that struck home at once, without the delay the Germans had thought inherent via their 'undetectable' mines.

Our interpreter, chastened by the experience of having been bamboozled by a 'private first class,' told me later that he was sorry to see me leave the regiment, since he felt that a sixth sense was an essential part of penetrating much of the persiflage some German prisoners practiced.

Just before I was called to the division headquarters as assistant G-1 I was sitting one morning in the Herrlisheim headquarters when I heard a loud explosion just outside our building that made me believe the Germans had fired an Anzio-Annie railroad gun at us. I got on the phone to call division and immediately afterward I received a dozen calls reporting an enormous explosion 'just outside' the headquarters.

It took an hour to learn that the explosion had been caused by some 5,000 British mines detonating in a rolling explosion that had seemed to telegraph itself to all points of the compass. Fortunately, the mines were piled inside a walled cemetery which muffled much of their concussive power and the main damage done was to expose some poor old buried bones to public view. These were soon re-interred.

It seemed that our mine-laying detachments of engineers had thought to improve their efficiency by arming thousands of mines in daylight to save time during the installation periods which, of course, occurred only at night. What no one seemed to know about British mines was that they were extremely delicate of mechanism and quite often exploded under minor vibrations. The Germans must have wondered what the explosion meant. It certainly sounded like a new high in psychological warfare.

During the time we were in the Herrlisheim area the Allied High Command, appalled at vehicular mayhem caused by blackout driving, decreed that the nights would be lit by anti-aircraft lights put into operation back of the lines to cast a skyward glow that would improve driving conditions.

Again, the German High Command must have wondered what kind of trick was being pulled on them. As usual, only the plight of the rear area operators was considered when this strategem was worked out. Front-line units were amazed and then angered at the need to send out patrols whose members were easily spotted by hostile observers, since they were silhouetted against the bright sky.

During the short time that the anti-aircraft lights were employed in this manner, a USO troupe came to play the Herrlisheim area. While I cannot remember who the performers were, I do recall that one of them was of the Jimmy Cagney persuasion: a tough guy. I had stated to the division special service officer that I felt it too dangerous to gather together 400–500 of our men for a show so close to the front, where direct-laying[1] guns could, and often did, send their snarling messengers into our midst. I was overruled.

We had an old church in the town that was set up as a theatre. The entertainment troupe came into the area after dark but under the shimmering glow of a backlit sky. Several of us met the entertainers and took them to our CP for dinner. It was a mixed group of men and women and we enjoyed talking with them.

When it came time to go to the theatre, I warned the group not to light any cigarettes outdoors.

'Why not?' said the tough guy. 'No bombers out at night any more, are there?'

'No,' I answered, 'but there could be other things.'

'Such as what?' the tough guy asked. Just as he did, he stumbled over something and went to his knees.

'You guys kill me,' he said, putting on his tough act. 'Why do you train people by putting dummies out for them to stumble over?' He apparently was feeling of the object he'd stumbled over. 'Helmets and everything,' he grumbled.

'For your information,' I responded, 'that was a dead German you stumbled over. We'd intended to have him removed before you got here. A patrol came in last night and we killed four of them. The rest were captured.'

'You're telling me that we're on the front lines?' came the subdued whisper.

'Right smack dab!' I said.

'Jesus Christ,' he whispered and when we got to the church he huddled with the rest of the troupe. 'We're leaving here right now,' the tough guy said.

'Fine,' I replied. 'Your vehicles are over here.' I showed them to a side street where the jeeps they'd come in were sheltering. I had to announce the cancellation of the show and received a great howl of protest.

Just before the final push into Germany, I was assigned to division headquarters as assistant G-1. I was glad to have a chance to do more to assist the regiments than I felt had been done in the past.

---

1. ' Direct laying' refers to shooting a cannon like a rifle, as opposed to 'indirect laying' where the trajectory is calculated and the target is typically farther away.

Chapter 30

Spring Offensive

Once I was assigned to the division headquarters, it was almost as though I had escaped the war. The division staff lived in what, to a dough-foot, could only be described as luxury. It was almost like a civilian job compared to anything I'd experienced so far in the war. Where, at regiment, we took potluck at every moment, whether it be eating, sleeping or risking death, at division we were out of range of light artillery and, as I think back over my experiences at the division level, I can't remember a moment of real danger while near the CP.

I slept in a room, had breakfast at the general's mess, worked at a desk, attended staff meetings, and started to put back on some of the weight I'd lost in the rough and tumble of daily fighting. It took me no more than a day to learn that, as I had suspected, the division staff was anything but first-rate.

I told the G-1, a handsome Texan named Bob Travis, whose great uncle had commanded the defenders of the Alamo, that I did not like the G-1 operation, which had responsibility for everyone in the division and attached troops, as individuals. Special staff heads in great numbers reported to the G-1. Strength reports were of prime importance, and I learned that no one from division had checked their accuracy by sending inspectors to the several regiments where, for lack of time and adequate personnel, insufficient attention was given to keeping a sharp eye on all details. The result in a number of cases had been the saddling of regiments with assignments that called for 90–100 percent effectiveness, where strength reports reflected such percentages, but when actuality found the regiments more nearly at 50–60 percent effective strength.

At the same time, I ran into the muscular captain whom I had not seen from the time I'd left General Wilbur's special school in North Africa where the captain had taken great pride in grilling us in the 110–20-degree temperatures, until I encountered him in the G-1 section. I asked him what he was doing there, since I sensed a defensive air about him as we talked. He tried giving me a fast shuffle about a special strength report he prepared each week for corps headquarters. I had reason to believe that, since corps was not an administrative body, such a report was serving no purpose.

I instructed the captain to show me the report, and then I went back through the files and found that the report had been a one-time requirement by II Corps before we went into combat at Salerno. I was pretty short with the captain when I presented him with the evidence that showed that, for the war to date, he and a couple of sergeants had put in their time to no good purpose.

'Why did you continue this report,' I asked him, 'when you knew it was of no value to anyone?'

'No one told me to stop,' he answered. 'I thought it was useful to corps'.

'I'm telling you to stop,' I said. 'Furthermore, since you've taken pains to hole up at this headquarters letting your muscles go soft, I've got other duties for you, starting right now.'

The look in his eye was one of wariness. 'What do you mean?' he asked.

'Why, Captain, I'm just going to show you what real men have been going through,' I responded. 'It will be in partial payment for your rotten attitude at Wilbur's school when you felt you had the upper hand. I'm sure you remember! You just follow me and I'll break you out of that shell you've built around yourself.'

'I'm going to see Travis about this,' he said.

'You go right ahead,' I stated, 'and I'll see to it that, instead of checking regimental headquarters for actual strength reports, you'll crawl on your guts to check the battalions.'

He stood there, a picture of consternation and defiance, and then slowly relaxed and nodded his head.

In the meantime, I had had a chance to talk with General Dahlquist about the many things I felt needed a change. He had told me that as far as he was concerned, I had carte blanche, that Travis would be going home among the first to leave when the war ended, and that he wanted the G-1 section in good shape to supervise the massive job of civilian, prisoner ,and surrenderee control when hostilities ended. The word had gotten around rather quickly that I was a 'take-charge' guy and that the general supported me all the way.

On the day that I put a stop to the 'special' corps report, I took the officer involved in my jeep and went forward to my old regimental headquarters. We were still on the Moder River line but each day produced a surcharged feeling, as pressures built to the crescendo that always preceded sharp action. Both sides were firing more artillery concentrations than had occurred in the depth of winter.

As we drew up behind a row of stables abutting the farmhouse where the regiment was located, a sudden salvo of heavy artillery struck in a courtyard not 50yd away. I ran toward a doorway, where I saw a soldier waving me into the building, and hit the floor inside as shell fragments tore through a window.

Several more rounds burst in the area and then nothing more happened for a while. I ran to the farmhouse and then thought to look for the captain who, grudgingly, had come with me. I found him under the jeep, his eyes closed, his face as white as a sheet. While I felt sorry for him, I knew that he'd had a very small taste of what the regiments had taken all the war.

'Get up, Captain,' I said, 'that's just Jerry's way of letting us know it's high noon.'

He got out from under the jeep and followed me into the regimental CP, his jaws clenched until the muscles stood out under his cheek.

'God, that was close!' he managed to say.

'You didn't get hurt, did you?' I asked. He shook his head.

'Then,' I said, 'it wasn't even close!'

We checked out the latest strength report of the regiment with a warrant officer, and, as I had thought, it was wrong in so many categories that it was worthless.

'Okay, Captain,' I said, 'you get that report up to date while I check around on some other items.' Before the day was over, we had visited all three regiments and I was boiling mad to learn that one of the regiments was deliberately reporting an understrength condition as it had done before, whenever serious action threatened. It also had more men on rest and rehabilitation than the other units.

Once I had the strength reports typed, which I insisted be done that night when the enlisted staff was about ready to leave, it being 5 pm, I took them to the general and went over them in detail. I made it pretty clear that I was not going to put up with the crap that the 142nd pulled any time there was a heavy fight in the offing. He was surprised at the discrepancies I'd found and congratulated me on getting things in shape.

'I haven't even got started yet,' I said. 'I plan to revise the SOP for the G-1 Section and I'm going to see to it, General, that instead of the G-1 staff sitting here like sacred cows, they get out and administer their jobs every day. We're changing the old system of lying doggo and waiting for the regiments to come to us.'

As I returned to the G-1 section, I heard the two sergeants who had helped prepare the corps 'special report' beefing about missing their nightly poker game.

I ducked my head around the corner and grinned at them. 'You fellers gamblers?' I asked.

One of them, trying to brass it out with me, knowing full well I'd heard their complaint said, 'I plan to set me up my own business when I get home.'

'Fine,' I said. 'Get your goods and chattels. I'm going to give you some real odds on that business of getting home.'

'What do you mean?' the other sergeant asked.

'When I tell you to get your goods and chattels, I mean everything you own. You two are now going to earn your stripes. There are some vacancies in the regiments and you're filling them as of now!'

The coldest kind of shocked silence settled on the room. Finally, as I eyed them, awaiting some movement, one said, 'Sorry, Major.'

'Get a move on,' I said and went back to my desk. No one else was working so I sent for a messenger and in a short time had the whole crew, except for Travis, at their places. When they were assembled, I gathered them in a circle and stood on a desk where they could get the idea as to who held the superior position.

'Gentlemen,' I said, 'for you, the war has just started. In case you don't know it, I'm sending two sergeants to regimental slots tonight. They complained about working after 5 pm. From now on, they'll be on duty 24 hours a day and they'll have something besides poker to worry them. So will you!

'You men can take your choice. You can put your weight behind the section's work or you can notify me that you want out and I'll see to it that you go to a "lower" rather than a "higher" headquarters.'

'There are no regular hours in the G-1 section from this moment on. You work until I tell you to stop. You will be given no second chance. Once you foul up, you're out. I know lots of better men than you who'd do your jobs and think they were in Heaven if given the chance. I've already circulated word to the regiments as to the types of men we want here.'

'Tonight we start re-writing the G-1 Section's SOP. I want every subsection head to give me a résumé of his assignment in detail. Accompanying that résumé will be that portion of the SOP that covers his work. Before morning, I want to have a new SOP ready for typing. No one is excused and if you miss a night's sleep, that's exactly what I have in mind. I want the AG to prepare his résumé at once and report to me in a half hour, ready to revise the pertinent part of the old SOP.'

'Whoever is not busy with such résumés will start sorting out all files into "Important" or "Unimportant" categories. Once this is done, I want "Important" papers subdivided into "Historical" and "Current" categories. I want no papers discarded until I've seen them, personally. I see no need to keep hundreds of copies of everything and until we have the SOP refined, we will retain no more than three copies of anything. My objective is to reduce the volume of files to 50 percent of their present size. Any questions?' None were forthcoming.

By 7 am the following morning we were almost finished with the SOP, a subject which no one had even thought of revising because of the burden of doing so after years of neglect. In two days, we had discarded more than twenty large cases of files, burning their contents and certifying their destruction. Once I had the ball moving, everyone pitched in and some even came up with solid suggestions for improvements. Travis never showed a sign of recognizing what I was doing.

In succession, I called in the special staff heads starting with the medical staff, and before we were done, we'd found a means of resting front-line troops who'd reached the limit of their endurance, by sending them back to Bains-les-Bains, a watering place we'd taken over as a rest camp, where they could sleep for several days, get clean, and enjoy respite from danger. At the same time such men were not out of division control and, in case of need, could be rushed back to the front in a few hours. Later, in Korea, I set up a similar system under circumstances where the medics were too soft on letting men off. Once our men got into medical channels we would not see them for months. It was interesting in both wars to note that tired men, given a couple of nights' real rest, were eager to rejoin their own units.

I had the special service officer arrange more entertainment and supply game equipment plus toilet articles and other items in constant demand. I increased the quotas for R and R for two of the regiments and fought for better allocation of trips to London and Paris as well as the Riviera, with the army staff.

I initiated forward planning to prepare for the routing of people home at war's end, and for obtaining replacements on a stepped-up basis. In doing this I flew in a small plane one day and made three forced landings in pastures in Belgium, due to socked-in conditions. At day's end, however, I had 5,000 replacements by raising hell with every headquarters I reached. I had them trucked to the division in special convoys so that the men could be trained properly before the spring offensive began.

Travis was very busy writing up citations for deserving men and units. I established a special team ready to go forward during the upcoming action to ferret out and recognize heroic actions rather than awaiting self-serving claims by fakers, as had happened too often in the past.

I put the military government and Red Cross units on notice that I wanted results and plans of action were to be approved by me before they were executed.

I checked out the Judge Advocate's Department and found it so lacking in discipline and proper action that I had many court-martial cases reviewed and verdicts set aside as a result of the lack of justice implicit in many of the proceedings. I requisitioned new personnel and worried higher headquarters so completely, when they failed to act, that some of them complained to Dahlquist. He simply called me to his office, congratulated me, and advised me to 'use the spurs.' He felt that division morale was at its peak for the whole war.

I worked 18 to 20 hours a day and though I kept a sharp ear out for complaints, I heard none, even though the rest of the G-1 staff stayed with me. The daily run to regiments by the muscular captain began to take on the aura of a lark, once he'd had his baptism of fire, and I was glad to learn that, on occasion, he'd gone to battalions to get correct figures when questions arose. I had noted that the longer men stayed away from the forward areas, the harder it was for them to take the first trip to the regimental precincts. Once there, however, there seemed to be a challenge to returning, time after time, if only for the purpose of discussing 'close calls' with less hardy characters who hadn't made their first journey into the void.

I had the chaplains of the division conduct more services and I warned them that they were needed in forward areas when battles erupted, rather than on trivial missions to the far rear when things got tough. Only one or two needed that reminder, the rest being among the most dedicated men I'd ever met.

A few snide remarks would be made at intervals at the general's mess, particularly when I first started marauding through the cabbage patch. Finally, Dahlquist said after one such remark, 'Take a lesson, you men, you're being out-classed in every respect.' That ended the resistance and started the move to a far more effective staff than had been the case prior to that time.

I went back to the 141st Infantry Regiment quite often in the course of my duties and on one occasion met General Stack there, as he was completing an inspection tour. We ate with the regimental staff and General Stack showed me a *Stars and Stripes* report that I had not seen, covering one of the funniest incidents of the war affecting my regiment.

It was the story of two GIs from one of our other regiments who, during the fighting in the Riquewihr–Mittlewihr area, had fallen on some fairly lush days when they found a wine cellar fully stocked with rare old wines. For them the war had stopped for a while as they sampled the various vintages and compared notes on them.

At that time Colonel McGrath, of the moustache, had taken command of one of our battalions. One day he called me in a great stir over the fact that snipers had driven him into the basement of the home where his CP was located and he wanted to know what the hell the regiment was doing to round up the snipers.

'Well, Mac,' I said, 'we're getting the same treatment. The trouble is that the sniping isn't localized. Yesterday, supplies to one of the other battalions were held up for almost 3 hours and the graves registration officer was pinned down under his jeep for an hour or more.'

'You get those bastards, hear?' McGrath yelled.

Several days elapsed with more reports of sniping being made to our headquarters in Riquewihr. Finally, we began to see that the pattern of sniping emanated from a vineyard just outside of Riquewihr. We hastily put together a task force of two TDs, infantry, and mortars to take the vineyard under fire.

As we did, all kinds of fire was directed from the center of the vineyard to targets lying anywhere around its perimeter. The TDs opened fire and sent a number of their 3in shells screaming into the vineyard. Mortars joined in the cannonading and the infantry, formed as skirmishers, started their walk through the low vines.

The battle reached a crescendo and I took shelter behind a shed near one corner of the vineyard. I could see GIs, on their bellies, working into the spot from which the hostile fire was coming. Suddenly all shooting stopped and I could hear voices exclaiming rather loudly over something.

Shortly, our men came back – escorting the two GIs who'd been on a drinking spree for a week. One was short and swarthy, the other tall and stoop-shouldered. They hadn't shaved for a week or ten days and they were grimy with dirt.

I later learned from the men who had finally captured the snipers that the two had dug a circular trench inside the vineyard and had stashed in it, not only German weapons and ammo, the use of which had completely fooled us, but a very large supply of wine.

Each of the men was brought before General Stack, then temporarily commanding our regiment, and while he managed to maintain his usual icy and acerbic mien, I caught him, once, covering a smile with one hand.

'I thought I'd have to laugh right out loud,' he said as we recounted the story when I met him on my G-1 rounds. 'That tall GI didn't care about anything we were telling him of the seriousness of his and his buddy's actions. He kept looking at the wine bottles we'd taken from him and you knew that his one care in the world was to get them back.'

To make the story complete and save it from becoming another tale of disaster, it should be noted that during a ten-day fusillade of snipers' bullets, no one was scratched, which says something about the capacity of the men to fire their weapons. If anything occurred, later, to cause the two snipers to regret their dalliance with the bottle, I never heard of it. They probably received minor company punishment.

The officer in charge of the task force that rounded up the offenders told us, after the men were led away, that he had heard them greet the GIs who'd come after them with the following statement:

'Where the hell have you been, you jerks? We been fightin' Germans for a week and no one came to help us. We been fightin' and fallin' back, fightin' and fallin' back. What kinda army is this, anyway?'!

Finally, the day came to break out of the Moder River line, an operation that was helped immeasurably by the fact that Allied Forces north of us had capitalized on a German error and on March 7, 1945, had seized the bridge at Remagen[1] and affected a bridgehead on the eastern shore of the Rhine River.

General Patton had also turned his army south to encircle a large number of German troops facing our position in the Saar Palatinate. The 36th Division was assigned the task of breaking the Moder River defenses, which the Germans had been building for several weeks, and then to breach the Siegfried Line, seizing Bergzabern and, thus, outflanking the Germans blocking passage of the French forces on our right.

In order to accomplish its first mission, the 36th Division had to effect crossings not only of the Moder River, but also the Zintel and Sauer[2] Rivers so that the 14th Armored Division could roll ahead to exploit the breakthrough. Important to the overall success of the operation was the need to clear the highway from Haguenau to Soultz in order to develop a main supply route for the corps. This road had been blocked for miles by abatis since it ran through heavy forests in places. Therefore, the effort to smash the defenses had to be made across open ground west of the forested area. Company K of the 143rd Infantry so conducted itself in the critical attack over terrain that offered little or no concealment that it received the Presidential Unit Citation, a matter that was handled by the special task force created at division headquarters to search out heroic actions.

Of small historical importance but operating as a challenge to our division was the fact that the German 36th Division opposed us. In another sharp fight at Mietesheim the 1st Battalion of the 143rd Infantry also won the Presidential Unit Citation. Fighting expertly and with the kind of guts the high command expected of one of its veteran divisions, the 36th's success completed its initial mission of crossing and bridging three rivers by March 17, having initiated its assault on March 15, 1945.

It should also be noted that the dirty job of opening the Haguenau–Soultz Road, on which much of the success of the division's action depended, fell to

---

1. Halfway between Cologne and Koblenz on the Rhine (i.e., deep inside Germany).
2. These three rivers run to the east (into the Rhine) out of the Vosges to Haguenau and north of that town.

the 141st Infantry. This job was also completed by March 17. On March 19 the division had crossed the last barrier to Germany and was facing the 'dragon's teeth' of the Siegfried Line near Wissembourg.

At about that time, I heard that there was a huge toll gateway at Schweigen which, I thought, would make a great public relations background, particularly if the Lone Star Flag of Texas were draped on it. Armond Puck, the provost marshall of the division, was dispatched to the scene and the photograph taken of him standing on a high balcony that straddled the road, as a customs barrier, made many newspapers stateside.

Any thought that the Germans would not man the Siegfried Line was squelched when our forces reached Ober-Otterbach, where dozens of pillboxes opened fire on our leading elements. On March 19, the 2nd Battalion of the 141st Infantry crossed into Germany, the first unit of the division to do so. This crossing was made a short way southeast of Wissembourg. Before long the division was engaged in its last major battle of the war, namely the breaching of the Siegfried Line.

Initially the 36th Division, located furthest from the Siegfried Line on March 15, 1945, was not expected to do more than demonstrate in front of that obstacle while other forces to the west of our position, possessed of armored siege guns, would make the vital penetration. However, once the forward movement started, the division smashed its way up to and through the Siegfried.

By March 24, the division had cleared the Siegfried defenses, showing the fallacy of the garrison mentality that had prompted the construction of both the Maginot and Siegfried Lines, and was drawn up along the Rhine.

During that battle I talked with some of the men of the 141st Infantry Regiment and learned that one of their company commanders, in trying to maintain control of his company in the hilly terrain, had – in true Texan style – 'borrowed' a horse for that purpose. He was bound to be out front with his company when it came time to wipe up the Krauts in their own country. In riding his horse during the night before a critical attack in the hills northwest of Ober-Otterbach, which succeeded in outflanking the famed dragon's teeth anti-tank defenses of that area, the captain came up missing. The attack went off as planned and the company did the job in an outstanding manner. Sometime during the next day a voice was heard calling for help and upon investigation, the captain was found in an anti-tank ditch with his horse, where both had fallen in the night. The horse had been killed and the captain badly hurt. So far as could be learned, no more episodes of that kind occurred later.

I had a peculiar experience or two as I entered Germany proper. The division headquarters moved to Wissembourg as soon as the dragon's teeth and the Siegfried outer defenses were breached. Long-range German artillery had the crossing point under fire when I approached the 'dragon's teeth.'

These 'teeth' were cement piers that were fastened in place by heavy cables imbedded in concrete that ran underground for the full length of the area they protected. With short piers at the front, the arrangement was such that, if tanks attempted to cross them, the forward parts of the tanks would rise higher and higher until their vulnerable bellies were exposed to anti-tank shells, fired from nearby defensive strongpoints.

Our engineers had dynamited the piers and in many places the heavy cables were exposed to view. My jeep was right in the middle of the roadway the engineers had blown through the dragon's teeth, when we were stopped by artillery fire just ahead of our position. I heard a heavy 'ping' and felt the jeep vibrate but could not account for what had occurred until my driver started to move the jeep forward again.

We could not budge an inch. On getting out and looking under the jeep, I found that a piece of cable, as big around as the barrel of a baseball bat, had sprung up from where it, apparently, had been caught beneath another cable and had jammed itself into the transmission of the jeep. We were high and dry. All kinds of racket ensued as impatient drivers behind us blew their horns as though they were Sunday drivers at home rather than hostile troops entering Germany through the vaunted Siegfried Line.

An engineer party came up and after assessing the damage and the peculiar accident, got an acetylene torch and cut the offending cable off while we waited for more artillery to catch us in the open. None came. Progress, however, was very slow as the troops were digging Germans out of secret tunnels, pillboxes, and fortifications that often extended for three or four stories below ground level and were serviced by regular elevators.

It was dark before we reached the outskirts of Wissembourg, and the constant play of artillery flashes showed that the resistance to our advance into Germany was tough. As we waited in a long column of vehicles and realized that we could expect a demoniacal defense of the Fatherland, I heard some sounds of boots scrambling down a hill beside my jeep and could make out, against the night sky, a column of men. I drew my .45 and waited. All around our men were smoking cigarettes as red circles of light disclosed, and talking in low murmurs as we awaited further movement forward. Most everyone was alert to possible surprise attack.

Suddenly, a voice speaking English in guttural accents said, 'We surrender!' He was evidently addressing me, as he seemed to be looking at me and stood fairly close to where I was leaning on the jeep.

I asked him how many men were with him and he said, '200.'

I ordered him, as I had the German officer who surrendered to me at Le Dramont, France, to have his men put their weapons down, right where they stood. After a series of whispered commands that were passed along in diminishing volume as they moved up the hill, I could hear sounds of weapons striking the ground.

My driver was talking with other drivers on his side of the jeep and I sensed that they were getting nervous. 'Take it easy, boys,' I said. 'We've got some PWs here and I don't want any mistakes made.' 'Okay, Major,' my driver whispered before he went back along the line to warn others to relax.

I made the German, whom I took to be an officer, understand that he would not be injured and that we would have less trouble if we said nothing to the rest of the convoy ahead of our position but simply marched ahead until I could turn him and his men over to our MPs. I told him to warn his men not to speak but simply to follow us. It was an eerie feeling walking beside the German, whose face I never did see, under circumstances where I could not be certain that all weapons had been abandoned on the hillside.

At the end of a 2-mile hike, accomplished while the division column continued its static condition, I found the provost marshall and a group of MPs. They were flabbergasted when I turned over the 200 or so PWs and when one MP asked me where I got them, I simply told him to take them away.

At Wissembourg I had some problems with civilian groups. We were told that we had fought our last fight and that we would now go into occupation of Germany west of the Rhine. This meant disposing of our troops to affect maximum control over the German population with little or no consideration of tactical requirements.

It was not long before we had all kinds of rear echelon troops in Wissembourg to include quartermaster companies, transportation companies, ordnance outfits, and the like.

The forward fighting elements soon had consolidated their bridgehead east of the Rhine and from there had pushed for Berlin. We were, for the first time, then, in the backwaters of the Second World War, a role with which we were not at all familiar. Although the troops were perfectly glad to stop the rat race, General Dahlquist was not. Corps, army, and then army Group displaced forward, each keeping its distance from the front, but all of them, sooner or later, passing us by. At each occasion, as old friends entered and then left Wissembourg, General Dahlquist was at their throats yelling something to the effect that 'a division that has contributed so much to the defeat of Germany deserves to be in at the kill.' It seemed that no one heard him.

I was on duty in the Wissembourg city hall one night when the telephone rang and upon answering it, heard the unmistakable sultry tones of 'Marlene Dietrich' – as the phone announced.

'Yes, Miss Dietrich,' I said. 'We're expecting you and your troupe to arrive in the division area tomorrow.'

'Please do one thing for me,' she said. 'Let me eat with officers other than those at division headquarters. I particularly don't want to eat at the general's mess.'

'I doubt that General Dahlquist will like that, Miss Dietrich,' I responded, 'but I'll see what I can do.'

She arrived the next noontime and, as she stepped out of a command car that bore a brigadier general's star, she presented a lovely sight to those of us who saw her. She was dressed in khaki slacks and shirt that enhanced her femininity. She greeted Max Justes, one of our French liaison officers, with a hug and kiss, and we went to the junior officer's mess for lunch, as she had suggested she would like to do.

I went about my duties that, by that time, were becoming onerous in as much as the supervision of military government was one of the functions assigned to G-1. I learned that a quartermaster truck company had caused a great deal of trouble by invading a religious institution where several nuns were raped. Because we were striving for civilized treatment of all concerned, this was one of the crimes that we were certain to treat summarily and with force. I set up an ambush on the institution's grounds that night and in the ensuing melee that occurred after midnight, several of the perpetrators – all of whom were drunk and disorderly – were shot and killed. The rest served long sentences in Leavenworth after courts martial.

The next day Miss Dietrich's secretary came to call on me. She was a red-headed, freckle-faced girl from Texas. 'Has Marlene told you she doesn't want to eat at the general's mess, yet?' she asked me.

'She called me before arriving,' I said, 'and said that she preferred to eat with the junior officers.'

'You can expect trouble then,' the girl said. 'She does this everywhere and then complains to the general about shabby treatment.'

'She doesn't have enough to keep her busy,' I commented, 'if she plays games like that.'

'It's her way of getting extra attention and of causing trouble, if she can,' the girl said. I gathered that the secretary had just about had it with La Dietrich.

Sure enough that evening after mess, which I had eaten at my desk, the general called on the telephone. He was well into his cups and his speech slurred a little as he barked at me.

'Doughty,' he yelled. 'How come you assigned Miss Dietrich to a mess, other than mine?'

'General,' I answered, 'you've just fallen into the little trap she prepares for all generals. Her secretary dropped by today to tell me to expect trouble. Miss Dietrich called me the other day and specifically asked not to be assigned to your mess. Now she thinks she can stir up trouble by twitting you about not asking her to dine with you.'

'I don't believe it,' the general said. I could hear him discussing my statement with someone whom I took to be Miss Dietrich. 'She denies it,' he finally said.

'Okay General,' I responded. 'Perhaps you and I can fight it out with potatoes at 50yd, just to please her.' This seemed to please the general for I heard him laugh and repeat the challenge before he hung up. About an hour later he, Marlene, and Max Justes stopped by the city hall where I was working. I went down the granite stairs to the sidewalk and noted that the general was quite drunk.

'Miss Dietrich is on her way to the Red-Cross girls' billet,' the general said. I didn't say anything but simply awaited the next move. 'She'll be there all night,' the general added as though he had delivered himself of some precious message.

'Fine!' I said and went back up the stairs.

Chapter 31

Victory at Long Last

Whie we sat in so-called occupation west of the Rhine, few of the old hands at the game of war objected to the peaceful conditions. With Russia and Allied Forces closing in on Berlin, it began to look as though we had fought our last battle. Spread thin to control population centers, contact between our units was maintained by motorized patrols. We occupied the Kaiserslautern–Zweibruecken area of Germany south of Frankfurt. We also

had troops in Ludwigshafen and Worms. During this time we, once again, went into heavy training to stay in condition.

As things turned out, we were ordered back to the front and on April 24, 1945, traveled to an assembly area 150 miles east of Heilbronn. Before we could collect all of our units there, the 7th Army line had moved over 100 miles further into Germany, a move expedited by the capture of a bridge across the Danube River by the 12th Armored Division. Once that crossing was effected, German resistance on our front began to crumble and fall.

We were attached to the 21st Corps and shortly thereafter relieved the 63rd Division at Landsberg, in whose prison Adolf Hitler had written *Mein Kampf*. We had made a run across Germany of some 300 miles in our effort to catch up with an active front. En route, I had been surprised at the cleanliness of German housewives who, despite the tremendous damage done to most areas, worked from dawn until after dark cleaning their homes inside and out and, as a final ablution, swabbing down their front walks. People, generally, were subdued and well behaved.

At Landsberg my old regiment initiated an attack southward toward Weilheim, which it captured, followed by the capture of Bad Tölz. Somewhere in that vicinity I came upon the villa of a German general named Wolff.[1] In it were trunks of uniforms, medals, and much of the impedimenta of a regular officer of the German army.

We must have been much of the same build for I donned one of his swastika-laden dress uniforms with a red-lined blue cape and walked into the general's mess one evening wearing it and a monocle. There was a stunned silence as, with my face fairly well shadowed, by the high-billed cap, I took a seat near the general. Then someone said, 'Doughty, you bastard!' and I was pummeled from right and left as everyone roared at the deception.

As usual, the 141st Infantry took the brunt of the fighting. As the division headquarters entered Landsberg I went to Stalag 3, a so-called 'killing camp' where I saw, at last, the atrocities visited upon Jews by the Nazis.

We captured a woman doctor there, and since we were under orders to try to establish a connection between such killings and the Nazi hierarchy, I had her put under guard. She, it turned out, had injected poison into the right arms of some 800 prisoners we had found along a railroad spur where the bodies had been run over by a train, after the poison had been injected.

One survivor, a Jew who had worked in a kitchen and had somehow escaped being murdered, gave us some background on what had occurred. The 800 bodies were those of Jews who had been told by prison authorities that, with Germany about to lose the war, all concerned would be transported south to rehabilitation camps in an effort to undo the abuse that had been their lot at German hands. The woman doctor, according to our informant, had told the Jews that she would

---

1. Supreme commander of all German SS forces in Italy.

administer sedatives to help them withstand the trip south, since they were walking skeletons and probably couldn't last the journey without help.

I sent for a special team from army to come to Stalag 3 to investigate the atrocities there, and so I had to stay in the area where typhus was prevalent for two days to assist the search for documents that might incriminate Hitler and his cohorts. No such documents were found.

In looking around the neighboring countryside I came upon a sight that was the cruelest I'd seen in the war. I walked through a pine forest which the German people had kept pruned and cleaned like a park. As I ducked under a low-hanging limb, I stopped short. In front of me in a row were what appeared to be eight men standing in foxholes. They were in the Jewish grey striped prison garb with the Star of David emblem on them. Suddenly I realized that these men were not in foxholes. These were the upper portions of men's bodies that had been cut in half by machine-gun fire.

Nearby, in a tree, I found the body of a Nazi guard who had hung himself when our troops had surrounded him. In later talks with men of the 141st Infantry I learned that the sights of Stalag 3 had so infuriated our men that, even though they knew the war was about over, they were spurred on to hunt down and kill the animals who had perpetrated such crimes.

I sent a party to pick up the torsos of the Nazi target practice range and went on to the railroad where the eviscerated bodies of the 800 Jews lay. We had sent for the people of Landsberg to come and see the sights of a camp they'd denied knowing about, in spite of the fact that ditches along the main road to Landsberg contained some 30,000 cadavers, many of them open to view as the covering process through use of bulldozers was often delayed.

At the railroad, I could only think back to a time in my life when I'd seen the body of a hobo near the Walpole, Massachusetts, railroad station, after he'd been run over by a train. However, that sight was as nothing compared with the awfulness of so many bodies jumbled together and forever cut to unrecognizable pieces.

I walked up the track toward Landsberg where I saw a GI prodding along a protesting old German man with a bayonet. The old man was carrying the severed arm of one of the murdered Jews in one hand and was holding his other hand over his heart in a distinct signal that he was suffering a heart spasm. Ordinarily, I would have stopped this brutality but having seen the depravity of Stalag 3, I did nothing. Shortly the old man collapsed and died and I had several citizens of Landsberg, including two women, carry the corpse to the Stalag and dump it on the human refuse that was being collected there for burial.

I called the sergeant of the guard to take me to the house where the woman doctor had been sequestered. As I entered the room, I knew in a moment that the woman was dead. Some ass, in trying to teach the Germans how some of their cruelty felt, had secured the woman's hands with a device that combined handcuffs with a steel ball containing hundreds of needles which, if placed between the wrists would effectively discourage any attempt to work out of the manacles. This was all that the doctor had needed to cut her own wrists and thereby avoid trial and execution for her depravity. I recommended a court martial for the offender.

Just before we reached Landsberg I had crossed the beautiful blue Danube River, only to find it turgid and green and unsightly. At some point between there and Kitzbühel, Austria, I was crossing another river on a pontoon bridge and had stopped about halfway across because of a road jam ahead. As I sat in the jeep with the top down talking with my driver, I could hear fast planes approaching us from our left. It was an extremely foggy and dull day but suddenly out of the mist appeared three zebra-striped planes flying in formation at about the 100ft level. Before we could react in any way, they roared over us and disappeared into the gloom. While I never learned what their mission was, I've secretly felt that this was a sortie, set up by Hermann Göring, to fly to Switzerland in an attempt to effect a separate peace with the Allies. I know that for a fleeting second I felt exactly like a sitting duck and, while the moment of truth never arrived, I fully expected to see tracers coming for me just as the war was about to end. All three planes were German fighters.

After I left Landsberg, I encountered more abysmal sights of freed Jewish prisoners, most of them zombie-like in their weakness, eating dead horses and then, themselves, dying a few minutes later. A train, filled with prisoners and cadavers, had been stopped by a shell through the engine and the smell and sight of its cars will remain a ghastly memory, always.

We, in the meantime, having been turned south away from Berlin, had been hearing stories of a national redoubt envisaged by Hitler as a place in the Alps from which German troops could hold out indefinitely against superior numbers. It all sounded reasonable enough, given the Nazi mentality, which could be thoroughly unreasonable.

As the war drew to a close, we encountered a series of amazing events none of which could be anticipated but all of which brought home to us the reality of the war's imminent end.

The first of these occurred at a castle near Weilheim – the Schloss Waldbichl – which we had taken over as a headquarters. Located in the country, it had huge camouflage nets concealing its battlements and, all-in-all, the first impression of the edifice was one of gloom and medieval antiquity; a place for vampires!

Admiral Horthy[2], whom we considered the fourth member of the Axis, was taken prisoner there together with many of his cabinet members. He was but a minor aberration in the major events occurring at that time. I was sitting before a huge fireplace in the commodious lobby of the castle playing chess with the division chaplain. There was a raised floor surrounding the fireplace and seated on it in divans and easy chairs were members of the division staff talking and

---

2. Miklós Horthy was a statesman who was regent of the Kingdom of Hungary until 1944.

laughing as we contemplated the possibility, long suppressed, that we might even make it through the war.

It was early evening, just after we'd eaten our dinner. Suddenly there came a loud knocking on the main portal and as the door opened we could see a very large, bearded American non-com standing there. He announced in a somewhat theatrical way the following news: 'Sirs, I have the honor to announce the capture of Field Marshal Gerd von Rundstedt.' As he stood aside, von Rundstedt, Germany's number one soldier, advanced into the room and raised his baton in silent salute to us.

Most of us had risen from our seats and I've often wondered what the effect of our relaxed attitudes must have been on the man who, if left alone by Hitler, might have blocked our D-Day invasion at the high water mark in Normandy.

Behind von Rundstedt came his son, a full colonel, and several German general staff officers with crimson stripes running down the sides of their trousers' legs. General Dahlquist came out of his office and within a few moments von Rundstedt was led into that office together with his son, who did most of the talking.

Von Rundstedt walked with a gimpy leg and the impression I retain was that he seemed smaller than I had thought him to be, but the look in his eye and the set of his jaw proclaimed a man of steel – a real presence. He was soon on his way back to higher headquarters but not before he had observed that our strategic bombing had won the war for us. Whenever a field commander needed men, munitions, or materiel, they were missing because 'you isolated the battlefield with your bombers.' He also said that when finally confronted with the reality of the successful invasion at Normandy, Hitler had turned to him and asked, 'What do we do now?' and von Rundstedt had said, 'Surrender, you fool.'

My friend, Paul Lefort, came in with another German high-ranking officer he'd found in bed in a small cottage in a neighboring hamlet. A frightened German housewife had run out of her house at dusk and told Lefort that such a man was hiding in her home.

Lefort entered the low-ceilinged house and in a back bedroom found a very large man shivering and shaking in bed. When ordered to get out of bed, the German had refused so Paul, with the help of his driver, had upended the bed and unceremoniously dumped the man, stark naked, onto the floor.

Paul refused to let him get back into uniform but accused him of espionage behind our lines while out of uniform. As a result, the prisoner was forced to put on some ill-fitting lederhosen that had belonged to the woman's dead husband. When the prisoner arrived at Schloss Waldbichl, he was a mess and it was like something out of a low-class comedy seeing him try to salute Field Marshal von Rundstedt while attempting to keep the lederhosen from falling around his ankles. He was kept overnight in a cell that had seen other uses under German occupation. We learned that he was Hugo Sperrle, the German air marshal, who had invented dive-bombing and had planned the blitz of London.

It was evident to me that the high brass of the German military forces were running for cover and had chosen an area where many large hospitals existed, on the premise that our air force would not bomb them there.

We moved out of our commodious schloss and proceeded into Austria, taking over the town hall of Kufstein for our headquarters. Rumors were endless as to when the war would end. We knew it must do so shortly if for no other reason than that the German soldiers, upon being driven out of Germany into Austria, began to surrender by the hundreds of thousands, even though they were fully armed and equipped. We could look down the Inn River Valley, once we reached Kufstein, and – as far as the eye could see – observe lines of beaten German soldiers plodding back toward Germany, all the fight gone out of them. The old German shibboleth that the German armies in the First World War were never defeated on the field of battle could not be revived for the Second World War. We had in front of us the vaunted German army and its demise was a certainty as we herded its surrenderees into vast encampments.

No one could take them off our hands, since PW enclosures all the way back to the Channel Ports were jammed. German strength had collapsed under the converging Allied and Russian armies.

As I sat at a desk on the second floor of the Kufstein Town Hall, a sentry came up to announce the arrival of a German colonel and four roughneck soldiers carrying machine pistols. I told him to show the colonel up but to keep the gunmen in their car. Upon glancing out of the town-hall window I saw the small vehicle at the curb swathed in white sheets and flying white flags.

The colonel, who spoke good English, turned out to be a son of General von Brauchitsch who'd tried to force the defenses of Stalingrad. He said he wanted to get back to General Jakey Devers or Ike Eisenhower to surrender a 'high Nazi personality' whose identity he was not at liberty to disclose.

I got word to General Dahlquist who refused safe passage to von Brauchitsch and instead said that the Nazi involved could either surrender to the 36th Division or to the Russians, who were rapidly closing in on Vienna.

Von Brauchitsch returned to his car and drove off. I watched him turn a corner where I lost sight of the car but shortly it returned having simply swung around a block. I'm sure the sight of so many German surrenderees on the main road had prompted the colonel's return.

He came to where I was waiting and asked if we would send an escort with him to assist in bringing in the Nazi. General Dahlquist, having been prompted by me to consider this alternative, since we were under strict orders to take the top men prisoner wherever possible, agreed to send General Stack, assistant division commander, with von Brauchitsch.

General Dahlquist made no bones about walking up to Colonel von Brauchitsch and telling him, nose-to-nose, that if anything happened to Stack, he – Dahlquist – would hunt von Brauchitsch down and settle matters with him personally. By this time, the German colonel had lost a good deal of his crispness and assured Dahlquist that he would do all in his power to keep Stack safe.

The 36th Division headquarters moved to Kitzbühel, Austria, that same day, which was May 7, 1945, even though the order had come down from on high to halt all fighting troops in place, as of May 5, 1945, since German Army Group 'G' had surrendered effective May 6, 1945.

While we had expected General Stack's return on May 7, the day he had gone deep into Austria to help safeguard the return to our lines of the 'high Nazi personality,' he did not return until May 8.

In the meantime we had taken over the Grand Hotel at Kitzbühel as our headquarters. I talked with General Stack, later, on the Riviera when we were there planning to celebrate the first anniversary of our landing at Le Dramont on August 15, 1944. When I asked him how things had gone after he left with Colonel von Brauchitsch, he said they had traveled some distance into Austria – 25 or 30 miles – when they came across a convoy of several vehicles drawn up along the side of the road.

It wasn't until he finally saw the portly figure of the 'high Nazi personality' that he knew who his prospective prisoner was. It was Reichsführer Hermann Göring[3] who was standing beside his armored vehicle near Radstadt, 35 miles southeast of Salzburg, Austria. With him were his wife, Emmy, and daughter, Edda, and a whole retinue of aides and servants.

Stack said that Göring wasn't entirely sure, even then, that he wished to surrender. They returned to a nearby castle where elements of the Florian Geyer SS Cavalry Division had been quartered until 36th Division troops had captured it that day.

Stack's driver had told me that he and the general had been disarmed, a factor I found hard to believe under circumstances where control of the castle where they stayed overnight was in our hands. In any event, since there was some possibility that German troops had been alerted to kill Göring when Hitler learned of the former's efforts to take command of German forces from Hitler, the decision was made to stay under cover until morning.

My first view of Göring and his family was at the portico of the Grand Hotel late in the afternoon of May 8, 1945. He was dressed in a plain grey uniform, minus all of his decorations (see plate), which he normally flaunted, judging by press releases of him in his heyday. He told us during interrogation that he had talked with Hitler by telephone a few days earlier and that Hitler had lifted the death sentence he had pronounced on Göring, provided that Göring would renounce all honors that had been bestowed on him by the Fatherland. We

---

3. Hermann Göring was chief of the German air force (Luftwaffe) during the war. He was designated to be Hitler's successor. He exercised that authority and tried peace negotiations as the war was recognized to have been lost – while Hitler was alive! Consequently, he was deemed a traitor, although this status was lifted provided he give up all his medals. This may have been among the reasons he 'escaped' to Austria to pompously attempt a noble surrender. Instead, the 36th Division arrested him as described in the memoir. He was tried for war crimes at Nuremberg in 1946, convicted, and sentenced to death by hanging. He escaped the hangman by poison pill. How he obtained access to such a pill is still unclear.

assumed, at the time, that this was Göring's ploy to gain sympathy and to change his image of a swashbuckler to something more appealing to, what he considered to be, the American viewpoint. However, it appears that other testimony later substantiated his story.

General Dahlquist was severely taken to task by General Eisenhower because of a story filed by a woman correspondent, who called from 6th Army Group Press Camp 60 miles to the rear, to learn of Göring's treatment by his captors. The story hit the headlines because it appeared that we had fêted Göring and had served him a chicken dinner. It is true that he received a chicken dinner but it was warmed-over canned chicken that we'd been served before Göring arrived.

It took several weeks to straighten out the bad publicity attendant upon such a rotten news story and in the interim Dahlquist was busted to Brigadier General. This injustice was corrected as soon as Ike learned the facts. Dahlquist, when he finally retired, was a full general – four stars on each shoulder.

While our division history contains one version of Göring's stay with us, it is incorrect. The history says that Göring arrived on the morning of May 8 and after interrogation was delivered to the chief of staff of Seventh Army.

He arrived in the afternoon, and after dinner was put up at the Grand Hotel under a guard headed by a Jewish lieutenant. That night, I could not sleep and after dressing went downstairs only to find most of the men of the headquarters sitting around and drinking some of the special liquors that we had captured from the German First Army, which had used the Grand Hotel as its headquarters prior to our arrival. It was too quiet to sleep and the peace was so momentous that we could scarcely assimilate it.

At daybreak, the Jewish lieutenant came running down the stairs brandishing a perfectly beautiful ring given him by Emmy Göring for having kept the family safe that night.

Strangely enough, too, we had asked the German First Army commander to send up some German officers capable of speaking English, so that we could have direct liaison with First Army's headquarters. They were quartered in the hotel with us and some yahoo, that night, had set fire to some paper and wood in front of their door.

I was ordered to go with one of the German liaison officers to the German First Army headquarters to deliver the outline of what was to be done with men, weapons, vehicles, and materiel. General Dahlquist, in commenting on what I was to do, said, 'Tell them! Let them know we're in charge! Let them know they've been defeated in battle!'

The German captain who accompanied me seemed nervous as we proceeded to a small Austrian town which I've always thought to be St. Johann, although my diary does not reflect that name. All of the German soldiers we saw were armed with machine pistols and wore scowls as they saw my uniform. We stopped in front of a three-storied country inn and, by running the gauntlet of armed and scowling soldiers, we proceeded to the top floor where small rooms were crowded beneath low eaves.

As we entered the room some twenty or thirty officers arose and stood at attention. Here in a group were more German general staff officers than we had seen all the war. The commanding general stood up last and in a deep, gutteral voice, introduced himself as 'Ritter von Hengl.'[4] The German liaison officer introduced me and I saluted the general who returned the salute with one very much like mine, rather than the comic opera 'Heil Hitler' gambit.

He started to speak in German and I put up my hand and said to the interpreter, 'I'll do all the talking. Simply tell the general that I am here as General Dahlquist's agent and that he, in turn, represents General Eisenhower.'

The interpreter looked so frightened that I thought he would not repeat what I had said. However, he stammered out something and the general shrugged and sat down.

I proceeded to outline where people and materiel were to be assembled, and then I told the interpreter to ask von Hengl how many men he had under his command.

In a long, drawn-out statement the general replied that he had been moving so rapidly lately that his records were not up to date. I could feel the eyes of everyone in the room on me as I questioned the general. I assumed that they were trying to assess the kind of treatment they might expect of us.

I told the interpreter to ask the general to explain more about such movement, particularly the direction of it. The answer came back, 'Southward!'

I then launched into a statement that I had been rehearsing since talking with Dahlquist. I kept my tone even and low but I said:

General von Hengl, I have been instructed by General Dahlquist commanding the 36th US Infantry Division to tell you that we are fully aware of your strength. You have some 300 men under your control now. We have taken 35,000 prisoners of war and some 180,000 surrenderees who have been coming into our zone of responsibility for days. The southward movement of which you speak has been a retreat. We want you to know that the armies of Germany have been defeated on the field of battle so that their invincibility will no longer be boasted of by the German general staff.

To orient you now on our attitude toward your army, let me state that, for us, the war has ended. We are only a fighting division not equipped to handle the tremendous administrative burden thrust upon us by the end of hostilities. We look upon your relationship with our headquarters as one of facing a mutual problem.

We are prepared to send home as soon as possible all but those personnel who have been termed by our high command as 'automatic arrests.' They are the SS. We anticipate using your staff to work closely with us in this effort. You will be housed and fed and guarded in that process. Any effort

---

4. General der Gebirgstruppe in the Wehrmacht who commanded the XIX Mountain Corps.

to conceal SS identities will be dealt with summarily. If you are agreeable to this solution, please so signify.

I had had to make this statement a sentence at a time to be certain that it was being translated just about as I had given it. I could sense an easing of tensions as men guardedly looked at each other and with raised eyebrows or drawn down mouths signaled what seemed to me to be an appreciation of the fairness of the statement I had made.

Von Hengl, heavyweight Junker that he was, clambered to his feet and started another speech. This time I let him go on for a short time but finally signaled him to stop. He had not acknowledged anything that I had said but had said something to this effect, 'I have told my officers that you Americans would be fair. Now I'm telling you or rather asking you why you do not convince your general that the German and American armies should join forces and together defeat the Russians who are the real danger to this world. They are at the end of their rope and we could drive them back to Moscow by fighting together.'

I responded that there was no place for political views in our talks. I also said that we, by being fair, never would turn on a nation that had helped us defeat a common enemy. I was, nevertheless, surprised that von Hengl, sitting in a small room under the eaves of a country inn, faced with utter defeat and loss of his command, could think in such terms, even though I recognized that such a solution would, if acted upon, salvage German pride.

I left shortly thereafter and after, again, running the gauntlet of scowls and machine pistols, was glad to reach the jeep and my driver. I had received von Hengl's okay to help with the demobilization of the German troops under our control. The German captain, still with me, smiled for the first time and said something to the effect that no one he knew in the German army had really expected honorable treatment upon surrendering. I looked at him for a moment and said, 'Nothing in your army's treatment of prisoners or civilians has been honorable. Therefore you have judged us by yourselves.' The nervous look, I was glad to note, returned to his face.

It was only mid-morning when I got back to the Grand Hotel where I found a festive mood among the major staff officers. They were planning to take the Red-Cross girls assigned to our division up the famed ski mountain in Kitzbühel, using a cable car for that purpose. I decided to go along and shortly we were at the control-house of the cable cars. There an old German wearing a uniform of some sort made every kind of protestation about our going up the mountain. We finally stood him at ease and he agreed to run the cars for our benefit. It was quite a sensation riding the car, crowded with people, and watching the twin car pass us on its way down. It was also a dizzying prospect to look down at the snow-covered mountain flank just as we passed over a high shoulder of the mountain-top and coasted into our own berth at the end of the run.

Some of us went out onto a promontory for a breathtaking view of miles and miles of mountain crests. This was the heart of the national redoubt we'd heard about for days. As we returned to pass the cable-car station and to make our way through a pass to the topmost peak, where we had heard a hotel was located, there came the unmistakable sound of someone working the bolt of a machine gun. We turned a corner and found ourselves under German guns once more. An entire mountain division of the German army was in position on the mountain.

We were escorted to the hotel where a German colonel wanted to know what we were doing there. He indicated that the presence of the Red-Cross girls had probably saved our lives. I had the impression that, despite his denial, he had been informed of the war's end and that he had been in contact with the German cable-car operator, probably by telephone.

As we stood on the porch watching ski troops go through their practice on slopes that formed a bowl, so that the sensation was one of perpetual motion, it was hard to believe that we were in trouble. The recommendation was made by us that the colonel in charge of the German troops send an escort back to Kitzbühel with the Red-Cross girls to verify the fact that Göring had surrendered and that the war, in fact, had come to a close.

It got to be a long day before the escort returned to confirm the report we'd given the German commander. I told him that I was the G-1 of the division that would process their return to civilian status and that under no circumstances should the mountain troops carry their weapons down the mountain. I was attempting to avoid further loss of life for I was certain that if our sentries saw ski troops racing downhill carrying weapons they'd open fire.

It was a good feeling, once again, to be on board our swaying transport and to return to the Grand Hotel where news of our adventure had been bruited about by the Red-Cross girls. It is my recollection, too, while on the subject of Red-Cross girls, that when Max Amann, publisher of *Mein Kampf,*[5] was taken prisoner by our troops, he had been sent back to a PW cage under the supervision of a couple of Red-Cross girls. Amann, it was reported, objected strenuously to being treated like something the cat dragged in and felt that it was beneath his dignity to be escorted by girls. He was minus one arm, as I recall it, and our girls would have been more than a match for him. He was taken in the vicinity of Tegernsee where he'd been hiding in his summer home.

All in all the 36th Division, at war's end, took the lion's share of high-ranking German and Nazi officials. This was made more heart-warming to the men who wore the T-patch by the fact that General Patton, still seeking notoriety wherever he could find it, swung fast-moving task forces across our zone of responsibility in a search for personalities. His actions were unwarranted, caused traffic jams, and netted him nothing but a lot of catcalls and rebel yells.

In addition to Göring, von Rundstedt, Sperrle and Amann, we captured Reichsminister Dr. Hans Franck, Gauleiter of Poland, Air Marshal Ritter von Greim who succeeded Göring in command of the Luftwaffe, SS General Sepp Dietrich (defender of Vienna against the Russians), and nineteen other

---

5. 'My Struggle' or ' My Battle'.

general officers of the German armed forces. In addition we liberated French leaders Edouard Daladier, Paul Reynaud, General Maurice Gamelin, General Maxine Weygand, Mme. Alfred Cailliau (de Gaulle's sister), M. Clemenceau (son of the French statesman), Jean Borotra (tennis star), and Leon Jouhaux (secretary of the Confederation General du Travail) from where they were being held prisoner in the twelfth-century Alpine castle of Itter. We also took Heinrich Himmler's home, having missed capturing him by 12 hours. For the record, the officer who captured von Rundstedt was Lieutenant Joseph E. Burke of St. Petersburg, Florida. I had sworn him in as a 2nd lieutenant the day before he took the German field marshal prisoner.

Chapter 32

Post-war Action

A lmost every day brought surprises to us in the snowbound fastnesses of the Bavarian Alps. One morning we awoke to the news that a very long German hospital train had been moved away from the Russian zone near Vienna and was sitting on tracks in the middle of a field near Kitzbühel. We had no way of evacuating the wounded to hospitals, for everything was jammed.

Just before the war had ended I had been traveling along a road that brought us to Oberammergau of Passion Play notoriety. The division surgeon and provost marshal were in our small entourage of three jeeps. As we passed through the streets of the quaint town, we had the feeling that we were the first American troops to enter its precincts. We stopped at the home of Mrs. Anton Lang, whose husband had played Christ for so many years, and I found her a delightful person. She told us that no other troops had been there and that the Germans had pulled out a day earlier as our division and another one had split around the town, leaving it untouched.

Mrs. Lang served us tea and cakes and before we left told us that the Germans, in order to make it difficult for the Allies to catch the SS troops, had impressed young Austrian boys into its infamous society. She also told us that there was a very large hospital back along the route we'd traveled into the town where she thought we should investigate conditions.

We were very much interested in the carved and painted scenes on the houses, all of them depicting biblical events and places. We turned off the main road as we retraced our steps and soon came upon a massive hospital area comprising some buildings but many more tents used as hospital wards.

A colonel in charge of the place reported to us, his face a swollen mess from an infected tooth. He had been awaiting safe passage to a town some 16 miles away where he could obtain an anesthetic for removal of the tooth. We had some reservations about him when we, later, learned that many of the thousands of amputees had lost parts of their bodies without the benefit of anesthesia.

The colonel, when asked what he needed for medical and other supplies, compiled a list of foods that he'd like – to include coffee, sugar, meat, and many other items that no one there had tasted in five years. So much for a cooperative attitude! I went with the division surgeon to a large hospital ward and, at once, noted a bizarre circumstance. Every other man in bed, up and down both sides of the ward, appeared hale and hearty. I asked the colonel what was wrong with them and he said it would be dangerous to move them. I had some enlisted men come in with sub-machine guns and ordered every healthy-looking man out of bed. It became readily apparent why they were there. All of them were SS troops who had had their special tattooed numbers removed from their arms by skin grafts. We marched them out of there en masse and the provost marshal radioed for a company of MPs to escort them to PW enclosures.

I communicated with army headquarters to tell them of the conditions in the camp where the only food we could discover was a root cellar full of half-rotten potatoes. We could feel a lot of sympathy for the amputees, and we initiated steps to better their circumstances as soon as the channels of communication cleared a bit.

On another occasion, I took a ride with Paul Lefort, who had appropriated one of Göring's Mercedes Benz sports cars and had 'French Liaison' painted on it. We drove down the Inn River Valley to the Brenner Pass and en route saw, literally, hundreds of jet planes sitting alongside the road. Manufactured in deep mine factories, they had never taken to the air for lack of fuel. They would have made a tremendous difference in the war's outcome.

The first jet[1] I'd ever seen in the war was near the Rhine after we'd moved from the Bitche area. I had been looking down a long slope through field glasses and was almost ready to call artillery fire down on a farm area where I'd seen a couple of helmeted heads moving in a pig sty. Suddenly a fast-moving German plane came into view and I saw tracers aimed at it from the pig sty, which I had thought was German-occupied. The tracers were hundreds of feet behind the plane, for its speed was so great that aiming bars on anti-aircraft sights weren't offset enough to lead such a plane correctly.

At the same time, the jet loosed a bomb at a bridge our engineers had put in earlier but the vacuum formed by the plane's passage carried the bomb along for a half-mile or more beyond the bridge. We weren't the only ones who were not accustomed to jet speed.

As we passed through sites where the Olympic Games had been played, we saw German prisoners clearing some of their old minefields under French guards. The French, it seemed, found it expedient to have the Germans lock arms, after an area was allegedly clear of mines, and walk across the soil to detonate any mines carelessly or otherwise left undetected. I found this barbarous.

I had to supervise so many tasks that I worked from morning to night overseeing PW dispositions or arranging to have displaced persons, of whom we had some 85,000 of 11 nationalities, sent home. One sad note concerned a number of Norwegian girls who, having fallen in love with German occupiers of their homeland, had followed them to Germany when troops were removed from Norway. These girls were real beauties and I finally arranged, through a severe but fair-minded Norwegian man of the cloth, to have them returned to their homes. Just before they left, our division artillery general threw a party for them

---

1. The engines of this jet played a large part in this memoir editor being an American because my father was one of its designers and was invited to emigrate to the US as a result.

at a local club and we succeeded in warming up the minister to a point where he said he'd do his best to hold recriminations to a minimum.

The German soldiers lived in encampments patrolled by our anti-aircraft flak wagons, as we called them. We had the German generals organize what had become a sloppy mass of humanity into provisional companies containing all of the men of former regular units who might have been taken by us. They set up kitchens and latrines and, daily, we sent jeeps fore and aft of a column of German trucks to Munich to obtain the dry stores of food that German armies lived on.

One German general, it seems, became very much attached to me. He was an artillery general and it was his job to see that organizations were properly administered and that discipline was high. We would meet each morning and I would accompany him on tours of inspection. Almost invariably he would try to shake hands with me but, as I had explained to him, we had no intention of fraternizing with him or any of the members of his army. Ike Eisenhower had listed this among other taboos for us.

The general, whose name escapes me, wore a monocle and I was fascinated at the size of the magnified blood vessels in his eye. There came a day when we were relieved by, of all units, the 42nd 'Rainbow' Division from New York. It had not been heard from by us since Christmas Eve when, during a similar relief, several of our men in the Strasbourg area had been killed by trigger-happy and scared soldiers of that division.

I had to stay behind to orient the newcomers on the work we had well in hand. I could scarcely abide the brigadier general who, allegedly, commanded the 42nd at that juncture. He was fat and pompous and full of false bellicosity that had apparently not been satisfied to date. I finally said to him, 'Look general. If you're so damned great at everything, why the hell weren't you people brought into the war earlier, because I'm sure it would have been over last year, if you could have been spared from stateside duty!'

He had argued against treating the demobilization of the German First Army as a mutual problem with that army's staff. Instead he was going to throw everyone in jail and, by God, snap the whip. The Ugly American in person! I told him that from anything I'd seen about his operation, he could use all the help available, particularly since the only linguists around were the German interpreters.

On the day that I was to leave the area to rejoin the 36th Division at Kaufbeuren, near Landsberg, where it was to undertake occupation duties, I arranged to see the German artillery commander for a last time. By that time he was fully aware of the change to be anticipated under the 42nd Division. It most likely is true that fighting men have an instinctive respect for each other, regardless of uniform. It is, I have noted, equally true that only when men have suffered under combat conditions do they develop those qualities that can permit them to treat enemies with magnanimity. But the man or unit who has sniffed at the perimeters of combat and been found wanting has lost something and, in trying to regain it, resorts to cruelty and bullying tactics.

As I saluted the German general, in turning him over to the tender mercies of his new captors, he suddenly grabbed my right hand and in an outpouring of German accompanied by tears that were magnified under the lens over his left eye thanked me, as the interpreter later translated, for the honorable manner in which the 36th Division had treated his men and officers. It was somewhat embarrassing for he held my hand in both of his until he was through expressing his gratitude. I later heard that the tactics of the 42nd Division had led to trouble and to the needless deaths of several men on both sides.

In leaving the area, I passed by the barracks where we had billeted the displaced persons. Near it was a house where we had incarcerated a number of German women who had actually fought in the trenches, so to speak, with German male soldiers. I could see them sitting around in a yard that had been sealed off with a high chain-link fence. It reminded me of an occurrence that had brought me to that yard a few days before.

A call had come in that told of rioting near the yard where the lady soldiers were being held. When I reached the place, thousands of displaced persons were howling at the German women who, to cause us as much trouble as possible, were parading stark naked around their yard. Obscenities were rampant.

I called the engineers and had them bring a somewhat antiquated fire engine to the scene and because there was a good-sized pond in the vicinity, we built up a strong stream of water to cool off the ladies in question. It was something to see the change come over their faces as they realized what was about to happen. I gave them a last chance to return to their rooms and to dress but received nothing but derisive hoots and gestures.

The stream hit the first girl in the guts and sent her scooting backwards on her butt down the slightly sloping yard. She was the ringleader and before we were through, she bore several bruises from the tumbling and sliding around that she was forced to do. All of the women felt the full force of that jet stream and in about 10 minutes they were making signs of surrender. The displaced persons, apparently, hadn't had such entertainment for years. Before we had caused any severe damage, I had the hose turned off and shortly thereafter the German women appeared, toweling their hair, but fully dressed. From then on, there was no problem of that nature.

Italian displaced persons were anxious to get home and sent a spokesman to talk with me. They wanted to be driven to the Brenner Pass, if it could be arranged, and from there they'd hike home. I found an old German truck which an Italian mechanic said he could repair and shortly they were on their way, some thirty-five of them, singing and crying. We had an escort go with them to pave their way and to prevent looting. It was, despite all that the Italians had done against our interests, a satisfactory feeling to see such happy people, particularly because they all had thought they would never see Italy again.

I should have mentioned earlier, when discussing the capture of Hermann Göring, that when I looked into the huge armored car he and his family had arrived in, I found tucked behind a jump seat a fine Walther pistol and holster that I appropriated for my own use. Just how Göring had managed to conceal it, then, I have no notion. I was also impressed with the fact that there were only four bright new bullets in the magazine. I had the sense then, and have had no reason to alter my opinion, that he planned to use it on his family and himself, had any untoward incident occurred en route to Kitzbühel from the castle near Radstadt. I still have the pistol and bullets. I carried that pistol from that time on in my rear pocket, while I was in Europe, as a substitute for my ungainly .45 caliber US army pistol.

When I reached Kaufbeuren, Germany, I found that the division headquarters was located in the town hall and that our billets were in an apartment house overlooking a monastery where cowled nuns worked inside a walled garden. Almost all of the inhabitants of Kaufbeuren, which had been a large air base, were the wives and children of deceased and missing German airmen, plus some older people. We were firm but fair in our dealings with the people but had a difficult time keeping some of our men in line, particularly when a bevy of pretty girls began to sunbathe in a park near the town hall.

One ghoulish reminder of Nazi Germany was put on display in a store window by our military government unit. It had found several bushels of human teeth, all containing gold caps or fillings that were spread, cornucopia-style, for public view and as a silent indictment of Nazi inhumanity.

Max Justes, one of our French liaison officers, came to me one day and said there was a French civilian wandering around the town repeating the sentence, 'They're eating the paper off the walls.' I went with Justes to see the man whom we found having wine at a sidewalk cafe. We could not get more out of the poor fellow, who was pretty far gone mentally, so we arranged for his shipment to Paris for hospitalization.

A short time later we moved to a more permanent occupation post at Geislingen, Germany. There our headquarters was located in the well-protected home of a silversmith. The area was lovely with an ancient ruins on a high hill overlooking the town. I mention the ruins because, within a short time, the 36th Division attached the Salzburg Symphony Orchestra to itself for rations, since the word had come to us that its members were starving.

During their stay with us, accompanied by a chorus of some thirty beautiful girls, the whole ensemble played and sang Brahms' 'Lullaby' from the heights containing the ruins while the moon lit up the night, making it a fairyland occasion. As a matter of fact, the whole evening was spent listening to a remarkable program that I doubt could be duplicated, given the special circumstances of the world's worst war having just ended.

The orchestra added a grace note to living under circumstances where we were all anxious to return home. It divided up into ensembles and played at our various messes. Its ladies, accompanied by a group of anti-aircraft gunners attached to our division, put on several plays a week, at a large communal hall that held several thousand people.

An 800-year-old tavern-cum-tollhouse served to house the ladies and, all-in-all, the residual effect of the presence of the musicians was one of gracious living.

At about this time General Dahlquist sent me to Frankfurt-am-Main to see General Willard Paul, SHAEF's G-1. I was to obtain approval to build a monument on the shore near Le Dramont, France, where the division had landed on August 15, 1944, commemorating that event. Word had come down that, unlike the First World War, there was to be no proliferation in the building of monuments and none was authorized at division level or lower.

I flew to Frankfurt in a division artillery light plane and on approaching the airfield wondered how we'd land, what with bomb craters disfiguring the landing areas. The pilot set us down in accordance with instructions and after twisting and turning, finally did a ground loop before we stopped.

I went to the main highway on foot and a passing air force general, a real young kid, stopped and picked me up. I was wearing no visible arms but had Göring's Walther in my hip pocket.

The general cautioned me to the following effect. 'Major, aren't you aware that this is hostile territory?' I could scarcely believe my ears.

'The war's over,' I said.

'Even so,' the youthful general said, 'you're taking a long chance barging around without a weapon.'

I noticed that he had two pistols on his belt. 'We're having all kinds of incidents here in Frankfurt,' the general added. 'How long have you been here,' I asked. 'About a week,' he responded. I almost let it go at that but couldn't resist saying, 'Welcome to the war, general. I've fought the German armies from Salerno on, with the 36th Division from Texas, and we've convinced them that they lost the war. I've just come from Austria where we captured Hermann Göring, Air Marshal Sperrle and a couple of dozen other generals who are working with us from 9 to 5 each day, sorting out the mess. The only reason you're having trouble is because you're showing fear wearing all that artillery.'

We rode in silence until we entered Frankfurt. Suddenly, two German men jumped out in front of the car we were in and flung their arms out to the side. The driver had all he could do to keep from hitting them. The general, pistol in hand, jumped out and threatened the Germans while a crowd gathered. I got out and walked up to the two Germans who were glaring at the general's pistol.

'Put the gun away, General,' I said. I took the Germans by the arm and walked with them to the sidewalk. The general holstered his gun and I gently pushed the Germans into the crowd. We were standing in front of the PX and all at once I gathered what was wrong. There, in plain sight of the public, were articles of wear and food that Germans hadn't been able to get for years.

I motioned to the two men who had jumped in front of our car to wait and went into the PX to get some cigarettes. Meanwhile the general had come inside too.

'What're you doing with those cigarettes?' he demanded to know. I turned on him pretty hard and said, 'General, it's a shame your rank got ahead of your common sense. I'm giving the two men a package of cigarettes each and then I'm going on my way. Thanks for the ride!'

I handed a pack of cigarettes to each man, smiled at the crowd who smiled back, and walked up the street to the large factory area where SHAEF was safely ensconced behind several barricades.

General Paul welcomed me as an emissary from General Dahlquist and while he hesitated about giving me written approval to erect a monument at Le Dramont, I reminded him that Dahlquist had mentioned that he, Dahlquist, was 'picking up all the chips that Paul owes me.' I got the approval and did some other business at the huge headquarters where everyone was heavily armed and went on my way, having cadged a chauffeur to drive me the several miles to the airport.

A few days after my return from Frankfurt, General Dahlquist slapped me on the shoulder and said, 'Doughty, how'd you like to go to the Riviera to arrange the details of the monument and the commemorative exercises for August 15?' I told him I'd like it fine but only if Paul Lefort, French liaison officer, went with me. Before we left I helped write a message that was to become part of two plaques, made of bronze from German guns, and phrased in English on one plate and French on the other. We left the plaques for the German silversmith to fashion.

Chapter 33

The Monument

Two more chapters of the memoir deal with Doughty's time on the Riviera after hostilities ended in Europe. The minds of the American military personnel were still clouded by the possibility of continuing hostilities in the Pacific theater. For now, Doughty's responsibilities focused on the details of a commemorative celebration that was to take place on August 15, 1945, a year after the successful invasion of Southern France that led, in part, to victory in Europe. Much of these two chapters dealt with questions like 'Where is the memorial going to be located?', 'Who is going to pay for it?', 'Who will determine the design?', etc. The bureaucracy of now more peaceful times had taken over every aspect of the ceremony preparations and the answers to the many questions that needed consideration were reached with frustration, but they were reached. Doughty's competence with the French language put him into the midst of most French-American arguments, much to his chagrin, although it allowed him to bend things to the way he saw them best executed.

In spite of the unfinished war, the mood of all concerned was celebratory. Hence there was much partying. Doughty and his French counterpart, Paul Lefort, were quite mobile in going here and there for business and pleasure with the car in which Göring surrendered.

The work necessarily involved a trip to Paris to coordinate plans for the many important government and military people planning the celebration on the Riviera. The trip description was dominated by the physical destruction of war and by interactions with a country whose economy was in ruin so that only valuable commodities were accepted as currency to obtain anything, including meals at restaurants that were barely open. The darker dimension described is that even Allied resources such as gasoline, tires, etc., were available only by interacting with the black market. Legitimate requisitions were made and logged with exaggerated numbers so that the dispensing people could sell the excess and still meet the book-keeping requirements of the military inspector-general.

With the dropping of the atomic bombs on Japan and that country's official surrender on August 15, the times were indeed jubilant.

For the ceremony on that day I was up at dawn arranging last-minute details. We had the general's party a couple of nights earlier and Bob Hope had shown up as planned. Cocktails and dinner had gone smoothly, and it was great to have so many veteran officers of the division present for the upcoming ceremony.

I was forced to return to Saint-Raphaël that night, since I had to be sure the whole thing went well. It was really a gala day, stirring with things martial and civilian. Important guests were lodged in a special stand in front of the fieldstone monument. Among them were the high hats of diplomats, gold braid of generals and admirals, ribbons, rosettes and pompoms, sashes and medals galore. As dawn broke, I was amazed to see the hills surrounding the area black with people who'd come from all over Europe to witness the spectacle. Over a hundred-thousand came to view and cheer.

Flagpoles in a huge semi-circle bore the colors of each nation present at the ceremony. In addition, church banners were also strung from more poles. In the center, draped in white cloth, was the monument we had commissioned.

The inscription on the monument reads:

OVER THIS DEFENDED BEACH, THE MEN OF THE 36th INFANTRY DIVISION STORMED ASHORE 15 AUGUST 1944 TOGETHER WITH THEIR FRENCH ALLIES. THEY BEGAN HERE THE DRIVE THAT TOOK THEM ACROSS FRANCE, THROUGH GERMANY AND INTO AUSTRIA TO THE FINAL DESTRUCTION OF THE GERMAN ARMIES AND THE NAZI REGIME.

At the moment before the formalities were to start, a dashing figure appeared in front of the reviewing stand in the form of General de Lattre de Tassigny, saluting all of the colors and then turning smartly to salute the dignitaries. Among the crowded stands and elsewhere were ancient veterans of France's wars – all decked out in sashes and ribbons and standing as straight as old bones would permit. General de Gaulle did not attend. He was too busy in Paris reorganizing the government.

Facing the reviewing stand was a dais equipped with a loudspeaker, and after the bishop of that district opened the memorial service with a prayer, I took the stand and, in about 10 minutes, described the manner in which the 36th Division from Texas had stormed ashore at this point and went on, in slashing attacks, to the north, to penetrate the Vosges barrier, close on the Rhine, and eventually participate in the kill of Naziism to include capturing Göring, von Rundstedt, and the other high-rankers we had taken. It was disconcerting, to say the least, to hear one's own words coming back as echoes from the hills long after they were spoken. I had to change my pace at least once to avoid the overlapping of echoes. My message was received with resounding applause, even though I'm sure very few understood what I had said.

Paul then took the stand and repeated what I had said but in French and again the crowd huzza-ed in great fashion. All of the military formations passed in review to include a fly-over by a large number of planes, a passage of warships off-shore and then a colorful parade of colonial troops as well as veterans of the 3rd, 36th, and 45th Divisions, all spit and polish.

All in all, the ceremony took about an hour-and-a-half and went off like clockwork. It was an excellent start for the day of commemoration and while I did not visit the other sites where additional services were held, I later learned from Dahlquist, who saw them all, that our execution stood head and shoulders over all the rest.

On September 9, 1945, exactly two years after I set foot on the Salerno sands, I was on board a Kaiser-built cement ship heading into a hurricane that made for an interesting voyage. On September 22, I was at the end of the line that had started in Boston, Massachusetts, coiled through Florida, the Carolinas, Missouri, and Massachusetts before leaping the ocean to Africa, then to Italy, France, Alsace, Germany, and Austria and finally, recoiling upon itself. I was – once more – a free man, glad to be home alive and unscarred.

It is possibly a fitting end to this saga to point out that, having left the US without fanfare of any kind, some of us looked forward to the moment when a grateful nation might receive us back with open arms and the demonstrations accorded to its heroes. We sailed past the Statue of Liberty silently and as we approached the New Jersey shore, a single small power boat came charging toward us. On its forward deck was a fairly buxom girl in a hula skirt and with a dilapidated oilskin over her shoulders to ward off spray from the bow. She gyrated a few times and, suddenly, the whole affair struck the hundreds of us watching as hilarious. We simply laughed and clapped to encourage the girl who, it has to be said, represented the nation's only, if not its best, effort to welcome us home.

Even then, since nothing could be offered as repayment for the time we'd spent in jeopardy, we were happy to receive this token of thanks. Most girls would have stayed home that cold morning.

But, to really bring us to the realization that returning heroes were a dime a dozen, we found that awaiting us at the dock were a number of Ladies in Pink, serving in a tired and fumbling way, creamed chipped beef on toast – or, as it is known wherever GIs collect – SOS ('shit on a shingle'). This was the crowning achievement of our return home. We had plastered the earth with such stuff wherever it was served. In New Jersey, that day, all of us simply said, 'No thanks' and headed for a waiting train and transportation to Camp Kilmer.

Sic Transit Gloria Mundi

Doughty's later military service included two years in Korea. He worked for the General Motors Acceptance Corporation and resided in New York state, and later in New England. He died in 2001 at the age of 91.

Glossary

Abatis	Debris (like trees, etc.) placed on roads to impede military movement
Ack-ack	Anti-aircraft gun, also called (in English) flak from the German abbreviation for Flugzeugabwehrkanone (aircraft defense cannon)
A-frame	A device for carrying a heavy load on one's back
Boche	A French (derogatory) term for a German. The British used 'Jerry' and the American infantry 'Kraut'
Brass	High-ranking officers
Casemate	Fortified (usually heavy concrete) artillery gun emplacement
Croix de Guerre	French military service medal (translation: War Cross)
Defile	A geographic term for a narrow pass or gorge between mountains or hills. It has its origins as a military description of a pass through which troops can march only in a narrow column or with a narrow front. On emerging from a defile (or something similar) into open country, soldiers are said to 'debouch'
Dog biscuit	A small round hard cracker for use with 'C' rations, often avoided
Dog tags	Identification discs
Echelons	A formation of troops, ships, aircraft, or vehicles in parallel rows with the end of each row projecting further than the one in front
Fire for effect	Shoot to kill
Half-track	Vehicle with tank treads in rear, normal tire wheels in front
Maquis	Rural guerrilla bands of French resistance fighters, called *Maquisards*
Nom de guerre	Wartime alias name
Overlay	A piece of transparent paper or plastic sheet which, when properly oriented on a map, shows the location of objects of military interest without the need to mark them on the map itself
Provost Marshal	Chief of the Military Police
Regimental exec	Second in command
Re-entrant	An S-bend in a river
Rondo	Code name for 141st Infantry Regiment

Salient	A piece of land or section of fortification that juts out to form an angle
SHAEF	Supreme Headquarters Allied Expeditionary Force. Created on February 13, 1944 out of the 'Supreme Allied Command' that was, in turn, created in April 1943. It was located in London until August 1944, in Versailles until May 1945, and in Frankfurt until July 1945 when it was discontinued
Stalag	Another German word formed from the beginnings of more words like Gestapo, Stasi, etc. Stammlager means a prisoner of war detention camp
Stuka	Sturzkampf (Flugzeug), dive attack (airplane)

Index